The *Wealth of Women:*

Understanding Islamic Financial Laws

Rabab Razik

The Wealth of Women: Understanding Islamic Financial Laws

First Published in 2025 by
THE ISLAMIC FOUNDATION

Distributed by
KUBE PUBLISHING LTD
MCC, Ratby Lane, Markfield, Leicestershire
LE67 9SY, U.K
Tel +44 (0)1530 249230
E-mail: info@kubepublishing.com
Website: www.kubepublishing.com

Author: Rabab Razik
Cover Design: Afreen Fazil (Jaryah Studio)
Typesetting: LiteBook Prepess Services

A Cataloguing-in-Publication Data record for this book is available from the British Library

ISBN: 978-0-86037-904-1
eISBN: 978-0-86037-909-6

Printed by: Elma Basim, Turkey

Dedication

I dedicate this book to my father Ali Abdel Razik, whose unconditional generosity, patience and compassion with my mother, my sister and me were in true emulation of our beloved Messenger, Prophet Muhammad ﷺ

Contents

Acknowledgments

First and last, I thank God for giving me the opportunity to learn about my faith and publish this work.

I would like to thank the women who shared their sensitive life experiences with me. They were key to the completion of this work. I would like to thank all team members of the American University for Human Science for their guidance. I thank Dr. Aziz Abdin, the President of the university for making this possible by supporting me when I entered my PhD program. I thank all defense committee members, especially Drs. Marwan Sadeddin and Marawan Shihata, who generously provided their knowledge and expertise. I thank Dr. Abed el-Fattah el-Samman for directing me to a plethora of resources and literature that were particularly valuable to my research. I would also like to give my special thanks to Dr. Ali al-Saadoon who mentored me while I conducted my research and writing – I could not have done it without his general consultation and guidance. Next, I am deeply grateful to Zehra Rizavi for her editing expertise and guidance, which played a significant role in bringing this project to fruition. I would especially like to thank my children – Yusra, Nada, Ehab and Munir – for their never-ending support as I pursued my studies, with special thanks to my daughters for dedicating much of their precious time to assist me, encourage me and be at my side during very hard times. I would also like to thank my mother Amal and sister May for their ongoing prayers and support. I, from the bottom of my heart, thank all the people who helped me along the way, including those I have not named, for their support throughout my PhD studies and book writing. I could not have done this without all of you.

Note on Translations

This book draws on numerous Arabic sources, including works written by scholars and Hadith collections in Arabic. Unless otherwise indicated, and with the exception of the Holy Qur'an, any translations of Arabic texts are my own. All translations of the Qur'an are taken from Sahih International's translation titled *The Qur'an,* unless otherwise noted. Any italicizations of Qur'anic translations are my own and made to highlight relevant text.

CHAPTER ONE

Introduction

When I am invited to lecture in prominent churches in the Chicagoland area, I am bombarded with the same questions I've been asked so often over the last 30 years: were you forced to marry your husband? Does wearing a headscarf mean you are married? Are Muslim women allowed to work? I enjoy addressing these questions about Muslim women because the overarching concern symbolizes a more universal struggle that all women share. As a Muslim American woman myself who has lived through the male-dominated workforce of the 1980s as well as the various waves of the American feminist movement, I know women are constantly pushing back against gender inequity, and that this is by no means an *Islamic* problem. As I point to old, detailed Islamic laws about a woman's financial independence and agency demonstrated through practices like wives keeping their maiden names after they marry, my audience is both interested and shocked. It's no surprise that I must often describe the same exact Islamic laws in classes I hold with Muslim American women – who are also sometimes shocked and especially eager to learn more.

My motivation for writing this book is drawn primarily from the lack of understanding or follow-through in securing women's rights under Islam specifically within Muslim communities. I have discovered that women in Muslim families are not necessarily enjoying all the rights Islamic law provides, despite those provisions being quite substantial. I became particularly interested in women's financial rights under Islamic law because financial rights and responsibilities are often a point of contention in the lives of many of the women with whom I speak.

The question of how Islamic law treats the financial situations and rights of women in Muslim families lies at the heart of this book. I've decided to focus on what may seem to many people to be unconventional rules surrounding the finances of women under Islamic law. But what financial rights does Islamic law unequivocally grant women? And to what extent are Muslim American women enjoying those rights?

These questions warrant closer examination. After spending the last three decades educating women in diverse communities about Islamic law, I have been struck – and sometimes dismayed – by the lack of knowledge, confusion, complaints, and concerns raised by single, married, and divorced Muslim women alike regarding their financial rights. I concluded that shedding light on the topic could make a real difference, not only for Muslim women who are directly affected but for the non-Muslim community as well.

The two original sources of Islamic law – the Qur'an (the Sacred Book of Islam) and the authentic Hadith corpus (the sayings and deeds of the Prophet Muhammad ﷺ, who is often referenced herein as "the Prophet") – do elucidate the protection and elevation of women's financial rights across every life stage. However, centuries of patriarchal attitudes that underpinned certain societies, and scholars' sometimes rigid adherence to contextualized *fiqh* (Islamic jurisprudence) rulings from a distant age and time have led to textual misinterpretations of certain Qur'anic verses and Hadith about women's issues. These misinterpretations have disparaged the status of women while ignoring multiple places in the same texts where her status is explicitly more dignified.

Uncovering the answers to these questions is crucial because the topic concerns the family unit, a focal point in Islamic law whose deterioration is believed to have a ripple effect and ultimately devastate the whole of society. Under Islamic law, every stone in the family unit – husband, wife, father, mother, son, daughter, brother, sister – has God-given rights, which include spiritual, physical, emotional, and financial rights. The stronger the commitment of each individual in this structure to secure the legal rights of the others, the stronger the foundation upon which the unit stands, radiating its stability and goodness into the larger community. However, if one party falls short in giving the others their due rights, that failing becomes a harbinger of the family unit's undoing.

Although each family member is equally important in Islam, this book gives special attention to the wife and the implementation of her financial rights. Among the plethora of studies and books on the importance of the family in Islam, no literature to date features case studies on the specific financial problems that women living in the U.S. face in their marriages to Muslim husbands. Therefore, this question forms the focal point of this book. My studies examine the types of financial problems women encounter throughout their marital lives and aim to find practical solutions that will both preserve the marriages of women (if preservable) and protect society from the ripple effects that occur when this part of the family unit is financially mistreated. The book presents real-life study participants who illustrate the financial obstacles that many American women from different ethnic or cultural backgrounds face today.[1] It explores how these women quietly tolerate the loss of their Islamic financial rights in order to sustain their marriages and, more importantly, what they can do to protect both their rights *and* their marriages.

This book examines the financial dynamics and practices of various Muslim families living in the U.S.. Through investigative interviews and study participants, the research qualitatively analyzes the real lives of 21 women married to Muslim husbands using a phenomenologist approach. The investigation sought to illuminate the degree to which the Islamic legal rights of these women were granted, and the consequences in cases where women were denied such rights. The research explored whether Muslim men in the U.S. today are adhering to the Prophetic example of respecting and protecting the financial rights of their wives. In other words, are the financial stability and independence of women living in Muslim households equal to those enjoyed by the Prophet's wives? When a woman is not granted her financial rights, what effects does that have on her physical and mental state? And finally, do the Muslim jurisprudential rulings of past ages regarding women and their Islamic finances still apply in the modern context, or is there a need for *fiqh* scholars to reopen *fiqh* practices to derive new rulings that apply to women today?

Ultimately, the book shows that many Muslim spouses of American women are not following the example of the Prophet ﷺ, nor are they compliant with providing their wives with their basic financial Islamic rights in accordance with the Shariah. The book also reveals that depriving a woman of her Islamic financial rights and independence often affects her psychological and physical well-being, as well as the likelihood of her meaningfully contributing to and participating in both family life and society.

A Brief History of Women's Financial Rights

Across history, civilizations have restricted women's financial rights in the name of religion, civil law, and cultural custom.[2] For example, Mosaic Law allegedly deprived a female of all inheritance rights if she had any male siblings.[3] In India, females received no share of inheritance under an agnatic law that only allowed males to inherit.[4] Under Roman law, women never became financially autonomous; unmarried women sat on the sidelines while their fathers or other male family members assumed complete control over their finances. Married women were no better off – they could neither execute a will nor take part in contractual agreements, and their husbands took charge of their wealth.[5]

Both the Hindu and Roman legal systems were influenced by so-called "priestly" laws developed by Hindu pandits, Jewish rabbis, and Christian priests which, in reality, proved contrary to the teachings of the Vedas, the Torah, and the Bible.[6] For example, holy texts describing the female as having been created as a mate or partner for man were interpreted in a literal, patriarchal sense to underpin a priestly law reading, "Man and wife are one, but the man is the one."[7]

It was under these priestly laws that the "patriarchal family" unit was formed as long as five thousand years ago, setting the ground rules for women's property rights.[8] Sir Henry Maine, a Victorian Era Professor and attorney who specialized in ancient law, described the patriarchal family unit as:

> A group consisting of animate and inanimate property of wife, children, slaves, land and goods, all held together by subjection to the despotic authority of the eldest male of the eldest ascending line, the father, grandfather or even more remote ancestor. The force which binds the group together is Power.[9]

Under this ancient legal system, men who were guardians over women – such as fathers and husbands – were trustees of the women's wealth, supplanting females from any power over its spending or disposal. Maine describes how both unmarried and married women fared under this patriarchal family system:

> The unmarried woman is for life under the guardianship of her male relatives whose primitive duty was manifestly to prevent her wasting her possessions, and to secure the ultimate reversion of these possessions to the family to whose domain those possessions had belonged…The great majority of women became by marriage, as all women had originally become, the daughters of their husbands… There can be no question that, in strict pursuance of this conception of marriage, all the wife's property passed at first absolutely to the husband and became fused with the domain of the new family; and at this point begins, in any

> reasonable sense of the words, the early history of the property of married women.[10]

English common law, developed during the Middle Ages and adopted by many European countries and the U.S., found its roots in this ancient patriarchal family system.[11] Herein we find the concept of coverture, a supremely androcentric concept passed down from the customs of the Anglo-Saxon period (410-1066).[12] Coverture is a legal doctrine whereby, upon marriage, a woman's legal rights are subsumed by her husband and she and her husband become one legal entity, with the husband exercising almost exclusive power over the unit's wealth: "Prior to marriage, a woman could sell her property as she wished, enter into a contract of any kind, execute her will and sue or be sued in her own name."[13] Coverture stripped a married woman of all these rights, transferring power into her husband's hands.[14] Such laws financially disabled married women in the U.S. until the 19th century (specifically 1838-1880), when a number of movements successfully reclaimed some rights for women.[15]

Women's Financial Rights under Islamic Law

It is important to view women's rights under Islamic law in historical context. In pre-Islamic Arabia, married women were treated like chattel – i.e., property to be inherited by the husband's heirs. The reforms enacted through the Qur'an and the Hadith, in contrast, were revolutionary for the times, with women gaining rights unparalleled in the world.[16] Thus the lower position of women in early Muslim society reflected neither the original spirit nor the content of the Qur'an. Rather, many social customs that subjugated women were remnants of laws developed in ancient and medieval times; unsurprisingly, as some of these customs infiltrated Muslim culture, they at times were mistakenly identified with Islam.[17]

Comparably, the Shariah, or the inalterable divine law derived from both the Qur'an and Prophetic tradition (Sunnah), established women's rights from as early as the 7th century.[18] Some of the most profound reforms the Qur'an made to customary law at the time were designed to improve the status and rights of women, including financial rights related to the marital gift (*mahr*), support during marriage, and inheritance.[19] Islam provided solutions that protected and elevated women's financial status at every life stage, effectively raising them from being mere property inherited by male family members to a position of being dignified individuals who themselves had a right to inherit, own, and distribute property.[20] Islam, in the 7th century, declared that a woman had the right to independently earn and invest, purchase, sell, rent, and bequest their wealth without the permission of a spouse or male family member. Arguably, the Shariah favors females over their male counterparts when it comes to financial matters, since the sacred law endows women with income sources that outnumber those available to Muslim men.[21]

While many Qur'anic verses (e.g. *al-Nisā'*, 2, 3, 4, 7, 12, 19; *al-Ṭalāq*, 1, 6; *al-Baqarah*, 236) establish the economic rights of women, these rights were made evident through the sayings and practices of the Prophet Muhammad ﷺ regarding his wives and female family members.[22] His respect for the financial rights of these women and his notable generosity toward them offered a living, breathing example of the financial protections and privileges God granted women.[23]

In Islam, a person's birth alone automatically confers upon him or her a legal identity and legal accountability to oneself and to others.[24] According to the scholars of *'Uṣūl al-fiqh* (the science of Islamic jurisprudence principles), every person is born a legal being (*dhimmah*) with certain rights and obligations.[25] The rights that come with one's mere existence are referred to as *ahliat al-wujūb*, while those which follow upon reaching adulthood are called *ahliat al-adā'*, since it is at puberty that a person becomes fully responsible to fulfill certain duties toward the Creator and creation alike.[26] Among the duties human beings have toward one another is that of protecting and honoring one another's right to wealth, as Islam equally permits both men and women to possess their own personal wealth.[27] This possession grants the freedom to do as one sees fit with one's wealth – buy, sell, invest, share, gift, rent or simply spend – without the approval or permission of another.[28]

A misconception exists that Islam favors males over females when it comes to financial matters. Upon closer examination, one finds that the reverse is true.[29] If we compare the sources Islamic law identifies as income specifically for Muslim men to those designated for Muslim women, the sources of wealth of women outnumber those of men.[30] Indeed, an entire chapter of the Qur'an titled "The Women", or Sūrah al-Nisā', is devoted to many of the ways in which God decrees that women's financial rights must be protected. It is also in this chapter that God delineates many of the sources of wealth allotted to a woman.[31] Sūrah al-Ṭalāq similarly serves to teach Muslim men how to abide by God's commands regarding women's financial rights during the dissolution of marriage. According to Imam al-Bukhārī ﷺ, the Companion of the Prophet, Ibn Masʿūd ﷺ referred to Sūrah al-Ṭalāq as "Sūrah al-Nisā' al-Quṣrā," meaning that it is a condensed, companion version to Sūrah al-Nisā', since they both pertain to the same subject matter and, in a way, complete one another.[32]

As evident by the Islamic primary sources that often highlight the financial rights of Muslim women, neither the Qur'an nor the Hadith ever intended to subjugate women in terms of economic status. However, it appears that, for whatever reason, society resisted the ideals of gender equality that those texts suggested, or did not have the drive to make changes to the cultural norms in a manner consistent with Islamic texts. As Islamic law began to be codified and instituted in the 8th century, it appears that many court judgments upheld the centuries-old traditions of male domination, and remnants of these conservative views continue to prevail today.[33] Similarly, as the study participants related in this book will illustrate, some patriarchal elements persist in husbands' financial treatment of their wives, despite the clarity of Islamic laws on this point.

The Subject of Economic Abuse

At times, the deprivation of a woman's financial rights can border on abuse. Today, the practice of economic abuse by husbands toward their wives has received greater recognition all over the world, including the U.S..[34] It has slowly, but surely, caught the attention of the U.S. Department of Justice, which has categorized economic abuse as a form of domestic violence.[35] Economic violence may take the form of limiting access to funds; controlling access to healthcare, employment, and education; exclusion from financial decision-making; and discrimination in terms of inheritance, property rights, and use of communal property.[36]

Arguably, economic abuse exists in Western societies, socially and legally, because of the deeply entrenched theory of coverture that justified indisputable male power over females.[37] The heritage of common law still exists, as American courts remain hesitant to interfere in what it considers an intact family circle, and supremacy was at times presumed for the male even when the woman earned equally or even more than he did.[38] Studies show that husbands who put such power into practice often make their wives beg for money or give them small amounts of spending money even if their husbands are wealthy.[39] While married, they may also deny them opportunities related to employment, job advancement, education, and access to credit cards or bank accounts; they may withhold from them information regarding assets and finances, interrogate them over every dime they spend, empty and close joint bank accounts, squander the family assets, put the family in debt, make purchases on their wives' credit cards, compel them to hand over their personal assets or earnings, place the children's financial responsibility on their wives, or place the financial burden of living expenses on their wives' shoulders.[40]

This may explain why, according to the American Academy of Matrimonial Lawyers, the second most common reason behind the failure of marriages and the consequence of divorce is financial problems.[41] Some study participants of non-Muslims living in America show that wives go through economic abuse whether they are employed and earning an income, or are housewives who are totally dependent on their husbands' earnings.[42] While U.S. courts generally take a hands-off approach to finances during a marriage, the Shariah closely regulates the financial rights of women during matrimony; still, in reality many Muslim husbands living in the U.S. do not appear to be providing their wives the basic financial rights they should enjoy pursuant to Islamic laws.

Luckily, the Islamic Shariah sets forth family financial laws for both spouses to follow. Of course, awareness of these laws can lead to their implementation, but too often, Islamic laws are simply ignored or—other times—misinterpreted or misapplied.[43] Academics suggest that, when it comes to Islamic law, the misinterpretation or misapplication of Islamic laws often relate to culture.[44] This is not to say that culture cannot be harmonized with the Islamic faith, but that the cultural practices men and women have must be in compliance with the fundamental tenets of Islam.[45] Cultural practices are frequently misattributed to religion.[46] And a more significant issue arises when interpretations of divine texts concerning women's issues conflict with the fundamental objectives of Islamic law.[47]

The Muslim faith organizes the family unit so that each member enjoys certain rights and obligations. Specifically, Islamic law requires every husband to carry the financial burden of supporting his family, particularly his wife and children. According to some scholars, his charge over them (*qiwāmah*) is defined as his obligation to provide support (*nafaqah*) for them.[48] His fulfilment of his financial responsibilities gives him ultimate leadership and authority, albeit with the condition that he must refrain from infringing on the rights of his family members and to continually consult (*shūrā*) with his wife and children who are affected by any ultimate decisions that could not otherwise be agreed upon.[49] Just the same, his failure in fulfilling his substantial financial duties would remove that right from him. According to interpretations (*tafsīr*) by some Qur'an scholars of Sūrah al-Nisā' verse 34, men are given headship (*qawwāmūn*) over their wives only on condition that they possess this traditionally masculine characteristic and role assigned to them.[50] Imam Abū Ḥayyān al-Andalusī ﵀ stated it may be possible that the term "*rijāl*" (translated as men) stated in the verse does not necessarily speak about a specific gender but about roles based on their ability to work and provide, adding, "It may be that a female is given preference over a male."[51] In fact, according to Imam al-Qurṭubī ﵀, the majority of Muslim scholars agree that "by virtue of what they spend" in verse 34 of Sūrah al-Nisā' means that the moment the husband becomes unable to spend on his wife, he loses any authority over her.[52] In either case, the man's role as the breadwinner, whether full or partial, does not give him the right to strip from his wife the sources of wealth granted to her by the Shariah. In Islam, she is regarded as an independent legal person whose financial independence must be secured outside as well as inside matrimony without any right of cultural or patriarchal interference.[53]

Significance of the Problem

This book is written from the perspective of a female who has worked in a male-dominated workforce, a lifetime student of Islam, an educator, a wife, mother, and grandmother. The fact that a woman is at the helm of this research sets it apart. Historically, it has been predominantly male scholars who derived the practical application of the Shariah (known as *fiqh*) when it comes to the financial rights of women.[54] While these men's contribution to *fiqh* is undeniable, it is important to incorporate educated female perspectives into the understanding and application of the Shariah, especially when the issues under consideration directly affect women, both in their day-to-day worldly lives and in their ultimate aim of seeking God's pleasure.

Further, existing research lacks any focus on American women living in the U.S. who are married to Muslim husbands. Therefore, I hope that this book makes a significant contribution to the corpus of literature on the subject.

This book comprises six chapters. The second chapter covers the historical and legal background of the financial rights of women according to the Shariah. That section describes the various sources of income Islamic law designates for women, and how they actually exceed those income sources men enjoy, refuting the argument that Islam is biased towards men. The third chapter presents an in-depth review of previous and current research on the subject of financial rights for women, including books authored by the scholars of the four main Sunni Islamic schools of thought, and those who followed them who adhered to their *fiqh* rulings or adopted some and derived new ones based on their own efforts (*ijtihād*). This review highlights different scholarly interpretations of certain Qur'anic foundational verses found in Sūrahs al-Nisā' (the Women) and al-Ṭalāq (the Divorce), from which most rulings have been derived regarding the financial rights of women in Islam. In addition, I examine key differences and controversies regarding these derived rulings in detail. I then delve into my research on the financial dynamics in Muslim households across the United States. In the fourth chapter, I first present the lives of women who shared their experiences with me as part of this study. In Chapter Five, I reveal my key findings, both those that were predicted based on my experiences counseling and teaching women over the years, and others that were unexpected. In the Conclusion of this book, I offer insight for actionable steps I believe can be taken to address gaps in our understanding and implementation of Islamic law, and propose future directions for research.

CHAPTER TWO

Women's Financial Rights Under Islamic Law

Having established that the Qur'an and Hadith, the two original sources of Islamic law, lay out the ground rules for women's financial rights across each phase of their lives, the next undertaking is to explore those laws in detail. Islamic law specifies financial provisions for women in the following instances: prior to and during marriage; upon divorce; in cases of the death of family members (inheritance); in terms of charitable giving; with respect to a woman's own personal earnings; and in other miscellaneous circumstances. The fact that women are afforded financial rights across each of these areas is undisputed. This chapter is devoted to providing an overview of the financial rights of women according to Islamic law, while the next chapter will examine more controversial issues and interpretations stemming from the same sources that delineate these rights.

In determining the precise financial rights that Muslim women possess under Islamic law, Sunni Muslims turn to three general sources: the Holy Qur'an, the example and teachings of the Prophet Muhammad ﷺ, and scholars of Islamic Law, including those from amongst the four major classical Sunni schools of thought – or the *madhāhib* (sing. *madhhab*).The Qur'an itself is the most important piece of literature on the subject, along with the best-known interpretations of the Qur'an, such as *Jāmiʿ al-Bayān ʿan Taʾwīl āy al-Qurʾān* by Abū Jaʿfar Muhammad ibn Jarīr ibn Yazīd al-Ṭabarī ﷺ and *Tafsīr al-Qurʾān al-ʿAẓīm* by Imam Abū al-Fidā' Ismāʿīl ibn Kathīr ﷺ. Specific Qur'anic verses – particularly in Sūrah al-Nisā' (the Women) and al-Ṭalāq (the Divorce) – address the rights of married, divorced, and widowed Muslim women, with their interpretations holding paramount importance. In addition, since many rulings were deduced from the life and words of Prophet Muhammad, books such as *Fatḥ al-Bārī* by al-Ḥāfiẓ Aḥmad ibn ʿAlī ibn Ḥajar al-ʿAsqalānī ﷺ, which offer meticulous detail on authentic narrations or the Hadith of the Prophet ﷺ and their historical context, also informed this research.[1]

Of course, the writings and rulings of the original scholars of the major classical schools of thought in Sunni Islam are key to any analysis of Islamic law: these men devoted their lives to both studying the Qur'an and Sunnah, developing processes for extracting Islamic law from the Qur'an and Sunnah, and— most notably— pioneered the science of applying Islamic law into distinctive contexts and in light of the cultural norms of their communities. It is no surprise that the vast majority of Muslims around the world, including those living in the U.S. today, adhere to the judgments of one or more of the legal schools of thought developed by these scholars. Throughout this book, I highlight the different rulings these four schools of jurisprudence hold on the financial rights of women, but also examine the views of Imam Ibn Ḥazm al-Ẓāhirī ﷺ, a student of Imams Mālik and al-Shāfiʿī ﷺ, who developed another school of thought that holds some unique Shariah-based views that are distinct from his teachers' views.[2] I also examine the views of other traditional and contemporary scholars who generally adhered to the processes and foundations established by the classical schools of thought. Given the purposes of my study, it is worth noting from the outset that, with very few exceptions, namely Dr. ʿĀbidah al-Mu'ayyad al-Aẓam's writings, the vast majority of literature on female-related issues in Islamic law was written by men rather than women.[3]

Building Blocks of Equality: The Foundational Role of the Qur'anic Chapter Al-Nisā' or "The Women" in Establishing Women's Rights in Islamic Law

Equality

In its very first verse, the Qur'anic chapter titled al-Nisā' (The Women) attests to the spiritual equality of two genders, reminding humankind that both men and women originated from a single soul. By referencing the origin of Adam ﵇ and his wife Ḥawwā' ﵇, the chapter highlights that both women and men possess the same essence, emphasizing their mutual capacity to complement and fulfill one another.[4] The introductory verse of the chapter also warns men and women to honor one another's rights, which in no uncertain terms would encompasses their financial rights:[5]

يَٰٓأَيُّهَا ٱلنَّاسُ ٱتَّقُواْ رَبَّكُمُ ٱلَّذِي خَلَقَكُم مِّن نَّفۡسٖ وَٰحِدَةٖ وَخَلَقَ مِنۡهَا زَوۡجَهَا وَبَثَّ مِنۡهُمَا رِجَالٗا كَثِيرٗا
وَنِسَآءٗۚ وَٱتَّقُواْ ٱللَّهَ ٱلَّذِي تَسَآءَلُونَ بِهِۦ وَٱلۡأَرۡحَامَۚ إِنَّ ٱللَّهَ كَانَ عَلَيۡكُمۡ رَقِيبٗا ١

O mankind, fear your Lord, who created you from one soul and created from it its mate and dispersed from both of them many men and women. And fear Allah, through what you ask one another, and [honor] the wombs [family ties]. Indeed, Allah is ever, over you, an Observer.[6]

On Protecting Orphaned Girls

In Sūrah al-Nisā', five subsequent verses similarly and more specifically emphasize the importance of safeguarding the financial rights of others. For instance, verses two and three of Sūrah al-Nisā' (4:2 and 4:3) instruct Muslims on the importance of protecting the wealth of a particularly vulnerable group within the community – orphans (defined by Islamic law as children who have not yet reached puberty and whose fathers have died), with special attention to female orphans of marriageable age:[7]

وَءَاتُوا۟ ٱلْيَتَٰمَىٰٓ أَمْوَٰلَهُمْ ۖ وَلَا تَتَبَدَّلُوا۟ ٱلْخَبِيثَ بِٱلطَّيِّبِ ۖ وَلَا تَأْكُلُوٓا۟ أَمْوَٰلَهُمْ إِلَىٰٓ أَمْوَٰلِكُمْ ۚ إِنَّهُۥ كَانَ حُوبًا
كَبِيرًا ﴿٢﴾

And give to the orphans their properties and do not substitute the defective [of your own] for the good [of theirs]. And do not consume their properties into your own. Indeed, that is ever a great sin.[8]

*

وَإِنْ خِفْتُمْ أَلَّا تُقْسِطُوا۟ فِى ٱلْيَتَٰمَىٰ فَٱنكِحُوا۟ مَا طَابَ لَكُم مِّنَ ٱلنِّسَآءِ مَثْنَىٰ وَثُلَٰثَ وَرُبَٰعَ ۖ فَإِنْ
خِفْتُمْ أَلَّا تَعْدِلُوا۟ فَوَٰحِدَةً أَوْ مَا مَلَكَتْ أَيْمَٰنُكُمْ ۚ ذَٰلِكَ أَدْنَىٰٓ أَلَّا تَعُولُوا۟ ﴿٣﴾

And if you fear that you will not deal justly with the orphan girls, then marry [others amongst] those that please you of [other] women, two or three or four. But if you fear that you will not be just, then [marry only] one or those your right hand possesses. That is more suitable that you may not incline [to injustice].[9]

Interestingly, many men derive from the above verse, the third verse in this chapter, only one objective – the right to marry as many as four women – disregarding the context in which the verse was revealed, thereby neglecting its real essence.[10] The first verse about orphans begins with God ﷻ warning men against taking in orphans to access their wealth. The subsequent verse issues a more specific warning: men who marry orphan girls should not take advantage of them. When 'Urwah ibn al-Zubayr ﵁ asked one of the wives of the Prophet ﷺ, 'Ā'ishah ﵂, about the meaning of this verse, she provided the historical context:

> O my nephew, this is about the orphan girl being brought up by her guardian, she shares her wealth with his so he becomes attracted to her because of her wealth and beauty so he wants to marry her without giving her an adequate *mahr*, which might have been given by another suitor. Such [guardians] have been disallowed, [on the basis of this verse], to marry such orphan girls unless they treat them fairly and give them the maximum *mahr* girls in their situation would have had. They are further commanded to marry other women [from amongst those permissible to marry] instead.[11]

So not only does the Qur'anic verse warn men against marrying orphans in order to gain access to their wealth, but the context in which the verse was revealed warns Muslim men against marrying those who were orphaned without giving them adequate *mahr*. And, as Imam al-Rāzī ﵀ points out, the words of 'Ā'ishah ﵂

explain that in this verse Allah ﷻ first forbids men from taking advantage of orphan girls, but then follows with a permissible alternative: in order to avoid committing such a grave injustice, God points out that He permits them to marry as many as four women who are not orphaned.[12]

Muslim scholars including Ibn Kathīr, al-Ṭabarī, al-Rāzī, and al-Qurṭubī ﷺ have held many interpretations of this verse. Some believed it forbid guardians from marrying orphans if the intent was to absorb the girls' wealth; others wrote that the injustice against which this verse warns consists of not paying orphaned girls the *mahr* she deserves before marrying her.[13] As, at that time in Arabia, men married an unlimited number of women and at times mistreated them, some scholars believe an equally important message is that men should not be unjust in their behavior with any woman they marry, not just orphans.[14] Others suggest that the verse was revealed to place a limit on the number of wives men could have because these men absorbed the wealth of the orphans they married in order to afford spending on their numerous wives, sometimes reaching ten or more.[15] Put simply, if a man could not afford to financially support four women without taking from an orphan's wealth, then he must marry fewer women.[16] Others concluded that exploiting orphan girls was a forbidden (*haram*) act, so Allah ﷻ gave them a permissible (*halal*) alternative of marrying more than one and up to four women.[17]

Ultimately, the third verse of Sūrah al-Nisā' cautions men against behaving unjustly toward their wives, and goes so far as to dissuade men from polygamy rather than encourage it.[18] In fact, Imam al-Ṭabarī ﷺ went even further, concluding from the verse that if a man fears committing injustice against even one wife, then it's best not to marry altogether.[19] His interpretation seems to have been supported by Prophet Muhammad ﷺ when he warned, "Whoever has two wives and is more inclined towards one of them (in material or immaterial matters), he will come on the Day of Judgment with half of his body leaning."[20]

On Inheritance

The next relevant verse is the seventh, which addresses the right of wives (and all women and girls) to inherit. This verse was revealed on behalf of a woman whose husband died, leaving her with three of their daughters.[21] When the time came to distribute the deceased man's wealth, his male cousins claimed charge over the wife and daughters – as was customary during the pre-Islamic era – keeping all of the deceased man's wealth, and leaving nothing for his female family members. When the Prophet ﷺ learned of this, he advised the wife of the deceased to remain patient until a verse of the Qur'an (4:7) was revealed specifically allotting the wife and her daughters certain inheritance rights:[22]

لِّلرِّجَالِ نَصِيبٌ مِّمَّا تَرَكَ ٱلْوَٰلِدَانِ وَٱلْأَقْرَبُونَ وَلِلنِّسَآءِ نَصِيبٌ مِّمَّا تَرَكَ ٱلْوَٰلِدَانِ
وَٱلْأَقْرَبُونَ مِمَّا قَلَّ مِنْهُ أَوْ كَثُرَ ۚ نَصِيبًا مَّفْرُوضًا ﴿٧﴾

For men is a share of what the parents and close relatives leave, and for women is a share of what the parents and close relatives leave, be it little or much – an obligatory share.[23]

On Economic Freedom

Next, in the nineteenth verse, the chapter addresses two forms of injustice against wives.[24]

يَٰٓأَيُّهَا ٱلَّذِينَ ءَامَنُواْ لَا يَحِلُّ لَكُمۡ أَن تَرِثُواْ ٱلنِّسَآءَ كَرۡهٗاۖ وَلَا تَعۡضُلُوهُنَّ لِتَذۡهَبُواْ
بِبَعۡضِ مَآ ءَاتَيۡتُمُوهُنَّ إِلَّآ أَن يَأۡتِينَ بِفَٰحِشَةٖ مُّبَيِّنَةٖۚ وَعَاشِرُوهُنَّ بِٱلۡمَعۡرُوفِۚ فَإِن
كَرِهۡتُمُوهُنَّ فَعَسَىٰٓ أَن تَكۡرَهُواْ شَيۡـٔٗا وَيَجۡعَلَ ٱللَّهُ فِيهِ خَيۡرٗا كَثِيرٗا ١٩

O you who have believed, it is not lawful for you to inherit women by compulsion. And do not make difficulties for them in order to take [back] part of what you gave them unless they commit a clear immorality. And live with them in kindness. For if you dislike them – perhaps you dislike a thing and Allah makes therein much good...[25]

The verse first bans a corrupt system which existed in pre-Islamic Arabia that allowed a deceased man's relatives to inherit a widow like a piece of property, taking complete advantage of her wealth, sometimes even imprisoning her until she could buy her freedom.[26] The second half of the verse tackles an injustice that emerged with the advent of Islam: most scholars interpret it as referring to a husband who dislikes his wife and makes her life difficult in order to pressure her to seek divorce, but then refuses to divorce her unless she agrees to relinquish certain property she owns (her *mahr*).[27] The verse concludes by requiring men to live in "kindness" with one's wife, which scholars unanimously agree point to the husband's religious obligation to financially provide for his wife generously.[28]

Finally, verse 32 of Sūrah al-Nisā' (4:32) unequivocally grants women, whether married or unmarried, the right to earn and own their own property:[29]

وَلَا تَتَمَنَّوْا مَا فَضَّلَ اللَّهُ بِهِۦ بَعْضَكُمْ عَلَىٰ بَعْضٍ ۚ لِّلرِّجَالِ نَصِيبٌ مِّمَّا اكْتَسَبُوا ۖ
وَلِلنِّسَآءِ نَصِيبٌ مِّمَّا اكْتَسَبْنَ ۚ وَسْـَٔلُوا اللَّهَ مِن فَضْلِهِۦٓ ۗ إِنَّ اللَّهَ كَانَ بِكُلِّ شَىْءٍ
عَلِيمًا ﴿٣٢﴾

And do not wish for that by which Allah has made some of you exceed others. For men is a share of what they have earned, and for women is a share of what they have earned. And ask Allah for his bounty. Indeed, Allah is ever, of all things, Knowing.[30]

The profound significance of this chapter of the Holy Qur'an transcends time, with its primary focus on advancing women's financial rights resonating not only in early Arabia but also in modern-day society where women are routinely denied basic financial rights before, during, and after marriage.[31] The remaining sections of this chapter will delve into three key dimensions of women's financial rights under Islamic law, specifically those bestowed upon wives, divorcées, and widows. Notably, this chapter underlines how, under Islamic law, women undoubtedly enjoy a considerable financial advantage as compared to their male counterparts, despite the unfortunate reality of being frequent victims of financial abuse.

Financial Rights Upon and During Marriage (*Zawāj* or *Nikāḥ*)

Islamic law provides women with several rights upon and during marriage: the right to a marital gift (*mahr*), financial maintenance (*nafaqah*), child support, and filial support.

The Marital Gift (Mahr) and the Rules Pertaining to it

According to Islamic law, once a marriage is contracted, the groom is obligated to give a gift of value to the woman he wishes to marry.[32] This gift, known as *al-mahr* or *al-ṣadāq,* can take the form of property, money, or any item of value and represents the man's sincere intention to marry this woman and his willingness to financially accommodate her.[33] Sūrah Al-Nisa (4:4) states:

وَءَاتُوا۟ ٱلنِّسَآءَ صَدُقَٰتِهِنَّ نِحْلَةً ۚ فَإِن طِبْنَ لَكُمْ عَن شَىْءٍ مِّنْهُ نَفْسًا فَكُلُوهُ هَنِيٓـًٔا مَّرِيٓـًٔا ﴿٤﴾

And give the women [upon marriage] their [bridal] gifts graciously. But if they give up willingly to you any of it, then take it in satisfaction and ease.[34]

Although it is a definite Sunnah of the Prophet ﷺ to identify the *mahr* in a written or verbal marriage contract, according to most scholars the delineation of the *mahr* is not a condition for the validity of the contract.[35] This fact is supported by the following verse of Sūrah al-Baqarah (2:236), which indicates that men may divorce their wives even when the obligatory *mahr* was never specified in the marriage contract (and, of course, there can be no divorce without the existence of a valid contract):[36]

لَّا جُنَاحَ عَلَيْكُمْ إِن طَلَّقْتُمُ ٱلنِّسَآءَ مَا لَمْ تَمَسُّوهُنَّ أَوْ تَفْرِضُوا۟ لَهُنَّ فَرِيضَةً ۚ وَمَتِّعُوهُنَّ عَلَى
ٱلْمُوسِعِ قَدَرُهُۥ وَعَلَى ٱلْمُقْتِرِ قَدَرُهُۥ مَتَٰعًۢا بِٱلْمَعْرُوفِ ۖ حَقًّا عَلَى ٱلْمُحْسِنِينَ ﴿٢٣٦﴾

There is no blame upon you if you divorce women you have not touched [consummated the marriage] nor specified for them an obligation...[37]

This interpretation is reinforced by a ruling made by the esteemed Companion Ibn Mas'ūd 🕮, when a married woman whose husband died prior to consummation wondered about her financial rights; he ruled that she receives *mahr al-mithl* (*mahr* of her equal), which is a determination of a *mahr* value based on what similar women have received, plus her inheritance right as a wife of the deceased.[38] Another Companion, Ma'qal ibn Sinān al-Ashja'ī 🕮, remembered this to be the Messenger's exact ruling in a similar situation involving a woman named Barwa' bint Wāshiq. As another example, the Messenger 🕮 married a couple without there being an alotted *mahr,* and the marriage was then consummated.[39] It was not until the husband was on his deathbed that he said:

> The Messenger 🕮 married me to such and such, but I never specified for her the obligatory *mahr* and I never gave her anything, so now I bear you to witness that I gift her my share from (the booties of the battle of) Khaybar so she took it and sold it for one hundred thousand.[40]

All the classical scholars of the schools of thought agree that if the precise value of the bridal gift is not delineated in the marriage contract, then the wife is due a *mahr* equal in value to those received by other women in comparable families, which is known as *mahr al-mithl.*[41] This rule applies when no *mahr* is specified, and there should never be an assumption that other jewelry gifted suffices as the *mahr* absent proof the gift was specified as *mahr,* as understood by the wife.[42] The classical scholars of the four major schools of jurisprudence also held that *mahr al-mithl* is due when the marriage has been consummated, even to women whose marriage was consummated by an invalid, corrupt (*fāsid*) contract, as in the example of a woman who married with a *walī* (marital advocate) but no witnesses.[43]

The *mahr* is a gift owned free and clear by a wife, and Islamic law does not permit a man to demand that his wife return the *mahr* to him for any reason, even if she hurls imprecations against him, as evident in at least one report.[44] In a narration by Saʿīd ibn Jubayr regarding a husband and wife who had invoked curses upon one another and separated (through either contract annulment or final divorce), a husband asked the Prophet about the *mahr* he had gifted his wife, hoping it would be returned to him because of his wife's insults, but the Prophet ﷺ replied: "No money is due for you, if you spoke the truth then indeed you consummated the marriage (already), and if you lied then it is further from you than you can imagine."[45]

Of note, the fourth verse of Sūrah al-Nisāʾ describes that a wife can, if she wishes and does so "willingly," choose to return some or all of the *mahr* back to her husband:[46]

وَءَاتُواْ ٱلنِّسَآءَ صَدُقَٰتِهِنَّ نِحۡلَةٗۚ فَإِن طِبۡنَ لَكُمۡ عَن شَيۡءٖ مِّنۡهُ نَفۡسٗا فَكُلُوهُ هَنِيٓـٔٗا مَّرِيٓـٔٗا ٤

And give the women [upon marriage] their [bridal] gifts graciously. But if they give up any of it willingly, then take it in satisfaction and ease.[47]

Marital Maintenance: The Husband and Father's General Obligation to Provide for his Wife, Children, and Others

Nafaqah is the Arabic word used to describe any sort of spending that is good, permissible, and pleasing to God.[48] As further described in this chapter, under Islamic law, the *nafaqah* of a wife is a fundamental and material term of any marriage, even when unwritten.[49]

The Qur'an (2:272) describes *nafaqah* as spending that grants its giver reward in the Hereafter:

﴿ لَّيْسَ عَلَيْكَ هُدَاهُمْ وَلَٰكِنَّ اللَّهَ يَهْدِي مَن يَشَاءُ ۗ وَمَا تُنفِقُوا مِنْ خَيْرٍ
فَلِأَنفُسِكُمْ ۚ وَمَا تُنفِقُونَ إِلَّا ابْتِغَاءَ وَجْهِ اللَّهِ ۚ وَمَا تُنفِقُوا مِنْ خَيْرٍ يُوَفَّ
إِلَيْكُمْ وَأَنتُمْ لَا تُظْلَمُونَ ﴿٢٧٢﴾

> ...And whatever good you [believers] spend is for yourselves, and you do not spend except seeking the countenance of Allah. And whatever you spend of good – it will be fully repaid to you, and you will not be wronged.[50]

For example, He ﷻ commanded people to spend on the poor, orphans, family members, and for the sake of keeping blood ties.[51] *Nafaqah* also includes spending in the way of building places of worship and schools, as well as maintaining grave yards.[52] On the other hand, Allah ﷻ forbids spending on impermissible activities or products such as intoxicants, gambling, or transactions involving usury.[53] Importantly, *nafaqah* refers not only to what one spends on him or herself, but to what a person spends on another person when it is the first party's responsibility as a Muslim to provide for and take care of the second party.[54] The one obligated to do so is rewarded in return. The Prophet ﷺ said Allah ﷻ said: "Spend (on others) O son of Adam and I will spend on you."[55] This is further indicated by the words of Allah ﷻ in Chapter 34:39:

قُلْ إِنَّ رَبِّي يَبْسُطُ الرِّزْقَ لِمَن يَشَاءُ مِنْ عِبَادِهِ وَيَقْدِرُ لَهُ ۚ وَمَا أَنفَقْتُم مِّن شَيْءٍ فَهُوَ
يُخْلِفُهُ ۖ وَهُوَ خَيْرُ الرَّازِقِينَ ﴿٣٩﴾

> Say, "Indeed, my Lord extends provision for whom He wills of His servants and restricts [it] for him. *But whatever thing you spend [in His cause] – He will compensate for it*; and He is the best of providers."[56]

In Islam, wealth is viewed as a tool for living life with dignity rather than the ultimate objective of life.[57] Of course, a Muslim is expected to earn and spend in a manner pleasing to God ﷻ because, as the Prophet ﷺ said, "Indeed good wealth is in the hands of a good person."[58] The Prophet ﷺ also advised that those blessed with wealth should first tend to their own needs before providing *nafaqah* for others: "Begin with yourself, then with those under your responsibility."[59] Generally, those blood-related relatives deserving of *nafaqah* fall into three categories: ascendants (*uṣūl*) or ancestors, descendants (*furūʿ*) or successors, and those of collateral kinship (*al-ḥawāshī*).[60] The ascendants (*uṣūl*) include the father, mother, grandfather, grandmother, and on up the ancestral line. The *furūʿ* or descendants are the sons, daughters, grandchildren, and on down the line.[61] Those of collateral kinship (*al-ḥawāshī*) include brothers, sisters, nephews, nieces, paternal and maternal aunts and uncles and their children.[62] Generally speaking, from an Islamic perspective those who fall under the *uṣūl* and *furūʿ* (parents and children) categories have a prioritized obligation to financially support one another under certain conditions.[63]

Before his obligation to provide support for his children and *uṣūl* family members, a Muslim man is obligated to financially support his wife and all her needs.[64] In fact, according to Islamic law, the *nafaqah* a man owes his wife is the most important category of *nafaqah* because it does not expire with time, but lasts as long as they stay married.[65] This differs from the *nafaqah* he is obligated to provide his children, which some scholars believe ends upon puberty. It also differs from the *nafaqah* provided to *usul* or *al-ḥawāshī* relatives, which is provided based on need and only when the wife and children's *nafaqah* rights, for instance, are fulfilled.[66] A husband's obligatory *nafaqah* toward his wife is not allocated to her because she is needy (as in the situation of other relatives), but, quite simply, a requirement during the matrimony.[67] On one occasion, a man who wanted to know how to spend his money in a way pleasing to Allah ﷻ asked the Messenger ﷺ:

> O Messenger of Allah, I have one dinar, he [the Messenger ﷺ] said: "Spend it on yourself." He [the man] then said: "I have another dinar." He [the Messenger ﷺ] said: "Spend it on your wife." He [the man] then said: "I have another," he [the Messenger ﷺ] said: "Spend it on your children." He [the man] said: "I have one more," he [the Messenger ﷺ] said: "Spend it on your servant." He [the man] said, "I have one more," then he [the Messenger ﷺ] said: "Spend it on whatever you please."[68]

From this Hadith, it is clear that a man must financially provide for his wife before anyone else, prioritizing his responsibility toward his wife over even his children.[69] It also indicates the responsibility of the husband to cover the costs of household help, which purportedly would support him, his wife, and children.[70] According to the schools of jurisprudence, a man is required to include household or maid services as part of the required *nafaqah* with some caveats:[71] in lieu of hiring help, for instance, a husband may personally offer the necessary household assistance himself (and his wife has the option to accept or reject that offer).[72] Importantly, although a man may have close relatives in need of *nafaqah*, his wife, followed by his children, will always take precedence. Only after his nuclear family members has been cared for does Islamic law permit him to tend to anyone else. The Ḥanbalī school of jurisprudence explains the reasoning behind this hierarchy:

> That is because the wife's *nafaqah* is contractually provided in exchange for something else [the marriage, companionship, and/or intimacy] whereas the *nafaqah* for relatives is provided out of compassion; therefore the wife's [*nafaqah*] was prioritized...and it is for this reason that it is a liability (on him) whether [his] financial situation is good or bad. Furthermore, the wife's *nafaqah* becomes an obligation because it serves his own needs. Therefore, it is prioritized over the financial needs of his relatives it is like him spending on his own self.[73]

Imam al-Shāfiʿī ﵀ cited the third verse of the Qur'anic chapter Sūrah al-Nisā', described earlier in this chapter, as further evidence of the gravity with which a Muslim man should treat the *nafaqah* he owes his wife.[74] Recall that the verse grants men permission to marry up to four women, but with the condition that if a man fears he cannot be fair to his wives, he must marry only one. Imam al-Shāfiʿī ﵀ interpreted the word "injustice" as referring to a man's failure to provide equal financial support to each of his wives.[75]

Based on the Qur'an, Sunnah, and unanimous scholarly consensus, the husband becomes fully financially responsible for providing for his wife once a couple has consummated the marriage – in fact, even if the couple has not yet been intimate, if the husband has not yet given the wife the initial portion of her *mahr* which they agreed would be immediately provided upon marrying (*muqaddam*), he remains responsible to take care of her.[76] The Prophet ﷺ once gave husbands the following advice: "Fear Allah regarding women, for you have taken them [as wives] as a trust from Allah and intercourse has been made lawful by the word of Allah, and it is your responsibility to provide for them with sustenance and clothing in a fair manner."[77] The Prophet ﷺ also advised men of their religious obligation to provide for their wives when he said, "O young men, whoever amongst you can afford to get married, let him do so, and whoever cannot afford, let him fast, for that will be a shield for him."[78] Thus if a man is unable to financially take care of a wife, he should not marry because he will be unable to fulfill the *nafaqah* requirements. Still, many young Muslim men today hurry into marriage to satisfy their physical desires without thinking through their wives' religious rights.

Even more troubling is when men refuse to find suitable employment, forcing their wives to work and provide not only for themselves, but also for their idle husbands. This sort of coercion stands in direct contradiction to Islam, which places the responsibility of *nafaqah* entirely on the man's shoulders and teaches that the wife should never feel pressured to provide for herself or her family.[79] Scholars interpret this as bringing harm to wives as stated in the sixth verse of Sūrah al-Ṭalāq: "Let them live where you live according to your means and do not harm them in order to oppress them."[80] They explain that the mere command to provide a home for your wife includes the cost of all living expenses, especially since— realistically— marriage itself may restrict her freedom to go out, earn, and spend on herself. When a husband stops working or becomes miserly toward his wife (whether during the marriage or during the divorce waiting period), he forces her to go out and earn in order to survive – an unacceptable situation in Islam.[81]

Nafaqah includes providing a home for one's wife, and scholars use a Qur'anic verse from Sūrah 65:6 as proof of this obligation. Using this verse, scholars infer that if a man is required by Allah to furnish a residence for his ex-wife for a certain period of time after the two have separated, then it logically follows that his wife has the same entitlement during their marriage:[82]

أَسْكِنُوهُنَّ مِنْ حَيْثُ سَكَنتُم مِّن وُجْدِكُمْ وَلَا تُضَارُّوهُنَّ لِتُضَيِّقُوا عَلَيْهِنَّ ۚ وَإِن كُنَّ أُولَاتِ حَمْلٍ
فَأَنفِقُوا عَلَيْهِنَّ حَتَّىٰ يَضَعْنَ حَمْلَهُنَّ ۚ فَإِنْ أَرْضَعْنَ لَكُمْ فَآتُوهُنَّ أُجُورَهُنَّ ۖ وَأْتَمِرُوا بَيْنَكُم
بِمَعْرُوفٍ ۖ وَإِن تَعَاسَرْتُمْ فَسَتُرْضِعُ لَهُ أُخْرَىٰ ﴿٦﴾

> Lodge them [ex-wives] [in a section] of where you dwell out of your means and do not harm them in order to oppress them. And if they should be pregnant, then spend on them until they give birth. And if they breastfeed for you, then give them their payment and confer among yourselves in the acceptable way; but if you are in discord, then let another woman nurse him.[83]

Along with providing his wife with a furnished home and domestic help, a husband is also financially obligated to provide her clothing. The basis for this obligation comes from the following Qur'anic verse, which is translated as follows: "...Upon the father [meaning husband] is the mothers' [meaning wives] provision and their clothing according to what is acceptable."[84] The Prophet ﷺ further reinforced this Qur'anic command when he said, "and it is our [the men's] duty to give them their blessings (*rizquhunna*) of sustenance and clothing sufficiently."[85] Scholars agreed that a husband must provide clothing that meet the wife's needs for all seasons, and go so far as to detail how their provision of clothing should include undergarments, outerwear, and shoes.[86] Scholars also describe how a husband must provide his wife with clothing in an amount appropriate to the customs and standards of their time and location.[87] The quantity of clothing must be sufficient to meet all her needs (*kifāyah*); some even suggest he must replenish his wife's wardrobe twice a year.[88]

Child Support During Marriage

Regardless of his financial status, a father is religiously obligated to financially support and spend on his young children, even if he has to borrow money.[89] In fact, according to Islamic law, a mother has the right to have the father of her children provide child support for their children, even during the marriage. This common-sense principle is made evident in the Qur'an (Chapter 2:233), the Sunnah, and by scholarly consensus:

۞ وَٱلْوَٰلِدَٰتُ يُرْضِعْنَ أَوْلَٰدَهُنَّ حَوْلَيْنِ كَامِلَيْنِ ۖ لِمَنْ أَرَادَ أَن يُتِمَّ ٱلرَّضَاعَةَ ۚ وَعَلَى ٱلْمَوْلُودِ
لَهُۥ رِزْقُهُنَّ وَكِسْوَتُهُنَّ بِٱلْمَعْرُوفِ ۚ لَا تُكَلَّفُ نَفْسٌ إِلَّا وُسْعَهَا ۚ لَا تُضَآرَّ وَٰلِدَةٌۢ بِوَلَدِهَا وَلَا
مَوْلُودٌ لَّهُۥ بِوَلَدِهِۦ ۚ وَعَلَى ٱلْوَارِثِ مِثْلُ ذَٰلِكَ ۗ فَإِنْ أَرَادَا فِصَالًا عَن تَرَاضٍ مِّنْهُمَا وَتَشَاوُرٍ فَلَا
جُنَاحَ عَلَيْهِمَا ۗ وَإِنْ أَرَدتُّمْ أَن تَسْتَرْضِعُوٓا۟ أَوْلَٰدَكُمْ فَلَا جُنَاحَ عَلَيْكُمْ إِذَا سَلَّمْتُم مَّآ ءَاتَيْتُم
بِٱلْمَعْرُوفِ ۗ وَٱتَّقُوا۟ ٱللَّهَ وَٱعْلَمُوٓا۟ أَنَّ ٱللَّهَ بِمَا تَعْمَلُونَ بَصِيرٌ ﴿٢٣٣﴾

Mothers may breastfeed their children two complete years for whoever wishes to complete the nursing [period]. Upon the father is the mothers' provision and their clothing according to what is acceptable. No person is charged with more than his capacity. No mother should be harmed through her child, and no father through his child. And upon the [father's] heir is [a duty] like that [of the father]. And if they both desire weaning through mutual consent from both of them and consultation, there is no blame upon either of them. And if you wish to have your children nursed by a substitute, there is no blame upon you as long as you give payment according to what is acceptable. And fear Allah and know that Allah is Seeing of what you do.[90]

According to the above verse, a father must finance his child's nursing needs for up to two years after birth. If both parents agree that the baby will suckle for less than two years, the Qur'an obligates the father to pay for the child's nursing needs for the length of time the baby is nursed. Of course, the father's duties to his child – and thereby to the child's mother – do not end with nursing; he must care for the child as long as the child is too young to earn on his own.[91] So, the child's mother must be provided child support through the entire marriage, and if divorced, until her waiting period is complete— and then while nursing or caring for her children.[92]

All scholars agree that fathers are solely responsible for the financial support of their children. In fact, a woman named Hind bint 'Utbah once complained to the Prophet ﷺ that her husband, Abū Sufyān, did not provide her with enough money to care for herself and child. The Prophet ﷺ replied, "Take [from your husband] what is sufficient for yourself and your child."[93] The scholar Ibn al-Mundhir explained, "Every person, from amongst the scholars that we learned from, agreed that the financial responsibility of the children who possess no source of income is upon their father."[94] Imam Abū Ḥanīfah went so far as to rule that the obligation towards a child includes a child, young or old, who is unable to work and earn because he or she is studying toward a career.[95] Interestingly enough, if a father passes away, the obligation to support the children does not revert to the mother. Rather, if the father passes away, the obligation to financially support the children passes to the deceased father's male heir, e.g. a brother or uncle.[96] Imam al-Ṭabarī ﵀ gives an alternative interpretation of the heir mentioned in verse 2:233, which reads "And upon the [father's] heir is [a duty] like that [of the father]": he suggests that it refers to a biological child who inherits and assumes the responsibility of providing for his mother after the father's passing.[97]

The Qur'an describes a father's children as those who emerge from between his backbone and ribs. which is the location of a man's reproductive system responsible for producing semen, known in the Arabic language as his *ṣulb*. Chapter 4:23 states:

حُرِّمَتْ عَلَيْكُمْ أُمَّهَٰتُكُمْ وَبَنَاتُكُمْ وَأَخَوَٰتُكُمْ وَعَمَّٰتُكُمْ وَخَٰلَٰتُكُمْ
وَبَنَاتُ ٱلْأَخِ وَبَنَاتُ ٱلْأُخْتِ وَأُمَّهَٰتُكُمُ ٱلَّٰتِىٓ أَرْضَعْنَكُمْ وَأَخَوَٰتُكُم
مِّنَ ٱلرَّضَٰعَةِ وَأُمَّهَٰتُ نِسَآئِكُمْ وَرَبَٰٓئِبُكُمُ ٱلَّٰتِى فِى حُجُورِكُم
مِّن نِّسَآئِكُمُ ٱلَّٰتِى دَخَلْتُم بِهِنَّ فَإِن لَّمْ تَكُونُوا۟ دَخَلْتُم بِهِنَّ فَلَا جُنَاحَ
عَلَيْكُمْ وَحَلَٰٓئِلُ أَبْنَآئِكُمُ ٱلَّذِينَ مِنْ أَصْلَٰبِكُمْ وَأَن تَجْمَعُوا۟
بَيْنَ ٱلْأُخْتَيْنِ إِلَّا مَا قَدْ سَلَفَ ۗ إِنَّ ٱللَّهَ كَانَ غَفُورًا رَّحِيمًا ﴿٢٣﴾

> … And [also prohibited in marriage are] the wives of your sons who are from your [own] *loins*…[98]

Chapter 86:7 also states:

يَخْرُجُ مِنۢ بَيْنِ ٱلصُّلْبِ وَٱلتَّرَآئِبِ ﴿٧﴾

> Emerging from between the *backbone* and the ribs.[99]

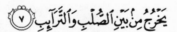

According to scholars, the description in these verses suggest that a man spending on his own children is tantamount to the father spending on himself, as they share his biological makeup.[100] In fact, as noted previously, according to some scholars, after a father's biological children have reached puberty, children have the religious right to continue to receive financial support from their father if they are unable to support themselves.[101] While sons who are able to support themselves would not enjoy a right to continued financial support, daughters, according to most scholars, are entitled financial support until they marry.[102] In requiring a father to financially provide for his daughter, even when she is able to support herself, women are afforded another financial advantage compared to their male counterparts. This paternal obligation stands in stark contrast to the attitudes prevalent in the pre-Islamic era, during which fathers buried their baby girls alive out of shame and disappointment.

Despite a father's firm obligation to financially support himself, his wife and children, some schools of jurisprudence rule that, if the husband-father is poor while the mother is wealthy, his wife could, out of her own free will, spend on her children as well as her husband as a form of voluntary charity (*ṣadaqah),* or even — if she so chooses, and according to only some — designate her charity to her family as part of the mandatory 2.5% charity every Muslim must give annually (*zakāt)* if they qualify as *zakāt* recipients.[103] If her expenditures on her family members were not specifically and willingly intended as a gift, however, then it becomes a debt owed by her husband. This debt is payable when his financial circumstances improve or upon his death, and is separate from her inheritance share.[104] In Islam, because the financial responsibility falls solely on the husband and father, a woman's voluntary act of charitable-giving to her husband and children holds extra value.[105] In one Hadith, Zaynab ﵂, the wife of Ibn Masʿūd ﵁, asked the Messenger ﷺ: "Is it possible for me to spend on my poor husband and some orphans under my care?" And he ﷺ replied: "Yes and for you is double the reward, one for helping a family member and one for giving charity." Still, there is no indication that a woman's voluntary *sadaqah* relieves a husband from his ultimate religious obligation to financially support his family. In failing to provide *nafaqah* to his wife and children, he not only neglects an undoubtedly obligatory marital and familial duty but also falls short of fully embodying the Prophetic directive of being best to his family: as the Prophetic saying goes, "The best of you are those who are best to your family [wife]."[106]

Filial Support for the Mother

According to Shariah, adult children are obligated to provide financial support to their mothers when they are in financial need, regardless of whether the mothers are married, divorced, or widowed.[107] Just as fathers are obliged to support their children financially during pregnancy, after birth, and even beyond puberty in cases of poverty or disability, men are obliged to financially support their elderly parents when in need of financial assistance:

وَإِذْ أَخَذْنَا مِيثَٰقَ بَنِىٓ إِسْرَٰٓءِيلَ لَا تَعْبُدُونَ إِلَّا ٱللَّهَ وَبِٱلْوَٰلِدَيْنِ إِحْسَانًا وَذِى ٱلْقُرْبَىٰ
وَٱلْيَتَٰمَىٰ وَٱلْمَسَٰكِينِ وَقُولُوا۟ لِلنَّاسِ حُسْنًا وَأَقِيمُوا۟ ٱلصَّلَوٰةَ وَءَاتُوا۟
ٱلزَّكَوٰةَ ثُمَّ تَوَلَّيْتُمْ إِلَّا قَلِيلًا مِّنكُمْ وَأَنتُم مُّعْرِضُونَ ﴿٨٣﴾

And [recall] when We took the covenant from the Children of Israel, [enjoining upon them], "Do not worship except Allah; *and to parents do good* [*iḥsānan*] and to relatives, orphans, and the needy. And speak to people good [words] and establish prayer and give *zakah* [or *zakat*]." Then you turned away, except a few of you, and you were refusing.[108]

The Arabic word *iḥsān* encompasses various forms of giving, whether spiritual or material. In Sūrah Luqmān, verse 15, the word "*maʿrūf*" or appropriate kindness is used to indicate how children must treat their parents, including providing financial support.[109] In fact, the verse was revealed on behalf of parents who were not Muslim, to illustrate the importance of mothers and fathers in all circumstances:

وَإِن جَٰهَدَاكَ عَلَىٰٓ أَن تُشْرِكَ بِى مَا لَيْسَ لَكَ بِهِۦ عِلْمٌ فَلَا تُطِعْهُمَا ۖ وَصَاحِبْهُمَا فِى
ٱلدُّنْيَا مَعْرُوفًا ۖ وَٱتَّبِعْ سَبِيلَ مَنْ أَنَابَ إِلَىَّ ۚ ثُمَّ إِلَىَّ مَرْجِعُكُمْ فَأُنَبِّئُكُم بِمَا كُنتُمْ
تَعْمَلُونَ ١٥

> But if they endeavor to make you associate with Me that of which you have no knowledge, do not obey them but *accompany them in* [*this*] *world with appropriate kindness [ma'rufan]*...[110]

In a Hadith reinforcing this principle, the Messenger ﷺ says, "The best food to eat is that which comes from your earnings and your children are from your earnings, thus consume whatever they give you in satisfaction and easiness."[111] In further underlining the esteemed status of a woman and mother, the mother is granted a status threefold higher than fathers: when a man questioned the Messenger ﷺ, saying "Who is most deserving of my care?" He replied: "Your mother, then your mother, then your mother, then your father, then close family members."[112]

The Qur'anic Chapter al-Ṭalāq (The Divorce)

An entire chapter of the Qur'an, titled al-Ṭalāq (The Divorce), is devoted to the topic of divorce. The chapter begins with the following verse:

يَٰٓأَيُّهَا ٱلنَّبِيُّ إِذَا طَلَّقۡتُمُ ٱلنِّسَآءَ فَطَلِّقُوهُنَّ لِعِدَّتِهِنَّ وَأَحۡصُواْ ٱلۡعِدَّةَۖ وَٱتَّقُواْ ٱللَّهَ
رَبَّكُمۡۖ لَا تُخۡرِجُوهُنَّ مِنۢ بُيُوتِهِنَّ وَلَا يَخۡرُجۡنَ إِلَّآ أَن يَأۡتِينَ بِفَٰحِشَةٖ
مُّبَيِّنَةٖۚ وَتِلۡكَ حُدُودُ ٱللَّهِۚ وَمَن يَتَعَدَّ حُدُودَ ٱللَّهِ فَقَدۡ ظَلَمَ نَفۡسَهُۥۚ لَا تَدۡرِي لَعَلَّ ٱللَّهَ
يُحۡدِثُ بَعۡدَ ذَٰلِكَ أَمۡرٗا ١

O Prophet, when you [Muslims] divorce women, divorce them for [the commencement of] their waiting period and keep count of the waiting period, and fear Allah, your Lord. Do not turn them out of their [husbands'] houses, nor should they [themselves] leave [during that period] unless they are committing a clear immorality. And those are the limits [set by] Allah. And whoever transgresses the limits of Allah has certainly wronged himself. You know not; perhaps Allah will bring about after that a [different] matter.[113]

In its opening verse, this chapter grants divorced women the right to continue to live in their marital homes for a period spanning three menstrual cycles (or three months for menopausal women) following the divorce. Ex-husbands are forbidden from coercing their wives into leaving their homes immediately upon divorce.[114] According to some scholars of the classical schools of thought, the divorcee also receives living expenses (Ḥanafī) such as food and clothing, while others (Mālikī and Shāfiʿī) provisioned this support only for those divorced via a revocable divorce (in which fewer than three divorces were uttered by the husband, thus allowing the couple to resume marital relations prior to her three-month waiting period).[115] The three-month waiting period allows for possible reconciliation, time to transition, and time to determine if the ex-wife might be pregnant. If she is, the Qur'an

commands that the husband provide for her and keep her in the
marital home through the birth.[116] If the divorced mother chooses
to nurse her child, her ex-husband owes her monetary compensation for nursing the infant:

أَسْكِنُوهُنَّ مِنْ حَيْثُ سَكَنتُم مِّن وُجْدِكُمْ وَلَا تُضَآرُّوهُنَّ لِتُضَيِّقُواْ عَلَيْهِنَّ وَإِن كُنَّ أُوْلَٰتِ حَمْلٍ
فَأَنفِقُواْ عَلَيْهِنَّ حَتَّىٰ يَضَعْنَ حَمْلَهُنَّ فَإِنْ أَرْضَعْنَ لَكُمْ فَـَٔاتُوهُنَّ أُجُورَهُنَّ وَأْتَمِرُواْ بَيْنَكُم
بِمَعْرُوفٍ وَإِن تَعَاسَرْتُمْ فَسَتُرْضِعُ لَهُۥٓ أُخْرَىٰ ٦

> Lodge them [in a section] of where you dwell out of your
> means and do not harm them in order to oppress them.
> And if they should be pregnant, then spend on them until
> they give birth. And if they breastfeed for you, then give
> them their payment and confer among yourselves in the
> acceptable way; but if you are in discord, then another
> woman may breastfeed the child for the father.[117]

Through this verse and others, jurists have also deduced the financial rights of married women, judging that if a divorced woman
is owed these rights, a woman in a stable marriage has more of a
right to them.[118]

Toward the end of this chapter, we come across a word that also
appeared in Sūrah al-Nisā' – ḥudūd. Ḥudūd, which translates to
boundaries or limits, is used in these two chapters to convey how
critical it is for spouses to honor the confines and rights God has
set both in marriage and in divorce.[119]

Financial Rights Upon Divorce

As alluded to above, Islamic law provides women certain sources
of financial support upon divorce. The classical scholars of the

schools of thought generally concur on the following financial sources: temporary maintenance under each method of divorce or separation; financial contribution post-divorce (*mutʿah*); compensation for breastfeeding; and compensation for childcare and child support. As discussed in Chapter 3, some of the classical schools of thought provide for additional sources of support. For instance, the Malikis provide a form of post-divorce financial support for women called the right of *kadd* and *siʿāyah*, which refer to her entitlement to the fruits of her labor, hard work, and contributions to the family's accumulated wealth as a homemaker.

Temporary Maintenance Upon Husband-Initiated Divorce

As indicated above, the classical scholars of the four schools of thought agreed that a wife divorced via a revocable divorce must receive *nafaqah* through the end of her three-month waiting period.[120] This financial support includes that she remain in the marital home but also receive all the necessities she received while married – food, clothing, living costs, etc. The ex-wife should typically reside in a separate quarter of the home, but if it becomes necessary for someone to move out, scholars agree it must be the husband.[121] If she prefers to move to a place of her own, the ex-husband is responsible to pay all her living expenses during this three-month waiting period, including rent.[122]

Regardless of whether a divorce is revocable or irrevocable, if the ex-wife is pregnant at the time of the divorce, scholars agree that the ex-husband must financially support her until she gives birth and if she nurses the baby, he must pay her for that service.[123]

Temporary Maintenance Upon Wife-Initiated Divorce (Khulʿ)

In a situation where a wife wishes to be divorced but her husband declines to initiate it through the conventional way (where he utters divorce), all jurists agree that the Shariah allows her to remove herself from the marriage *(khulʿ)*.[124] When the wife chooses to utilize the *khul'* method to dissolve the marriage, she typically initiates a formal legal procedure through a third party, although, as discussed in Chapter 3, some believe the *khul'* can be done directly between wife and husband.[125] Jurists rule that this type of separation requires the wife to either return the entire *mahr* he gave her or give him some other type of agreed-upon amount of money.[126] They base such ruling on verse 229 of Sūrah al-Baqarah "But if you fear that they will not keep [within] the limits of Allah , then there is no blame upon either of them concerning that by which she ransoms herself [gives up]," and on a Prophetic tradition regarding the wife of a Companion by the name of Thābit ibn Qays who informed the Messenger of her wish to be released from her marriage to her husband and his reply was, "Would you be willing to return to him the garden [he gifted you with as *mahr*]?, and she replied, "Yes" and returned it, then the Messenger commanded her husband to separate from her. In cases of *khulʿ*, the majority of classical jurists agree that the ex-husband should provide the three-month (or one month according to some) *nafaqah* typically provided a woman upon divorce.[127]

It is important to note that jurists do recognize a third way for a woman to initiate bringing an end to a marriage: by seeking a divorce or annulment through *a judge* when she suffers certain harms in the marriage. This is discussed further in Chapter 3, and, of course, has implications on a woman's receipt of temporary maintenance.

Temporary Maintenance (Nafaqah) Post Al-Mulāʿanah (Oath of Imprecation) Divorce or Contractual Annulment

Drawing from a historical event during the Prophet's time, all scholars agree that if a husband takes an oath declaring that his wife committed adultery, and he is the only witness to her crime, this oath immediately and irreversibly ends the marriage.[128] Imam al-Shāfiʿī ﷺ described this oath as a declaration that caused the couple to part in such a way that they would never unite again even if the wife was to remarry then divorce to be able to legally remarry an ex-husband after an irrevocable divorce.[129] In this ritual oath, known as *al-mulāʿanah*, the husband testifies four times to Allah ﷻ that his wife is guilty of adultery, and a fifth time oath invoking Allah's wrath upon himself if he is lying. Conversely, the wife can refute his accusation by swearing four times to Allah ﷻ that her husband is falsely accusing her and that she is in fact innocent, also taking a fifth oath invoking God's wrath upon her if she is lying. The Qur'an outlines this procedure in the following verse, which was revealed when a companion accused his wife of adultery but failed to produce four witnesses to support his claim. Consequently, he was found guilty of slander (as per verse 24:4) and faced the prescribed punishment for his offense:[130]

وَٱلَّذِينَ يَرْمُونَ أَزْوَٰجَهُمْ وَلَمْ يَكُن لَّهُمْ شُهَدَآءُ إِلَّآ أَنفُسُهُمْ فَشَهَٰدَةُ أَحَدِهِمْ أَرْبَعُ شَهَٰدَٰتٍۭ بِٱللَّهِ ۙ إِنَّهُۥ لَمِنَ ٱلصَّٰدِقِينَ ﴿٦﴾

And those who accuse their wives [of adultery] and have no witnesses except themselves - then the witness of one of them [shall be] four testimonies [swearing] by Allah that indeed, he is of the truthful.[131]

*

وَٱلْخَٰمِسَةُ أَنَّ لَعْنَتَ ٱللَّهِ عَلَيْهِ إِن كَانَ مِنَ ٱلْكَٰذِبِينَ ﴿٧﴾

And the fifth [oath will be] that the curse of Allah be upon him if he should be among the liars.[132]

Because of the finality of this type of divorce to certain scholars, this divorce draws questions about the financial support a woman could subsequently receive from her ex-husband; nonetheless, and as further discussed in Chapter 3, most scholars treat this type of divorce similar to a *revocable* divorce rather than an irrevocable divorce—granting women the right to receive some financial support in certain instances.

Post-Divorce Alimony (Mut'ah)

According to the Qur'an, if a husband divorces his wife prior to consummating the marriage or prior to spending any time with one another in seclusion, and their marriage contract **does specify** an exact amount of *mahr*, then the husband owes his wife half the agreed-upon amount of the *mahr* at the time of divorce:[133]

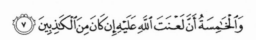

وَإِن طَلَّقْتُمُوهُنَّ مِن قَبْلِ أَن تَمَسُّوهُنَّ وَقَدْ فَرَضْتُمْ لَهُنَّ فَرِيضَةً فَنِصْفُ مَا فَرَضْتُمْ إِلَّآ
أَن يَعْفُونَ أَوْ يَعْفُوَا۟ ٱلَّذِى بِيَدِهِۦ عُقْدَةُ ٱلنِّكَاحِ ۚ وَأَن تَعْفُوٓا۟ أَقْرَبُ لِلتَّقْوَىٰ ۚ وَلَا
تَنسَوُا۟ ٱلْفَضْلَ بَيْنَكُمْ ۚ إِنَّ ٱللَّهَ بِمَا تَعْمَلُونَ بَصِيرٌ ﴿٢٣٧﴾

And if you divorce them before you have touched them and you have already specified for them an obligation, *then [give] half of what you specified* – unless they forego the right or the one in whose hand is the marriage contract foregoes it. And to forego it is nearer to righteousness. And do not forget graciousness between you. Indeed Allah, of whatever you do, is Seeing.[134]

Scholars ruled that a woman whose marriage contract **did not specify** a *mahr* and was divorced by her husband before the consummation of the marriage, or before both spouses were with one another in seclusion (*khalwah*), is entitled to receive a compensational gift known as *al-mutʿah*.[135] *Mutʿah* is also defined by some scholars to be compensation given to the woman following any type of divorce initiated by a husband, whether before or after consummation (See further discussion in Chapter Three). In Arabic, the literal meaning of the word is "that which may be useful and betters one's life." Several verses in the Qur'an convey this meaning, for example:

وَلِلْمُطَلَّقَٰتِ مَتَٰعٌۢ بِٱلْمَعْرُوفِ ۖ حَقًّا عَلَى ٱلْمُتَّقِينَ ﴿٢٤١﴾

And for divorced women is *a provision* according to what is acceptable – a duty upon the righteous.[136]

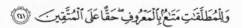

لَّا جُنَاحَ عَلَيۡكُمۡ إِن طَلَّقۡتُمُ ٱلنِّسَآءَ مَا لَمۡ تَمَسُّوهُنَّ أَوۡ تَفۡرِضُواْ لَهُنَّ فَرِيضَةٗۚ وَمَتِّعُوهُنَّ عَلَى
ٱلۡمُوسِعِ قَدَرُهُۥ وَعَلَى ٱلۡمُقۡتِرِ قَدَرُهُۥ مَتَٰعَۢا بِٱلۡمَعۡرُوفِۖ حَقًّا عَلَى ٱلۡمُحۡسِنِينَ ٢٣٦

There is no blame upon you if you divorce women, you have not touched nor specified for them an obligation. *But give them [a gift of] compensation* - the wealthy according to his capability and the poor according to his capability - *a provision* according to what is acceptable, a duty upon the doers of good.[137]

Compensation for Breastfeeding After Divorce

As noted previously, the classical scholars of the schools of thought agree that, upon divorce, the father must compensate the mother who chooses to nurse her child.[138] Even when a biological mother is unable to nurse her baby and another woman steps in to do the job, the nursemaid must also be paid accordingly:

۞ وَٱلۡوَٰلِدَٰتُ يُرۡضِعۡنَ أَوۡلَٰدَهُنَّ حَوۡلَيۡنِ كَامِلَيۡنِۖ لِمَنۡ أَرَادَ أَن يُتِمَّ ٱلرَّضَاعَةَۚ وَعَلَى ٱلۡمَوۡلُودِ
لَهُۥ رِزۡقُهُنَّ وَكِسۡوَتُهُنَّ بِٱلۡمَعۡرُوفِۚ لَا تُكَلَّفُ نَفۡسٌ إِلَّا وُسۡعَهَاۚ لَا تُضَآرَّ وَٰلِدَةُۢ بِوَلَدِهَا وَلَا
مَوۡلُودٞ لَّهُۥ بِوَلَدِهِۦۚ وَعَلَى ٱلۡوَارِثِ مِثۡلُ ذَٰلِكَۗ فَإِنۡ أَرَادَا فِصَالًا عَن تَرَاضٖ مِّنۡهُمَا وَتَشَاوُرٖ فَلَا
جُنَاحَ عَلَيۡهِمَاۗ وَإِنۡ أَرَدتُّمۡ أَن تَسۡتَرۡضِعُوٓاْ أَوۡلَٰدَكُمۡ فَلَا جُنَاحَ عَلَيۡكُمۡ إِذَا سَلَّمۡتُم مَّآ ءَاتَيۡتُم
بِٱلۡمَعۡرُوفِۗ وَٱتَّقُواْ ٱللَّهَ وَٱعۡلَمُوٓاْ أَنَّ ٱللَّهَ بِمَا تَعۡمَلُونَ بَصِيرٞ ٢٣٣

…And if you wish to have your children nursed by a substitute, there is no blame upon you as long as you give payment according to what is acceptable. And fear Allah and know that Allah is Seeing of what you do.[139]

Post-Divorce Compensation for Childcare (Ujrat al-Ḥaḍānah) and Child Support (Nafaqat al-Walad)

Most scholars agree that a divorced mother whose waiting period has ended while she continues to retain custody of her children who have not reached puberty is entitled wages for child-care, known in Arabic as *ujrat al-ḥaḍānah*.[140] This ruling is based on the following Qur'anic verse:

۞ وَٱلۡوَٰلِدَٰتُ يُرۡضِعۡنَ أَوۡلَٰدَهُنَّ حَوۡلَيۡنِ كَامِلَيۡنِۖ لِمَنۡ أَرَادَ أَن يُتِمَّ ٱلرَّضَاعَةَۚ وَعَلَى ٱلۡمَوۡلُودِ
لَهُۥ رِزۡقُهُنَّ وَكِسۡوَتُهُنَّ بِٱلۡمَعۡرُوفِۚ لَا تُكَلَّفُ نَفۡسٌ إِلَّا وُسۡعَهَاۚ لَا تُضَآرَّ وَٰلِدَةُۢ بِوَلَدِهَا وَلَا
مَوۡلُودٞ لَّهُۥ بِوَلَدِهِۦۚ وَعَلَى ٱلۡوَارِثِ مِثۡلُ ذَٰلِكَۗ فَإِنۡ أَرَادَا فِصَالًا عَن تَرَاضٖ مِّنۡهُمَا وَتَشَاوُرٖ فَلَا
جُنَاحَ عَلَيۡهِمَاۗ وَإِنۡ أَرَدتُّمۡ أَن تَسۡتَرۡضِعُوٓاْ أَوۡلَٰدَكُمۡ فَلَا جُنَاحَ عَلَيۡكُمۡ إِذَا سَلَّمۡتُم مَّآ ءَاتَيۡتُم
بِٱلۡمَعۡرُوفِۗ وَٱتَّقُواْ ٱللَّهَ وَٱعۡلَمُوٓاْ أَنَّ ٱللَّهَ بِمَا تَعۡمَلُونَ بَصِيرٞ ﴿٢٣٣﴾

Mothers may breastfeed their children two complete years for whoever wishes to complete the nursing [period]. Upon the father is the mothers' provision and their clothing according to what is acceptable. No person is charged with more than his capacity. No mother should be harmed through her child, and no father through his child. And upon the [father's] heir is [a duty] like that [of the father]. And if they both desire weaning through mutual consent from both and consultation, there is no blame upon either of them. And if you wish to have your children nursed by a substitute, there is no blame upon you as long as you give payment according to what is acceptable. And fear Allah and know that Allah is Seeing of what you do.[141]

To that end, the classical scholars also held that divorced women have a right to receive support for their own living expenses if they are pregnant, until childbirth. This *nafaqah* right is derived from Chapter 65:6:

أَسْكِنُوهُنَّ مِنْ حَيْثُ سَكَنتُم مِّن وُجْدِكُمْ وَلَا تُضَآرُّوهُنَّ لِتُضَيِّقُوا۟ عَلَيْهِنَّ ۚ وَإِن كُنَّ أُو۟لَٰتِ حَمْلٍ
فَأَنفِقُوا۟ عَلَيْهِنَّ حَتَّىٰ يَضَعْنَ حَمْلَهُنَّ ۚ فَإِنْ أَرْضَعْنَ لَكُمْ فَـَٔاتُوهُنَّ أُجُورَهُنَّ ۖ وَأْتَمِرُوا۟ بَيْنَكُم
بِمَعْرُوفٍ ۖ وَإِن تَعَاسَرْتُمْ فَسَتُرْضِعُ لَهُۥٓ أُخْرَىٰ ٦

> ...*And if they should be pregnant, then spend on them until they give birth.* And if they breastfeed for you, then give them their payment and confer among yourselves in the acceptable way; but if you are in discord, then there may breastfeed for the father another woman.[142]

The wages provided to a woman for carrying and taking care of her and her ex-husband's children is oftentimes viewed as separate from child support, which relate to the expenses children accrue. Under Islamic law, after the waiting period and upon the finalization of a woman's divorce, a father is also obligated to pay his ex-wife child support, or *nafaqit al-walad*.[143] The obligation to pay child support stands whether or not the divorce is revocable or irrevocable.

Women's Inheritance Rights

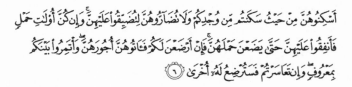

The Qur'an specifically delineates the individuals entitled to inheritance after the death of a family member. These individuals are commonly referenced throughout this book as lawful "heirs" to a deceased family member. Under Islamic law, there are four possible grounds for inheritance: certain blood relationships, a valid marriage contract (regardless of consummation), emancipation from servitude, and subscription to Islam.[144] The first two categories are self-explanatory. The third, a category not applicable in modern-day society, referred to a freed slave who had an Islamic right to a share of the former owner's estate. The fourth refers to instances when a person of a different faith dies without any heirs in a Muslim land: in those cases, their wealth goes to the state's treasury and is distributed to needy members of the Muslim community.[145] A Muslim girl or woman can inherit through any of these four channels.

The Wife's Right to Inheritance

If a husband and wife have a valid marriage contract, Islamic law decrees that the wife is due a share of her deceased husband's wealth. Her inheritance right remains intact if she is divorced through a revocable divorce and is still in her three-month waiting period.[146] The following Qur'anic verse stipulates that a widow is owed a share of inheritance:

۞ وَلَكُمْ نِصْفُ مَا تَرَكَ أَزْوَاجُكُمْ إِن لَّمْ يَكُن لَّهُنَّ وَلَدٌ ۚ فَإِن كَانَ
لَهُنَّ وَلَدٌ فَلَكُمُ الرُّبُعُ مِمَّا تَرَكْنَ ۚ مِن بَعْدِ وَصِيَّةٍ يُوصِينَ بِهَا أَوْ
دَيْنٍ ۚ وَلَهُنَّ الرُّبُعُ مِمَّا تَرَكْتُمْ إِن لَّمْ يَكُن لَّكُمْ وَلَدٌ ۚ فَإِن كَانَ لَكُمْ
وَلَدٌ فَلَهُنَّ الثُّمُنُ مِمَّا تَرَكْتُم ۚ مِّن بَعْدِ وَصِيَّةٍ تُوصُونَ بِهَا أَوْ دَيْنٍ ۗ وَإِن
كَانَ رَجُلٌ يُورَثُ كَلَالَةً أَوِ امْرَأَةٌ وَلَهُ أَخٌ أَوْ أُخْتٌ فَلِكُلِّ وَاحِدٍ مِّنْهُمَا
السُّدُسُ ۚ فَإِن كَانُوا أَكْثَرَ مِن ذَٰلِكَ فَهُمْ شُرَكَاءُ فِي الثُّلُثِ ۚ مِن بَعْدِ
وَصِيَّةٍ يُوصَىٰ بِهَا أَوْ دَيْنٍ غَيْرَ مُضَارٍّ ۚ وَصِيَّةً مِّنَ اللَّهِ ۗ وَاللَّهُ عَلِيمٌ حَلِيمٌ ﴿١٢﴾

> ...And for the wives is one fourth if you leave no child. But if you leave a child, then for them is an eighth of what you leave, after any bequest you [may have] made or debt...[147]

Based on the above verse, scholars agree that the amount a wife is entitled to inherit depends on whether her husband has living children.[148] If he does, she receives one-eighth of his wealth; if he does not, she inherits one-fourth. Her inheritance is also reduced to one-eighth if she has grandchildren (male or female) from a son who has passed away.[149] A wife inherits her husband whether the marriage was consummated or not, as long as the marriage contract was legitimate. A wife whose husband dies while she is still in her three month waiting period from a revocable divorce has a right to her full share of inheritance just as if she is still married.[150] Scholars have opined that a woman in some instances receives less than a man because Islam places the financial responsibility of supporting the family on every Muslim male, while females are not legally obligated to provide others financial support at any stage of their lives.[151]

The Mother's Right to Inheritance

The following Qur'anic verse in Chapter 4:11 lays out the inheritance rights of a woman whose child has passed away:

يُوصِيكُمُ ٱللَّهُ فِيٓ أَوۡلَٰدِكُمۡۖ لِلذَّكَرِ مِثۡلُ حَظِّ ٱلۡأُنثَيَيۡنِۚ فَإِن كُنَّ نِسَآءٗ فَوۡقَ ٱثۡنَتَيۡنِ
فَلَهُنَّ ثُلُثَا مَا تَرَكَۖ وَإِن كَانَتۡ وَٰحِدَةٗ فَلَهَا ٱلنِّصۡفُۚ وَلِأَبَوَيۡهِ لِكُلِّ وَٰحِدٖ مِّنۡهُمَا
ٱلسُّدُسُ مِمَّا تَرَكَ إِن كَانَ لَهُۥ وَلَدٞۚ فَإِن لَّمۡ يَكُن لَّهُۥ وَلَدٞ وَوَرِثَهُۥٓ أَبَوَاهُ فَلِأُمِّهِ ٱلثُّلُثُۚ فَإِن كَانَ
لَهُۥٓ إِخۡوَةٞ فَلِأُمِّهِ ٱلسُّدُسُۚ مِنۢ بَعۡدِ وَصِيَّةٖ يُوصِي بِهَآ أَوۡ دَيۡنٍۗ ءَابَآؤُكُمۡ وَأَبۡنَآؤُكُمۡ لَا
تَدۡرُونَ أَيُّهُمۡ أَقۡرَبُ لَكُمۡ نَفۡعٗاۚ فَرِيضَةٗ مِّنَ ٱللَّهِۗ إِنَّ ٱللَّهَ كَانَ عَلِيمًا حَكِيمٗا ﴿١١﴾

…And for one's parents, to each one of them is a sixth of his estate if he left children. But if he had no children and the parents [alone] inherit from him, then for his mother is one third. And if he had brothers [or sisters], for his mother is a sixth…[152]

The portion of inheritance a mother receives depends on whether or not the deceased left behind children and/or siblings. Moreover, just as a mother receives one-sixth of her child's estate if the deceased had children or siblings, she also receives one-sixth of the estate if the deceased left behind a spouse.[153] Whether a woman is a mother or a wife, her right to inheritance is guaranteed.

The Daughter, Son's Daughter, and Sister's Right to Inheritance

Certain categories of heirs, such as daughters, cannot be excluded (*yaḥjub*) from inheritance.[154] When a parent passes away, his or her minor or adult daughters will always inherit from the deceased parent. A parent's granddaughter, however, will not inherit from the deceased except if she is the daughter of the parent's predeceased son. In other words, a granddaughter will inherit from her paternal grandparents if her father is not alive at the time of her paternal grandparent's death.[155] This provision is outlined in verse 11 of Sūrah al-Nisā' referenced earlier. In instances where a granddaughter will inherit from her grandparent, scholars agree that she will inherit the same portion as the deceased grandparent's daughters.[156]

Finally, in certain instances, a woman may inherit from her siblings who pass away. This is delineated in the last half of verse 12 of Sūrah al-Nisā':

۞ وَلَكُمْ نِصْفُ مَا تَرَكَ أَزْوَاجُكُمْ إِن لَّمْ يَكُن لَّهُنَّ وَلَدٌ ۚ فَإِن كَانَ
لَهُنَّ وَلَدٌ فَلَكُمُ الرُّبُعُ مِمَّا تَرَكْنَ ۚ مِن بَعْدِ وَصِيَّةٍ يُوصِينَ بِهَا أَوْ
دَيْنٍ ۚ وَلَهُنَّ الرُّبُعُ مِمَّا تَرَكْتُمْ إِن لَّمْ يَكُن لَّكُمْ وَلَدٌ ۚ فَإِن كَانَ لَكُمْ
وَلَدٌ فَلَهُنَّ الثُّمُنُ مِمَّا تَرَكْتُم ۚ مِّن بَعْدِ وَصِيَّةٍ تُوصُونَ بِهَا أَوْ دَيْنٍ ۗ وَإِن
كَانَ رَجُلٌ يُورَثُ كَلَالَةً أَوِ امْرَأَةٌ وَلَهُ أَخٌ أَوْ أُخْتٌ فَلِكُلِّ وَاحِدٍ مِّنْهُمَا
السُّدُسُ ۚ فَإِن كَانُوا أَكْثَرَ مِن ذَٰلِكَ فَهُمْ شُرَكَاءُ فِي الثُّلُثِ ۚ مِن بَعْدِ
وَصِيَّةٍ يُوصَىٰ بِهَا أَوْ دَيْنٍ غَيْرَ مُضَارٍّ ۚ وَصِيَّةً مِّنَ اللَّهِ ۗ وَاللَّهُ عَلِيمٌ حَلِيمٌ ﴿١٢﴾

And if a man or woman leaves neither ascendants nor descendants but has a brother or a sister, then for each one of them is a sixth. But if they are more than two, they share a third, after any bequest, which was made or debt, as long as there is no detriment [caused]. [This is] an ordinance from Allah, and Allah is Knowing and Forbearing.[157]

Imam Mālik held that a ṣister or brother may only inherit if the deceased has no living close male relative (son, grandson, father, or paternal grandfather living), and all scholars agree with this view.[158] If, for example, the heirs left by the deceased are one daughter, a son's daughter (but no son), and one sister, then the daughter would receive half of the estate, the son's daughter one sixth, with the rest going to the sister, whereas if the only heirs were a daughter and a sister, they would divide the estate equally between them. In a case in which the deceased had no children and only one sister (maternal or paternal), the deceased's sister would be entitled to one-half.[159] If there were two siblings, each would be entitled to one-sixth. If there were more siblings (males or females), they would all share one-third while taking into account that the male's share is twice that of the female.[160]

A man bears financial responsibility not only for himself, but for his wife, children, parents, and family members when in need; whereas a woman's or girl's inheritance share is exclusively hers. Consequently, sisters (or brothers) become heirs only when the deceased had only living female children or no children.

Charitable Financial Rights

Islamic law offers different channels through which Muslim men and women may both give and accept charity. Some forms of charity are obligatory upon a person, such as giving 2.5% of one's wealth each year (*zakāt al-māl*) or giving charity at the conclusion of Ramadan (*zakāt al-fiṭr*), while others are voluntary, such as alms giving (*ṣadaqah*), gift giving (*hibah*), or giving through an endowed trust fund (*waqf*). A Muslim can also bequeath a portion of his or her wealth for charity upon his or her passing. Another form of charity is given for atonement (*kaffārah*). Under Islamic law, both Muslim men and women may be recipients of these various types of charity. However, because Islamic law ultimately relieves women of having financial responsibilities in general, women are eligible to access these charitable resources in more ways than men are.[161]

Rights to Making and Receiving a Bequest (Waṣiyyah)

As noted previously, Muslim men and women may prepare a will or bequest (*waṣiyyah*) during their lifetimes which delineates how up to one-third of their wealth and valuables should be distributed as charity upon their deaths.[162] Chapter 4:12 of the

Qur'an, which references the specific inheritance rights of family members, distinguishes inheritance from *wasiyyah,* and underlines the applicability of the rules of inheritance and *wasiyyah* to women specifically:[163]

> ۞ وَلَكُمْ نِصْفُ مَا تَرَكَ أَزْوَاجُكُمْ إِن لَّمْ يَكُن لَّهُنَّ وَلَدٌ ۚ فَإِن كَانَ
> لَهُنَّ وَلَدٌ فَلَكُمُ الرُّبُعُ مِمَّا تَرَكْنَ ۚ مِن بَعْدِ وَصِيَّةٍ يُوصِينَ بِهَا أَوْ
> دَيْنٍ ۚ وَلَهُنَّ الرُّبُعُ مِمَّا تَرَكْتُمْ إِن لَّمْ يَكُن لَّكُمْ وَلَدٌ ۚ فَإِن كَانَ لَكُمْ
> وَلَدٌ فَلَهُنَّ الثُّمُنُ مِمَّا تَرَكْتُم ۚ مِّن بَعْدِ وَصِيَّةٍ تُوصُونَ بِهَا أَوْ دَيْنٍ ۗ وَإِن
> كَانَ رَجُلٌ يُورَثُ كَلَالَةً أَوِ امْرَأَةٌ وَلَهُ أَخٌ أَوْ أُخْتٌ فَلِكُلِّ وَاحِدٍ مِّنْهُمَا
> السُّدُسُ ۚ فَإِن كَانُوا أَكْثَرَ مِن ذَٰلِكَ فَهُمْ شُرَكَاءُ فِي الثُّلُثِ ۚ مِن بَعْدِ
> وَصِيَّةٍ يُوصَىٰ بِهَا أَوْ دَيْنٍ غَيْرَ مُضَارٍّ ۚ وَصِيَّةً مِّنَ اللَّهِ ۗ وَاللَّهُ عَلِيمٌ حَلِيمٌ ﴿١٢﴾

> ... And for you is half of what your wives leave if they have no child. But if they have a child, for you is one fourth of what they leave, *after any bequest* they [may have] made or debt...And if a man or woman leaves neither ascendants nor descendants but has a brother or a sister, then for each one of them is a sixth...[164]

The Prophetic tradition emphasizes writing down such bequests through a Hadith stating, "It is the duty of a Muslim who has something which is to be given as a bequest not to keep it for two nights without having his will written down regarding it."[165] Historically, it was also encouraged to assign such bequests to women in the community. In some traditions, the Companions of the Prophet specifically advised a man to include a particular woman in his bequest. Imam Mālik ﵀ recorded that 'Umar ibn al-Khaṭṭāb ﵁ encouraged a wealthy young man whose heirs lived in another town to leave a portion of his wealth in charity for his cousin, Umm 'Amr ibn Sulaym al-Zuraqī, who was not his heir, but lived nearby.[166] The young man bequeathed her with a water well worth thirty thousand dirham.[167]

Obligatory Almsgiving (Zakāt al-Māl or Obligatory Sadaqah), Voluntary Almsgiving (Ṣadaqah) and Donation (Hibah)

Once a Muslim reaches puberty, if he or she possesses a certain amount of wealth that is left unused or is otherwise saved for one full year, Islamic law mandates him or her to purify these savings (*niṣāb*) by giving a portion to those less fortunate.[168] This act is called *zakāt al-māl* or an obligatory *ṣadaqah*.[169] This obligatory charity serves as form of social security for the men and women who are eligible to receive it.[170] Muslims can give *zakāt* either to the Islamic state (if existent), which then has the responsibility to distribute it among those eligible to receive it, or directly to the recipients. If for any reason the state is unable to fulfill the task of adequality providing for the needy in the community, the collection and distribution of *zakāt* becomes the religious responsibility of wealthy Muslims in the community.[171] In support of this view, Imam Ibn Ḥazm ﷺ said, "And it has been made obligatory upon the rich of every state to become in charge of their poor, and (if they do not do so) the head of state is to force them to if the *zakāt* or [*ṣadaqah*] money given to them by the Muslim [community] does not suffice."[172] In the case of a non-Muslim state, Muslim leaders (*imams*) in the community become responsible to administer this duty. Those eligible to receive *zakāt* also have the right to receive *zakāt*. Imam Abū Ḥanīfah ﷺ said, "It is the duty of the religious leaders (imams) to deliver the rights to their owners [the poor and needy] …and it is not permissible for these imams to take from this wealth [*zakāt* money] except what is enough for them and their families to live on."[173]

In the following verse, the Qur'an lays out the eight categories of people who qualify to receive this obligatory charity. Of course, women who fall under these eight categories qualify to receive this obligatory charity:

﴿ إِنَّمَا ٱلصَّدَقَٰتُ لِلْفُقَرَآءِ وَٱلْمَسَٰكِينِ وَٱلْعَٰمِلِينَ عَلَيْهَا وَٱلْمُؤَلَّفَةِ قُلُوبُهُمْ وَفِى
ٱلرِّقَابِ وَٱلْغَٰرِمِينَ وَفِى سَبِيلِ ٱللَّهِ وَٱبْنِ ٱلسَّبِيلِ ۖ فَرِيضَةً مِّنَ ٱللَّهِ ۗ وَٱللَّهُ عَلِيمٌ
حَكِيمٌ ﴿٦٠﴾

> *Zakah* [or *zakāt*] expenditures are only for the poor[,] and for the needy[,] and for those employed to collect [*zakah*] [,] and for bringing hearts together [for Islam] [,] and for freeing captives [or slaves] [,] and for those in debt[,] and for the cause of Allah[,] and for the [stranded] traveler - an obligation [imposed] by Allah. And Allah is Knowing and Wise.[174]

Besides *zakāt al-māl,* there are other non-obligatory forms of charity known as *ṣadaqah* (charity) or *hibah* (gift). Scholars define both *ṣadaqah* and *hibah* as "granting ownership [to someone] without [asking for or expecting] anything in return."[175] However, the intention behind these two forms of voluntary-giving are different. When one makes a donation to someone with the goal of drawing nearer to Allah ﷻ, the person has given *ṣadaqah,* whereas when one gives to another in order to win this person's affection and gratitude, the gift giver has given *hibah.*[176] While strengthening human relations through gift-giving is encouraged in Islam, *ṣadaqah* remains the more valuable form of voluntary giving, as its aim is to please Allah ﷻ. Allah ﷻ reinforces the importance of *ṣadaqah* in the Qur'anic verse which is translated as follows: "Indeed, the Muslim men and Muslim women, the believing men and believing women…*the charitable men and charitable women*…for them Allah has prepared forgiveness and a great reward."[177]

As for who is most deserving of voluntary charity – both *ṣadaqah* and *hibah* – Allah ﷻ commands that close family members and individuals facing financial difficulties, whether male or female, should receive first priority:

يَسْـَٔلُونَكَ مَاذَا يُنفِقُونَ ۖ قُلْ مَآ أَنفَقْتُم مِّنْ خَيْرٍ فَلِلْوَٰلِدَيْنِ وَٱلْأَقْرَبِينَ وَٱلْيَتَـٰمَىٰ
وَٱلْمَسَـٰكِينِ وَٱبْنِ ٱلسَّبِيلِ ۗ وَمَا تَفْعَلُوا۟ مِنْ خَيْرٍ فَإِنَّ ٱللَّهَ بِهِۦ عَلِيمٌ ﴿٢١٥﴾

They ask you, [O Muhammad], what they should spend. Say, "Whatever you spend of good is [to be] for parents and relatives and orphans and the needy and the traveler. And whatever you do of good – indeed, Allah is Knowing of it."[178]

Breaking Fast Obligatory Charity (Zakāt al-Fiṭr)

Another source of income women may be eligible for is *zakāt al-fitr.* Every Muslim, male or female, young or old, is obliged to pay what is known as *zakāt al-fiṭr* – a charity one gives upon completing the fast of the month of Ramadan with the intention of relieving the underprivileged from having to go without their needs or ask anyone for help on the celebratory event of Eid al-Fiṭr.[179] Ibn ʿUmar ﵁ explained:

> The Messenger ﷺ commanded for *zakāt al-fiṭr* to be amounted to a *ṣāʿ* [three Kilograms] of dates or a *ṣāʿ* of

> barley upon the slave and the free, the male and the female, the young and the old from amongst the Muslims. And he commanded that it is paid before the people's outing to the prayer [of Eid al-Fiṭr].[180]

Lifelong & Survivorship (Al-ʿUmrā wa Al-Ruqbā) and Endowment (Al-Waqf) Forms of Gifts

Islam permitted certain charitable practices from the pre-Islamic era because of their beneficial outcomes; women, of course, also stand to benefit from these types of sources of financial support. Among these practices are gifts (*hibah*) that people gave one another during their lifespans and conditioned upon survivorship, known as *al-ʿumrā wa al-ruqbā*. For example, a person would say to another, "This home is yours during your entire life."[181] The Shariah permitted these types of gifts to both males and females without any distinction.

One form of charity that may be given by either men or women is *al-waqf*, the freezing or dedication of wealth of any kind in order to benefit particular people or the community at large and thereby please Allah ﷻ. So long as the giver specifies the way in which this charity will serve the people – for example, specifying that a property will become a mosque for the local community – it qualifies as *a waqf*, or an Islamic endowment. *Al-waqf* is a voluntary form of charity, and because it cannot be inherited, sold, or gifted to a person, but rather remains perpetually in service of the community, it is an elevated category of charity known as *ṣadaqah jāriyah* which will continue to benefit the giver even after his or her death. The Messenger ﷺ said, "When a man dies, his deeds come to an end except for three things: ceaseless charity (*ṣadaqah jāriyah*); a knowledge which is beneficial, or a virtuous descendant who prays for him (for the deceased)."[182] One of the first and most famous historical examples of charity in the form of *waqf* is that of ʿUmar ﷺ. ʿUmar's son relayed that his father asked the Prophet ﷺ how to best use land that he had acquired in Khaybar:

> O Messenger of Allah, I have acquired property more valuable than any I ever had before so what do you advise me to do with it [to please Allah]...and the Messenger replied: 'If you wish you may keep the capital and give its produce as *ṣadaqah*. So Ibn ʿUmar narrated: thus ʿUmar gave it [land acquired in Khaybar] as *ṣadaqah* declaring that this property must not be sold, gifted or inherited. He devoted it for the poor and close family members and the emancipation of slaves and for jihad the sake of Allah and for those visiting. It is also permissible for the one managing it to eat from its goodness and feed his friends from it in a reasonable manner.[183]

Of course, women or girls may stand to benefit from a *waqf* that has been established, underlining yet another source of financial support they may enjoy.

Expiations (Kaffārāt), Vows (Nudhūr), and Sacrifices (Aḍāḥī)

An expiation (*kaffārah* is singular form of *kaffārāt*) is an obligatory form of charity incumbent upon both men and women in which one pays a set price in order to atone for having wrongfully sworn using one of the names of Allah ﷻ. This form of charity is also required to make up an obligatory act, like when a person deliberately does not fast during Ramadan. With respect to *kaffārah* for wrongfully using the name of God, Imam al-Shāfiʿī ﷺ explicated *al-kaffārāt* in the following manner:

> Expiations are given in two conditions, and they are: You saying, "I swear by Allah I shall do such and such." Then (by saying this) you have the choice of doing it if it is a permissible act or of not doing it in which you would be required to pay expiation. In the case that it is an impermissible act you are commanded to expiate…"[184]

The following Qur'anic verse in Chapter 5:89 delineates the various ways in which one can give *kaffārah*:

لَا يُؤَاخِذُكُمُ ٱللَّهُ بِٱللَّغْوِ فِيٓ أَيْمَٰنِكُمْ وَلَٰكِن يُؤَاخِذُكُم بِمَا عَقَّدتُّمُ ٱلْأَيْمَٰنَ ۖ فَكَفَّٰرَتُهُۥٓ
إِطْعَامُ عَشَرَةِ مَسَٰكِينَ مِنْ أَوْسَطِ مَا تُطْعِمُونَ أَهْلِيكُمْ أَوْ كِسْوَتُهُمْ أَوْ تَحْرِيرُ رَقَبَةٍ ۖ
فَمَن لَّمْ يَجِدْ فَصِيَامُ ثَلَٰثَةِ أَيَّامٍ ۚ ذَٰلِكَ كَفَّٰرَةُ أَيْمَٰنِكُمْ إِذَا حَلَفْتُمْ ۚ وَٱحْفَظُوٓا۟ أَيْمَٰنَكُمْ ۚ
كَذَٰلِكَ يُبَيِّنُ ٱللَّهُ لَكُمْ ءَايَٰتِهِۦ لَعَلَّكُمْ تَشْكُرُونَ ﴿٨٩﴾

> Allah will not impose blame upon you for what is meaningless in your oaths, but He will impose blame upon you for [breaking] what you intended of oaths. So, *its expiation* [*kaffārah*] is the feeding of ten needy people from the average of that which you feed your [own] families or clothing them or the freeing of a slave. But whoever cannot find [or afford it] – then a fast of three days [is required]. That is the expiation for oaths when you have sworn. But guard your oaths. Thus does Allah make clear to you His verses that you may be grateful.[185]

An example of an oath that would require an expiation is *al-ẓihār*, a practice in which a man swears by Allah upon his wife that she, from that point on, shall be as a mother to him, insinuating that he will no longer have sexual relations with her.[186] Because this is unlawful type of oath in Islam, such an oath demands an expiation. God describes this unlawful oath in Chapter 58:2 of the Qur'an:

الَّذِينَ يُظَاهِرُونَ مِنكُم مِّن نِّسَائِهِم مَّا هُنَّ أُمَّهَاتِهِمْ ۖ إِنْ أُمَّهَاتُهُمْ إِلَّا اللَّائِي وَلَدْنَهُمْ ۚ
وَإِنَّهُمْ لَيَقُولُونَ مُنكَرًا مِّنَ الْقَوْلِ وَزُورًا ۚ وَإِنَّ اللَّهَ لَعَفُوٌّ غَفُورٌ ﴿٢﴾

Those who pronounce *thihar* [or *ẓihār*] among you [to separate] from their wives – they are not [consequently] their mothers. Their mothers are none but those who gave birth to them. And indeed, they are saying an objectionable statement and a falsehood. But indeed, Allah is Pardoning and Forgiving.[187]

While expiations are an obligatory form of charity, vows or *al-nudhūr* (sing. *nadhr*) are voluntary. *Al-nudhūr* refers to that which a Muslim man or woman promises or pledges to Allah ﷻ in the event that Allah ﷻ fulfills a specific need. For example, a person might commit to feed a certain number of poor or even perform *umrah* upon the fulfillment of a certain need.[188] The purpose of such vows is to express gratitude to Allah ﷻ for granting help and thereby grow closer to Allah ﷻ.[189] The Prophet ﷺ discouraged making such vows, warning that these pledges of charity do not change one's destiny but may leave a person feeling frustrated if his or her need or request is not fulfilled: "It does not bring good. Indeed, it is only a means by which something is extracted from the miserly."[190] It is also not proper etiquette to say to Allah ﷻ, "If you give me such and such, I will commit to performing an act of worship and if you do not, I will not." Still, a person must follow through on a *nadhr* once it has been made, such that even if one was to die, family members must fulfill such pledge on behalf of the deceased, as long as the vow is lawful and not an unlawful act such as consuming alcohol or taking someone's life. If impermissible, then the Prophet ﷺ forbade abiding by it when he stated, "Whoever makes a vow to obey Allah must obey Him and whoever makes a vow to disobey Him must not disobey Him.[191] Imam Ibn Ḥazm ﵀ said:

> And the *nadhr* is for males and females, for the virgin who has a father and the one who does not, for the female who is married and the one who is not, for the slave and the free, all which we have mentioned are considered equal because Allah ﷻ commanded all to be loyal to fulfill their pledges (*nudhūr*) and commanded His Messenger ﷺ of this in general without specifying anyone over the other..."[192]

Islam does detest certain vows, such as a vow to divorce one's wife. In such case, the man has the option to pay an expiation instead of following through on the vow.[193]

Another voluntary financial deed both men and women can undertake when financially able is sacrificing consumable animals such as cows and sheep for the sake of Allah ﷻ. They do this as a way of showing gratitude for all which He ﷻ gives them. In verse 2 of sūrah 108 of the Qur'an, Muslims are enjoined to carry out these actions on various occasions and in significant life events: "So pray to your Lord and sacrifice [to Him alone]." The meat from the sacrifice can be distributed to men or women based on need and the desire of the giver. On whether the act of sacrifice is *sunnah* or obligatory, scholars distinguished between those who are endowed with wealth and able to sacrifice, and those underprivileged persons who are not, based on whether or not they possess wealth in the quantity of two hundred *dirhams* (612.36 grams) of silver, twenty dinars of gold, or their equivalent in value. Of course, those who are wealthy and expected to participate in these acts of charity should not be indebt to others if they wish to enjoy the spiritual reward of animal sacrifice—Islamic law prioritizes fulfilling a religious obligation over a voluntary good deed. Imam al-Shāfiʿī ﵀ ruled that a person who fosters an orphan or is in charge of an underaged person's estate should not use this young person's wealth to make animal sacrifices. Even when other scholars permitted using the wealth of a young person under one's care to perform a sacrifice in cases where the minor is extremely wealthy, they agreed that the spiritual reward of the sacrifice would belong to the minor.[194]

Of course, this act of goodness is an important gesture that can be taken by both men and women alike; when eligible, women or girls who are less fortunate could be recipients of such acts of charity as well.

A Woman's Right to Receive Charity Funds from the State's Treasury (Bayt al-Māl)

In a Muslim nation, the state's treasury, or *bayt al-māl*, collects various types of funds, including *zakāt*, and must use these funds to serve the public. *Bayt al-māl* should prioritize the ones who need the most help. In Islamic law, women who do not have husbands or relatives to take care of their financial needs are identified as a group most urgently in need of receiving assistance from the state's treasury. While Islamic law does not obligate people of other faiths who live in a Muslim state to pay the same charitable dues as their Muslim counterparts, it does offer Christians and Jews, for instance, many of the same financial protections and rights as their Muslim peers, including the right to receive financial support. Scholars cite two historical examples to support this idea. Both Companions Khālid ibn al-Walīd, a military commander of the Muslim army during the lifetime of the Prophet ﷺ, and ʿUmar ؓ wrote letters, one to the people of al-Ḥīrah and the other to the commissioner in Basra (in Iraq), instructing them to give from *bayt al-māl* to the poor Jews and Christians living among them. ʿUmar ؓ wrote, "Pay good attention to those amongst the people of the book who have grown old and became weak and their earnings lessened, and give them from *bayt al-māl* of the Muslims whatever they need."[195]

A Woman's Right to Her Personal Earnings

Employment Earnings

According to the Shariah, the main purpose of employment is to secure the sustenance needed to live a healthy and honorable life.[196] For some, working is a religious obligation, whereas for others it is both permissible and optional. Men are generally mandated to provide women and girls in their households or communities with all their basic living necessities such as residence, food, drink, clothing, and medical needs. Under the Islamic framework, a woman or girl is guaranteed financial support by a male family member whether it be her father or brother (if she is unmarried) or husband (if married).[197] Still, she may earn a living on her own.[198] The fact women may independently earn and own money is evident in the following verse:

وَلَا تَتَمَنَّوْا۟ مَا فَضَّلَ ٱللَّهُ بِهِۦ بَعْضَكُمْ عَلَىٰ بَعْضٍ ۚ لِّلرِّجَالِ نَصِيبٌ مِّمَّا ٱكْتَسَبُوا۟ ۖ
وَلِلنِّسَآءِ نَصِيبٌ مِّمَّا ٱكْتَسَبْنَ ۚ وَسْـَٔلُوا۟ ٱللَّهَ مِن فَضْلِهِۦٓ ۗ إِنَّ ٱللَّهَ كَانَ بِكُلِّ شَىْءٍ
عَلِيمًا ﴿٣٢﴾

And do not wish for that by which Allah has made some of you exceed others. *For men is a share of what they have earned, and for women is a share of what they have earned.* And ask Allah of his bounty. Indeed, Allah is ever, of all things, Knowing.[199]

Earnings Through Rental Property (Ijārah)

Scholars interpret the Qur'an as having given women the full right to engage in various financial transactions, including the right to rent and earn from properties they own.[200] One verse that demonstrates a woman's right to earn a livelihood by renting her property describes women who are employed to nurse a newborn, suggesting that she essentially rents out her milk supply for the use of a baby who is not hers:

۞ وَٱلْوَٰلِدَٰتُ يُرْضِعْنَ أَوْلَٰدَهُنَّ حَوْلَيْنِ كَامِلَيْنِ ۖ لِمَنْ أَرَادَ أَن يُتِمَّ ٱلرَّضَاعَةَ ۚ وَعَلَى ٱلْمَوْلُودِ
لَهُۥ رِزْقُهُنَّ وَكِسْوَتُهُنَّ بِٱلْمَعْرُوفِ ۚ لَا تُكَلَّفُ نَفْسٌ إِلَّا وُسْعَهَا ۚ لَا تُضَآرَّ وَٰلِدَةٌۢ بِوَلَدِهَا وَلَا
مَوْلُودٌ لَّهُۥ بِوَلَدِهِۦ ۚ وَعَلَى ٱلْوَارِثِ مِثْلُ ذَٰلِكَ ۗ فَإِنْ أَرَادَا فِصَالًا عَن تَرَاضٍ مِّنْهُمَا وَتَشَاوُرٍ فَلَا
جُنَاحَ عَلَيْهِمَا ۗ وَإِنْ أَرَدتُّمْ أَن تَسْتَرْضِعُوٓا۟ أَوْلَٰدَكُمْ فَلَا جُنَاحَ عَلَيْكُمْ إِذَا سَلَّمْتُم مَّآ ءَاتَيْتُم
بِٱلْمَعْرُوفِ ۗ وَٱتَّقُوا۟ ٱللَّهَ وَٱعْلَمُوٓا۟ أَنَّ ٱللَّهَ بِمَا تَعْمَلُونَ بَصِيرٌ ﴿٢٣٣﴾

... And if you wish to have your children nursed by a substitute, there is no blame upon you as long as you give payment according to what is acceptable. And fear Allah and know that Allah is Seeing of what you do.[201]

Earnings Through Selling Property

In the same vein, women may also buy or sell any of their own property, and have full rights to any income generated from such sales.[202] The only exception to this right comes up when someone is unable to make financial decisions because of his or her mental health, but that ruling applies to both genders. Imam Ibn Ḥajar al-ʿAsqalānī ﷺ said in his commentary of *Ṣaḥīḥ al-Bukhārī*: "...and indeed the female who had reached puberty is able to handle for herself all matters related to selling or otherwise even if she was married."[203] He also said, "It is permissible for the adult female to handle her wealth without the permission of her husband and also (freely) communicate with strangers regarding selling and buying."[204]

Compensation for Women in Cases of Injury or Death (Diyah)

Finally when 'an eye for an eye' is not imposed, women have a right to be compensated monetarily for any injury inflicted upon them, while their heirs also have a claim to similar compensation in instances where they have been killed.[205] In Arabic this is called *diyah*. Imam al-Shāfiʿī ﷺ said, "The wife and the free woman and the grandmother and the son's daughter and every heir whether male or female deserves the right of eye for and eye (*qiṣāṣ*) and for *diyah* (payment).[206] This right is clearly indicated in the following verses:

وَكَتَبۡنَا عَلَيۡهِمۡ فِيهَآ أَنَّ ٱلنَّفۡسَ بِٱلنَّفۡسِ وَٱلۡعَيۡنَ بِٱلۡعَيۡنِ وَٱلۡأَنفَ بِٱلۡأَنفِ
وَٱلۡأُذُنَ بِٱلۡأُذُنِ وَٱلسِّنَّ بِٱلسِّنِّ وَٱلۡجُرُوحَ قِصَاصٞۚ فَمَن تَصَدَّقَ بِهِۦ
فَهُوَ كَفَّارَةٞ لَّهُۥۚ وَمَن لَّمۡ يَحۡكُم بِمَآ أَنزَلَ ٱللَّهُ فَأُوْلَٰٓئِكَ هُمُ ٱلظَّٰلِمُونَ ٤٥

And We ordained for them therein a life for a life, an eye for an eye, a nose for a nose, an ear for an ear, a tooth for a tooth, and for wounds is legal retribution. But whoever gives [up his right as] charity, it is an expiation for him. And whoever does not judge by what Allah has revealed – then it is those who are the wrongdoers.[207]

وَمَا كَانَ لِمُؤۡمِنٍ أَن يَقۡتُلَ مُؤۡمِنًا إِلَّا خَطَـٔٗاۚ وَمَن قَتَلَ مُؤۡمِنًا خَطَـٔٗا فَتَحۡرِيرُ
رَقَبَةٖ مُّؤۡمِنَةٖ وَدِيَةٞ مُّسَلَّمَةٌ إِلَىٰٓ أَهۡلِهِۦٓ إِلَّآ أَن يَصَّدَّقُواْۚ فَإِن كَانَ مِن قَوۡمٍ
عَدُوّٖ لَّكُمۡ وَهُوَ مُؤۡمِنٞ فَتَحۡرِيرُ رَقَبَةٖ مُّؤۡمِنَةٖۖ وَإِن كَانَ مِن قَوۡمِۭ
بَيۡنَكُمۡ وَبَيۡنَهُم مِّيثَٰقٞ فَدِيَةٞ مُّسَلَّمَةٌ إِلَىٰٓ أَهۡلِهِۦ وَتَحۡرِيرُ رَقَبَةٖ
مُّؤۡمِنَةٖۖ فَمَن لَّمۡ يَجِدۡ فَصِيَامُ شَهۡرَيۡنِ مُتَتَابِعَيۡنِ تَوۡبَةٗ مِّنَ ٱللَّهِۗ وَكَانَ
ٱللَّهُ عَلِيمًا حَكِيمٗا ٩٢

And never is it for a believer to kill a believer except by mistake. And whoever kills a believer by mistake – then the freeing of a believing slave and *a compensation payment* presented to the deceased's family [is required] unless they give [up their right as] charity...[208]

The classical scholars agree that these verses apply to both women and men, and that, upon the state conviction of a murderer, for instance, retribution (*qiṣāṣ*) may be taken without any gender discrimination. Thus if a man murdered a woman, his life can be rightfully taken in exchange.[209]

CHAPTER THREE

Scholarly Controversies and Varying Interpretations

Chapter Two presented an overview of the financial rights Islamic law provides for women in general terms – those interpretations of the Qur'an and Hadith regarding which most jurists and scholars can agree. However, many issues remain where scholars differ in their textual interpretations of Islamic jurisprudence related to women's financial rights. This chapter is devoted to discussing those controversies and variations in opinion. Many of the verses under discussion in this chapter appear in the primary Qur'anic chapters referenced in this book, Sūrah al-Nisā' and Sūrah al-Ṭalāq, while others are drawn from different sections of the Qur'an.

Differing Opinions on the Marital Gift or *Mahr*

As noted in Chapter Two, the right to *mahr* is a key financial right of a married Muslim woman. According to Islamic law, it is obligatory upon a man to give a gift of value, known as *al-mahr* or *al-ṣadāq,* to the woman he marries:[1]

وَءَاتُوا۟ ٱلنِّسَآءَ صَدُقَـٰتِهِنَّ نِحْلَةً ۚ فَإِن طِبْنَ لَكُمْ عَن شَىْءٍ مِّنْهُ نَفْسًا فَكُلُوهُ هَنِيٓـًٔا مَّرِيٓـًٔا ﴿٤﴾

And give the women [upon marriage] their [bridal] gifts graciously. But if they give up willingly to you anything of it, then take it in satisfaction and ease.[2]

Based on the interpretation of this verse provided by the Companion Abū ʿUbaydah ibn al-Jarrāḥ ﵁, the word *niḥlah* means "graciously" or "in good will." As such, with regard to the aforementioned Qur'anic verse, the majority of scholars – in fact, all schools of thought, except the Mālikī school and some Shāfiʿī scholars – interpret the *mahr* as a gesture of goodwill that is not given with the expectation of receiving something in return.[3] In other words, these scholars argue that the *mahr* is not tantamount to a man purchasing a woman as his wife, but is rather a gift which honors the wife and solidifies the beginning of a permissible and legitimate (*halal*) partnership, thereby allowing the couple to consummate their marriage.[4]

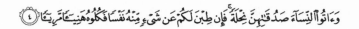

A minority of scholars, however, interpret the *mahr* as a man compensating a woman in exchange for access to her body, i.e. in exchange for sexual intercourse.[5] Such a view seems problematic to most Muslim scholars because it insinuates one human taking ownership of another, a concept that Islamic law abolished.[6] Further, interpreting the *mahr* as some sort of purchase price for one's wife also appears flawed because it conflicts with the Qur'an's description of the marriage contract being "a solemn covenant" as stated in verse 21 of Sūrah al-Nisā'. The intention of marriage was to bring a man and woman together by choice to share their lives, find comfort in one another, fulfill each other's physical needs, and serve as a shield and shelter for one another.[7] As the contemporary scholar Ḥassān al-Ṣaffār points out in an article entitled "al-Ṣadāq," if what the Mālikī school suggests is the correct interpretation of *mahr,* then why does the Qur'an command that the wife be gifted half the agreed-upon *mahr* if divorced prior to the consummation of the marriage? In such case, the husband did not gain access to his wife's body in return for the *mahr*.[8]

Last, most scholars agree that the *mahr* is first and foremost a rightful duty of a Muslim husband to God ﷻ. Dr. Wahbah al-Zuḥaylī رحمه الله describes the bridal gift in his work *Islamic Jurisprudence and its Proofs* [*al-Fiqh al-Islāmī wa Adillatuhu*] as a type of *hibah* (gift) from Allah ﷻ to honor wives from the start of the union.[9] This opinion likely explains why the Companions Ibn ʿAbbās رضي الله عنه and Qatādah رضي الله عنه defined *niḥlah* as a religious obligation, which neither spouse has the right to void even by agreement.[10] This view is based on several Qur'anic verses found in Sūrahs al-Nisā' and al-Aḥzāb, including the following:

۞ وَٱلْمُحْصَنَٰتُ مِنَ ٱلنِّسَآءِ إِلَّا مَا مَلَكَتْ أَيْمَٰنُكُمْ ۖ كِتَٰبَ ٱللَّهِ عَلَيْكُمْ ۚ وَأُحِلَّ لَكُم
مَّا وَرَآءَ ذَٰلِكُمْ أَن تَبْتَغُوا۟ بِأَمْوَٰلِكُم مُّحْصِنِينَ غَيْرَ مُسَٰفِحِينَ ۚ فَمَا ٱسْتَمْتَعْتُم بِهِۦ
مِنْهُنَّ فَـَٔاتُوهُنَّ أُجُورَهُنَّ فَرِيضَةً ۚ وَلَا جُنَاحَ عَلَيْكُمْ فِيمَا تَرَٰضَيْتُم بِهِۦ مِنۢ بَعْدِ
ٱلْفَرِيضَةِ ۚ إِنَّ ٱللَّهَ كَانَ عَلِيمًا حَكِيمًا ﴿٢٤﴾

And [also prohibited to you are all] married women except those your right hands possess. [This is] the decree of Allah upon you. And lawful to you are [all others] beyond these, [provided] that you seek them [in marriage] with [gifts from] your property, desiring chastity, not unlawful sexual intercourse. So for whatever you enjoy

> [of marriage] from them, give them their due compensation *as an obligation*. And there is no blame upon you for what you mutually agree to beyond the obligation. Indeed, Allah is ever Knowing and Wise.[11]

All schools of thought, with the exception of the Mālikī school, agree that the value of the *mahr*, or even the very concept of *mahr*, need not be written explicitly in the marriage contract for the contract to be valid.[12] Scholars draw this inference from the following Qur'anic verse, which states that men may divorce their wives even if they never specified the obligatory *mahr* for their wives in the marriage contract. Through backwards deduction, scholars reason that there can be no divorce without the existence of a valid contract in the first place:[13]

لَّا جُنَاحَ عَلَيْكُمْ إِن طَلَّقْتُمُ ٱلنِّسَآءَ مَا لَمْ تَمَسُّوهُنَّ أَوْ تَفْرِضُوا۟ لَهُنَّ فَرِيضَةً ۚ وَمَتِّعُوهُنَّ عَلَى
ٱلْمُوسِعِ قَدَرُهُۥ وَعَلَى ٱلْمُقْتِرِ قَدَرُهُۥ مَتَٰعًۢا بِٱلْمَعْرُوفِ ۖ حَقًّا عَلَى ٱلْمُحْسِنِينَ ﴿٢٣٦﴾

> There is no blame upon you if you divorce women you have not touched nor specified for them an obligation...[14]

Even if the marriage contract need not mention the *mahr* in order to be valid, the bridal gift remains a religious marital obligation of the husband. As ʿAbd al-Raḥmān al-Jazīrī ﷺ explains in his book, *Kitāb al-Fiqh ʿalā al-Madhāhib al-Arbaʿah,* all four jurists of the major schools of religious jurisprudence ruled that the wife has the absolute right to refuse intimate relations with her husband until she receives her specified *mahr* (in full or part).[15] Imams Aḥmad, al-Shāfiʿī, and Abū Ḥanīfah ﷺ further ruled that in such instance the husband remains responsible to take care of his wife financially because she has good cause for abstaining from sexual relations.[16] The imams ⌘ also ruled that until she receives her bridal gift, the wife is free to leave the household and travel out of town without her husband's permission, stating, "If he gives her the *mahr* minus one dirham, she has the right to abstain herself (physically) from him and to go wherever she pleases, until she receives her rightful gift payment."[17] The rule does have exceptions. First, scholars agree that if the wife permits consummation, she cannot afterwards decide to abstain from marital relations; by consummating the marriage, she signals acceptance of the delay in receiving her *mahr*.[18] Second, if, prior to the marriage, the couple agreed that all or some part of the *mahr* would be deferred until after intimacy, known as *mu'akhkhar mahr*, then the wife cannot rightfully refuse marital relations on the basis of not having received the full *mahr*.[19] However, Imam Ibn Rushd ⌘ points out in his jurisprudence book *The Distinguished Jurist's Primer* [*Bidāyat al-Mujtahid*] that not all schools of jurisprudence accept postponement of the *mahr* and even some of those who do, such as the Mālikī school, rule that it must be paid to the wife by a date agreed upon by both bride and groom.[20] Some recommend that a portion of the deferred *mahr* be paid in advance, while others leave the matter an open debt until either divorce or death. These differences can be traced back to varying interpretations of the marriage contract itself— some scholars interpreting it as a sales contract, while others considering the contract "an act of worship."[21]

Given the indisputable evidence that the *mahr* is a religious obligation upon a Muslim husband, what happens when a husband cannot pay the *mahr*? Does the wife then have the right to divorce or possibly annul (*faskh al-ʿaqd*) her marriage? Different Muslim schools of jurisprudence hold different opinions.

The Ḥanbalī and Ḥanafī schools took on the more conservative view by not permitting annulment to preserve the marriage, but stated a wife can abstain from consummating the marriage until her *mahr* is paid in full. Both the Shāfiʿī and Mālikī schools ruled that a wife could annul the contract or divorce her husband if the husband had agreed to gift her the *mahr* in full prior to the couple consummating their marriage and has yet to deliver on this promise (meaning the union has not yet been consummated).[22] The likely reason for this opinion is that, prior to consummation, the marital bond is not as strong as it becomes once the couple has been intimate and possibly even had children. If, *prior to consummation*, the husband claims he cannot afford to pay the *mahr* he specified in the contract, then, according to the Mālikī school, the wife may seek a hearing with a judge.[23] The judge will determine whether the husband's claim of financial hardship is compelling by combing through the man's income, assets, and investments and decide how much time to allot the husband to pay the *mahr*. The Mālikī school ruled that even if no evidence of the man's possession of income is found, if his outside appearance indicates that he is well-off while he insists not to pay the *mahr* he specified, the judge can go so far as to jail him until he agrees to pay the wife what he owes her.[24] They also ruled that if it proves too time-consuming and onerous for the wife to prove his ability to pay, the wife can choose to forgo this protracted process and immediately divorce her husband.[25] The Shāfiʿī school permitted contractual annulment on condition that it becomes evident to the judge that the husband is unable to pay the *mahr* and only after he is given three days to seek the money, even if he has to borrow the amount.[26] These rulings underscore the seriousness with which Islamic law regards this financial right of the wife – i.e., its denial is grounds for a swift divorce. Allah ﷻ uses the following weighty words to describe the *mahr* and thereby remind the reader that a man must not shirk this critical financial responsibility:

وَكَيْفَ تَأْخُذُونَهُۥ وَقَدْ أَفْضَىٰ بَعْضُكُمْ إِلَىٰ بَعْضٍ وَأَخَذْنَ مِنكُم مِّيثَٰقًا غَلِيظًا ﴿٢١﴾

> And how could you take it while you have gone in unto each other and they [your wives] have taken from you a solemn covenant?[27]

Scholars of all four major Sunni schools of thought believe that even if the marriage contract does not enumerate a bridal gift, the absence of this information does not justify denying the wife her *mahr*.[28] In fact, the jurists held that even if a woman herself requested that her *walī* (the person giving her away in marriage) not stipulate the amount of the *mahr*, or came to an agreement with her future spouse to marry without a *mahr* altogether, she is still entitled to receive a *mahr*.[29] As stated earlier, under all schools of thought, scholars agree that if the precise value of the bridal gift is not delineated in a valid marriage contract, then the wife is owed a *mahr* equal in value to the other women in comparable families (known as "*mahr al-mithl*").[30]

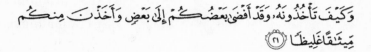

Of course, many differences in opinion exist as to the criteria for establishing a fair comparison of the deserved *mahr al-mithl*. Most scholars generally agree that a woman's married sisters (if any) constitute the first point of comparison. Some argue that the next comparison point should be married female cousins from the woman's father's side of the family, while others instead prioritize finding the woman's equals in wealth, moral character, education, beauty, and prior marital status (i.e. a previous marriage) to determine the *mahr* value. To this end, the Shāfiʿī school of jurisprudence rules: "If [the woman] held a special trait that none in the family possessed, a special *mahr* that meets her worthiness is stipulated for her."[31] Similarly the Ḥanbalī school of thought states:

> Equal *mahr* is ruled by the judge in analogy to women related to her like the mother, maternal aunt, paternal aunt and sister and the ruler puts into consideration who is her equal in wealth, beauty, intelligence, manners and age... and consideration is placed upon whom is closest to her... and if her family female members did not resemble her then women in her hometown are compared to her.[32]

The majority of the four major schools of jurisprudence uphold the principle that *mahr al-mithl* is due even to women whose marriage was consummated by an invalid defective (*fāsid*) contract, as in the case of a woman who married without witnesses present.[33] In fact, the Ḥanbalī school ruled that women who had been raped also deserve *mahr-al-mithl.*[34]

The schools of thought also differ over the wife's right to *mahr al-mithl* prior to consummation.[35] Some differences are based on the legal rulings derived from Chapter 2, verse 237 of the Qur'an, which refers to a woman who gets divorced prior to consummation and thus becomes entitled to a post-divorce financial contribution called *mutʿah.* The debate centers on whether, based on the wife's situation, she deserves *mahr al-mithl* or *mutʿah.* With respect to contracts that do not specify a *mahr*, Imam Mālik ﷺ, for example, ruled that such contracts are not only defective, but cause for marriage annulment, leading a woman to lose her right to *mahr al-mithl* but become entitled to *mutʿah* instead.[36] Other scholars ruled that the wife would be entitled to *mahr al-mithl* even prior to consummation, based on the Hadith of the Companion Ibn Masʿūd ﷺ. When once questioned about a woman whose husband passed prior to the consummation of their marriage with a contract that did not specify a precise *mahr* amount, he ruled that she was due *mahr al-mithl*.[37] His judgment was heard by another Companion who confirmed this to be correct since he remembered the Messenger ﷺ making the same ruling for another woman by the name of Baruʿ bint Wāshiq al-Ashjaʿiyyah.[38]

While the four major schools of thought agree upon the concept of *mahr al-mithl*, they hold different opinions on the minimum amount of *mahr* a man can gift his wife. The Ḥanafī school ruled that a man cannot give less than ten dirhams. The Mālikī school required that the bridal gift be no less than three dirhams of pure silver. The other two schools did not specify a minimum requirement[39] Some contemporary scholars like al-Zuḥaylī suggest that today, a *mahr* amount should not be less than what the Messenger ﷺ gave his wives, 400-500 dirhams, equal to 1487.5 grams of silver. The Prophet's wife 'Ā'ishah said, "The *sadaq* [*mahr*] of the Prophet to his wives was five hundred dirhams." However, because the price of silver fluctuates, scholars suggest that the most accurate way to calculate this amount in today's currency is by comparing the cost of livestock since that value is stable. According to the Companion Arwah al-Bariqi the Prophet gave him one dinar (equal to 12 dirhams) to purchase one sheep. And since one sheep today costs about $200 (equal to the one dinar), the value of the 500 dirhams (the cost of 42 sheep) today would amount to $8,440.

An exception of a much higher *mahr* (of four thousand dirhams) was given to the Prophet's wife Umm Ḥabībah ﷺ who lived in another country when the Messenger married her.

> The Prophet ﷺ married her while she resided in Abyssinia [Ethiopia today] and the King Negas married them by a power of attorney that he ﷺ sent him. At the time the Messenger ﷺ was living under siege in Mecca and King Negas gave her a *mahr* of four thousand dirham and paid all of her bridal expenses, a matter that was not disapproved by the Messenger ﷺ.[40]

Still, according to Zaydān, the majority of scholars agree that there is no set minimum or maximum amount of *mahr,* and that the *mahr* must simply meet the following conditions: it is of monetary value, derived from a permissible source (*halal*), something useful, and a gift that belongs fully to the wife.[41] Regarding an impoverished man, several Prophetic traditions suggest that materials of value other than money can serve as *mahr.* For example, when ʿAlī ﷺ asked for the hand of Fāṭimah ﷺ – the daughter of the Prophet ﷺ – in marriage, the Prophet ﷺ asked the destitute suitor to offer his armor as the bridal gift.[42] Most scholars agree that the aim is to make marriage accessible to everyone, while still allowing every woman to feel honored. It is important to note that although the *mahr* may have at times appeared as a symbolic gesture during the age of the pious, today this bridal gift often functions as a source of financial security in cases of divorce.

Instances when Half of the Mahr is Due

There are also circumstances in which the wife is owed only half the amount of the agreed-upon *mahr*. These cases include divorce prior to the total seclusion (*khalwah*) of both spouses in a private setting – a scenario in which some degree of physical intimacy may occur – and of course, divorce prior to consummation.[43] Scholars derived these rulings directly from Qur'anic Chapter 2:237:

وَإِن طَلَّقْتُمُوهُنَّ مِن قَبْلِ أَن تَمَسُّوهُنَّ وَقَدْ فَرَضْتُمْ لَهُنَّ فَرِيضَةً فَنِصْفُ مَا فَرَضْتُمْ إِلَّا
أَن يَعْفُونَ أَوْ يَعْفُوَا الَّذِي بِيَدِهِ عُقْدَةُ النِّكَاحِ ۚ وَأَن تَعْفُوا أَقْرَبُ لِلتَّقْوَىٰ ۚ وَلَا
تَنسَوُا الْفَضْلَ بَيْنَكُمْ ۚ إِنَّ اللَّهَ بِمَا تَعْمَلُونَ بَصِيرٌ ﴿٢٣٧﴾

And if you divorce them before you have touched them [consummated the marriage] and you have already specified for them an obligation, then [give] half of what you specified – unless they forgo the right or the one in whose hand is the marriage contract forgoes it. And to forego it is nearer to righteousness. And do not forget the graciousness between you. Indeed Allah, of whatever you do, is Seeing.[44]

Scholars also deduced that this ruling applies if, before consummation or spousal seclusion (*khalwah*), the husband takes an oath to abstain from any conjugal relations with his wife (*īlā'*), a practice customary in the pre-Islamic era. The husband would refuse intimacy with his wife sometimes for years in order to harm her, by keeping her hanging as stated in Sūrah al-Nisā', neither divorced nor truly married.[45] Verse 226 of sūrah 2 of the Qur'an prohibited this act and prescribed consequences upon those who put it into practice.[46]

A wife is also owed half the *mahr* if prior to consummation, the husband swears an oath of imprecation (*li'ān),* in which spouses become forever separated due to a man accusing his wife of adultery while being the only witness.[47] Imam Ibn Taymiyyah ﵀

noted that in a case where the husband and wife swear an oath of imprecation after the marriage has been consummated, all schools of thought agree that she receives her full *mahr*.[48]

Half the *mahr* may also be owed if the husband proves physically unable to consummate the marriage (*ʿunnah*).[49] According to the four schools of thought, the wife's word on impotence is sufficient and she is entitled to take the matter to an Islamic court where a judge may declare the two divorced. Half the *mahr* is also due to the wife if information prohibiting a couple's marriage is revealed – for example, if both spouses partook in suckling (*riḍāʿah*) from the same wet nurse.[50]

Relinquishing her Right to the Mahr

As mentioned in Chapter Two, according to verse 4 of Sūrah al-Nisā', a wife can choose to return some or all of the bridal gift back to her husband. However, if a wife returns the bridal gift to her husband and then changes her mind, many scholars agree that the husband must then return the *mahr* back to his wife. They base this ruling on the fact that if a wife regretted her decision to return the gift to her husband, she did not truly make that decision from a place of sincerity and willingness, as instructed in the Qur'anic verse. Therefore, she is entitled to change her mind and ask that the *mahr* be restored. Several historical examples fortify this view. In one instance, a dispute came before the judge and Successor Shurayḥ ﵀ in which a husband complained that his wife had returned the *mahr* to him, yet was now retracting her decision. Shurayḥ ruled in the wife's favor, saying, "If she did this [returned the *mahr*] out of her heart, she would not ask for it back."[51] A similar case appeared before Caliph ʿAbd al-Malik ibn

Marwān.[52] A wife had returned her *mahr* of one thousand dinars back to her husband, but when he decided after a mere month of marriage to divorce her, she asked that the bridal gift be given back to her.[53] ʿAbd al-Malik ibn Marwān ruled that the man return the bridal gift back to his ex-wife in full, and recited the following verse as the basis for his ruling:

وَإِنْ أَرَدتُّمُ ٱسْتِبْدَالَ زَوْجٍ مَّكَانَ زَوْجٍ وَءَاتَيْتُمْ إِحْدَىٰهُنَّ قِنطَارًا فَلَا تَأْخُذُوا۟ مِنْهُ شَيْـًٔا ۚ أَتَأْخُذُونَهُۥ بُهْتَٰنًا وَإِثْمًا مُّبِينًا ﴿٢٠﴾

> But if you want to replace one wife with another and you have given one of them a great amount [in gifts], *do not take [back] from it anything.* Would you take it in injustice and manifest sin?[54]

One of the most compelling statements to buttress scholars' viewpoint that a husband must honor a wife's request to receive back a *mahr* she has returned to him is one made by ʿUmar ibn al-Khaṭṭāb ﵁ to the judges commissioned under him: "Women give out of their goodwill or out of fear; therefore whenever a woman gives [and] then asks back for it, that is her prerogative and Allah knows best."[55] This view was later adopted by Imam Ibn Abī Laylā ﵀, as well as Imam al-Shāfiʿī ﵀, who said:

> If a woman hands her husband any charity (*ṣadaqah*) or gave up her *mahr* to him…then provides evidence at a later time that her husband compelled her to do this… then her doing so is considered null and void.[56]

In a situation where a wife is ill and on her deathbed pardons her husband of her deferred *mahr*, which she never received, the jurists of the major schools of thought again held different opinions. While Imam Abū Ḥanīfah ﵀ ruled that such bequest to pardon his obligation is unacceptable, Imams Mālik, al-Shāfiʿī, and Aḥmad ﷺ permitted such pardon only if she had also earlier relinquished the owed *mahr* while in good health.[57] If she did not, then her heirs would have to agree to relinquish the *mahr*, because upon her death the *mahr* owed to her belongs to her heirs. And even upon relinquishing her right to *mahr* (which would have otherwise been inherited), all three Imams conditioned that the wife must utter her wish in the presence of a witness, in the form of a sworn statement (*yamīn*).[58]

Differing Opinions on Marital Maintenance or Nafaqah

As a woman enters marriage, she not only receives her bridal gift, the *mahr*, but attains a special right to *nafaqah*, defined in her case as marital maintenance— a testament to the honor and respect she deserves as a partner in the journey of matrimony. The *nafaqah* due to one's wife includes providing a home for her, tending to her healthcare needs, and supplying her with household help, clothing, and food. All scholars agree that it is a man's religious obligation (*farḍ*) to provide *nafaqah* to his wife before extending such support to any other individual, making her the most important recipient of *nafaqah*. Subsequently, the obligation extends to his children. Opinions differ between the schools of jurisprudence on whether the remaining categories of *nafaqah* (*nafaqah* due to needy relatives, etc.) are obligatory upon a Muslim man or simply encouraged. Interestingly, with respect to a Muslim woman's obligation to financially support others, most scholars agree that with the exception of her parents and grandparents (if they are poor) none of the *nafaqah* categories are obligatory upon her;

if she chooses to take care of her family members financially, it can be a gift or act of charity. Of course, when she willingly spends on her financially struggling husband or other family members, her financial support is a form of voluntary charity or may even – according to most scholars – be considered a part of her obligatory charity (*zakāt*) if the recipients fall among the eight permissible *zakāt* categories stated in sūrah 9, verse 60 of the Qur'an.[59] If neither was her intent, then what she spends on her household and husband, for instance, becomes a debt her husband owes her when his financial situation improves or upon his death, separate from her share of inheritance.[60] Imam Abū Ḥanīfah ﷺ and his school disagreed with the notion that a wife could provide her husband *zakāt*, because her *nafaqah* is his responsibility regardless.[61] Imam al-Shāfiʿī ﷺ allowed it only if what she gives him is spent solely on his living expenses and not on hers, since he is responsible to spend on her.[62]

Once a husband has taken care of his wife's *nafaqah*, scholars differ on the next person in line to being entitled to *nafaqah* from him. Imam Abū Ḥanīfah ﷺ stated if a man can only afford *nafaqah* for one more person, it should be his mother. She is given priority over his father due to the response of the Prophet ﷺ when he was asked who a person ought to treat with the most kindness and respect: "Your mother…your mother…your mother, then your father, then the closest relative (next in line)."[63] contrast, Imam al-Shāfiʿī ﷺ said a man must provide *nafaqah* first for his wife, but then his small child, followed by his mentally handicapped child (whether young or old), then his mother followed by his father, then his adult children, and, finally, his grandparents.[64] Imam Mālik ﷺ agreed with the same sequence, with one exception:

he ruled that a man's children deserve *nafaqah* before his parents, even if they are adults.[65] Despite these divergent opinions, one will always find that a woman, whether a wife or mother, take precedence over a man when it comes to receiving *nafaqah*.[66]

The provision of *nafaqah* includes providing a home for one's wife. Using the Qur'an and Sunnah, scholars have issued specific rulings on the type of home a Muslim husband is obligated to provide for his wife as part of her due *nafaqah*. If the residence fails to meet the criteria set by Islamic law, the wife has the right to refuse to move into the home and to refuse to consummate the marriage, but — even then — the husband remains obligated to provide for her financially.[67] Only in serious breaches of the marriage, or when a marriage contract is proven defective or invalid, do some scholars ever find no entitlement to *nafaqah*.[68] According to Islamic law, the residence must be either owned or rented by her husband.[69] It must also offer the wife privacy and security (i.e. located in a safe area).[70] The wife does not bear the responsibility of furnishing the home or purchasing household supplies; as part of his duty to provide for his wife, the husband must ensure that the home is fully furnished and, as his financial means allow, in keeping with the quality of home where his bride lived prior to marriage.[71] As noted in the Ḥanbalī school of thought, it is the husband's duty, as part of *nafaqah*, to improve and renovate the home over time to meet the couple's changing needs.[72]

Scholars also ruled that in certain cases the husband must arrange for household help, such as maid service, for his wife. All of the schools of jurisprudence ruled that, for instance, a woman who comes from a well-off family in which she was accustomed to domestic help is entitled to the same level of help in her new home with her husband.[73] They also agree that if she is ill, she is deserving of this type *nafaqah* so long as her husband can afford it. In fact, Imam al-Shāfiʿī and Imam Abū Ḥanīfah ﷺ agreed that in fulfilling the Qur'anic injunction to "live with [his wife] in accordance to what is fair and kind" as the Qur'an commands in Sūrah al-Nisā' verse 19, it is incumbent upon any husband to engage at least one domestic servant for her.[74] Imam Mālik ﷺ went even further, obliging a husband to hire even more help for her if needed.[75] According to Imam Ibn Ḥazm ﷺ, a wife's right of household help is absolute and unconditional.

> It is not the duty of the woman to serve her husband in any way, not in baking, cooking, dusting furniture, sweeping floors, sewing his cloth or anything else, but if she does (any of this) it is good of her.[76]

Imam Ibn Ḥazm's statement clarifies the wife's position as the man's companion rather than a house servant – although the latter has become a commonly-held opinion today. When some Muslim men argue that many of the female Companions did serve their husbands, these scholars explain that those women *chose* to serve their husbands; Islam did not mandate it. It is also the opinion of Imams Mālik, al-Shāfiʿī, Abū Ḥanīfah, Aḥmad ibn Hanbal, Ibn Ḥazm, and their followers ﷺ, Imams Ibn Taymiyyah, Ibn Qudāmah, al-Nawawī, al-Sarakhsī, al-Kāsānī and al-Ṭaḥāwī ﷺ that it is not her duty to cook, clean and serve the husband or children, and if a wife does so, it is tantamount to a voluntary act of good will. Under Islamic jurisprudence, the marital union is a mutually beneficial relationship where the wife's role in the marriage involves honoring and being trusted by her husband, showing kindness to him, and meeting his intimate needs, but simply does not require or condone his exploiting her as a servant.[77]

Scholars concur that the husband's duty of *nafaqah* includes the obligation to supply his wife with clothing suitable for all seasons, consistent with the prevailing norms or customs of the time and place.[78] Similarly, most scholars hold the opinion that *nafaqah* includes providing for one's wife's personal care, as it is important for both the health of the marriage and the woman's sense of self to feel that she looks her best. Personal care includes, among other things, a woman's hygiene products, hair products, and according to some scholars (e.g. Mālikī school), even perfume and makeup. Surprisingly, scholars disagree as to whether medical care is included in the *nafaqah* a husband owes his wife. Some scholars opine that a husband must cover the costs of medical care – including but not limited to medication, doctor visits, childbirth, surgeries, or hospitalization – as part of *nafaqah*.[79] They deduce that if a husband is obligated to provide his wife with "sustenance," as the Prophet ﷺ said, then sustenance includes all things that preserve one's life and health – food, water, and medical care.[80] These scholars also interpret Allah's command to live in kindness with one's wife as obligating a husband to provide and care for his wife in times of sickness.[81] As Dr. Wahbah al-Zuḥaylī said, "Is it proper to fulfill the duty of treating one's wife in the best manner only when she is in good health and when she's ill he tells her to go back to her parents?"[82] Failing to provide for a wife's medical care appears to conflict with the following words of God:

وَمِنْ ءَايَٰتِهِۦٓ أَنْ خَلَقَ لَكُم مِّنْ أَنفُسِكُمْ أَزْوَٰجًا لِّتَسْكُنُوٓا۟ إِلَيْهَا وَجَعَلَ بَيْنَكُم مَّوَدَّةً وَرَحْمَةً ۚ إِنَّ فِى ذَٰلِكَ لَءَايَٰتٍ لِّقَوْمٍ يَتَفَكَّرُونَ ﴿٢١﴾

And of His signs is that He created for you from yourselves mates that you may find tranquility in them; and He placed between you affection and mercy. Indeed, in that are signs for a people who give thought.[83]

Despite strong evidence in favor of the idea that a wife's medical care falls under *nafaqah*, the Shāfiʿī, Ḥanafī, and Ḥanbalī schools of jurisprudence disagree. The Mālikī school appears to hold both views dichotomously.[84] Some Mālikī scholars clearly indicated that medical care is indeed part of her *nafaqah*.[85] The argument adopted by other scholars posits that a husband is only responsible for the absolute basics of life, with the presumption that his wife is healthy—akin to the upkeep of a healthy building, not one in disrepair.[86] This analogy posits that just as a tenant renting a building is not accountable for repairing its crumbling foundation, the husband is similarly is not obligated to cover the expenses of healing his wife's ailments. That argument was rejected by renowned scholar Dr. ʿAbd al-Karīm Zaydān, whose jurisprudential works on the status of women, *al-Jāmiʿ fī al-Fiqh al-Islāmī al-Mufaṣṣal fī Aḥkām al-Marʾah wa al-Bayt al-Muslim,* achieved a King Faisal International Prize in Saudi Arabia. He rejects the argument and analogy upon which it is based.[87] Similarly, Imam ʿAbd al-Raḥmān al-Jazīrī vehemently opposed this view in *Kitāb al-Fiqh ʿalā al-Madhāhib al-Arbaʿah,* commenting, "If the sick wife is not treated by her husband who has the money to save her from her pain, then who else will treat her from amongst those who have money? Is it not common sense that he takes care of her treatment and pays for the medicine she needs?"[88] Dr. 'Abida al-Mu'yed al-Aẓam opined that the husband's non-expenditure on his wife's medical needs is baseless.[89]

Retranslating and Reinterpreting a Controversial Qur'anic Verse about Wives

After understanding the significant financial burden Islam places on a husband, a seemingly contentious Qur'anic verse, often translated as follows, becomes clear:

ٱلرِّجَالُ قَوَّٰمُونَ عَلَى ٱلنِّسَآءِ بِمَا فَضَّلَ ٱللَّهُ بَعۡضَهُمۡ عَلَىٰ بَعۡضٖ وَبِمَآ أَنفَقُواْ مِنۡ
أَمۡوَٰلِهِمۡۚ فَٱلصَّٰلِحَٰتُ قَٰنِتَٰتٌ حَٰفِظَٰتٞ لِّلۡغَيۡبِ بِمَا حَفِظَ ٱللَّهُۚ وَٱلَّٰتِي تَخَافُونَ
نُشُوزَهُنَّ فَعِظُوهُنَّ وَٱهۡجُرُوهُنَّ فِي ٱلۡمَضَاجِعِ وَٱضۡرِبُوهُنَّۖ فَإِنۡ
أَطَعۡنَكُمۡ فَلَا تَبۡغُواْ عَلَيۡهِنَّ سَبِيلًاۗ إِنَّ ٱللَّهَ كَانَ عَلِيّٗا كَبِيرٗا ﴿٣٤﴾

Men are in charge of women by [right of] what Allah has given one over the other and what they spend [for maintenance] from their wealth. So righteous women are devoutly obedient, guarding in [the husband's] absence what Allah would have them guard. But those [wives] from whom you fear arrogance [*nushūzuhuna sing. nushūz*] – [first] advise them....[90]

Too often, readers – both Muslim and non-Muslim – interpret this verse 34 to mean that Allah created men as superior to women since they have been placed in charge of women. First, in the aforementioned translation as well as many others, the phrase "in charge" is translated from the Arabic word "*qawwāmūn* (*sing. qawwām*) ," and the well-known Arabic dictionary *Lisān al-'Arab* defines "*al-qawwām*" as a person who protects and is just.[91] So, in this verse, Allah ﷻ designated men as protectors of women. In fact, the English translation of this same verse by Yusuf Ali and Mohsin Khan provides, as the translation of the beginning of this verse: "Men are the protectors and maintainers of women…"[92] If we delve into the meaning of *qawwamun* further, *qawwām* comes from the root *qawm*, which is defined as a sizeable group of people. Thus, the true meaning of the Arabic word *qawwamun* encompasses the responsibility of leading and protecting not only women, but the family as a whole.[93] The first line of this verse also makes clear that Allah ﷻ chose men to fulfill this leadership role because He required men to provide for their wives and family members. Arguably, it stands to reason that if a man fails to fulfill the key condition of this role by financially providing for his wife and family, he is no longer deserving of the leadership position or of having the final say in the household.[94]

While there is disagreement about why and when the marital financial obligation is triggered, this verse undoubtedly makes clear that men must financially provide for their wives. Specifically, many scholars maintained that the *nafaqah* or financial maintenance that a husband owes his wife is a financial right that begins from the consummation of the marriage because they see this obligation of maintenance as an exchange for the husband's fulfillment of his sexual needs.[95] Some scholars reason that we can infer this start date of *nafaqah* from the Sunnah of the Prophet ﷺ as his *nafaqah* upon 'Ā'ishah رضي الله عنها did not begin after the marriage contract, but rather commenced two years later once the marriage had been consummated.[96] Interpreters of the Qur'an, however, point out that the words of Allah ﷻ in the 34th verse of Sūrah al-Nisā' mentioned above along with the following words that appear in the second Chapter of the Qur'an, verse 233, indicate that during pregnancy, childbirth, and nursing, a husband is obligated to provide for his wife, regardless of whether his sexual needs are met at those times: "...and it is incumbent upon him who has begotten the child to provide in a fair manner for their [mother and child] sustenance and clothing."[97] Therefore, some scholars, including Imam Abū Ḥanīfah ﵀, go so far as to argue that if a man marries a young woman who is not yet ready to consummate the marriage, but is his wife and companion in every other sense, she still deserves *nafaqah*.[98] The Shāfiʿī jurist al-Māwardī ﵀ reasons that this was the view of Imam al-Shāfiʿī ﵀ because the situation resembles illness— since, when ill, a wife may be unable to have sexual relations with her husband but would, in his view, unquestionably retain the right to *nafaqah* under Islamic law.[99] Similarly, Imam Ibn Ḥazm ﵀ said, "Indeed the *nafaqah* (for the wife) is an exchange for marriage and not an exchange for sexual intercourse."[100] This viewpoint stands out as a compelling and equitable one, particularly in light of the fact that when a man decides to marry a young woman, he is surely cognizant of both her age and her readiness or lack thereof to consummate the marriage.[101] The claim that the Messenger did not begin financially supporting ʿĀ'ishah ﵂ until the marriage was consummated appears to be an assumption by some scholars, as there was no Prophetic tradition that indicated that he ﷺ did not at all financially provide for her ﵂ after the marriage was contracted.[102] The Ḥanafī scholar al-Kāsānī clarified that a man must pay his wife *nafaqah* if the marriage was not consummated and she remains in her parents' household if, (1) he did not request that she move into his home and/or (2) she has certain legitimate reasons for refusing to move into his home.[103] Legitimate reasons that justify her refusal to move into her husband's home after the contractual agreement include instances where she has not received her prompt *mahr* or if her husband failed to provide a suitable home for her.[104]

Another important point to note regarding verse 34 of Chapter 4 of the Qur'an is the appearance of the word *nushūz*, a word sometimes translated in Qur'anic translations as "recalcitrant." or "arrogant." Scholars held different opinions on whether or not wives considered recalcitrant should receive *nafaqah*.[105] Those who held that a recalcitrant wife does not deserve *nafaqah* reason that the act of *nushūz* goes against the marriage contract, even though verse 34 of Sūrah al-Nisā' instructs husbands to take three progressive steps against *nushūz* wives and none of those measures include withholding *nafaqah*.[106] They reason that *nushūz* in the verse represents the wife's disobedience of her husband in matters that become his right once the marriage is contracted in exchange for him providing financial support to her, including her withholding herself from intimacy, leaving the marital home without his knowledge, or refusing to move into his home or travel with him.[107] Still, according to Imam Abū Ḥanīfah ﷺ, a wife who does not allow her husband to have intimate relations with her is not defined as *nāshiz*, but a woman who leaves the husband's home (*iḥtibās*) without his knowledge is so defined (since that particular requirement is a condition in his jurisprudence for a wife's receipt of *nafaqah* rights).[108]

It is important to note that the Islamic term "*nāshiz*," at times translated as recalcitrant or rebellious/defiant, is an adjective used to describe a person, while "*nushūz*" is a noun referring to that state of being. For example, a wife might be described as a *nāshiz* wife, and she would thus be labeled as being in a state of *nushūz*. However, before we accept that *nushūz* means rebellious, we must consider that one of the key sources in determining the exegesis and meanings of the words in the Qur'an is by turning to the use of the same words in other parts of the Qur'an. In fact, Islamic thinker Jamal al-Banna was of the opinion that since all interpretations of the Qur'an are by scholars who, while doing their best, are nonetheless human and susceptible to errors – the only acceptable form of interpretation is interpreting the Qur'an through the Qur'an itself.[109] So, if we examine all the verses that contain the word *nushūz* (or its derivatives), we see that this adjective does not, in fact, translate to recalcitrant. In verse 128 of Sūrah al-Nisā', the word *nushūz* is used to describe an act committed by the husband rather than the wife:

وَإِنِ ٱمْرَأَةٌ خَافَتْ مِنۢ بَعْلِهَا نُشُوزًا أَوْ إِعْرَاضًا فَلَا جُنَاحَ عَلَيْهِمَآ أَن يُصْلِحَا بَيْنَهُمَا
صُلْحًا ۚ وَٱلصُّلْحُ خَيْرٌ ۗ وَأُحْضِرَتِ ٱلْأَنفُسُ ٱلشُّحَّ ۚ وَإِن تُحْسِنُوا۟ وَتَتَّقُوا۟ فَإِنَّ ٱللَّهَ
كَانَ بِمَا تَعْمَلُونَ خَبِيرًا ﴿١٢٨﴾

And if a woman fears from her husband *contempt* [*iʿrāḍ*] or *evasion* [*nushūzan*], there is no sin upon them if they make terms of settlement between them – and settlement is best. And present in [human] souls is stinginess. But if you do good and fear Allah – then indeed Allah is ever, with what you do, Acquainted.[110]

In this verse of Sūrah Al-Nisaa' the words *nushūz* and *iʿrāḍ* stand for the same meaning because the word "or" or "*aw*" is placed between the two. According to Imam al-Ṭabarī ﷺ, in this verse the descriptive *nushūz* refers to the husband treating his wife poorly and with contempt and no longer wanting to remain in the marriage.[111] Since the word *nushūz* in the above verse refers to a husband who treats his wife contemptuously and who no longer wants to remain in the marriage, we can infer that the word "*nāshiz*" does not describe a recalcitrant wife, but rather a wife who treats her husband poorly and does not want to remain married to him.

Another point of disagreement amongst scholars is whether or not *nafaqah* can be waived by a woman and the effect of the waiver of such a fundamental right: Imam Ibn Kathīr ﵀ and others argue that in the scenario involving *nushūz* (when defined as *defiant*), when a husband intends to divorce his wife, a wife may relinquish her right to *nafaqah* as a way of persuading her husband to remain in the marriage.[112] Imam Ibn Kathīr ﵀ viewed this concession by the wife to be the settlement (*iṣlāḥ*), mentioned later in the same verse. It is unclear how this was derived however. While some may accept Imam Ibn Kathīr's interpretation of verse 128, meaning that a wife can choose to forgo her right to *nafaqah* as a way of convincing an uninterested husband to remain married to her, this interpretation seems inconsistent with the purpose of the revelation of this verse. According to a Hadith within *Ṣaḥīḥ al-Bukhārī*, ʿĀ'ishah ﵂ explained that the above verse was revealed in response to Sawdah ﵂, the wife of the Prophet ﷺ, who, because of her older age, gave the nights the Prophet ﷺ spent with her to ʿĀ'ishah ﵂. ʿĀ'ishah ﵂ explained: "[This verse] refers to a man who is married to an old woman and he does not desire her and wants to divorce her. So, she says, 'I forfeit my right on you,' so this verse was revealed."[113] What is apparent from this Hadith, however, is that Sawdah ﵂ waived her right to nights of intimacy with the Prophet ﷺ

but did not relinquish her *nafaqah.* Yet many scholars such as Imam Ibn Kathīr ﷺ assume that a woman in a similar situation might relieve the man from *nafaqah* and from payment of his deferred *mahr.*[114]

What we do know: according to most authentic Hadith, the Prophet ﷺ accepted Sawdah's offer to give up her right to nights of intimacy with him, but there are no authentic traditions that indicate that he ﷺ no longer desired Sawdah ﷺ or intended to divorce her; this in fact could have been her own disinterest in intimacy as a result of her age. It is important to note that even if a woman chooses to give up her husband's conjugal visits for whatever reason, it is her full legal prerogative to change her mind at any time.[115] It follows that, if a woman chooses to forgo some of her financial rights for some reason, it is also her right within Islamic law to reverse her decision and once again receive that particular financial right. The main takeaway of the aforementioned verse 128 is that, in an ideal case scenario, it is best for a husband and wife to come to an agreement that satisfies both parties and keeps the marriage intact.

As mentioned earlier, one of the requirements upon scholars writing an exegesis of the Qur'an is to interpret words and phrases by first examining other instances therein where the same words and phrases are used.[116] Therefore, it is incongruous to interpret the word *nushūz*, when it refers to men, to mean a husband who treats his wife contemptuously and plans to divorce her; yet when the same word is used to describe women, to interpret it to mean a rebellious wife who disobeys her husband. In conducting an exegesis of the Qur'an, scholars generally agree that when different verses discuss the same subject matter, those verses should be interpreted as having similar meanings. This form of interpretation is known as *al-tafsīr al-mawḍūʿī*, or "interpretation by subject."[117] When determining the meaning of the word *nushūz*, the concept of *al-tafsīr al-mawḍūʿī* may be applied to both verse 34 and verse 128 of the fourth Chapter of the Qur'an, as both verses are about the same subject matter – marriage and how husbands and wives treat one another. It is more logical and accurate to derive the meaning of the word *nushūz* through these two verses rather than through others in the Qur'an where *nushūz* (or its derivatives) is used in entirely different contexts. Therefore, it seems that the correct translation of the word *nushūz* in Chapter 4, verse 34 of the Qur'an – a translation based on a sister verse in the same chapter regarding the same subject – appears to be a woman who regards her husband with contempt and wants to divorce him.

Once we have established the correct meaning of the word *nushūz*, as it is used in this particular verse, it seems clear that because the word *nushūz* describes not a wife who is rebellious and disobedient (as stated in most translations), but rather a wife who seeks to divorce her husband, scholars cannot use verse 4:34 to argue that wives who disobey their husbands should not receive financial maintenance during their marriages. And according to Imam Ibn Ḥazm ﵀ and other scholars, there is no evidence to suggest that a wife who no longer wishes to remain in her marriage should be denied *nafaqah* throughout the remainder of her marriage.[118]

So, the view based on Qur'anic text appears to be that a woman shall at all times remain entitled to *nafaqah* throughout her marriage. A straightforward and empathetic view of human behavior also opposes a ruling that wives who are viewed as defiant may not remain entitled to their *nafaqah*. The Qur'an teaches us that men and women are created from the same soul and are equally human in their emotions. Just like her husband, a wife will at times experience anger and irritability toward her partner and may be disagreeable or defiant. The inevitable fluctuations of life, compounded by the distinct pressures and demands faced by women specifically — ranging from their monthly cycles to the challenges of hormonal shifts, pregnancy, childbirth, postpartum struggles, nursing and child-rearing, all while striving to fulfill religious duties and meet familial expectations – will inevitably lead to moments of frustration and irritability in women's lives.[119] A foundational understanding of human psychology reveals the unreasonable nature of asserting that a wife who disagrees with her husband, does not fully accept or abide by his decisions, or expresses frustration towards him, is not entitled to financial support. Such ruling would open the door for a narcissistic or miserly spouse to escape the *nafaqah* he owes his wife simply by accusing her of recalcitrance. A wife would never feel secure in her own home and marital life could not survive. The grandchild of prominent jurist ʿAlī al-Ṭanṭāwī, Islamic thinker Dr. ʿĀbidah al-Mu'ayyad al-Azam, a Shariah professor and author of 16 books on women's matters, strongly criticizes the opinion that a husband is not obligated to provide *nafaqah* to a rebellious or disobedient wife. She argues that such an attitude dehumanizes women, reducing them to mere bodies devoid of feelings or desires, akin to machines that unquestioningly obey commands without the ability to think or refuse.[120] In her opinion, *nushūz* in verse 4:34 refers to a woman who engaged in the act of pre-adultery and not of a rebellious wife. She bases her view on the Prophet's ﷺ final sermon, regarding the husband's rights in a marital relationship. The final sermon suggests that certain behaviors, like allowing someone to lay in your bed, which are considered pre-cursors to adultery are prohibited (*lā ya'tīna bi-fāḥishah*), and that a husband could take certain progressive steps if they do occur—including abstaining from sharing the marital bed.[121] Remarkably, these consequences mirror those outlined for individuals in a state of *nushūz* in verse 34 of Chapter 4 of the Qur'an.[122] According to Dr. al-Azam a husband is not entitled to deny financial support to his wife merely because she demonstrates anger, rebellion, or disobedience.

No scholar disagrees that Prophet Muhammad ﷺ sets the pinnacle example of a husband who appropriately fulfils his religious duties to his wife. Of course, the Prophet never shirked his duty to financially provide for his wives, and certainly never did so citing their "rebelliousness" as the reason. He and his wives had their share of disagreements, but a Muslim marriage is based in part on mutual patience and tolerance, and the Prophet ﷺ never withheld the *nafaqah* he owed his wives as a result of their disagreements. Imam al-Ghazālī ؒ interpreted the words of Allah in verse 19 of Chapter 4 of the Qur'an, "And live with them [your wives] in kindness," to mean, among other things, that a husband must show patience and kindness toward his wife in all her states – both when she is agreeable and when she is upset and dissenting – just as she accepts her husband in all his states.[123] Examples of the forbearance of the Prophet ﷺ abound: in one incident, he invited some Companions for a meal to the home of one of his wives. Another of his wives learned of the gathering and took it upon herself to send her servant over with a beautiful plate of rice and meat for the guests. The wife who was hosting the gathering felt resentful at this gesture and pushed the plate from the servant's hand onto the floor, where it shattered into pieces. Instead of reacting with anger, the Prophet ﷺ calmly brought out another plate, knelt on the ground and picked up the fallen food to placing it onto the unbroken dish. The Prophet ﷺ gently excused his wife's behavior, explaining to his guests, "Your mother got jealous."[124] Not only did he not admonish his wife, but he reminded his Companions that, as his wife, she is a *mother* of the believers. In another instance, Abū Bakr ؓ, while standing on the doorstep of the home of the Prophet ﷺ, overheard his daughter ʿĀʾishah ؓ who was also the wife of the Prophet ﷺ raise her voice against her husband. Once he had received permission to enter, Abū Bakr ؓ strode in, grabbed his daughter out of anger and exclaimed, "How dare you raise your voice like that to the Messenger!" The Prophet ﷺ quickly intervened, pulling Abū Bakr ؓ away from ʿĀʾishah ؓ and calming him down.[125]

Not only did the Prophet ﷺ never withhold *nafaqah* from his wives as a result of them disagreeing with him or becoming upset with him, but he never characterized his wives' opposition as recalcitrant or *nāshiz*. In fact, many traditions reveal that the Prophet ﷺ did not admonish women when they were assertive in their relationships. For example, unlike Meccan women, the women of Medina were particularly confident and active in the public sphere, and accustomed to fully participating in decision-making both within and outside their homes. Apparently, upon immigrating to Medina and marrying Medina's women many Meccan men were frustrated by their wives' assertiveness. In one instance, ʿUmar ؓ said to Ibn ʿAbbās ؓ during the Hajj (pilgrimage):

> We, the people of Quraysh, used to have authority over women, but when we came to live with the Anṣār, we noticed that the Anṣārī women had the upper hand over their men, so our women started acquiring the habits of the Anṣārī women. Once I shouted at my wife (about a matter) and she shouted back at me, and I disliked that she dared to answer back at me. She said, 'Why do you take it ill that I responded right back at you? By Allah, the wives of the Prophet do answer back at him, and some of them abstained from speaking with him for the whole day until night.' ['Umar thought] What she said scared me and I said to her, 'Whoever amongst them does so, will be a great loser.' Then I dressed myself and went to Ḥafṣah ['Umar's daughter and the wife of the Prophet ﷺ] and asked her, 'Does any of you keep Allah's Messenger angry all day long until night?' She replied in the affirmative.[126]

When 'Umar ؓ voiced a similar complaint to the Prophet ﷺ, the Prophet simply smiled in response and did not criticize the women of Medina nor advise that their husbands reassert themselves. If these wives were characterized as disobedient, or *nāshiz*, because they at times disagreed with or corrected their husbands, the Prophet ﷺ would have issued some sort of reprimand. His smile indicates that he did not regard such behavior as *nushūz*.

The Prophetic tradition is filled with examples and directives about showing kindness to a wife, as well as examples of how the Prophet handled difficult situations in his marriages. The Prophet's example exphasized maintaining marital harmony, reflecting Islam's efforts to discourage divorce while acknowledging that divorce remains permissible and halal.[127]

Continued Interpretations of Nushūz as a Wife's Rebelliousness, and the Types of Nushūz

In verse 128 of Chapter 4 of the Qur'an, the word *nushūz* describes a husband who treats his spouse contemptuously and wishes to leave the marriage. In the following verse 11 of Sūrah al-Mujādilah, we see yet another meaning of the term *nushūz*:

يَٰٓأَيُّهَا ٱلَّذِينَ ءَامَنُوٓا۟ إِذَا قِيلَ لَكُمْ تَفَسَّحُوا۟ فِى ٱلْمَجَٰلِسِ فَٱفْسَحُوا۟ يَفْسَحِ ٱللَّهُ لَكُمْ ۖ وَإِذَا
قِيلَ ٱنشُزُوا۟ فَٱنشُزُوا۟ يَرْفَعِ ٱللَّهُ ٱلَّذِينَ ءَامَنُوا۟ مِنكُمْ وَٱلَّذِينَ أُوتُوا۟ ٱلْعِلْمَ دَرَجَٰتٍ ۚ وَٱللَّهُ بِمَا
تَعْمَلُونَ خَبِيرٌ ﴿١١﴾

O you who have believed, when you are told, "Space yourselves" in assemblies, then make space; Allah will make space for you. And when you are told, *"Get up"* [*anshizu,*] *then get up* [*fa'anshizu*]*;* Allah will raise those who have believed among you and those who were given knowledge, by degrees. And Allah is acquainted with what you do.[128]

Based on the above translation and the interpretation of Imam Maḥmūd al-Ālūsī رحمه الله, the word *nushūz* in this verse refers to a person who is directed to get up and depart from a gathering in which the Prophet ﷺ is also present.[129] Consequently, some scholars then hold that *nushūz* refers to a wife's rebelliousness when she departs or leaves the marital home without her husband's permission. These scholars justified their ruling by pointing out that if a woman left her marital home without her husband's consent, she would be physically unavailable for intimacy. This reasoning, however, appears to conflict with how the Prophet ﷺ treated his wives. The following tradition demonstrates that women are permitted by Allah ﷻ Himself to leave their homes to take care of their needs, and do not require their husbands' permission. ʿĀ'ishah ﵁ said:

> Once Sawdah bint Zamʿah went out at night for some need, and Umar saw her, and recognizing her, he said (to her), "By Allah, O Sawdah! You cannot hide yourself from us." So, she returned to the Prophet ﷺ and mentioned that to him while he was sitting in my dwelling taking his supper and holding a bone covered with meat in his hand. Then the Divine Inspiration was revealed to him and when that state was over, he ﷺ was saying: "O women! You have been allowed by Allah to go out for your needs."[130]

Because women are permitted by Allah ﷻ to leave their homes to take care of their needs, the majority of scholars, including both Imam Abū Ḥanīfah and Imam al-Shāfiʿī ﵏, held the opinion that a woman who leaves her home without her husband's knowledge is not behaving in a rebellious, or *nāshiz*, manner if her reasons for traveling outside of her home are need-based. In Islamic law, there's a fundamental principle prioritizing the fulfillment of basic needs.[131] Islam is a pragmatic faith and women, not unlike men, have many commitments and exigencies that require them to leave their homes – visiting parents or relatives, doctor's appointments, household errands, and picking up or dropping off their children, for example. Scholars have also held that if a wife included a stipulation in her marriage contract to pursue an education or employment after marriage, which obviously necessitates her regular departure from her marital residence, then her departure for such purposes is considered her Islamic right, and her husband cannot withhold *nafaqah* as a result.[132]

While the majority of scholars agree that a husband is not permitted to deny his wife *nafaqah* for leaving her home to take care of her needs, there is some disagreement among scholars as to whether or not a woman traveling for Hajj (pilgrimage to Mecca) without her husband's knowledge is tantamount to her being recalcitrant and if her husband can withhold *nafaqah* as a result.[133] Imam Abū Yūsuf and Imam Aḥmad ibn Ḥanbal ﷺ ruled that she is still entitled *nafaqah*, while Imam Abū Ḥanīfah and al-Shāfiʿī ﷺ disagreed, since the pillar of Hajj is open anytime during one's lifetime and one need not rush to do it.[134] However, Imam Aḥmad ibn Ḥanbal ﷺ reasoned that when a woman travels to perform Hajj, she is carrying out a religious obligation commanded by Allah ﷻ, much like her praying five times a day or fasting in the month of Ramadan, and no person can deny a Muslim's fulfillment of obligations toward Allah ﷻ.[135] As the Prophet ﷺ said, "[There is] no obedience to any creation upon a sinful act," and failure to perform one's mandated Hajj would be a sin.[136]

In her book *Mā Ḥudūd Ṭāʿat al-Zawj?* (*What are the Boundaries to Obeying the Husband?*), Dr. ʿĀbidah al-Aẓam argues that women do not require their husbands' knowledge or approval to leave the home for any reason – regardless of whether their reasons are need-based or not – and a husband simply cannot deprive his wife of her *nafaqah* for stepping out of her home. She points out that it is inconsistent and illogical to claim that a woman cannot step outside her home without her husband's permission except out of necessity, when Islam grants a woman complete freedom to manage her own wealth, for instance:[137]

> A woman who has wealth needs to go to the banks to keep up with what she owns and she must go to governmental offices to sign contracts, yet some men make things difficult and stop them from going… and if she is disabled to take care of her rights, she can lose what is hers…and more importantly, what if she inherits and her brother or mother share with her the property, if her husband stops her from going, harm comes to all the heirs, not just his wife.[138]

Dr. ʿĀbidah al-Aẓam shared Imam Ibn Ḥazm's opinion that a woman is perfectly within her rights to leave her home for any reason without her husband's permission, and to deny a wife financial maintenance for doing so is unjust. The Imam highlights that if a wife leaves her household out of anger at her husband, she is still entitled to continue to receive *nafaqah*. He cited as evidence a narration relayed by the Companion Shuʿbah regarding al-Ḥakam ibn ʿUtaybah who, when asked if a woman who left her home out of anger deserves financial maintenance, replied yes.[139] This opinion is shared by the prominent Kūfī (from Kufa in Iraq) Imam al-Ḥakam ibn ʿAṭiyyah ﷺ who said, "A man is not relieved from *nafaqah* because of his wife's *nūshuz* [which he defined as leaving the household] since *nafaqah* did not become demanded of him for being the only male able to enjoy her company."[140] Most other scholars including Imam al-Shāfiʿī ﷺ ruled that leaving her home for necessities is not a cause of losing *nafaqah*.[141]

Many scholars from the Ḥanbalī and Shāfiʿī schools also interpret the word "*nūshuz*" as referring to a woman who refuses intimacy with her husband.[142] They derive this definition based on their interpretation of *nafaqah* – that it is given upon consummation of the marriage and therefore should only continue to be given if intimate relations between husband and wife continue.[143] Thus, their definition of the word *nūshuz* does not rest on a Qur'anic verse or on a Hadith but rather upon these scholars' *ijtihād* – meaning their use of independent reasoning to arrive at a ruling – that *nafaqah* does not become due except after the consummation of the marriage. It is important to note that even in cases where scholars define *nushūz* as refusing intimacy, there are circumstances in which the majority of scholars agree that a wife has the Islamic right to refuse intimacy but remains entitled to *nafaqah*, such as when a wife declines to consummate the marriage because her husband has yet to give her owed and due *mahr*.[144] Imam Abū Ḥanīfah ﵀ ruled that while a husband can withhold *nafaqah* from his wife for refusing to have sexual relations with him altogether, he cannot deny her *nafaqah* if she declines having sexual relations on occasion because she is uninterested, so long as she remains living in the same home as her husband.[145] Imam Ibn Ḥazm ﵀, however, argued that there is nothing in the Qur'an, Sunnah, sayings of the Companions, or in analogy (*qiyās*) to another ruling to suggest that *nafaqah* is a religious obligation upon a Muslim husband only once the couple consummates the marriage and begins to live in the same home; nor is there any evidence to suggest that the husband can suspend the *nafaqah* due to his wife if she refuses intimacy. Imam Ibn Ḥazm ﵀ said, "There is no question that if Allah ﷻ intended to make an exception for the (married) underaged girl [who is not yet ready to consummate her marriage] or the *nāshiz* [to not receive *nafaqah*], He would never have been negligent from making this known to us, Allah is Exalted above such an action."[146] Imam Ibn Ḥazm ﵀ therefore ruled that once the marriage contract has been signed and the man and woman are husband and wife, the husband is responsible to financially provide for his wife and cannot withhold her *nafaqah* for any reason at all, including whether the marriage has been consummated, whether the wife is underage and not yet ready to consummate the marriage, or whether she is *nāshiz*.[147] As evidence in support of his ruling, the Imam cited a letter written by ʿUmar ibn al-Khaṭṭāb ﷺ, the second Caliph, to his army commanders, "See all those [soldiers] who prolonged their absence [from their wives] and demand them to send their due *nafaqah* or return back [to their wives] or separate [through divorce], and whoever of them chooses to separate is obliged to pay maintenance from the day he left [his wife to serve as a commander]."[148] Imam Ibn Ḥazm ﷺ emphasizes that when ʿUmar ibn al-Khaṭṭāb ﷺ issued this order, he specified no category of wives from whom husbands were permitted to withhold *nafaqah*.

While some Companions of the Prophet ﷺ, such as al-Nakhaʿī, al-Shaʿbī, Ḥamad ibn Abī Sulaymān, al-Ḥasan, and al-Zuhrī ﷺ claim that *nafaqah* is given in exchange for marital intimacy, this opinion is not substantiated by the Qur'an and Sunnah.[149] As mentioned earlier, Imam Ibn Ḥazm ﷺ once said, "Indeed the *nafaqah* (for the wife) is an exchange for marriage and not an exchange for sexual intercourse." He critiqued those who argue that if a wife refuses intimacy, a husband can withhold her *nafaqah* in retaliation, saying, "What's really puzzling is that they make it permissible to be unjust to the *nāshiz* by taking away her rights due to her injustice to her spouse by withholding his (sexual) right, when (in reality) this in itself is what typical injustice is."[150]

Imam Ibn Ḥazm's reaction to the claim that a husband can suspend his wife's financial maintenance if she refuses sexual intercourse was to dismiss it entirely, saying, "That is an excuse (to defer from paying *nafaqah*) that is too weak to deserve correction."[151] Imam Ibn Ḥazm's reasoning coincides with the essence of Islam – a faith that prioritizes gentleness, consideration, tolerance, and mercy among all humans, especially between spouses:

وَمِنْ ءَايَٰتِهِۦٓ أَنْ خَلَقَ لَكُم مِّنْ أَنفُسِكُمْ أَزْوَٰجًا لِّتَسْكُنُوٓا۟ إِلَيْهَا وَجَعَلَ بَيْنَكُم مَّوَدَّةً وَرَحْمَةً ۚ إِنَّ فِى ذَٰلِكَ لَءَايَٰتٍ لِّقَوْمٍ يَتَفَكَّرُونَ ﴿٢١﴾

> And of His signs is that He created for you from yourselves mates that you may find tranquility in them; and He placed between you affection and mercy. Indeed, in that are signs for a people who give thought.[152]

Given the clarity in Qur'anic verses regarding the relationship between spouses, Dr. 'Ābidah al-Aẓam suggests that it is possible that verse 34 of Sūrah al-Nisā', regarding which there is much dispute amongst scholars, was abrogated altogether once it became out of context with the decline of slavery.[153] She notes that it is in this Chapter, that many verses were abrogated such as 4:15-16 (in exchange of 2:24) and 4:43 (in exchange with 5:90).[154]

The Value of Nafaqah

There are clear guidelines in both the Qur'an and Sunnah regarding what type of financial support falls under the umbrella term *nafaqah,* but what then is the precise amount of *nafaqah* that a husband owes his wife for her day-to-day needs? Imam Abū Ḥanīfah and Imam Mālik ﷺ left the value of the *nafaqah* entirely upon the couple to decide, with the assumption that they would fairly evaluate what the husband owes his wife given her needs and the customs of the time and place.[155] They simply suggested that the minimum even a poor man must give to his wife and their children is the amount that any human requires to survive. Imam al-Shāfiʿī ﷺ, on the other hand, disagreed with this open-ended approach, saying even if the Qur'an and Sunnah offered no specifications, it is necessary to set an amount by which husbands must abide in order to avoid abuse and spousal disputes. So, for example, he calculated that the dry groceries (e.g. seeds, rice, barley, wheat, or bread) a husband of meager means must purchase for his wife should be one *mudd*, or approximately 171 dirhams daily.[156] This amount is estimated as a container the size of 75L or 544 grams.[157] A wealthy man must provide twice this amount of dry goods for his wife, while a man with a moderate income falls in between. Imam al-Shāfiʿī even delineated what a wife's servant or house help should receive as *nafaqah*, providing that the wife's servant would receive one *mudd* in all three cases.[158] Imam al-Shāfiʿī ﷺ derived these measures from the expiations scholars had set, which required feeding the poor as a form of atonement. Imam al-Shāfiʿī ﷺ, and scholars who shared his approach, determined the standard minimum amounts of various essentials that would fall under the *nafaqah* ruling and in case of disputes, the couple could take the matter before a judge who could issue a settlement.[159] The majority of scholars, however, simply said that Allah ﷻ left the amount unspecified because an undefined amount can be more easily adjusted to accommodate all contexts. Thus, the *nafaqah* should be a reasonable and fair amount paid to the wife on a regular schedule (daily, weekly, monthly) that meets the standards of the time period and place in which the couple lives.[160] They reasoned that the needs of each household and wife will be different. For example, one wife may come from a well-to-do home where she was accustomed to certain amenities; another may have special medical needs; another may need to host family members often. The circumstances are limitless, and so Imam Ibn Rushd ﵀ claimed that to define and thereby limit the amount of *nafaqah* a husband owes his wife would, in fact, violate the wife's right and correlates neither with the Qur'an nor the example of the Prophet ﷺ.[161]

There is no doubt that providing his wife with a home is part of the financial maintenance a Muslim husband owes. As mentioned earlier, the majority of scholars rule that the home into which a man brings his wife must be a property either owned or rented by him, must offer the wife both safety and privacy, and must be furnished. But is there a certain spaciousness and quality of the home a husband is obligated to provide as part of the *nafaqah* due to his wife? Scholars agree on a general rule that a husband should strive to provide a home that is akin to that which she experienced before marriage, but they differed on the nuances of this directive. Imam al-Shāfiʿī ﵀ ruled that it is the husband's duty to ensure that the home he provides satisfies his wife, regardless of his financial circumstances. Some Ḥanafī jurists were of the opinion that the type of home depends entirely on the husband's means, while the Mālikī and Ḥanbalī jurists, as well as some Ḥanafī scholars like Imam al-Kasaf, said both the means of the husband and the needs of the wife deserve equal consideration— basing their opinions on the Prophet ﷺ directing Hind, Abū Sufyān's wife, to "Take from your husband's money the amount enough for you and your child."[162] Some Ḥanafī scholars fell somewhere in the middle, believing that, in determining what financial support a husband should provide his wife, the husband's financial position cannot be entirely ignored due to verse 7 of Sūrah al-Ṭalāq.

At the same time, these Ḥanafī scholars ruled that if a husband is unable to afford a home that meets the standards his wife is accustomed to, then the cost of such a home becomes a debt he owes her and should strive to pay because her right to a home that aligns with her needs should not be lost.[163] So, if the husband and wife both came from similar financial backgrounds, the matter was simple: he could easily offer her a home and amenities that corresponded with those to which she was accustomed. If their financial backgrounds differed, the matter became more complex and unless the couple could come to an agreement, a judge could review and settle the matter.[164]

Just as Islamic law obligates a husband to pay the financial maintenance due to his wife, it also requires a man married to more than one woman to provide equally for each of his wives. Some scholars, including Imam Ibn Taymiyyah, Ibn Ḥajar, al-Ṣanʿānī, and al-Shawkānī ﵏, held that a man must pay the exact same *nafaqah* to each wife. They based their rulings on the following Hadith: "Whoever has two wives and leans toward (favors) one of them (over the other), he will come on the Day of Resurrection with half of his body leaning."[165] Other scholars, such as Imam Ibn Qudāmah and al-Qurṭubī ﵏, disagreed and ruled that a man can provide more or less to one wife over another based on status and satisfaction, on the premise that a wife's *nafaqah* ought to correlate to the lifestyle that she was accustomed to prior to marriage.[166]

Once we understand the gravity of fulfilling a wife's right to *nafaqah*, the question arises: what are the consequences for a man who fails to fulfill this religious obligation? Two scholarly opinions propose solutions: either the wife takes the matter to an Islamic judge to annul the marriage, or she seeks divorce.[167] Separation through annulment becomes one option for a woman.[168] According to Imam Abū Ḥanīfah رحمه الله, the marriage should not be annulled as a result of a husband's failure to pay the *nafaqah* owed to his wife if the reason he failed to pay was because he was poor. Rather, the Imam ruled that the unpaid *nafaqah* becomes a debt the husband owes his wife and must pay once he is financially able.[169] The judge is then expected to keep track of the amount owed to her.[170] The Imam compares this situation to the *mahr* which Islamic law requires a husband to gift his wife once the marriage is contracted, although it can be deferred if the husband needs more time. The Imam believed such a ruling was most beneficial and advantageous to the wife because she would be retaining her right to *nafaqah*, while the alternative of annulling the marriage altogether (*ibṭāl or faskh*) would leave her with no marital rights at all.[171] In support of the ruling that would give a husband more time to fulfill his obligation towards his wife, Imam Abū Ḥanīfah رحمه الله pointed to the following Qur'anic verse:

وَإِن كَانَ ذُو عُسْرَةٍ فَنَظِرَةٌ إِلَىٰ مَيْسَرَةٍ ۚ وَأَن تَصَدَّقُوا خَيْرٌ لَّكُمْ ۖ إِن كُنتُمْ
تَعْلَمُونَ ﴿٢٨٠﴾

And if someone is in hardship, then [let there be] postponement until [a time of] ease...[172]

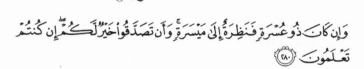

Unlike Imam Abū Ḥanīfah رحمه الله, the jurist Imam Ibn al-Qayyim رحمه الله sometimes ruled that a marriage without appropriate *nafaqah* be annulled and sometimes not. Specifically, he approached his ruling on whether a marriage should be annulled due to a husband's failure to provide *nafaqah* based on the husband's financial status at the time of marriage.[173] If the husband initially gave the wife the impression that he was wealthy or financially sound, but after they married claimed to have meager means, the Imam ruled that she would be entitled to an annulment. The wife would also be granted annulment if the husband appeared well-to-do prior to the marriage, but after marriage simply refused to provide financially for his wife. However, if, when she married him, the wife knew and accepted her spouse's poverty, annulment would not be granted.[174]

In line with this thought process, according to Imam Mālik, Imam Aḥmad ibn Ḥanbal, and Imam al-Shāfiʿī, if a woman is surprised to find that her husband has no money to provide for her, she is within her right to end the marriage through a third party judge (or imam if no Islamic judge exists). The imams differed, however, on whether the couple's separation by the judge would be considered an annulment of the contract or a divorce. Imams al-Shāfiʿī and Aḥmad ibn Ḥanbal ruled the contract should be annulled whereas Imam Mālik said that this type of separation is considered one revocable divorce.[175] They also ruled that if the wife lived with the husband without receiving her financial rights for any time period during the marriage, he owes her this amount even after the annulment of the contract or divorce.[176] The Imams specify that his debt includes her food, clothing, home rental, and cost of household services she would have been entitled to:[177]

> When the husband holds back from spending on his wife, if she [chooses] to stay patient the amount [he did not spend] becomes a debt on him even if this was not ruled on by a judge; and if she cannot remain patient, she has every right to annul [the marriage contract].[178]

This was the opinion of many Companions and their followers including ʿUmar, ʿAlī, Abū Hurayrah, Saʿīd ibn al-Musayyib, al-Ḥasan, and ʿUmar ibn ʿAbd al-ʿAzīz. They believed it was an injustice for a husband to remain married without fulfilling her religious right (and his obligation) to provide for her financially, and that a wife had the absolute right to end such a marriage either through divorce or annulment. Their ruling is rooted in the following command that appears in the Qur'an: "...keep [her] in an acceptable manner or release [her] with good treatment."[179] The ruling is further supported by the tradition of the Prophet ﷺ, when he sheds light on a woman's emotional state when her husband refrains from providing for her, as expressed in her saying: "Either you feed me or divorce me."[180] The majority of scholars agree on this doctrine because it reflects a fundamental principle of Islamic law – to safeguard the rights of every Muslim and refrain from causing harm to others. The Prophet ﷺ commanded believers to "[cause] no harm to oneself nor to others."[181] To deliberately withhold *nafaqah*, or even to be unable to pay *nafaqah*, while refusing to divorce one's wife is indeed denying her of her God-given right and causing her harm. Imam Ibn Ḥanbal and al-Shāfiʿī went a step further, ruling that if a wife chooses to patiently remain married to her husband despite him not fulfilling her right to *nafaqah*, she has the right to refuse physical intimacy with him, leave the home for any reason – to work or otherwise – without his knowledge or permission, and decline to meet any of his demands or requests.[182]

Traditional scholars address not only cases in which the husband is either unable or unwilling to financially provide for his wife, but also cases in which the husband is physically absent from the home, because he voluntarily chose or was compelled to leave, as in the case of abduction or imprisonment. They ruled that if the husband plans to travel for a substantial time, including traveling to perform Hajj, he is obliged to leave his wife the appropriate *nafaqah* during his absence.[183] For example, Ḥanafī scholars ruled that, in such cases, the wife should be given full access to any of his savings, such as in a bank account, trust, or amount owed to him as a debt, and that she should be able to withdraw her due *nafaqah* from these savings.[184] Ḥanafī scholars also delineate how a wife might go about legally accessing his property in his absence: for instance, because it is impermissible to sell a missing person's property under Islamic law, in order to collect her *nafaqah* by selling her husband's property, she must prove that she is, in fact, her husband's legal wife by a legal marriage contract; that she is still in her three-month waiting period following divorce; or that she was not deserted by her husband due to her *nushūz* (based on one of the many definitions of *nushūz*). Some Ḥanafī scholars insisted that she must give an oath before a judge testifying to her identity.[185] Others ruled that because requiring a woman to stand in a court and give a public oath might coerce her to reveal private or embarrassing details of her marriage, simple documentation of the marriage is sufficient:

> In many cases, people (men) leave behind their wives without *nafaqah* or someone to spend on them. They do this out of revenge and disappear so that no one is able to find them by travelling to (another) city or a village. Thus, if the first opinion was taken it will service the evil (intents) of these men and their will…resulting in their wives being severely tormented, thus the second view is the most correct.[186]

Ḥanafī scholars also ruled that the wife has the right to request someone else to bear the financial obligation her husband has neglected, and to ask a judge to select a person to provide for her (*kafīl*), for as long as her husband remains missing. Because the Mālikī school considers the withholding of intimacy a *nāshiz* act that voids a wife's right to *nafaqah*, it requires that a wife affirm to a judge that she permitted a sexual relationship between her and her husband before giving her access to her absent husband's income (in case that was the reason her right to *nafaqah* ceased).[187] The question sometimes arises about a wife's right to receive *nafaqah* if she is employed since some scholars associate her right to *nafaqah* with her availability for intimacy or presence in the home.[188] In this instance, one prominent scholar, Jamaal Zarabozo, underlines Imam Ibn Ḥazm's view that *nafaqah* is required once the marriage is contracted, irrespective of and not specifically associated with other marital commitments.[189] Zarabozo also highlights the significance customs (*ʿurf*) play in Islamic legal interpretation: because it is so customary for women to work outside the home, her engagement in this *ʿurf* should not interfere with her right to *nafaqah*; in fact, some scholars opine that, in addition to having to provide her with *nafaqah*, a husband should not interfere with her right to work altogether. Notably, Imam al- Shāfiʿī ﷺ ruled that amongst the things a woman cannot be prevented from doing is to go out for work.[190]

Differing Opinions on Child Support During Marriage and Upon Divorce

Several Qur'anic verses indicate that a mother is due financial and material support for her children, regardless of whether she is married to the father or divorced. For instance, verse 6 of Chapter 65 provides that financial support is required even upon divorce:

أَسْكِنُوهُنَّ مِنْ حَيْثُ سَكَنتُم مِّن وُجْدِكُمْ وَلَا تُضَارُّوهُنَّ لِتُضَيِّقُوا عَلَيْهِنَّ ۚ وَإِن كُنَّ أُولَاتِ حَمْلٍ
فَأَنفِقُوا عَلَيْهِنَّ حَتَّىٰ يَضَعْنَ حَمْلَهُنَّ ۚ فَإِنْ أَرْضَعْنَ لَكُمْ فَآتُوهُنَّ أُجُورَهُنَّ ۖ وَأْتَمِرُوا بَيْنَكُم
بِمَعْرُوفٍ ۖ وَإِن تَعَاسَرْتُمْ فَسَتُرْضِعُ لَهُ أُخْرَىٰ ﴿٦﴾

Lodge them [your ex-wives] [in a section] of where you dwell out of your means and do not harm them in order to oppress them. *And if they should be pregnant, then spend on them until they give birth.* And if they breastfeed for you, then give them their payment and confer among yourselves in the acceptable way; but if you are in discord, then there may breastfeed for the father another woman.[191]

لِيُنفِقْ ذُو سَعَةٍ مِّن سَعَتِهِ ۖ وَمَن قُدِرَ عَلَيْهِ رِزْقُهُ فَلْيُنفِقْ مِمَّا آتَاهُ اللَّهُ ۚ لَا يُكَلِّفُ اللَّهُ نَفْسًا
إِلَّا مَا آتَاهَا ۚ سَيَجْعَلُ اللَّهُ بَعْدَ عُسْرٍ يُسْرًا ﴿٧﴾

Let a man of wealth spend from his wealth, and he whose provision is restricted - let him spend from what Allah has given him. Allah does not charge a soul except [according to] what He has given it. Allah will bring about, after hardship, ease.[192]

۞ وَالْوَالِدَاتُ يُرْضِعْنَ أَوْلَادَهُنَّ حَوْلَيْنِ كَامِلَيْنِ ۖ لِمَنْ أَرَادَ أَن يُتِمَّ الرَّضَاعَةَ ۚ وَعَلَى الْمَوْلُودِ
لَهُ رِزْقُهُنَّ وَكِسْوَتُهُنَّ بِالْمَعْرُوفِ ۚ لَا تُكَلَّفُ نَفْسٌ إِلَّا وُسْعَهَا ۚ لَا تُضَارَّ وَالِدَةٌ بِوَلَدِهَا وَلَا
مَوْلُودٌ لَّهُ بِوَلَدِهِ ۚ وَعَلَى الْوَارِثِ مِثْلُ ذَٰلِكَ ۗ فَإِنْ أَرَادَا فِصَالًا عَن تَرَاضٍ مِّنْهُمَا وَتَشَاوُرٍ فَلَا
جُنَاحَ عَلَيْهِمَا ۗ وَإِنْ أَرَدتُّمْ أَن تَسْتَرْضِعُوا أَوْلَادَكُمْ فَلَا جُنَاحَ عَلَيْكُمْ إِذَا سَلَّمْتُم مَّا آتَيْتُم
بِالْمَعْرُوفِ ۗ وَاتَّقُوا اللَّهَ وَاعْلَمُوا أَنَّ اللَّهَ بِمَا تَعْمَلُونَ بَصِيرٌ ﴿٢٣٣﴾

…*upon the father* is the mothers' provision and their clothing according to what is acceptable. No person is charged with more than his capacity. No mother should be harmed through her child, and no father through his child. *And upon the [father's] heir is [a duty] like that [of the father].* And if they both desire weaning through mutual consent from both of them and consultation, there is no blame upon either of them. And if you wish to have your children nursed by a substitute, there is no blame upon you as long as you give payment according to what is acceptable. And fear Allah and know that Allah is Seeing of what you do.[193]

In the latter verse (2:233) of Sūrah al-Baqarah, the Arabic text uses the words *"mawlūdun lahu,"* translated as "born from him," instead of just the word father. Thus the intent is to confirm an association or belonging between him (the father) and the child.[194] This highlights two main points: first, that mothers gave birth to children who belong to their biological fathers, to confirm the importance of the baby's full lineage and identity being known.[195] Second, that the father of a child is financially responsible for him or her.[196] Scholars from three of the four major schools of thought ruled that a father's financial responsibility extends beyond his children to his biological grandchildren while others, such as Imam Mālik 🌸, held that he is only religiously obligated to provide for his direct progeny.[197]

After a father's biological children have reached puberty, they have the religious right to continue receiving financial support from their father if they are unable to support themselves. For example, if a son cannot earn money due to a health problem, the father remains obligated to financially provide for him. There is controversy regarding whether a father is still responsible to financially support his older son who can work. Imam Abu Bakr al-Sarakhsī ﷺ said in his work *al-Mabsūṭ*: "If they (children) are males who have reached puberty, their father is not obligated to spend on them since they are able to earn on their own, with the exception of those who are sick, blind, paralyzed…"[198] Dr. Zaydān raises the question in his jurisprudential encyclopedia: "What if the son is able to work but cannot find work?" He still replied that the father was obligated to support his son since the matter is based on need. He supports his view using the book "*Al-Durr Ul-Mukhtar,*" in which the 18th-century jurisprudence scholar Ibn ʿĀbidīn ﷺ said: "*Nafaqah* is obligatory for his (a father's) older son who is unable to find work as in the situation of every female…"[199] Imam Abū Ḥanīfah ﷺ, however, did not agree that the older able-bodied son deserves *nafaqah;* whereas for Imam al-Shāfiʿī ﷺ there were two narrations with different views, the more well-supported view being that the son should be financially supported.[200] Imam Ibn Ḥanbal ruled that *nafaqah* should be provided to a mature son who is able to work but cannot find work, basing his view on the Prophetic tradition regarding the financial difficulties of the Companion Hind in which the Prophet advised her to take from the wealth of her husband Abū Sufyān what is was satisfactory to provide for her and her children. He supports his view saying that the word *children* encompassed the father's progeny in general – that is, of all ages and circumstances.[201]

Some scholars are of the opinion that a father is only religiously obligated to provide for his daughter (who has reached puberty) if she is not earning enough money to support herself, in which case he should assist her when she falls short of paying her expenses.[202] This view however is a minority opinion. According to most scholars (including Imam Abū Bakr al-Jazā'irī ﷺ), daughters are entitled financial support until they marry.[203] The Ḥanafī book of jurisprudence *Al-Hidāyah* stated that femininity inherently implied a tendency towards dependency.[204] Consequently, according to the Ḥanafī *fiqh*, a Muslim daughter is entitled financial support whether her father is Muslim or non-Muslim.[205] According to not only the Ḥanafī school, but the Mālikī and Shāfiʿī schools, a father who is not Muslim but who has Muslim children is obligated to financially support them under Islamic law. Scholars of the Ḥanbalī school held two opposing views in this regard.[206] Imam 'Ala' al-Din al-Kāsānī ﵀ stated, for instance, that, in an Islamic state, if a Muslim woman had children whose father was Christian, it was obligatory for a person of the Christian faith to financially provide for the living costs of his young children.[207]

Differing Opinions on Temporary Maintenance (Nafaqah) for the Widowed

The four schools of jurisprudence held diverging opinions on a widow's right to financial maintenance after her husband's death during her four-month and ten-day waiting period.[208] The Ḥanafī school ruled that she is not entitled to any financial support through the estate (and outside of inheritance distributions), even if she is pregnant with her deceased husband's child. It did, however, opine that she is entitled to residency during her four-month, ten-day mourning period if the home was owned by her deceased husband.[209] The Ẓāhirī *madhhab* held she does not receive maintenance or residence since it all belongs to the heirs at this point (including partially herself). The scholars in the Ḥanbalī school provide two views, one declining and another affirming her right to *nafaqah* as a widow. But according to Dr. Zaydān, in his book *al-Jāmiʿ fī al-Fiqh al-Islāmī al-Mufaṣṣal fī Aḥkām al-Mar'ah wa al-Bayt al-Muslim,* the most sound, well-supported view is the one shared by the Mālikī and Shāfiʿī schools, who agreed that the estate does not need to provide for her and her unborn child's food and clothing expenses, but that she is to remain in her deceased husband's home for a certain amount of time. They based the latter part of the opinion on an authentic narration in which a widow by the name of Farīʿah bint Mālik bint Sinān asked the Prophet ﷺ whether she should return to her parents' home upon her husband's death. His initial reply was affirmative, but soon after he asked her to repeat her circumstance and question and then said, "Remain in your household until your waiting time period comes to an end." She then said: "So I spent four months and ten days in my (husband's) home."[210] From then on, the Companions of the Prophet ﷺ abided by this ruling.

Financial Rights Upon Divorce

The schools of jurisprudence disagreed on the *nafaqah* owed to the wife who had been divorced three times by her husband, as the third and final divorce is irrevocable. Based on Islamic law, an irrevocable divorce is one in which the husband utters to his wife "you are divorced" once, then a second time, then a third time during their marriage, or in a triple repudiation all at once. In both situations a husband cannot go back to his wife unless she remarries another man and gets divorced from him.[211]

Imams Mālik, al-Shāfiʿī, and Aḥmad ﷺ ruled that since this divorce is final and binding, the wife is not entitled to financial support for food and clothing but should receive residence for the

Islamic three-month waiting period that follows the divorce. Imam Abū Ḥanīfah ﷺ disagreed, ruling that for the duration of this waiting period, she is owed everything that typically falls under *nafaqah*.[212] Still, although Imam Malik ruled that the divorced wife was entitled to only residence during the waiting period, some Mālikī scholars saw no difference between a revocable and irrevocable divorce with regards to *nafaqah* rights during the ex-wife's waiting period.[213]

Those against the divorcee's right to *nafaqah* following an irrevocable divorce based their view on a Hadith of Fāṭimah bint Qays ﷺ in which she said, "My husband divorced me three times during the life of the Prophet ﷺ, and he did not rule that I receive *nafaqah* or residence." On the other hand, those in support of her receipt of *nafaqah* after the third irrevocable divorce based their opinion on the Companions ʿĀ'ishah ﷺ and ʿUmar ﷺ who stated that one cannot diverge from the word of God, which provides in the first verse of Chapter 65 of the Qur'an : "Do not turn them out of their [husbands'] houses."[214]

When it comes to dividing the house, household items, furnishings, and belongings (*matāʿ al-bayt*) between the divorced couple, scholars had further differences of opinion. Some held that ex-wives should take the items that naturally belong to women and ex-husbands should take those items that generally belong to men.[215] Imams Abū Ḥanīfah, Mālik, and Aḥmad ﷺ shared this opinion based on a statement made by one of the Companion's of the Prophet, Alī ibn Abī Ṭālib ﷺ, "Feminine possessions belong to women and male possessions belong to males."[216] Imam al-Shāfiʿī ﷺ, however, disputed this point of view and ruled that everything should be split between the two based on ownership at the time of divorce.[217] He argued that that there are instances in which traditionally feminine items, such as jewelry, may be owned by the ex-husband and other more traditionally masculine items, such as tools, owned by the ex-wife; thus, each deserves possession of the items they own through purchase, inheritance, or other possible avenues.[218] To support his view, Imam al-Shāfiʿī ﷺ pointed to the example of Fāṭimah ﷺ – she owned a metal armor that her husband gifted her as her *mahr,* the armor being the most valuable item he had possessed at the time he got married. Imam al-Shāfiʿī ﷺ offered other examples as well:

> I saw a woman whose sword (that she held) was placed between her and myself. It was a sword, which she inherited through her father and it was of great value, plus an armor and a Qur'an book. They were hers alone and not the property of any of her siblings. I also saw another (male) who inherited items from his mother and sister and felt bad to sell them, thus gifting them to the women in his family.[219]

Opinions on Temporary Maintenance after Wife-initiated Divorce (Khulʿ)

Classical jurists, including Ḥanbalī al-Shāfiʿī, al-Ẓāhirī, ʿAṭā' and al-Awzāʿī, generally agree that if a wife initiates divorce through *khulʿ*, she is entitled to temporary maintenance during the three month waiting period (or one month based on some jurists). Ḥanafī Jurist al-Shawkānī highlights in his book, "*Fath al-Qadeer*" the Ḥanafī stance that, "...Indeed for the wife that removes herself from the marriage (*mukhtali'a*) is *nafaqah* and residence."[220]

A minority of Ḥanafī scholars, however, suggest that a wife may relinquish her right to post-divorce temporary maintenance to effectuate the *khulʿ*. However Dr. ʿAbd al-Karīm Zaydān disagreed saying a wife cannot waive her right to nafaqah given how fundamental it is to the marriage contract. He stated her right to residence is the right of Allah that cannot under any circumstances be taken from her based on the first verse of Sūrah al-Ṭalāq, "Do not turn them out of their [husbands'] houses, nor should they [themselves] leave [during that period]." He further quotes Ḥanafī Jurist al-Shawkānī regarding what exactly is meant for her to relinquish when she initiates *khulʿ*, "This [loss] is restricted to the *mahr* and a past *nafaqah* [that was spent on her] when it was obligatory [upon him] which differs from the divorce waiting period *nafaqah* and [her right] to residence." Imam Ibn Hazm of the Zahiri school of Islamic jurisprudence also ruled that upon *khulʿ* any amount of *mahr* a man owes his wife is to be given to her if it differs from the agreed upon financial compensation in the *khulʿ* contract.[221]

There are many reasons why a wife would resort to *khulʿ* rather than filing for divorce through a third party or waiting for her husband to initiate a divorce, namely the desire for a speedy separation, as at times and based on varying situations, divorce can take a long time. Also, some women prefer to take the *khulʿ* route because some classical jurists' rule that she is completely relieved from matrimony after only one month [rather than a three-month divorce waiting period]. But what happens if the husband does not agree to *khulʿ*, which involves her relinquishment of some monetary item or amount? Scholars of jurisprudence today have addressed this question and different Muslim countries have developed laws to address this issue. However, according to Al-Azhar

Fatwa Global Center, a wife can file for *khulʿ* from her spouse in a court or with a third party judge without her husband's consent, as long as — in its view — the wife presents financial compensation in exchange. Al-Azhar made this decision while acknowledging the plight of a wife who might resent continuing to live with her husband and feels unable to remain within the boundaries of Allah ﷻ while married to him.[222]

Some prominent jurists within the four major schools of thought (Ḥanafī scholar al-Jassas and Shafīʿi scholar Ibn Ḥajar al-ʿAsqalānī) rule that *khul'*, which involves some sort of financial relinquishment (of the *mahr* gift, for instance), must be done through a third party. This was the ruling of the successors of the Prophet's Companions, al-Ḥasan ibn ʿAlī and Muhammad Ibn Sirin. Others (including Imams Malik and al-Shafīʿ) believe *khul'* can be done directly between the wife and husband, when the wife requests *khul'* and husband agrees to the *khul'* by uttering she is removed from the marriage by *khul'*. The scholars who do not agree that *khul'* can be done privately by the husband's utterance of *khul'* argue that such dissolution actually amounts to a traditional male-led divorce since, in that case, the husband is ultimately granting the dissolution of the marriage, in which case no financial relinquishment provided in *khul'* should be required. The schools of thought differed as to the type of separation between spouses that *khulʿ* falls under. Their differences directly affect some or even all of the wife's rights to temporary maintenance and her inheritance rights in case the husband dies during her *khulʿ* waiting period. Some held that *khul'* is a revocable type of divorce, some held that it is an irrevocable divorce, and some go so far as to consider it an annulment of the marriage contract. In determining the type of divorce or dissolution *khul'* falls under, some scholars look at the husband's intention when he uttered the word *khulʿ* and whether or not he mentioned the parties' agreement on some sort of financial relinquishment. For example, the Ḥanafī jurists ruled that unless the husband uttered the *khulʿ* of his wife along with the value of financial compensation expected from her, the dissolution would be considered a male-led divorce and not *khulʿ*. When a value of the financial relinquishment is specified, however, with his *khulʿ* utterance, then the dissolution should be considered an irrevocable divorce. The Maliki school ruled that *khulʿ* privately agreed-to by the husband is considered an irrevocable divorce, whether financial relinquishment or compensation was specifically uttered by the husband or not. The Ḥanbalī jurists differed based on two narrations for Imam Ahmad ibn Hanbal, one that the *khulʿ* separation is considered an annulment of the marriage, while the other, that it is an irrevocable divorce. Amongst the Shafiʿī jurists, there are also two opinions: one in support of *khulʿ* being an annulment of the marriage contract, while the other, a revocable divorce but only if the husband specifically said "I am removing you out of matrimony *without* any financial compensation in return," finding that if —however — he did not mention any financial compensation and uttered more generally, "I am removing you out of matrimony" it becomes an irrevocable divorce. Imam ibn Hazm rejected the claim that a single instance of a couple agreeing to *khulʿ* could amount to an irrevocable type divorce, finding that the primary Islamic sources only identified a divorce as irrevocable with three utterances of divorce (separately or at once).[223] Also, according to some of the classical jurists, the classification of this type of separation depends on a wife's agreement and follow-up to her husband's *khul'* proposal.

All in all, when *khul'* is done privately between a wife and her husband, there is significant debate among classical jurists about the requirements of such a process and the classification of such a divorce. What's more is that today, scholars are unsure about what Imam Ahmad ibn Ḥanbal's accurate view on this form of *khulʿ* is: according to the first, he agrees with Imam al-Shāfiʿī ﷺ that providing some sort of compensation is still a condition for the type of *khulʿ* done directly between wife and husband. According to the second view, Imam Ahmad agrees with all the other Imams, including Imam Abū Ḥanīfah, Mālik ﷺ who ruled that there should be no requirement of financial relinquishment if the *khul'* is privately initiated by the wife and agreed to by the husband, since this form of marriage dissolution is essentially no different from a male-led divorce that rests on the husband's utterance of divorce.[224]

In the case of *khulʿ*, all the wife's financial rights – including any debt the husband owes her or the *nafaqah* she is due during her waiting period – remain intact unless she otherwise waived those rights. The one financial right that should not be relinquished as a condition to end the marriage through *khul'* is the husband's obligation to provide his ex-wife a home during her three-month waiting period.[225] The Mālikī and Ḥanafī schools ruled that a man could not be relieved of this duty as "this is the Right of Allah and it impermissible to drop it:"[226]

يَٰٓأَيُّهَا ٱلنَّبِيُّ إِذَا طَلَّقۡتُمُ ٱلنِّسَآءَ فَطَلِّقُوهُنَّ لِعِدَّتِهِنَّ وَأَحۡصُواْ ٱلۡعِدَّةَۖ وَٱتَّقُواْ ٱللَّهَ
رَبَّكُمۡۖ لَا تُخۡرِجُوهُنَّ مِنۢ بُيُوتِهِنَّ وَلَا يَخۡرُجۡنَ إِلَّآ أَن يَأۡتِينَ بِفَٰحِشَةٖ
مُّبَيِّنَةٖۚ وَتِلۡكَ حُدُودُ ٱللَّهِۚ وَمَن يَتَعَدَّ حُدُودَ ٱللَّهِ فَقَدۡ ظَلَمَ نَفۡسَهُۥۚ لَا تَدۡرِي لَعَلَّ ٱللَّهَ
يُحۡدِثُ بَعۡدَ ذَٰلِكَ أَمۡرٗا ١

Prophet, when you [Muslims] divorce women, divorce them for [the commencement of] their waiting period and keep count of the waiting period, and fear Allah, your Lord. *Do not turn them out of their [husbands'] houses*, nor should they [themselves] leave [during that period] unless they are committing a clear immorality. And those are the limits [set by] Allah. And whoever transgresses the limits of Allah has certainly wronged himself. You know not; perhaps Allah will bring about after that a [different] matter.

Scholars disagree about whether a wife , in the context of *khul'*, can choose to give up the *nafaqah* of a baby or toddler who is still being nursed, her wages for nursing, or wages she might be entitled to for caring for the child.[227] The majority of schools permit the financial relinquishment of these rights, whereas Imam Ibn Ḥazm ﵀ disagreed, saying, "To remove herself from the marriage by that which she does not own is invalid and unjust."[228]

The majority of scholars agreed that if a husband deprives his wife of her right to *nafaqah* and mistreats her to pressure her into seeking *khulʿ*, where she agrees to pay an amount to dissolve the marriage, such a *khul'* is deemed invalid. In such cases, the husband must return to his wife what he coerced her into paying.[229] Imam Abū Ḥanīfah ﵀ disagreed, ruling that even if she was coerced to initiate *khulʿ* in exchange of some financial relinquishment she made to her husband, the *khulʿ* would still be valid; but he added, "He will face consequences for committing such sin and injustice (against Allah in the Hereafter)."[230] Based on all these views, Dr. Zaydān suggests that the most appropriate course of action in cases of a private *khul'* agreement, where a wife relinquishes a monetary amount to remove herself from a marriage in which she is mistreated, is to recognize the *khul'* as valid, resulting in a legal separation. Dr. Zaydān suggests that we consider this type of *khul'*—as some of the classical scholars rule—akin to an irrevocable divorce since, given that she initiated the divorce, it more permanently removes her from any potential harm caused by her husband.[231] He also opined that, because she was mistreated until she sought *khul'*, any monetary amount a wife pays in this situation is unfair and must be returned back to her as supported by the words of God in Sūrah al-Nisā': "And do not make difficulties for them in order to take [back] part of what you gave them..."[232]

Opinions on Post-divorce Financial Support or Mutʿah

After a divorce is finalized, an ex-husband may be required to provide a post-divorce lump sum amount to his ex-wife for alimony, called *mut'ah*. The value of this *mut'ah* is not specified by jurists. Qur'anic exegetes differed in opinion on how *mutʿah* is defined and when it becomes rightful for a divorced wife. Some considered it a gift or provision for divorced women whose marriages were both not yet consummated and for whom no *mahr* was specified based on Chapter 2:236, which reads: "There is no blame-upon you if you divorce women you have not touched [not consummated the marriage] nor specified for them an obligation [*mahr*]. *But give them [a gift of] compensation* [*wa matti'ūhunna*]," while others relied on Chapter 2:241 and considered it also a gift or provision for any divorced woman in any situation.[233]

According to Imam al-Ṭabarī's interpretation (*tafsīr*), the word "*wa matti'ūhunna*" (*and* give them [a gift of] compensation...) in verse 236 of Sūrah al-Baqarah is a separate amount in addition to the agreed-upon deferred *ṣadāq* or owed *mahr* a man is required to pay upon divorce. He also held the view that the *mut'ah* is not specified for a particular type of divorce, but rather for every marriage dissolution.[234] He basis his opinion on the words of Allah in the following verse 241 in Chapter 2 of the Qur'an, directed to all divorced women in any state:

وَلِلْمُطَلَّقَٰتِ مَتَٰعُۢ بِٱلْمَعْرُوفِ ۖ حَقًّا عَلَى ٱلْمُتَّقِينَ ﴿٢٤١﴾

And for divorced women is *a provision* [*matā'un*] according to what is acceptable – a duty upon the righteous.[235]

When a man divorces his wife before the consummation of the marriage, the wife is still entitled to receive half the *mahr* or *ṣadāq* (if she hasn't received the *mahr* yet) as stated in verse 236 of Sūrah al-Baqarah. Imam al-Tabari explains this has nothing to do with her extra right she might have to *mut'ah,* however. Both types of divorcées, the one for whom a *ṣadāq* (*mahr*) was estimated and the one for whom no *ṣadāq* (*mahr*) was estimated, are entitled to receive *mut'ah.*[236] This opinion is similar to that of Imam Ibn Ḥazm ﵀, who ruled:

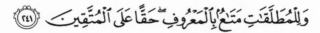

> *Mut'ah* is an obligation upon every man who divorces [his wife] ... whether he consummated the marriage or

> not, or whether he agreed upon a certain *mahr* amount or not…and the judge is to enforce upon him [the husband] to pay it whether he likes it or hates it. *Mut'ah* does not become nullified if the husband revoked divorce prior to the ending of the waiting period nor is it nullified if [either] the husband dies or the wife dies. [In case of his death] The *mut'ah* is to return to her or her heirs and is taken from his wealth [estate].[237]

Imam Mālik ﷺ presents two traditions in his book *al-Muwaṭṭa'* that indicate *mut'ah* is applicable for either type of divorce, one without consummation in which no *mahr* was specified and following any other divorce generally. In the first, 'Abdullāh ibn 'Umar ﷺ said, "For every divorcee is a *mut'ah* except for the one whom a *ṣadāq* (*mahr*) amount was set yet she was never touched (through consummation) – then her right is half what was set for her."[238] In the second, Ibn Shihāb said, "For every divorcee is a *mut'ah*."[239] The Imam did not specify how much the *mut'ah* should be, saying: "In our view, there is no set amount for the *mut'ah*, whether it is small or great." In one example of a substantial *mut'ah* payment, al-Ḥasan ﷺ, the grandson of the Prophet and son of 'Alī ﷺ, gave his ex-wife a *mut'ah* payment of $10,000 dirhams.[240]

Alternatively, some jurists held that the Shariah established *mut'ah* specifically for the divorcée before consummation as a type of consolation in consideration of her emotional well-being. Some argued that such consolation is not mandatory, but rather a voluntary act by the husband; others such as Imams Ibn Ḥazm, Mālik and Ibn Abī Laylā ﷺ strongly dispute the sources of such opinions. Ibn Ḥazm wonders how they support their view when the

Qur'anic verses say, "Indeed those whom Allah enjoined this upon [in verses 236 and 241 of Sūrah al-Baqarah] are only the people of *taqwā* (*al-muttaqīn*) and the people of *ihsan* (*al-muḥsinīn*)."[241] He states: "Every Muslim on the face of this earth who utters there is no god but Allah and Muhammad is the Messenger of Allah falls under the category of the pious people (*al-muttaqīn*) just by their pronouncement [of this testimony]."[242]

The Value of Deferred Mahr

A final point of disagreement exists regarding deferred *mahr*, when a couple who marries establishes that part of the *mahr* will be paid upon the marriage and the rest of the *mahr* will be deferred. If the deferred amount is specified at the time of marriage, after 20 or 30 years of marriage, a question arises: should the wife receive the exact amount agreed upon at the time of the marriage, or should she receive an adjusted amount that accounts for inflation? Scholars agree that if the deferred *mahr* was recorded in the form of gold or silver, then its value will be based on the value of gold or silver at the time the wife is provided the deferred *mahr*. Ibn Qudāmah, for instance, ﷺ explained, "It is obligatory to return an equal amount in all things of weight."[243] If the deferred *mahr* was recorded in currency, three different opinions apply. The majority of scholars ruled that a deferred bridal gift is akin to any debt, so its value remains the same and should not be adjusted for inflation. A second view is that if the agreed-upon amount deflated in value by one-third, then the wife must receive its current value. This is the opinion of Shaykh al-Albānī ﷺ who said, "Indeed the dinar is to be returned back to the person with the same purchase strength it possessed the day it was borrowed."[244] The third and final view that appears more sound and fair to contemporary scholars, is to give the wife a fair settlement accounting for inflation and considering the value of the *mahr*, especially if the initial *mahr* amount was small and symbolic.

Post-divorce Right to Marital Property Settlement or Kadd and Si'āyah

Most scholars recognized only two forms of financial support for divorced women: deferred *mahr* (deferred bridal gift) and *mut'ah* (post-divorce compensatory amount). Imam Malik was the exception; he went beyond deferred *mahr* and *mut'ah*, addressing an additional form of financial support – *kadd* and *si'āyah*. According to Imam Mālik ﵀, these terms refer to a woman's right to a share of the wealth that the couple earned as a unit while married.[245] In other words, *kadd* and *si'āyah* represents a pension the ex-wife should receive for all she did throughout the marriage– because, as mentioned earlier, the wife is not religiously obligated to help provide for the family or otherwise contribute to the family's financial success. Her efforts would include work she did as a homemaker, work she did outside the home, money she lent her husband, and essentially any way in which she served her spouse and children that is not mandated by Islamic law, but without which the husband would not have prospered as he did. An American Muslim attorney describes this right as follows:

> The right of *kadd* and *si'ayah* refers to the management and distribution of property acquired during marriage upon divorce or [upon] death of one of the spouses. According

> to this longstanding jurisprudential tradition, the wife, and in some cases siblings, are entitled to a share of the accumulated marital wealth proportionate to her efforts and contribution to the financial well-being of her family. They did not limit the wife's contribution to her work outside the house, in agricultural or commercial activities for instance, but also included her work in the house.[246]

Evidence of such pension is actually embedded within the Qur'anic principals of equality and justice. The main *āyat* in support of this law are in Chapter 53, verses 39, 40 and 41:

وَأَن لَّيْسَ لِلْإِنسَٰنِ إِلَّا مَا سَعَىٰ ﴿٣٩﴾

And that there is not for man except that [good] for which he [or she] strives.[247]

وَأَنَّ سَعْيَهُۥ سَوْفَ يُرَىٰ ﴿٤٠﴾

And that his [or her] effort is going to be seen –

ثُمَّ يُجْزَىٰهُ ٱلْجَزَآءَ ٱلْأَوْفَىٰ ﴿٤١﴾

Then he [or she] will be recompensed for it with the fullest recompense.[248]

The concept of *kadd* and *si'āyah* makes sense because, once a woman is divorced, apart from receiving her deferred *mahr* (if there is one) and *mut'ah*, she is left to fend for herself. Many Muslim wives choose to focus on taking care of their families and rely on their husbands to act as the sole providers, as is a wife's right in

Islam. However, after living in a state of total financial dependence upon her husband over the previous 10, 20, or even 30 years of marriage, a divorced woman might suddenly finds herself alone, without professional work experience and with very little in savings to support herself, while her ex-husband might possess nearly every penny accumulated during their life together. The concept of *kadd* and *si'āyah* rectifies this inequity and grants credit to all deserving parties.[249]

For this reason, Mālikī scholars from several Muslim countries, such as Morocco, issued rulings declaring that upon divorce or the husband's death, the wife deserves a share of the wealth accumulated during their marriage. These legal rulings (*fatwas*) came under the category of *fiqh al-nawāzil* which translates to laws derived for minorities.[250] Moroccan scholar Imam al-'Abbāsī explained:

> It is customary among the jurists of Masmouda and Jezoula tribes [two southern Moroccan tribes] that the wife is a partner to her husband in the wealth they accumulate through their work and efforts during the time they spend together and cooperated. The husband should not monopolize the wealth by registering it in his name. His wife is his partner through her efforts and partnership, if he divorces her, she has an equal share in it [the wealth].[251]

Scholars also point to the example of one woman— Ḥabībah bint Zurayq – as evidence to support the concept of *kadd* and *si'āyah.* Ḥabībah and her husband worked together and built a successful business manufacturing and selling clothes, but upon her husband's death, his family demanded their share of inheritance, which came out to be three-quarters of the estate. Ḥabībah complained to 'Umar ibn al-Khaṭṭāb ⬥, the Caliph at the time, and he ruled in her favor, saying that because she and her husband jointly strived and sacrificed to build their business, she was entitled to half the estate plus her share of inheritance.[252]

Compensation or Wages to Mother for Nursing During the Marriage or After Divorce

While there is no doubt that a father must provide *nafaqah* for his wife and child while his wife is nursing regardless of whether he and the child's mother are married or divorced, scholarly opinions diverge on whether mothers should receive separate wages for nursing independent from the broader *nafaqah* owed to a wife during the marriage or to an ex-wife for the first three months after divorce. All scholars agree that if a mother nurses her child post the three-month waiting period, she must receive wages for nursing the child.

The Ḥanafī, Mālikī and Ẓāhirī schools held that a wife does not need to be paid separate wages for nursing her baby while married or during her waiting period after a revocable divorce, but that wages for nursing are due to her after an irrevocable divorce. In one narrow exception, however, the Mālikī school held that wages should be provided to a wife in instances when she came from a very wealthy family in which nursing a baby was not customary (as happened during that time). In such cases, if she chooses to nurse, it ruled that her husband should pay her separate wages in addition to *nafaqah*..

The Shāfiʿī and Ḥanbalī jurists disagreed with the Ḥanafī, Mālikī and Ẓāhirī jurists, ruling that every wife was entitled wages for nursing their child regardless of whether they are married or not married. The Shāfiʿī school made three declarations regarding this matter:

1. A mother is to nurse her child with colostrum (*al-labaʾ*) – the milk released following childbirth –, and she is entitled for wages similar to [those wages provided to] others [wetnurses].
2. Following her nursing [her child] with colostrum[,] if there is no wetnurse available to nurse the child except the mother, she becomes obligated to nurse [her child] and she has the right to receive wages from the child's wealth if he is an owner of wealth and if not, from the one responsible for the *nafaqah*.
3. In the case that a wetnurse is available, the husband is (preferred) to hire his wife instead during matrimony or [there]after.

Further, some contemporary scholars opine that if a wife is not paid wages for nursing during the marriage, her *nafaqah* amount should increase based on need. This view is based on Imam Ibn Qudāmah's ﷺ, when he stated in his famous work "*Al-Mughnī*," "And if a mother nurses her child while married to his father – or anytime while still wed – and she is in need of an increase in her *nafaqah* [amount], he [her husband] is required to comply. He based his ruling on Chapter 2:233 of the Qur'an, where God stated: "Upon the father is the mothers provision and their clothing according to what is acceptable," and because she has the right to whatever is satisfactory; thus if her need is increased, her *nafaqah* is increased accordingly.[253]

Most schools of thought held that the father is religiously obligated to pay a wetnurse to nurse his baby if the wife is unwilling to nurse the child. If the child has wealth to his or her name, the wetnurse should be paid from the child's wealth. If neither the father nor child has wealth, other male family members must pay the wetnurse. Imam Ibn Ḥazm ﷺ, however, disagreed with the idea that the wages of a wetnurse should be paid from a child's wealth, ruling that under no circumstances should a child pay for his or her own nursing needs.[254]

Post-divorce Compensation for Providing Childcare or Ujrat al-Ḥaḍānah

As described previously, both during the marriage and post-marriage, children have a right to financial support or *nafaqah* from their fathers *(nafaqat-al-walad)*, perhaps akin to what Americans consider "child support" in the United States (albeit only enforceable when a couple is not married in the United States).

Under Islamic Law, however, there is an additional type of financial compensation provided to a mother who is the primary caretaker of her children: *ujrat al-ḥaḍānah.* Three of the four major schools of thought, with the exception being the Mālikī school of jurisprudence, agreed that the divorced mother who remains the primary caregiver of her pre-prepubescent child or children has a right to this additional payment known as *ujrat al-ḥaḍānah (compensation for childcare)*.[255] Imam Abū Ḥanīfah ﷺ stated that separate compensation should be provided to the ex-wife after the three-month waiting period, and that the compensation should additionally cover the caretaker's residence unless she is financially independent and has her own residence. The Mālikī school did not agree that wages or compensation should separately be provided to the mother for taking care of the children and that only *nafaqah* for the children should be provided, but did note that if she does not have the means to provide for a home for her and the children, the father should provide one.[256] Imam Abū Ḥanīfah ﵀ confirmed that the responsibility to pay a mother for her role in providing childcare, *ujrat al-ḥaḍānah,* rests upon the father, or the next responsible adult male in line, and that the mother's financial right to childcare compensation is distinct from child support payments (*nafaqat al-walad*) or from a mother's right to payment for nursing the child. The cost of any childcare assistance the mother might need, e.g. a nanny or babysitter, also falls under the *ujrat al-ḥaḍānah* payment. Finally, both Imam Abū Ḥanīfah and Imam al-Shāfiʿī ﵀ rule that a mother should serve as primary caretaker of her children at her ex-husband's expense even when a relative offers to care for the children for free, but that if the father is destitute and simply cannot pay *ujrat al-ḥaḍānah*, the child's mother can either act as primary caregiver for her child without financial compensation or hand over custodianship to the relative who is willing to care for the child for free.[257] Imam Abū Ḥanīfah ﵀ preferred these two alternatives to deducting this payment from the child support payment which covers the children's living expenses. Imam Aḥmad ﵀ held that a mother should be given custodianship and paid for it regardless, even if others are willing to care for the children at no cost.[258]

Post-divorce Child Support (Nafaqat al-Walad)

If the wife initiated ending the marriage (*khulʿ*), all her financial rights within Islam, including the right to child support, remain intact unless she specifically waived certain waivable financial rights in exchange for her husband's agreement to divorce.[259] The only instance in which the ex-husband is not religiously obligated to pay child support is if the couple divorced as a result of the husband taking an oath denying paternity (*mulāʿanah*), which essentially means taking an oath accusing the wife of adultery and denying paternity of her child. In such cases, the child is neither due child support nor inheritance rights.[260] Contemporary scholars have addressed whether DNA testing would change this ruling. Some said yes while others disagreed, contending that test results lack absolute certainty.[261]

Of important note, Islamic law does not permit a man to deny that a child is his based on mere suspicion.[262] In fact, Prophet Muhammad ﷺ warned of the religious gravity of wrongfully denying paternity, stating, "...no man that unjustly rejects his child while looking at him [the child] except that Allah conceals His Gracious Self from him [such a man] [in the Hereafter] and exposes him in front of the first and last of creation."[263] According to the Shāfiʿī, Mālikī, and Ḥanbalī schools, "If the husband becomes certain without doubt that the pregnancy of his wife or the child she conceived on his marital bed is not his, he must disavow that child or her pregnancy having resulted from him."[264] According to the Shāfiʿī scholar al-Shīrāzī ﷺ, a man cannot deny the paternity of his child if the mother gives birth at or after six months of pregnancy.[265]

Losing the Right to Temporary Maintenance (Nafaqah) Subsequent to the Oath of Imprecation (al-Mulāʿanah) Separation or Contractual Annulment

The majority of scholars ruled that if a marriage ends as a result of the husband taking an oath of imprecation, that marriage is annulled and the ex-wife is not owed temporary maintenance (*nafaqah*) nor the right to residence (*sakan*) which is normally owed to one's ex-wife during her three-month waiting period. They reasoned that the ex-husband is not obligated to pay either because the couple's union was annulled, rather than dissolved through divorce, thereby nullifying any marital rights associated with a marriage. Imam Abū Ḥanīfah ﵀ disagreed, ruling that an oath of imprecation does not nullify the marriage; he considered the dissolving of such a marriage divorce and opined that in such cases, an ex-wife is entitled temporary maintenance and a residence.[266]

Financial Rights of Inheritance

In order to inherit any form of wealth or property under Islamic law, both the deceased and heir must be Muslim, a qualification explained in a narration by Usāmah ibn Zayd who relayed that Prophet Muhammad ﷺ said, "No Muslim inherits [from] a disbeliever (*kāfir*), nor a disbeliever [from] a Muslim."[267] According to scholarly consensus across the four schools of thought, the people of the book (Christians or Jews) would therefore fall outside of the purview of Islamic inheritance laws.[268] Most of the Companions of the Prophet also held this opinion, including Abū Bakr, ʿUmar, ʿUthmān, and ʿAlī ﵃. Still, there is a minority view relayed by

Companions 'Umar, Mu'ādh, and Mu'āwiyah 🙵, maintaining
that a Muslim can inherit from someone outside of the Islamic
faith, but not vice versa. This minority view is based on a tradition narrated by Mu'ādh 🙵 that the Messenger 🙵 said, "Islam
increases and does not decrease."[269] Mu'ādh 🙵 further explained
his view, stating, "And because we marry their women, that is
women from the People of the Book, and they cannot marry our
women, then just the same, we can inherit from them and they
cannot inherit from us."[270]

According to some Shāfi'ī scholars, a Muslim's financial right to
inheritance remains intact and obligatory so long as he or she has
not murdered or otherwise killed the deceased. Others ruled that
the culprit's right to inherit is based on whether the murder was
deliberate or accidental.[271]

Grandmother's Right to Inheritance

While a mother or wife's financial right to inheritance are absolute, a grandmother, paternal or maternal, may be excluded from
receiving inheritance altogether if the mother of the deceased is
still alive.[272] According to Imam Mālik 🙵, the grandmother is to
inherit one-sixth of her grandchild's estate only if the mother of
the deceased (female) is not alive. This is agreed upon by all major jurists.[273] Imam Mālik 🙵 derived this ruling from an instance
in which a maternal grandmother asked the Companion Abū
Bakr 🙵 for her inheritance rights upon the death of her grandchild.
After verifying from two Companions, al-Mughīrah ibn Shu'ba and
Muhammad ibn Maslamah 🙵, that the Prophet 🙵 had said that a
grandmother is to inherit one-sixth of her deceased grandchild's

estate if the deceased's mother has also passed on, Abū Bakr 🕮 granted this grandmother her share. Soon after, the deceased's paternal grandmother appeared and asked 'Umar ibn al-Khaṭṭāb 🕮 for a share of the inheritance. He replied that the two women may split the one-sixth between them.[274] Imam Mālik 🕮 was of the opinion that the maternal grandmother is more entitled to the share of the inheritance as compared to the paternal grandmother, as she is considered as having a closer bond to the deceased grandchild.[275] There was disagreement regarding the case that the paternal grandmother happens to be closer to the deceased's grandchild. Imam Abū Ḥanīfah 🕮 and some Shāfiʿī scholars held that the closest lived relation blocks the other from receiving a share, even if she happens to be the paternal grandmother. Imams Mālik, Aḥmad and other Shāfiʿī 🕮 scholars disagreed and ruled that in such case, the one sixth is split between the two grandmothers.[276]

Sister's Inheritance Right

Scholars sometimes contend that the designated inheritance shares for women at times surpass the specific amounts outlined in texts. For instance, some rule that a woman may be entitled to the remainder of an estate if no other heirs are alive. Specifically, Allah 🕮 decreed in Chapter 4:176 that if a deceased man has no children or parents but only one sister, she should inherit half of his wealth: *"If a man dies, leaving no child but [only] a sister, she will have half of what he left."*[277] As for the other half of his estate, Islamic inheritance laws delineate who the shares must go to. If no other heirs exist, even though Imam al-Shāfiʿī, al-Awzāʿī and Mālik 🕮 ruled that it would be transferred to *bayt al-māl*, the stronger scholarly view (including that of Imam Abū Ḥanīfah 🕮), based on what the majority of Companions of the Prophet transmit, is that the sister would be eligible for the entire estate.[278]

Differing Opinions Regarding Charitable Financial Rights

Bequest (Waṣiyah)

Scholars disagree somewhat as to who is qualified to create a will. Some held that a person must have reached puberty to be eligible to bequest his or her wealth. Imam Mālik ﷺ held an opposing opinion, giving room, for instance, to wealthy, orphaned girls, whose estate was controlled by an unjust guardian, to bequest their wealth to a more trustworthy person.[279] Ibn Ḥajar al-ʿAsqalānī ﷺ shared Imam Mālik's view, declaring, "And (drawing up a will) does not require being Muslim, or being an adult or being divorced or widowed or the permission of a husband."[280]

As to the amount one may bequest in a will, most scholars agree that it should not exceed one-third of one's wealth.[281] In one narration, the Prophet Muhammad ﷺ advised against allocating more than one-third of one's wealth upon death as even charity in order to protect the inheritance rights of female heirs. If a person dedicates more than one-third of his or her wealth as charity, the person's female heirs, who have a religious right to a portion of the remaining wealth, may have insufficient funds to live comfortably after the passing of their loved ones. On one occasion, Saʿd ibn Abī Waqqās ﷺ, a man nearing his death, asked the Prophet Muhammad ﷺ:

> O Messenger of Allah, my ailment has overcome me as you can see and I have wealth, but no one inherits me except my only daughter. Should I bequest two-thirds of my wealth in charity? The Messenger ﷺ replied, "No." I said, "How about half?" He ﷺ replied, "No you may give one-third but this is (still) too much (*kathīr*) for indeed for you to leave your heirs rich is better than to leave them in poverty, dependent on (other) people. And you will not give anything for the sake of Allah except that you will be rewarded for it even a tiny crumb that you feed your wife."[282]

Some scholars hold the opinion that a Muslim should bequest less than one-third of his wealth, citing the above narration and the following as evidence: Ibn 'Abbās ؓ, a Companion of Prophet Muhammad ﷺ, once said, "If the people came down in their bequest from a third to a fourth, it would be dearer to me as the Messenger ﷺ said, 'A third, and a third is too much.'"[283]

Views on Obligatory Charity (Zakāt Al-Māl)

The first two groups who qualify for *zakāt* in verse 60 of Sūrah al-Tawbah are the poor (*fuqarā'*) and the needy (*masākīn*).[284] Many scholars agree that a poor or needy woman is given *zakāt* priority over a poor or needy man, while Imam Aḥmad ؒ ruled that both genders share equal priority.[285] A man is eligible for *zakāt* if he is unable to find work and has no wealthy relatives who can financially assist him. Islamic law does not require a woman to provide for herself unless she chooses to earn a living and so, according to the Ḥanafī school of thought, if a woman has no provider – father, brother, husband, etc. – the Islamic state must by default financially provide for her using its *zakāt* funds or funds from the state's treasury box (*bayt al-mal*).[286]

A woman is also considered eligible for *zakāt* if she is studying toward a degree – for example, a teaching degree or medical license – that would benefit or serve other Muslims.[287] A wife is also eligible for *zakāt* if her husband fails to provide her with enough to meet her needs in a manner that is equivalent to the care to which she was accustomed prior to marriage.[288] In fact, Imam Abū Ḥanīfah ﵀ ruled that even if a woman's husband is wealthy, if he pays her insufficient *nafaqah*, she deserves *zakāt*.[289] In addition, because her husband, not her father, is religiously obligated to provide for her, a woman with insufficient financial support can accept a share of her parents' *zakāt*.[290] In the past, this ruling allowed parents to allocate a portion of the charitable contributions they received to support their married daughters who were in need.[291]

The next four categories of individuals who qualify to receive *zakāt* may not necessarily be impoverished and might be quite wealthy, yet the Qur'an instructs that they can accept this form of charity: employees who collect the *zakāt*, those who support Muslims and protect them, those in bondage, those in debt for the cause of Allah, and those who are traveling in a foreign land with insufficient funds to live on.[292] The Prophet ﷺ said, "Whoever has sustenance should give it to those who do not have sustenance."[293] The Messenger ﷺ, as head of state, specifically commanded that individuals in debt receive a share of *zakāt*:

> I am more deserving [to take responsibility] of the believers than their own selves. Thus, whoever dies while in debt

> and does not leave anyone who can pay it for him, then it becomes our duty to pay it off and whoever leaves behind wealth then it is handed to his [or her] heirs.[294]

Verse 6 of Sūrah al-Aḥzāb reaffirms this responsibility of the Messenger (as head of the Muslim nation) to take care of those under his leadership. Furthermore, in the second verse of Sūrah al-Māidah, God commands the believers to assist one another, "And cooperate in righteousness and piety." Imam ibn Ḥajar al-ʿAsqalānī explained in his book *Fatḥ al-Bārī* that just as the Messenger ﷺ as head of state indicated his responsibility to care for those in need, it is incumbent upon every leader of a Muslim nation to support those, including women in need, by providing from the state's treasury box (*bayt al-māl*) housing, sustenance, and—if they choose— assistance in acquiring work until they are economically secure.[295] Traditional scholars thus found that it was the responsibility of every Muslim leader to financially support women who are not properly provided for. Such support included and was not limited to a residence that is managed by a righteous woman, housemaids to assist them, a mosque in which to pray, and a religious scholar (preferably a woman) responsible to teach them their religion and address problems they face. These same scholars relay that the objective is not only to protect women and secure their well-being, but ideally to train them to secure a profession so they can earn an income independently. When a Muslim nation is economically unable to provide this form of social security (or for instance, when residing in a nation that is non-Muslim) Imam ibn Hazm stated, "It becomes an obligation upon the wealthy to take care of the needs of those underprivileged," and to otherwise provide them with such services.[296]

Scholars generally rule that family members, such as the mother or wife, who are owed financial support (*nafaqah*) cannot receive *zakāt* from those who are already religiously obligated to financially support them unless, as some scholars view, the women are considered "in debt" as stated in the Qur'anic verse delineating the eight categories of people who are eligible for *zakāt*. So, for example, according to one view, a man married to a woman in debt may give his wife his *zakāt*. Imam al-Shāfiʿī 🕮 said:

> And if a woman [his wife] or his adult son were in debt and then became ill and in need, or his father was in debt, he may give them *zakāt* for falling under the category of those in debt [*al-ghārimīn*] and just the same, if they fall under the categories of the wayfarer or the poor and needy since he is not obliged to [directly] pay their debt..."[297]

Zakāt Al-Māl: The Global Issue of Denying Women Obligatory Charity

As evidenced throughout this book, Islamic law imposes a duty on every Muslim to mitigate poverty, particularly amongst financially vulnerable women, with a goal of guaranteeing their financial stability and security. However, the current, general economic status of women today underscores the persistence of poverty amongst them, revealing a significant gap between Islamic principles and their realization. According to statistics gathered by world human rights organizations, women represent the largest proportion of people in severe poverty. For example, the *Tadamun* (Solidarity) European Mediterranean Women's Foundation declared, "There are a billion and two hundred poor men and women in the world that live on less that one dollar per day. But the fact is that women make up the greatest (number) of them and are the most in extreme impoverishment."[298] Nations have verified that the number of women in poverty amounts to one-third of the poor population worldwide.[299] The *zakāt* system, rooted in divine ordinance, is notably overlooked, and substituted by various manmade constructs that fail to ultimately support and uphold the rights of women. Under Islamic law, every nation is obliged to equally provide the necessities for every family member, male or female, young or old – to take a portion from the rich and give it to the poor. They are obliged to require husbands to financially support their wives so that women are never in a state of poverty. In fact, when a husband's responsibilities to his wife fall short, under certain conditions, other male family members can allocate a portion of their annual *zakāt* to provide for her.[300] In fact, some scholars, including Imam al-Shāfiʿī ﵀, ruled that a person's *zakāt* may also be given to family members (e.g. wife, daughter, mother, grandmother) who already receive financial support from their husbands if they fall under one of the eight *zakāt* categories specified in Chapter nine, verse 60 of the Qur'an.[301] Of course, a Muslim's obligation to generally pay *zakat* to eligible women and men is an important tenant of the faith, inseparable from one's obligatory prayers:

وَأَقِيمُوا۟ ٱلصَّلَوٰةَ وَءَاتُوا۟ ٱلزَّكَوٰةَ وَٱرْكَعُوا۟ مَعَ ٱلرَّٰكِعِينَ ﴿٤٣﴾

And establish prayer and give *zakah* [or *zakat*]and bow with those who bow [in worship and obedience].[302]

For those who fall short in paying their dues, the Messenger ﷺ warned:

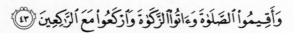

> Whoever is made wealthy by Allah and does not pay the *zakāt* of his wealth then on the Day of Resurrection his wealth will be made like a bald-headed poisonous male snake with two black spots over his eyes. The snake will encircle his neck and bite his cheeks and say, "I am your wealth; I am your treasure."

Following this warning, the Prophet ﷺ recited Chapter 3 verse180 of the Qur'an:[303]

وَلَا يَحْسَبَنَّ ٱلَّذِينَ يَبْخَلُونَ بِمَآ ءَاتَىٰهُمُ ٱللَّهُ مِن فَضْلِهِۦ هُوَ خَيْرًا لَّهُم ۖ بَلْ هُوَ شَرٌّ لَّهُمْ ۖ سَيُطَوَّقُونَ مَا بَخِلُوا۟ بِهِۦ يَوْمَ ٱلْقِيَـٰمَةِ ۗ وَلِلَّهِ مِيرَٰثُ ٱلسَّمَـٰوَٰتِ وَٱلْأَرْضِ ۗ وَٱللَّهُ بِمَا تَعْمَلُونَ خَبِيرٌ ﴿١٨٠﴾

> And let not those who [greedily] withhold what Allah has given them of His bounty ever think that it is better for them. Rather, it is worse for them. *Their necks will be encircled by what they withheld on the Day of Resurrection.* And to Allah belongs the heritage of the heavens and the earth. And Allah, with what you do, is [fully] Acquainted.[304]

The fact that women represent the most impoverished in the world today is especially disturbing given the final sermon of the Messenger ﷺ during Hajj at the Mount of 'Arafah:

> Fear Allah in your dealings with women, for you have taken them as your wives under Allah's trust and consummated the marriage by His permission…and it is your responsibility to feed them and clothe them in a goodly manner… O people, there shall be no prophet after me nor a nation after you, so worship your Lord and perform your five

prayers and fast your month of Ramadan and pay off your due *zakāt* from your wealth to cleanse with it your souls and perform Hajj and obey your leaders. Do this, and you shall enter your Lord's Paradise [*Jannah*].[305]

Obligatory Charity at the End of Ramadan (Zakāt al-Fiṭr)

With exception of Imam Abū Ḥanīfah 🕮, the majority of scholars agreed that the husband carries the religious responsibility of paying his Muslim wife's share of *zakāt al-fiṭr*. If his wife is Jewish or Christian, she is not required to give this form of charity.[306] Some scholars are of the opinion that there are certain circumstances that allow a husband to refuse to pay his wife's *zakāt al-fiṭr*; these include her being *nashiz* at the time of payment, or the couple not yet having consummated their marriage.[307] For example, Imam Aḥmad 🕮 ruled a husband cannot pay *zakāt al-Fiṭr* on behalf of his young wife who is not yet physically able to consummate the marriage.[308] As for a divorced woman whose divorce is revocable and who is in her three-month waiting period, the jurists agree that her husband must pay her share of *zakāt al-Fiṭr*. Also, the majority of scholars ruled that if the divorce is revocable or irrevocable but the woman is pregnant with her ex-husband's child, the ex-husband remains responsible to pay his ex-wife's share of *zakāt al-fiṭr*. This was the ruling of Shafī'ī jurists Imam al-Haramayn 'Abd al-Malik ibn Yūsuf al-Juwaynī and Imams al-Ghazālī. If, however, the couple's divorce is irrevocable and she is not pregnant, it is no longer the ex-husband's religious duty to pay his ex-wife's *zakāt al-fiṭr* during the pregnancy.[309]

A Woman's Right to Give Voluntary Charity or Ṣadaqah from her Husband's Wealth

With exception of Imam Mālik ﷺ, the majority of scholars agree that, although according to Islamic law the husband is charged to provide for his wife and family, the wife can spend the family's wealth toward voluntary charity (*ṣadaqah*) without her husband's permission.[310] They held that since Muslims, both men and women, ought to be generous and because husbands are directed by Allah to live with their wives "in kindness," a wife does not require her husband's permission to give in voluntary charity.[311] To further clarify, most scholars agree that a wife may give in *ṣadaqah*, both wealth that is strictly her personal possession as well as wealth which she and her husband share, without first seeking her husband's approval. Asmā' ﷺ, the daughter of Abū Bakr ﷺ, asked Prophet Muhammad ﷺ:

> O Messenger of Allah I have no wealth except what al-Zubayir brings home, am I able to give charity from it? He replied: Give charity (for the sake of Allah) as much as you could and do not hoard, lest Allah would withhold (His blessings) from you.[312]

According to the majority of scholars (including Imams al-Shāfiʿī, Abū Ḥanīfah, Ibn Ḥazm al-Ẓāhirī, and Sufyān al-Thawrī ﷺ) any female who has reached puberty is free to dispose of any portion of her wealth as she pleases; she does not require the permission or input of any family member. Imam al-Shāfiʿī ﷺ refuted scholars who did not agree by citing verse 229 of Sūrah al-Baqarah, "There is no blame upon either of them concerning that by which she ransoms herself." In citing further evidence in support of this ruling, Imam Ibn Ḥajar al-'Asqalānī 🕮 gave reference to an instance when, after a Eid al-Fiṭr sermon, the Prophet 🕮 had Bilāl 🕮 spread out his cloak in the form of a collection bucket and encouraged the women present to give *sadaqah*. The female listeners complied generously and removed their jewelry, placing it onto the cloak. Imam al-Qurṭubī 🕮 commented on the women's response, pointing out that the tradition neither says that these women's husbands were present nor that these women sought their husband's permission or approval before giving this *sadaqah*, all of which reinforces the ruling that a woman may dispose of her wealth as she pleases. Another Prophetic example reinforces this ruling. In one instance Maymūnah 🕮, the wife of the Prophet Muhammad 🕮, gave away what was at the time considered her personal property without consulting with the Prophet 🕮, yet he did not question or disapprove of her decision.[313]

Gift or Endowment (Hibah)

Just as the Prophet 🕮 encouraged women to give voluntary charity in the form of *sadaqah*, he also advised them to give charity in the form of gifts, or *hibah*. According to Islamic law, a woman, regardless of marital status, can give from her wealth anything she wishes to anyone she chooses. Conversely, a woman can be gifted anything by anyone. Within Islamic law, a gift is valid so long as the gift was clearly offered by its giver and accepted by the recipient.[314] An exchange between Abū Bakr 🕮 and his daughter 'Ā'ishah 🕮 is one of several traditions which confirm this definition of 'gift'. In the moments before his death, Abū Bakr 🕮 said to his daughter, "I had [attempted to gift] you with a gift, [which] if you had accepted it then, it would have been yours, but today it is for all heirs."[315] It appears that although her father offered her a gift, ʿĀ'ishah ﵂ neither accepted it nor took possession of it – therefore, it did not belong to her. Ibn ʿAbbās ﵄ and other scholars inferred from this tradition that gift-giving is incomplete and invalid unless the person to whom the gift was offered takes possession of it.[316] As an important side-note, some scholars say that when Abū Bakr ﵁ offered a special portion of his wealth to ʿĀ'ishah ﵂, it was done with the knowledge and acceptance of her siblings, because it is generally best for parents to gift their children equally so that no ill feelings develop between siblings.[317]

Scholarly opinion differed on what gift equality meant when it came to men and women. Only some Shāfiʿī and Mālikī scholars ruled that if a person gives a gift to multiple recipients at the same time, then the male recipient must receive twice that given to the female to match Islamic laws regarding inheritance. Others disagreed, ruling that there is no evidence to support the inference that the laws of gift-giving must coincide with the laws of inheritance and that both genders should receive whatever the person giving the gift sees fit to give. In fact, some scholars said that, if anything, Islamic law favors gift-giving to women over men, as Ibn ʿAbbās ﵄ once narrated that the Prophet ﷺ exhorted, "Treat your children equally regarding gifts and if I was to favor anyone, I would certainly favor the females."[318]

Scholars agree, however, that once a gift has been offered and accepted, it is impermissible for a person to demand that the recipient return the gift for any reason. The one exception to this rule is a father who asks that a child return a gift because he would prefer to divide his wealth in a more equitable manner amongst his children. The Prophet ﷺ admonished his people about taking back a gift, stating, "It is not permissible to give a gift and take it back except for a father taking back a gift he gave his offspring."[319]

Islamic Endowment (Waqf)

Women may receive any sort of endowment or *waqf* by their fathers or family members if stated in writing.[320] If a parent who had two children, a son and a daughter, were to say, for example, "Such land is *waqf* for my children," both would have equal right to the land and its benefits as long as they live.[321] Scholars agree that he is free to split the shares of such a *waqf* property any way he pleases. He can do so based on the inheritance rules, with the male receiving twice the female's share, or do the opposite by giving the daughter a share twice that of the son. Imam Aḥmad ؒ, however, said it is better to give one child more than the other for the sake of need, rather than preference.[322] Also if the land is identified as a *waqf* type of *ṣadaqah*, once all the children pass away, the property should be transferred to the poor and needy because its usefulness and goodness is intended to be everlasting.[323] If it is the owner's wish, he may add to his recorded statement (*waqf ṣīghah*), "Such land is *waqf* for my children, my grandchildren, and their children." Although Imam Mālik ؒ viewed that such charity can only be given to the son's children, since only they carry the father's name, Imam al-Shāfiʿī and Abū Yūsuf ؒ disagreed, saying the daughter's children may unquestionably serve as recipients.[324]

Expiations (Al-Kaffārāt)

As mentioned previously, in certain instances when a Muslim makes an oath that is untruthful or inappropriate, he must give a form of charity to atone for the wrongful oath called an expiation or *al-Kaffārāh* (singular of *al-kaffārāt*). Scholars held different opinions on who is eligible to receive charity in the form of an expiation – in other words, who can a person feed in order to atone for his or her wrongful oath – and they disagreed on the form of an expiation. The Shāfiʿī and Ḥanbalī schools of thought ruled that the expiation must be in the form of food or clothing, whereas Ḥanafī scholars maintained that it can be paid in currency or partially in food and partially in currency.[325] Imam al-Shāfiʿī رحمه الله held that a wife is eligible to receive a *kaffārāh* owed by her husband to atone for a wrongful act that he committed if the *nafaqah* he spends on her does not suffice her needs.[326] The Imam generally conditions all those deserving of these expiations to be Muslims in need.

A Wife's Income and Education

According to the Islamic Shariah, every wife, divorcee, or widow has a right to her own income.[327] This idea is supported by the Qur'anic verse 32 of Chapter Four which indicates that she may earn such an income through her own employment:[328]

وَلَا تَتَمَنَّوْا مَا فَضَّلَ ٱللَّهُ بِهِۦ بَعْضَكُمْ عَلَىٰ بَعْضٍ ۚ لِّلرِّجَالِ نَصِيبٌ مِّمَّا ٱكْتَسَبُوا۟ ۖ
وَلِلنِّسَآءِ نَصِيبٌ مِّمَّا ٱكْتَسَبْنَ ۚ وَسْـَٔلُوا۟ ٱللَّهَ مِن فَضْلِهِۦٓ ۗ إِنَّ ٱللَّهَ كَانَ بِكُلِّ شَىْءٍ
عَلِيمًا ﴿٣٢﴾

And do not wish for that by which Allah has made some of you exceed others. For men is a share of what they have earned, *and for women is a share of what they have earned.* And ask Allah of his bounty. Indeed, Allah is ever, of all things, Knowing.[329]

The above verse from 7th century Arabia demonstrates not only the idea that women may earn an income just as men might, but that their earnings are their own.[330] The Shariah unequivocally encourages both men and women to strive to receive the earth's blessings in verses 3 and 4 of Chapter 92:

وَمَا خَلَقَ ٱلذَّكَرَ وَٱلْأُنثَىٰٓ ٣

And [by] He who created the male and female.[331]

إِنَّ سَعْيَكُمْ لَشَتَّىٰ ٤

Indeed, your efforts [strive] are diverse.[332]

Scholars point to various circumstances when women in Islamic history or throughout the Qur'an needed to find employment. In one example presented in the Qur'an, two unmarried women worked to support their family when their father was too ill to carry on his responsibility as breadwinner.[333] Chapter 28, verse 23 describes the story of two girls in the town of Madyan who had no choice but to strive to provide sustenance for themselves, their family, and animals in order to survive:

وَلَمَّا وَرَدَ مَآءَ مَدْيَنَ وَجَدَ عَلَيْهِ أُمَّةً مِّنَ ٱلنَّاسِ يَسْقُونَ وَوَجَدَ مِن دُونِهِمُ
ٱمْرَأَتَيْنِ تَذُودَانِ ۖ قَالَ مَا خَطْبُكُمَا ۖ قَالَتَا لَا نَسْقِى حَتَّىٰ يُصْدِرَ ٱلرِّعَآءُ ۖ وَأَبُونَا شَيْخٌ
كَبِيرٌ ٢٣

And when he [Prophet Moses] came to the well of Madyan, he found there a crowd of people watering

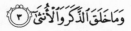

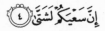

> [their flocks], and he found aside from them two women driving back [their flocks]. He said, "What is your circumstance?" They said, "We do not water until the shepherds dispatch [their flocks]; and our father is an old man."[334]

Asmā' bint Abī Bakr, the female Companion of the Prophet ﷺ, was another example of a woman who worked hard to make a living, although she was forced to do so, as her husband al-Zubayr was quite poor. In addition to caring for her household, she took on additional household duties like repairing the water bucket and attending to his animal's needs, which involved walking long distances in search of food. She explains:

> Al-Zubayr married me, and he had no wealth, no slaves, nothing except his horse. I used to feed his horse, looking after it and exercising it. I crushed date-stones to feed his camel. I used to bring water and repair the bucket, and I used to make bread, but I could not bake it, so some of my Anṣārī neighbors, who were kind women, used to bake it for me. I used to carry the dates from the garden that the Prophet ﷺ had given to al-Zubayr on my head, and this garden was two-thirds of a *farsakh* away. One day I was coming back with the dates on my head. I met the Messenger of Allah ﷺ, who had a group of his Companions with him. He called me, then told his camel to sit down so that I could ride behind him, but I felt embarrassed to ride with the men and I remembered al-Zubayr and how jealous he was for he was more jealous than all the people. So, the Messenger ﷺ understood that I was shy and he ﷺ just left. When I got home to al-Zubayr I told him the Messenger of Allah ﷺ saw me carrying the dates on my head and

> his Companions were with him and he asked me to ride [on the camel] but I felt shy from him and I remembered your jealous nature. he [al-Zubayr] said, "By Allah, it is worse for me to see you carrying the dates on your head than to see you riding behind him." Later, Abū Bakr sent me a servant, who relieved me of having to take care of the horse; it was as if I had been released from slavery.[335]

The irony behind the story lies in the extent of the responsibilities she assumed and could handle. While a few use this Hadith to show the extent a wife should do for her husband, most scholars reject this view as incorrect.[336] Remarkably, all the chores, which she initially took on when her husband was busy at war, were voluntary, as evidenced by her father's response in sending someone to assist her and alleviate these burdens.[337] Importantly, and contrary to some outlier opinions about Islam's permissibility or encouragement of a woman's engagement outside the home, the Hadith shows that the Prophet ﷺ never disapproved the work she did outside her home, even upon seeing that she traveled a long distance.[338] On the contrary, he ﷺ offered assistance, which she felt uncomfortable accepting.

These examples indicate the Qur'an and Sunnah's endorsement of women working outside the home when circumstances demand, but what if a woman, for instance, without financial necessity, seeks to leverage her education or skillset to make a positive impact in her community? Scholars affirm a woman's right to do so but ultimately leave the question to the jurisdiction of the household, affirming its permissibility so long as a woman's husband (or father, if unmarried) does not oppose it.[339] As noted previously, scholars rule that a husband or father's approval is not required in certain instances, like when, for example, those responsible to financially support her fall short of their obligations. As another example, approval is unnecessary for a widow or divorcée who must work to earn a living for herself and her children, particularly if no men in the family step up to assist her.[340] In one incident, the Companion Jābir ibn ʿAbdullāh ﷺ related the situation of his divorced aunt, who took initiative to earn an income on her own by farming during her waiting period. He explained:

> My maternal aunt was divorced, and she wanted to collect the harvest from her date-palm trees. A man rebuked her for going out to the trees. She went to the Prophet ﷺ who said, "No, go and collect the harvest from your trees, for perhaps you will give some in charity or do a good deed with it."[341]

This tradition may explain why the Prophet's wife ʿĀ'ishah ﷺ gave a legal opinion (*fatwa*) that a woman could go out to earn a living for her general needs during her three-month waiting period following her divorce.[342] In fact, when ʿĀ'ishah's brother-in-law was killed, she took her sister to perform ʿUmrah during her three-month waiting period. For that reason, when Imam al-Ghazālī ﷺ was asked by the parents of their widowed daughter whether they may take her to ʿUmrah during her waiting period to relieve her depression, he remembered ʿĀ'ishah's ruling and gave them permission to do so.[343]

Education for women was actively promoted during the life of the Messenger ﷺ. In fact, in one tradition the Prophet ﷺ said, "Seeking knowledge is an obligation upon every Muslim."[344] The Messenger ﷺ himself championed the employment of women who had specialized training they could use to service the community. In one example, he ﷺ set up a special tent in the mosque to hospitalize those injured on the battlefield, employing a female physician, Rufaydah al-Aslamiyyah. Under his direction, men like Saʿd ibn Muʿādh ﷺ were sent to her to receive proper medical treatment.[345] Other female Companions also worked in the medical field, including Umm Kabsah, Umm ʿAṭiyyah, Ḥamnah bint Jahsh, Umm Salīm, and Umm Muṭāʿ ﷺ.[346] These examples in early Islamic history serve as evidence that women with specialized educational backgrounds and skill-sets are not hindered but rather encouraged to pursue careers in their field.[347] Additional examples of women employed during the life of the Prophet ﷺ included midwives who assisted in childbirth, such as the midwife Salmā who delivered the Prophet's son, Ibrāhīm. These women carried out their duties in the households of their patients, plainly demonstrating that the early female adherents to Islam at times worked outside their homes.[348] Some female Companions of the Prophet also worked as farmers, and their communities depended on the crops they cultivated. In fact, one woman who was a farm owner grew vegetables that she would pick, add meat to and cook every Friday to serve at the mosque following the prayer.[349] The Companion Sahl ibn Saʿd ﷺ said, "After finishing Friday or the *Jumuʿah* prayer we used to greet her and she would give us that food which we would eat with our hands, and because of that meat we used to look forward to Friday."[350] Women during and after the life of the Messenger also owned their own businesses – for example, the Prophet's wife Khadījah ﷺ and others including Khawlah, Saqafiyyah bint Mukarramah, and al-Khamiyyah ﷺ, used to buy, sell, and trade perfume.[351]

Equal Pay

Islamic law and principles would also require equal pay between women and men when they share the same responsibilities and workload.[352] This concept is supported by Sūrah al-Aḥzāb, which generally upholds the idea of men and women being equally entitled reward for the good that they do:

إِنَّ ٱلْمُسْلِمِينَ وَٱلْمُسْلِمَٰتِ وَٱلْمُؤْمِنِينَ وَٱلْمُؤْمِنَٰتِ وَٱلْقَٰنِتِينَ وَٱلْقَٰنِتَٰتِ
وَٱلصَّٰدِقِينَ وَٱلصَّٰدِقَٰتِ وَٱلصَّٰبِرِينَ وَٱلصَّٰبِرَٰتِ وَٱلْخَٰشِعِينَ وَٱلْخَٰشِعَٰتِ وَٱلْمُتَصَ
وَٱلْمُتَصَدِّقَٰتِ وَٱلصَّٰٓئِمِينَ وَٱلصَّٰٓئِمَٰتِ وَٱلْحَٰفِظِينَ فُرُوجَهُمْ وَٱلْحَٰفِظَٰتِ وَٱ
ٱللَّهَ كَثِيرًا وَٱلذَّٰكِرَٰتِ أَعَدَّ ٱللَّهُ لَهُم مَّغْفِرَةً وَأَجْرًا عَظِيمًا ﴿٣٥﴾

Indeed, the Muslim men and Muslim women, the believing men and believing women, the obedient men and obedient women, the truthful men and truthful women, the patient men and patient women, the humble men and humble women, the charitable men and charitable women, the fasting men and fasting women, the men who guard their private parts and the women who do so, and the men who remember Allah often and the women who do so - for them Allah has prepared forgiveness and a great reward.[353]

It is worth noting that, historically, in the U.S., because women weren't viewed as breadwinners or "real workers" who had to support their families, any income they did receive was considered "special money" or "allowance," giving way to a culture where women were generally paid less than men for the same jobs men had even when women became important contributors in the workforce.[354] Laws in the early twentieth century aimed to specifically benefit and protect male breadwinners, rather than women who could not be "real workers" given their household and child-rearing duties, leaving us with traces of coverture that remain today.[355] In her research about the subject matter, one attorney, Arianne Renan Barzilay, comments:

> Today, the concentration of wealth and power in the market is linked to top executive ranks and the most lucrative professions, which are still disproportionately male. Despite advances in women's marketplace labor participation and earnings, women still earn less than men, and mothers, in particular, have even lower earnings.[356]

Furthermore, regardless of whether women earn the same or more than men, it is often presumed that he is the one who owns any property.[357] Discrepancies in pay persist in not only the west, but in the Arab world as well: one women's advocacy organization in Jordan known as Tadamun in fact attributes the state of poverty women are in worldwide to the fact they often work without pay and often receive less pay than their male co-workers.[358] Statistically, the unpaid amount for these hard-working women amounts to $11 trillion, which is not only disturbing but deeply affects the economy of every nation.[359] A significant portion of women who work for no or little pay are often engaged in farm labor, and have little to no education. Essentially, those primarily responsible for providing nutrition to their households and communities are the most underpaid, undervalued, and receive the least credit for their efforts.[360] In Islam, even when men are assigned the responsibility of being a financial provider, men and women alike are rewarded and compensated equally for the work they do.

Differing Views on a Woman's Right to Compensation Upon Injury or Death (*Diyah*)

The issue of equal compensation for men and women arises in a different context but is met with disagreement that is paramount to this discussion— specifically, when providing monetary compensation for the death or injury of a woman or man. Generally, Islam recognizes the death penalty as retribution *(qiṣāṣ)* for someone who murders a woman just as it does when a man is murdered, as confirmed by a letter the Prophet wrote to the Companion ʿAmr ibn Ḥazm ﵁, saying, "The man is killed for the woman (whom he kills)."[361] As an alternative to imposing the same injury to the perpetrator of harm (*qisas*), God does provide people with the option of forgiving (*ʿafw*) those who killed or injured them or their loved ones so long as monetary retribution is provided (*diyah*).[362] According to the Qur'an and Prophetic tradition, a woman, like a man, is entitled to monetary compensation when someone injures or kills her, but there is disagreement about whether or not the same monetary compensation would be provided for the death of a man versus a woman.[363]

Thus, as outlined by Hadith, the family of the deceased can choose whether or not to enforce an "eye for an eye" ruling (*qiṣāṣ*) (if living under an Islamic government that implements the Shariah) or to accept *diyah* instead.[364] In applying *qiṣās,* however, Imam al-Shāfiʿī ﵀ held that *qiṣāṣ* cannot be implemented unless all heirs agree to take revenge on behalf of their dead. In cases where *diyah* is implemented instead, he rules that each heir may receive the value of *diyah* he or she is entitled based on their inheritance rights.[365] The same rule applies in cases where a husband strikes his wife intentionally causing her physical harm: scholars similarly agree that the wife has the right to have *qiṣāṣ* enforced.[366] Otherwise, consistent with the Islamic rules of *qiṣāṣ,* her husband may need to pay her *diyah.* Payment for *diyah* may be in the form of material or currency.[367]

There is disagreement about the value of *diyah* provided for a death or injury of a woman as compared to the death or injury of a man—some holding that, although the *qisas* is the same for the death or injury of a man and woman, the value of the *diyah* following the death or injury of a woman is less than that of a man's. As described in this section, the argument that a woman's *diyah* should be different than a man's *diyah,* however, is not based on directions from verified primary Islamic texts or sources. Specifically, the classical jurists of the four schools of thought hold that if a female is killed and her family pardons the killer and accepts monetary compensation (*diyah*) on her behalf, the monetary retribution should amount to half the *diyah* of a male.[368] For example, Imam al-Shāfiʿī ⚜ considered the value of *diyah* for a male to be one hundred camels, and, for females, if no *qisas* is implemented, fifty camels.[369] Of course, at the time, he ruled that the family could request to be paid in currency.[370] Similarly, when *diyah* is paid for an injury, the Ḥanafī and Shāfiʿī schools held that a girl or woman's *diyah* amount is half that of the male.[371] The Mālikī and Ḥanbalī schools, however, hold that a girl or woman's *diyah* is equal to the male if her injuries amount to one-third of the total *diyah* amount.[372] They then, based on certain traditions (that are categorized as weak, less reliable sources by Hadith scholars) and analogies to rulings on a woman's inheritance share, held that once the female's injuries rise above the one-third portion, she receives half from that point on.[373]

Imam Ibn Qudāmah ﵀ attributed the classical rulings about the *diyah* of women being less than the *diyah* of men to some successors or *salaf* of the Prophet's Companions (such as Ibn al-Mundhir) but then presents opposite views of other successors (such as Ibn 'Ulayyah) who rejected their view.[374] Those successors of the Companions who rejected the view of a woman's *diyah* being lower argue that such rulings do not coincide with the Prophetic tradition that states, "For the believing soul is one hundred camels,"[375] which does not distinguish between men and women.[376] More importantly, it does not coincide with the Qur'anic verses about the sanctity and equality of human life in verse 92 of Sūrah al-Nisā' which does not make such gender distinctions.[377]

Importantly, to support a distinction between the genders, the classical jurists of the schools of thought present both (1) prophetic traditions that are legally questionable (referring to 'weak' Hadith, for instance) or (2) statements from successors of the Companions of the Prophet that are subject to opposing interpretations. The jurists of the schools of thought do not reference any authentic traditions of the Messenger ﷺ when explaining their reasoning for imposing distinct monetary values for *diyah* based on gender.[378] Specifically, in his famous book "*Nayl al-Awṭār,*" Imam al-Shawkānī's comments on the less reliable traditions used to claim the value of *diyah* is different for a man and woman, saying that there was no proof that the Prophet made those statements.[379] In finding gender-based distinctions in *diyah* values,

Imam al-Shawkānī discusses the evidence the classical scholars rely on from the generation after the Prophet's Companions: for instance, traditional scholars refer to a statement made by Saʿīd ibn al-Musayyib ⁂ about a woman's lower *diyah* when a man injured a woman, causing her to lose her fingers.[380] But scholars disagree about the meaning of the word "sunnah" which appears in that statement. Imam al-Kāsānī ⁂ regarded the word "sunnah" in that statement as simply referring to the customs of the people rather than the Sunnah of the Prophet, which would lead to a different interpretation of the tradition.[381]

Because a woman who is killed or injured (or her family) has an indisputable, absolute right to impose the process of *qiṣāṣ* by taking the life of her killer or subjecting the perpetuator to the same exact injury, it logically follows that her *diyah* would be equal to that of a male, since this is a much lesser punishment.[382] Furthermore, many hold that it is inappropriate to compare a woman's inheritance share with compensation for injuries or loss of life. Scholars believe inheritance rights are designed to consider a man's higher living expenses under the Islamic legal framework, but the purpose of retribution is to merely compensate people for harm and injury. Moreover, there are situations under Islamic inheritance laws where female heirs receive equal or even greater shares than their male counterparts — so this selective application gives rise to a flawed comparison. Prominent scholars who supported the view that the woman's *diyah* should be equal to the man's include Imam al-Ghazālī, Shaykh Maḥmūd Shaltūt, Shaykh Rashīd Riḍā, Shaykh Muhammad Abū Zahrah, and Dr. Yūsuf al-Qaraḍāwī ⁂, the latter of whom said in what I've translated as follows:[383]

> The view that the majority of scholars held of the woman's *diyah* being half of a man's is not supported by the Qur'an, the Sunnah, an absolute consensus (*ijmāʿ mutayaqqan*), nor of an analogy or the interest of the public (*maṣlaḥah*)... and those who held that the woman receives equal *diyah* as the man support this by making every soul equal to another, which is what most scholars of today found who had good insight of the texts, good insights of the Shariah's objectives and good insight of our age and time.[384]

In a conference held at the Supreme Council for Family Affairs in Qatar on December 22, 2004, Dr. Yūsuf al-Qaraḍāwī ﵀ presented research on the subject matter, after which the council established without doubt, that the *diyah* of the female is equal to the male based on verse 92 of Sūrah al-Nisā'.[385]

The perspectives of Imam al-Ghazālī, Shaykh Maḥmūd Shaltūt, Dr. Yūsuf al-Qaraḍāwī and similar scholars about how *diyah* should be the same for men and women is consistent with important, authentic primary Islamic texts that are gender neutral:[386] (1) "And We ordained for them therein a life for a life, an eye for an eye, a nose for a nose, an ear for an ear, a tooth for a tooth, and for wounds is legal retribution," (2) "And whoever kills a believer by mistake – then the freeing of a believing slave and a compensation payment presented to the deceased's family," (3) and the Prophetic tradition "For the believing soul is one hundred camels."[387]

CHAPTER FOUR

Study of the Lives of 21 American Women

Chapter Four forms the heart of this book – a summary of the stories of 21 women living in America who are or were married to Muslim men. I conducted thorough, structured interviews with these women between March 2019 and January 2021. The study aimed to ascertain the main financial conflicts faced by Muslim-American women of different cultural backgrounds – including whether or not they enjoyed their financial rights under Islamic law. Specifically, I examine whether or not these women received certain financial rights to begin with, whether or not they were able to maintain their rights, and if they were able to manage their own personal income without threat or manipulation. I did begin each interview by providing an overview of the Islamic financial rights of women during marriage, divorce, and widowhood.

I took a phenomenological approach when interviewing these women. Phenomenology is concerned with understanding social and psychological phenomena from the perspectives of the very people who have lived or are living out those phenomena.[1] This approach is characterized by in-depth interviews of a limited number of participants (10-20).[2] Lengthy, informal interviews are the preferred method in gathering and compiling stories in this type of study, as they allow the researcher to better understand and more accurately relay to the readers the setting, context, nuances, and complexities of the subjects' unique stories. Consistent with this approach, I spent approximately 50 hours interviewing each woman, and spent a great deal of time in follow up communications.[3] In addition to examining the technicalities of whether or not these women enjoyed their financial rights under Islamic law, I delved into how each woman felt about the fulfilment of such rights, or lack thereof.

The Women I Interviewed

I interviewed American women who married Muslim men. According to the PEW Research Center, more than 63 percent of American Muslims over the age of 18 were born abroad and 37% were born in the U.S..[4] I attempted to choose a sample of households somewhat consistent with the PEW statistic.[5] As such, most of the women I interviewed were in households where both husband and wife were born abroad, but I did make sure to include some households in which at least one of the spouses were born in the U.S..

Ultimately, a total of 21 women participated. All women were U.S. citizens, residing in various parts of the country, and had children throughout their marriages. All women were between the ages of 38 and 65 and were also either currently or formerly married for at least 15 years (inclusive of one or more marriages), so as to ensure that the women experienced various life stages where they might have changing financial needs and rights.

This, however, is where the more obvious similarities between the women end. In some households both partners belonged to the same country of origin, while in other homes the husband and wife were from different backgrounds with clashing cultural or money managing practices, for instance. The study participants were of different races, and some women subscribed to a religion other than Islam during their marriages to their Muslim husbands. Some of the subjects felt pressured into matrimony; others made what they felt were good or bad, but nonetheless independent, choices. Some marriages remain intact today, while others ended upon the husband's death or in divorce. Among the interviewees are women who, as a result of experiencing financial abuse at the hands of their spouses, became psychologically affected and/or physically ill and are seeking treatment; others felt able to recover quickly and move forward with their lives after the abuse ended. Others found forgiveness in their hearts for their deceased ex-husbands upon learning of their passing.

The women's reactions during and at the conclusion of the interviews were no less varied than their backgrounds and stories. Some were eager to share their stories and felt relief at the opportunity to finally openly speak about their experiences, even though doing so brought to the surface pain that had been buried in their hearts for years. Others felt anxious and reluctant at the prospect of dredging up painful memories they had fought to forget. The women's willingness to speak candidly with me differed among those still married and those who were divorced. The former seemed more guarded during the interviews, taking care not to tarnish their husbands' public image for fear that their husbands would find out about their participation in the study or out of a desire to protect their marriages. As expected, the divorcees were much less reticent, speaking with a freedom and ease that the married participants did not enjoy.

The willingness of women to participate in the study and their degree of responsiveness to the questions also varied. Some women agreed to be part of the study, but refused to participate once the questionnaire was sent to them. Some initially felt that they were not the right candidates, but then agreed to participate once I explained the purpose of the study. Some hesitated at the start of the interview, but became increasingly comfortable as we discussed each topic. Others, who I relieved from participating in the study, initially consented to join the study, but were noticeably uncomfortable and taciturn when required to reveal details regarding the financial aspects of their marriages. The one motivation shared across all the women who participated in this study was a genuine desire to draw on their experiences to benefit other women. The one emotional response shared across nearly all study participants once they learned more about their financial rights under Islamic law, was pride in their Islamic faith and that their forbearance in the face of the denial of their financial rights will be rewarded by God – if not in this life, then in the Hereafter.

I of course did not have the opportunity to interview women from every corner of the beautifully diverse American Muslim demographic, but — given my own constraints and the reluctance of women generally to participate in a study like this — did my best to capture a small snapshot. The demographic characteristics of the interviewees are presented in Table 1:

Table 1. Demographic Characteristics of Study Participants

Subject Race/Nationality		
Caucasian	5	23.8%
African American	1	4.7%
Arab	5	23.8%
Iranian	2	9.5%
South Asian	6	28.6%
American-born to Arab parents	1	4.7%
American-born to South Asian parents	1	4.7%
Place of Birth		
United States	8	38.1%
Outside of the United States	13	61.9%
Husbands' Nationalities*		
American	1	4.3%
Arab	8	34.7%
Iranian	3	13.0%
South Asian	8	34.7%
Southeast Asian	1	4.3%
Bangladeshi	1	4.3%
British	1	4.3%
Age of Subject		
38-45	4	19.0%
46-55	9	42.8%
56+	8	38.1%

* For two subjects, both their first and second husbands were included in this data. It is important to note that all but one of the husbands in this study were not born in the U.S..[6]

Education Level		
Completed high school while married	1	4.8%
High school	3	14.3%
Some college	2	9.5%
Associate degree	1	4.8%
Bachelor's degree	7	33.3%
Graduate and/or professional degree	7	33.3%
Socioeconomic Status – Family of Origin		
Low-income	3	14.3%
Average/middle-class	7	33.3%
Upper middle-class	6	28.6%
Above average/wealthy	5	23.8%
Faith Origins		
Christian – Muslim convert prior to marriage	3	14.3%
Christian – Muslim convert after marriage**	4	19.0%
Muslim	14	66.7%

** One subject left Islam after divorce.[7]

It is important to note that before diving into the substance of my interviews, I made sure to gather information about the other diverse demographics of the women I interviewed, including, relevantly, her and her spouse's ages, their level of education, and their family's financial status upon matrimony. These details are particularly important because *Fiqh* scholars base their rulings related to *nafaqah* on both the husband's means and the standard of living of the wife before marriage.[8] It is also important to note that, of the 21 women who participated in this study, twelve of the women remain married, eight women were divorced, and one was in the process of divorce.

Addressing the Hesitation of Many Women: Is Silence the Answer?

Before describing the stories of the women I interviewed, I believe it is worth addressing the elephant in the room that so often silences women who are facing any kind of abuse in their marriages: is it morally wrong to expose the sordid details of our own marriages or to read about the problems in the marriages of others? The Islamic ideals of moral behavior forbid frivolous gossip and certainly backbiting, but with the express approval of the Prophet ﷺ, ʿĀ'ishah رضي الله عنها, the wife of the Prophet, permitted women to break their silence about their husbands' behavior in general (good and bad) for instructive purposes.[9] ʿĀ'ishah رضي الله عنها narrated a Hadith about 11 women (their identities were kept anonymous except for one who appeared most content in her marriage) who gathered and spoke unreservedly regarding their husbands' character and behavior so that other couples could learn what is and is not Islamic behavior within a marriage and how to address any injustice.[10] It is important to note that among these 11 couples, the husbands whose wives had praised them were referenced by name in related narrations, while the husbands who were failing to fulfill their wives' rights were not identified by name. It appears that the aim of the latter wives disclosing their husbands' misbehaviors was not to shame these men, but rather to illustrate how a good and loving Muslim husband should treat his wife.[11]

From among these 11 women, the wives who complained appeared to have lost the sense of security and protection (*iḥtiwāʾ*) their marriages were supposed to provide.[12] For example, the third woman to share her story expressed a fear of revealing details about her husband's misbehavior, "If I describe him (and he hears of that), he will divorce me, and if I keep quiet, he will keep me hanging (neither divorcing me nor treating me as a wife should be treated)."[13] The wives in the group who felt secure and loved also shared their stories. According to one narration, after each wife told her story, the Messenger ﷺ reflected on which women within this group of 11 was married to a husband who fulfilled his duties as a husband and exemplified praiseworthy character as a partner. He compared himself to one particular husband, saying, for "I am to you (ʿĀ'ishah) as Abū Zarʿ was to his wife Umm Zarʿ."[14] We find in another Hadith, Umm Zarʿ, who interestingly enough was no longer married to Abū Zarʿ by the time this story was relayed, characterizing her ex-husband as having been extremely generous and kind towards her, his children, his mother, and his wife's parents:[15]

> My husband [was] Abū Zarʿ, and what is Abū Zarʿ [i.e., what should I say about him]? He has given me many ornaments and my ears are heavily loaded with them and my arms have become fat [i.e., I have become fat]. And he has pleased me, and I have become so happy that I felt good about myself. He found me with my family who were mere owners of sheep and living in poverty and brought me to a respected family having horses and camels and threshing and purifying grain. Whatever I say, he does not rebuke or insult me. When I sleep, I sleep till late in the morning, and when I drink water (or milk), I drink my fill... [16]

Umm Zarʿ went on to say that she remarried a good man, but she couldn't help but admit that his generosity did not compare to that of Abū Zarʿ. She said, "He gave me many things, and also a pair of every kind of livestock and said: 'Eat [of this], O Umm Zarʿ, and give provision to your relatives." She added, "Yet, all those things which my second husband gave me could not fill the smallest utensil of Abū Zarʿ."[17]

Much like the goal of the 11 women who gathered to speak about their marriages, the purpose of the study participants in this chapter is not to present idle complaints or to slander, but rather to uncover the ways in which women married to Muslim men have found their financial rights under Islamic law fulfilled, denied, or curtailed. Through these candid, detailed revelations, we can begin to learn what changes Muslim Americans must make in deriving, understanding, and applying the *fiqh,* as it pertains to the financial rights of a wife, so that women are safe and secure in their marriages. As Jacquette Timmons, the author of *Financial Intimacy,* said, "Most people operate from the paradigm that experience is the best teacher. But learning from what others have or have not done is an excellent way to get the lesson without having to take the test! It can be just as insightful, but much less stressful."[18]

As I delve into the stories of the remarkable women I had the privilege of interviewing, it is important to share that I obtained consent from them before sharing their stories, and that I also went to extensive measures to protect their identities within these pages. To safeguard the privacy of the women I present in this chapter, I avoided disclosing or changed details that could identify them or their families, such as their actual countries of origin, marriage duration, milestone dates, and/or other details that were not ultimately relevant to my analysis. Instead, I describe the family's situations in general terms. Each participant's story is shared using a fictitious name or pseudonym. I additionally advised participants not to discuss their involvement in the study with anyone.

The Stories of 21 American Women

Participant 1 – Dana

Dana married a Muslim man from a different cultural background, herself converting to Islam after marriage. Prior to her marriage she was Christian but never believed Jesus was God. She came from a lower-income family while her husband came from an incredibly wealthy one; both were well educated with college degrees. They met while working in the same restaurant. He pressured her into marriage by convincing her that he must obtain a green card because if he was deported to his home country, he could be killed. A trusting person, Dana believed his ruse and agreed to a brief marriage in order to save his life. She neither had a *walī* present to advocate for her at the time the marriage was contracted, nor was she aware of her right to a *mahr* as a woman marrying a Muslim man. It was only when the couple divorced years later that she learned her husband's claim that he had clandestinely recorded a *mahr* of measly twenty-five cents in their marriage contract.

Although her husband came from an affluent family, at the time of their marriage, he had lost access to all of his wealth for political reasons. The two married and lived in college housing, depositing their earnings into a joint account. She would have liked to keep her income in a private account but, as she explained,

"I was shamed into sharing it from the very beginning of our marriage." What was to be a short-term marriage stretched into one that lasted for decades: Dana became an invaluable asset to him, becoming his mentor and helper in every aspect of his career, while forgoing building a career for herself. She became an indispensable support through his many jobs, as he was often fired for sexually harassing coworkers.

Not long after they married, Dana became pregnant and her husband forced her to have an abortion. He made sure she understood that her marriage to him was just a temporary one. Knowing this, when questioned why she stayed in the marriage and did not seek divorce her response was:

> Since I had severe childhood trauma, I was geared to identify with my abuser (Stockholm Syndrome). My father was a sociopath-logical narcissist; I married one to complete my healing. After three years of absolute pain, I did seriously look into divorcing. But my husband would throw out things like "I am all alone here and you have your family". He was very good at triggering my guilt.

After he made her abort their child, he made travel plans to his home country, leaving her to singlehandedly work and earn to carry all financial responsibilities, including house payments, groceries and transportation, without any help. She later discovered his six-month visit was for the purpose of finding another wife. His plan did not succeed because, while in his native country, the government mandated that he join the military, so he covertly fled back to America to escape military service. Once he returned, they purchased a home together; they paid equally for the property.

At this stage, he decided that he wanted children of his own and the couple had many in quick succession. All the while Dana continued to tirelessly assist him with his own job and career growth and when, in the final weeks of her pregnancies, she would plead that they hire help to relieve her of the housework, he would first acquiesce, but then say he himself would help her and always fail to fulfill his promise. She quickly learned that their finances were a subject she was not permitted to raise. "I learned over time to self-censor in order to keep harmony. If I overpaid for something I definitely kept it to myself, creating anxiety [within me] over the fact that I was being dishonest in a way."

After the birth of her first child, she was diagnosed with temporomandibular joint disorder (TMJ), a condition that left her in chronic pain. Their insurance did not cover the cost of treatment, and he dismissed the problem as psychological in order to save money until one day Dana finally collapsed. She recounted:

> I felt abandoned, unloved, and mistreated. I was just a broken thing that couldn't perform the way he wanted it to perform. It upset him greatly that I wouldn't just fix myself. It was all in my head and I was simply making things up so I wouldn't have to do things. It was a great source of friction and to avoid getting yelled at, I wouldn't share all that was happening [with my health].

Not only would her husband withhold payment for basic necessities like medical care until the situation reached a critical stage, he also seized any money that came his wife's way. When her mother died, Dana inherited $5,000. He coerced her into depositing it into their joint account and then spent the entire sum to purchase an ostentatious handmade rug. Dana described her husband's greed and obsessiveness regarding money as a form of worship:

> His God was money. Everything was about money. I used to love to read books for pleasure, but he harassed me saying I was wasting time and that if I chose to read, I should read about how to make money. From then on, I only read nonfiction that was professionally geared to assist him at his job. It was a terrible thing to buy something that wasn't at the best price. For instance, I bought new tires for my car (we agreed that was needed), but when he found that I didn't get the best price he yelled at me and fought for an entire week afterwards. I was reduced to tears. The currency of love was money. He would withhold money [or threaten to withhold money] whenever he disapproved of something. That also applied to the children many times. That was the way his family of origin functioned. We had many arguments about the importance of money. My stance was that it wasn't as important as other things and he would respond by holding back money and would say, "See how important it is? You can't live without it." I would agree that one needs it as a means to survive, but it shouldn't be the main focus of one's life. We never saw eye to eye. As a grand punishment for me filing for divorce, he vowed to destroy me financially through litigation. The so-called justice system is set up for just that purpose I found. The lawyers and judge were more than happy to comply. The amount of money that was spent could have paid off all of our children's student loans.

To add insult to injury, Dana revealed that her husband repeatedly cheated on her. Over the years, the adultery and emotional abuse took a toll on her health until Dana became too ill to even follow through on leaving her husband, as she could no longer care for herself. "I always felt [like I was] dying inside." Her deterioration had a ripple effect on her children, and they remember their mother being a deeply unhappy and bitter person. Their father's ill-treatment of their mother unquestionably caused them to resent him:

> They were abhorred and each had a different reaction. The two older ones were most upset about my inability to stand up for myself. This resulted in my son despising women until he could heal that. My oldest daughter…had a strong reaction to both of us – cutting herself off from her father after the divorce (mainly because of how he treated me during the divorce, which was nasty). She was surprised to find, through therapy, that she had a stronger reaction to my victimhood, so that was an item for us to work out.

Dana recognized the breadth of the damage her husband had wrought on her psyche and personality, and she sought out therapy in an effort to cope. Although she herself paid for sessions amounting to tens of thousands of dollars, Dana would sneak out surreptitiously to meet with her counselor because if her husband discovered she was spending money on her healing, he would have been enraged.

Over the years, with Dana as his full-time assistant, her husband did amass a good deal of wealth. Then came a time when his infidelity gave her the courage to ask for divorce:

> I initiated the divorce when I found checks for thousands of dollars written to another woman and heard him talking on the phone with a woman like he was a love-sick teenager. He never talked to me like that ever! I knew I was in trouble. I had confronted him before and he denied things and I immediately felt guilty. But a situation was set up (by angels?), where I would hear a lengthy conversation so there was no doubt. Since he had secret accounts and was driving us into debt by not giving me enough to pay the bills, and threatening that if I couldn't figure out how to run the household on this budget that he would sell the house, I went into panic. At this point I was completely disabled from the narcissistic abuse (PTSD, DID, fibro-myalgia, chemical sensitivity, etc.) and so I didn't know how I would survive. It took faith and knowing that if I stayed I would die. One of the worst things you can do to a narcissist is to file for divorce. It took three years and went to trial. He vowed he would destroy me through the divorce process.

When the two finally divorced, she discovered that he had managed to funnel their savings back to his home country under a false name, ensuring that she would not receive any share of the wealth. At the time of the divorce, her husband earned a yearly income of $250,000, yet during the divorce proceedings, he convinced the judge that Dana had no right to any portion of it. The divorce process stretched on for years – years of financial torture, as Dana terms it – and when the protracted proceedings finally came to an end, the decision was not in favor of Dana. The judge ruled that her ex-husband did not have to pay her a penny in alimony.

Dana received half of the value of their home, which she spent to pay off her daughter's university student loans, and half of her ex-husband's 401K, of which $80,000 went towards her attorneys' legal fees. Interestingly, at the time of the divorce, the government of her ex-husband's home country released his frozen assets, making him an incredibly wealthy man. At times, Dana wishes she had filed for divorce in his home country where the courts would have divided the couple's wealth in accordance with Islamic law and she would have walked away with much more than she has. She knows her husband would have fought to carry out the divorce in the U.S. because "He used Islam if it was to his favor and used the American legal system if that was best for him."

She recently discovered that he donated $40,000 to the community *masjid* and surmised that it is neither generosity nor religiosity that motivated her ex-husband's charity, but rather wanting to be seen and applauded by people. Meanwhile, she relies on government disability to survive and hopes she never has to resort to asking her children for financial help. Sadly, after the divorce was finalized, Dana left Islam, citing both her Muslim husband's awful treatment of her, as well as the silence of the larger Muslim community when she reached out for help. She complained that "the imam treated divorce like dirty water" and that Muslim leaders are simply not trained to counsel women in abusive marriages and support them through the process of divorce. She felt she simply did not belong in the Muslim community. Today, she still keeps a copy of the Qur'an in her home and has the good of Islam treasured inside her heart.

Participant 2 – Sara

Sara was a devout Christian woman who married a Muslim man from a different cultural background. Both she and her husband were born and raised in their respective home countries overseas, but moved to America as adults. She came from a reasonably well-off family and she herself had steady work with good pay, whereas her husband came into the marriage with hefty debts and had landed his first job only a few months prior to the wedding. At the time of marriage, Sara had no clue that as a woman marrying a Muslim man, she was entitled to something called a *mahr*, but thankfully a Muslim friend of hers who was attending the wedding spoke up and pointed out that this gift was due to the bride. The husband suggested a mere twenty-five cents, but Sara's friend refused and countered with $5,000. The husband grudgingly conceded, and although there was no verbal or written agreement that the *mahr* would be deferred, Sara never received any portion of this safeguard, not even upon her later divorce. Being a Christian woman, Sara did not know, and therefore could not advocate for, her financial rights within Islam, but her Muslim friend did his best to represent the bride's interests. Her friend insisted on a prenuptial agreement guaranteeing that the wealth Sara had accumulated before marriage, through inheritance, gifts, work, or any other means, would remain entirely hers in order that she may use this cushion towards caring for her sons from her previous marriage. It is true that the substance of such a prenuptial agreement is a default rule within Islam, but since she resided in the U.S., her friend felt the need to set this as a condition to guarantee her and her children financial security.

From the very beginning of the relationship, Sara began to shoulder the responsibility of paying for things. She paid for the wedding, including the hall rental, food, and beverages for both the bride and the groom's guests, and she then foot the bill for the couple's honeymoon. They flew abroad for their honeymoon and she noted that, along with financing the trip, he used her money to buy extravagant gifts for his relatives. All the while, he refused to provide her with simple necessities like a bottle of water in sweltering weather. In fact, she recalls one day resorting to sucking on a wet wipe to quench her thirst. She was not able to use her money to purchase items she needed because, upon marrying him, she was brainwashed to give him control over all her money in order to be a good obedient and loving wife.

As mentioned earlier, Sara's husband only began working a few months prior to the wedding so, from the very start of the union, she earned nearly double what he did. He cited the disparity in their salaries as justification for his insistence that she take full responsibility for all household spending. He also repudiated any obligation to spend on her and her three sons, saying he should not be burdened with having to provide for children from her former marriage (even though her ex-husband paid child support to help care for his and Sara's kids, which happened to be deposited into the couple's joint account). Being from a different religious and cultural background, Sara acquiesced, accepting this refusal as the norm in her new husband's faith and traditions. She later discovered that although her husband claimed to be financially struggling at the time of marriage, he had purchased a condominium a few months prior to the wedding.

Once married, the couple moved into a fully-furnished home that the wife had bought while single. Her status change from being single to married did not in any way ease her financial burden, but rather she found that her financial responsibilities only swelled once she became a wife. She continued to pay the mortgage and taxes for the home in which they lived, as well as cover the cost of the car insurance and health insurance from her own savings account. Her husband made one contribution to the monthly bills—he purchased the groceries. However, she could not make requests or add any items to the shopping list. She explained, "I cooked whatever he brought." In fact, years into the marriage Sara learned that, although she would regularly spend time preparing homemade spaghetti sauce from scratch, her husband could have simply bought canned sauce from the store.

Despite the fact that Sara paid all the household bills with the exception of the grocery bill, and that her monthly paycheck was directly deposited into the couple's joint account, her husband remained dissatisfied. He complained that even though he contributed to the household spending, the house was in her name only. She ultimately capitulated to the relentless pressure from him and added his name to the house title. She hoped this would appease him and their incessant fights over money matters would subside, but shared ownership only allowed him the opportunity to unilaterally pull out almost three-quarters of their equity in the home and use it to renovate the house and purchase a car for himself.

Not long after marriage, Sara had three children with her second husband. In order to keep up with the bills, she took on additional work alongside her full-time job. Working more than one job and being a mother and a homemaker left her exhausted, but she was determined to do all she could for her husband and children. Her patience finally snapped when her three sons from her first marriage began to feel that their stepfather did not treat them with the same kindness and generosity he showed his biological children. This was especially true when it came to food. Sara noticed that her children from her past marriage were limited as to how much they could eat at the dinner table, whereas her children with her second husband could eat their fill, taking seconds and thirds if they wanted. Her husband would even go so far as to sift through his stepchildren's school lunch boxes, pluck out the meat from the sandwiches and eat it himself. These petty, parsimonious behaviors, and others such as turning off the hot water whenever his stepchildren took a shower, were more than she felt able to tolerate. She could see that her children from her first marriage were frustrated and bewildered as to why they lived under such restrictions when their mother worked tirelessly to give them a comfortable life. In reality, all her earnings – approximately $7,000 per month – were under her husband's control, and he would dole out a measly $150 monthly allowance to her. So in reality, her name on the account was just for show and he did not give her access to the account she mostly contributed to, except what he permitted. Over the years, he reduced even this paltry amount to $75 a month, chastising her for spending too much of the allowance on his stepchildren. His miserly attitude towards her children from her first marriage, in addition to his generally disdainful treatment of her, is what finally broke Sara. For years on end, he would daily ridicule her intelligence, calling her "stupid." She admitted:

> I pretty much started believing it despite the fact that I was head of a department…managing over 100 employees…I just couldn't understand why he was not giving me my $150 month allowance *from my own salary*, but whatever he said I believed. And he always gave excuses.

Finally, she could no longer bear the degradation and financial abuse. She reached out to the imam of the local mosque for counseling to save the marriage, but was unsuccessful. Soon after, her husband traveled to his home country and returned with a new bride. However, he could not marry his second wife in an American court since polygamy is illegal in the U.S.. He also did not consider that the Islamic faith requires Muslims to abide by local laws and rulings on marriage restrictions (see AMJA codes, appendix E, 5).

Sara felt deeply betrayed and could not help but wonder why her husband fully financially supported his new wife, who did not work, when he had always insisted on Sara carrying almost all the financial burden in their marriage. She tried to seek an Islamic divorce through their local mosque imam, but her husband refused, hoping to pressure her to remove herself from the marriage (*khulʿ*). He believed that if she initiated the *khul'*, he would not owe his wife her unpaid marital gift (*mahr*) as the *mahr* is typically considered financial relinquishment in exchange for the *khul'*. Sara fought back, refusing to allow her husband to hold her hostage in the marriage or blackmail her. She presented proof to the imam of how she had essentially been the provider for the family from the very beginning of the marriage, when in fact Islam mandates that the husband be the one to financially support his wife and children, and the imam granted her a traditional divorce, not *khulʿ*, and judged that her husband owed her $250,000. Her husband, however, did not abide by this ruling and only gave her $80,000.

When Sara reflects on her second marriage, she credits her job and her volunteer work at her children's school for preserving her sanity. Both restored, in some measure, the confidence and sense of worth that were daily chipped away by her partner at home. She broke out of her abusive marriage, but the years of financial abuse left psychological scars that remain until this day. The greed, injustice, callousness, and exploitation she endured at the hands of her Muslim husband created an aversion to Islam itself in the hearts of her parents and extended family members. They all say they would never consider reverting to Islam because of how her Muslim husband treated her. When questioned about what made her convert to Islam, she replied that her urge to learn about the religion drove her to oversee the Muslim Student Association at her work place, after which she learned about Islam. It was her relentless pursuit of Islamic education that gave her and her children strength to put this horrible experience behind them and move forward, *Alḥamdulillāh*.

Participant 3 – Nabila

Nabila, a Muslim woman born overseas, was only a teenager when she married a man whom her parents arranged for her to marry from her native country, one who had falsely represented himself as being much younger than he had been prior to their marriage. It was only after the wedding that she and her family were alarmed to learn that her new husband was 20 years older than her. But ending the marriage at this point was never an option. The *mahr* amount agreed upon in the marriage contract was a mere $100 because Nabila's husband alleged that the *mahr* was a symbolic gift rather than one that factored in either the bride's financial status prior to marriage or the groom's capacity to give. Regardless, Nabila never received this $100 gift before, during or after the marriage.

Although her husband had a high-paying job, she saw red flags of his miserliness from day one of the marriage. She felt the lifestyle to which she had been accustomed prior to marriage had been downgraded. His withholding behavior persisted after marriage. Nabila recalls:

> I felt like his maid who did things for him, but when it came time for him to show me that he cared by taking me out or buying me something nice or just spending on me, he wouldn't. I felt disrespected and unloved and so I (equally) lost respect and love towards him.

Soon after the wedding, the couple had children in quick succession and Nabila noted that expanding their family only intensified her husband's miserly behavior. She hoped earning her own income would help matters, but she did not have a college degree, and when she tried to persuade her husband to pay for a college education, he flatly refused. Although he claimed that he worried their children would be neglected if she enrolled in college, Nabila knew he simply wanted to avoid paying the tuition. Nabila desperately wanted to work, not only to bring in additional income that she could spend on herself and her children, but also to boost her self-confidence, which would take a daily beating from his incessant fault-finding. When he would return home from work at the end of the day, he would often pass belittling remarks such as, "What have you been doing all day – nothing!" Her husband showed no appreciation or empathy for the efforts Nabila made in the way of raising their children and keeping up with all household responsibilities of cooking, cleaning, and laundry. She felt she needed house help, but never dared to ask (it was only for a few months, when she fell terribly ill following childbirth, that her husband reluctantly hired temporary domestic help). As the years passed and their children grew, she continued pressing her husband to allow her to work outside the house. He could no longer recycle his earlier objection that their small children would be neglected if she did not remain at home full-time and he ultimately relented to her pleas, but on the condition that her paycheck would be automatically deposited into their joint account, which he alone controlled. Her new job did not bring her any additional spending money, but it did set her free, she said. For years she had felt like a slave under a master, but now she began to meet new people and feel valued and respected by her manager and coworkers.

Despite Nabila's work offering a reprieve, her husband's financial abuse became unbearable with time and finally she asked for a divorce. He refused to sign divorce papers (within the American legal system) unless she gave up all her financial rights, including her earnings placed in their joint account or jointly-owned stocks. Another condition was to give up any alimony rights granted by either the U.S. courts or the Islamic Shariah. He threatened to just flee back to his native country if she did not comply.

She had to accept his demands, and all their accumulated wealth went to him. He also did not want to pay child support. Nabila tried to singlehandedly provide for her children but after some time it became clear that she was financially unable, and none of her male family members had the means to help. Eventually, she felt pressured to voluntarily give up her physical custody of her children, all of whom were under 11 years old while she pursued an education and career. He assured her that once she began to earn enough money to support the kids, he would return the children to her, but his promise quickly proved to be specious because before the divorce was even finalized, he moved back, with the children in tow, to his home country and remarried. Nabila's marriage was instantaneously dissolved by the U.S. court since her husband never showed up to the final divorce hearing. Nabila was devastated about the loss of her children, but she moved back into her parents' home and took charge of her life by working during the day and attending to college classes in the evening. Her children grew up overseas and she finally saw them once they had reached adulthood and did not need their father's permission to travel back to the United States.

In time, Nabila rebuilt her life and even remarried. Her second husband was a wealthy man who earned four times more than she did. She feels he was certainly better than her first partner; he provided her with a comfortable home and an abundance of food, although he too was somewhat tightfisted when he offered her a *mahr* amount of a mere $500 – which she never received – and insisted she pay for household electric bills, as well as all personal needs, including house help. Nabila found these conditions bizarre, but she accepted them and preserved her marriage because they were nothing compared to the financial humiliation she experienced in her first marriage.

Nabila believes she learned two key lessons from her two marriages – lessons she has handed down to her children, especially the daughters. The first, and most important, lesson is to acquire an education, no matter the obstacles to earning your degree. The second is to work, earn, and become financially independent. Money is tantamount to power and respect. Her marriages taught her that, unfortunately, to the world and the men in it, a woman's value lies in her earnings.

Despite the formidable hardships Nabila endured, she maintains a resilient, positive outlook. Her missing her children and worry about their well-being caused her to supplicate daily to Allah to take care of them. She feels her pain pulled her closer to Allah and for this she is thankful. She said, "If I had to do it all again for the price of becoming near Him ﷻ, I would not hesitate one bit. *Alḥamdulillāh* for everything!"

Participant 4 - Aya

Aya married right out of high school. Her marriage took place abroad, as her husband was not a U.S. resident. Once married, her husband became eligible to apply for a green card and, within a few months of their union, moved to America. In his native country, Aya's husband had been a college-educated business owner who earned an income comparable to that of his new wife's family income, but still Aya's parents insisted that the *mahr* function as a symbolic gift, recording it as only five dollars. The bride was instructed not to take even this small amount and she did as she was told. After his papers were finalized, Aya and her new husband moved to the United States and into her parents' home where everything was provided for them. It is unclear what happened to his business back home, but to Aya's knowledge, when her husband arrived in the U.S., he was penniless. He was unsuccessful in his efforts to find work in his field of study and ultimately accepted a job at a restaurant for low pay. Meanwhile, she immediately became pregnant and had no choice but to find work to relieve her parents from their financial burden and try to independently survive.

Once he became a U.S. citizen, Aya's husband immediately applied for his mother and five siblings to immigrate to America. Within a short time, his mother arrived to the U.S. and settled into Aya's parents' home. Worried and embarrassed at the financial stress on her parents, Aya pressed her husband to move into their own apartment. He resisted, painting his in-laws as unwelcoming, arguing, "So, your parents want to kick us out?" Aya persisted and after some time, the couple finally shifted into a rental apartment. Even then, her parents gifted the couple $3,000 to purchase furniture and home appliances for their new place. Aya's mother-in-law moved in with the couple to their new home and continued to live with them for the next four years, a matter in which the daughter-in-law had no say because to oppose this living arrangement would be akin to being a selfish wife.

Soon after the couple began life in their new home, the husband's five siblings and their families obtained their paperwork and landed in the U.S.. They would each visit the couple twice a year, staying for six to eight weeks at a stretch. Aya's small apartment was nearly always filled with guests whom she had to serve and entertain. All the while she continued working and because her income was significantly larger than her husband's, she was the one who paid the rent and he took care of the utilities and groceries. Both their earnings would go in a joint account, but while hers provided for their family, a hefty chunk of his would be channelled to his relatives overseas.

As their family grew, they moved from the apartment into a home. Once again, she alone bore the cost of the mortgage, although the deed recorded the husband and wife as jointly owning the property. When they later sold the home to invest the equity into launching a business, Aya assumed that the contract would include her name along with her husband's and the topic of ownership never came up; she only later discovered that her husband was the sole owner of their business. Over the years, as the business burgeoned, expanding into a chain, and as her children became increasingly independent, Aya asked to take part in the family business. Her husband flatly refused and would become distant and reticent when she brought up the subject.

His uncommunicative attitude only intensified when the two decided to draft a will. On the day of the appointment with the attorney, he simply told her that the will would be written according to Islamic law. She did not understand what this meant, but he remained tight-lipped and refused to explain any further. When Aya sat down with her husband and their attorney, the attorney informed her that all wealth and property was in her husband's name. Shocked, she asked about the income she had earned while working for nearly 15 years of their marriage life. In fact, his prosperous business was purchased from selling the home she paid for in full. The attorney was taken by surprise, completely unaware that she had ever been employed. When Aya delineated her long employment history for him, the attorney replied, "This changes everything!" Aya's husband stormed out of the meeting at this point and later harshly reprimanded her for mentioning her earnings. The matter quickly thickened into a huge conflict. Her husband felt he still had the upper hand and took the dispute to the imam of their local mosque, but once the imam learned of Aya's many years of earnings, he sided with the wife and informed the husband that Islamic law mandated that this portion of wealth was hers entirely. Aya was astonished that the imam supported her, and says that for the first time in her life, she realized the equity inherent in her religion, and felt grateful to be a Muslim. Her husband, still wanting to be the sole owner of all the wealth and property acquired over the course of their marriage, implored her to forget and forgo her past earnings. She stood her ground and insisted upon her Islamic right to her earnings. From that day on, her husband parted from her, moving to another bedroom in their home. This living arrangement has continued for years now and she remains puzzled as to what she did to bring about this estrangement. "Living under one roof but separated keeps me in tears. What did I do to deserve this?"

Over the years, Aya's husband successfully painted her as an avaricious woman in the eyes of their children, who now believe their father separated from their mother due to her money-hungry tactics. Having grown up as the child of divorced parents, Aya never wanted to resort to this measure, but she feels she has reached a dead end in her marriage. Having lost all trust in her husband, she has built up the courage to file for divorce. "I always thought my husband [wa]s there to protect me," she said wistfully.

Participant 5 - Jasmine

Jasmine was a devout Christian woman studying to become a priest when she met a Muslim man online who was in search of a spouse. Still in the midst of finalizing a divorce from her non-Muslim husband, Jasmine began communicating with this potential match who resided overseas. As the two chatted, she developed an interest in Islam, a faith she had never before examined. She did her homework, building a friendship with a Muslim woman in her community who taught her the basics of the religion. Her knowledge of Islam led Jasmine to question the Trinitarian theology and by Ramadan of that same year, she had discontinued her pastor studies and entered Islam. Her Muslim male friend proposed and she quickly made travel plans to visit her fiancée in his country so they could marry.

Their families both came from upper-middle class backgrounds and Jasmine and her fiancé were more or less equally educated, with her having a Master's degree and him holding a Bachelor's. Still most of their family members opposed the union due to the age difference. She was significantly older than he was and to further complicate matters, she had children from her previous marriage. She tried to gain his father's approval by giving a reminder of the Prophet's wife Khadījah رضي الله عنها and how much older she was than the Messenger ﷺ with no success. Before the two married, one of the groom's brothers, who had come to the States to study, met with Jasmine, and upon his return to his country, he discouraged his brother from following through with the marriage by speaking ill of Jasmine. This attempt to halt the marriage did not succeed and the couple became husband and wife.

Jasmine's father had passed away and she did not have a Muslim male friend or family member to act as her *walī,* or guardian. The Imam performing the ceremony spoke little English, so a distant relative of the groom, one of the few that supported this marriage, stepped in as her guardian, to make sure that the marriage documents were well understood in both English and their tongue language.

Jasmine understood the fundamentals of Islam, but was not familiar with her financial rights as a wife. No one, including the imam or her *walī*, explained these to her prior to the signing of the marriage contract. Rather, she understood the marriage contract and ceremony to be rooted in the cultural traditions of her husband's country, not in Islam. She did not try to understand all the minute details of the contract because of how unsupportive both her family and his were of their marriage. Jasmine, not wanting to further agitate any of the groom's already disapproving family members and feeling self-conscious that she was a divorced woman bringing children from her first marriage into this union, kept quiet. She neither asked questions nor protested, even though she never explicitly received the $10 *mahr* amount specified in the contract.

The couple consummated the marriage at a hotel at the groom's expense, and immediately afterwards Jasmine returned to the U.S. while her new husband awaited visa approval to follow her. The paperwork took several years and during this time, her husband never sent her any money to help with her living expenses, and she herself paid for the handful of visits she made to his country to see him. Upon receiving his visa, he arrived in the U.S. with some money his parents had given him to begin his life in his new country. He settled into a fully-furnished home Jasmine had purchased in her name. She worked full-time, paying all the bills and fully supporting her husband until he found employment. He landed a job that paid ten dollars an hour, and once he had this income, he pitched in financially and took care of most of the utilities, with the exception of gas and cell phone costs. Within a few years, his yearly earnings had climbed to $55,000, an amount that was much more than Jasmine's income. He then continued to pay for the same share of their living expenses as before, but would contribute a share towards the mortgage.

Both generally took care of their personal needs with their own earnings. When it came to groceries, he bought his own food with his income and she purchased the food for herself and her children with her paycheck, although on occasion, if they happened to be grocery shopping together, he would pay the bill for the two of them. The reason behind the division appeared to be their differing food quality needs. She and her children chose to consume humanely-raised chickens, free-range eggs, and organic fruits and vegetables, while he would eat the less costly non-organic meats, fruits and vegetables. Jasmine's husband also expected her to foot the bill for her wardrobe and personal needs. She refrained from pressing him to buy these items for her and instead took care of her own needs, because he was extremely frugal, while she was more openhanded in her spending and wanted to sidestep any arguments with him over financial matters.

Jasmine does give her husband credit for helping her pay off her graduate school student loans, until they went into automatic forbearance due to COVID-19. She also acknowledges that if their house required maintenance or repairs, he would step up and share the cost with her. And he took on the responsibility of purchasing certain household items like laundry detergent, toilet paper, and paper towels for everyone to use, including her children from her previous marriage (it is important to note that Jasmine's former husband provided well for her children from her first marriage, diligently paying his child support).

At the end of the interview, Jasmine gently wept for not knowing the breadth of her financial rights as a wife, lamenting that had she known the privileges Islamic law afforded her, "Simple things could have [been done to] alleviate so much burden [from her]." She reflected more on the guidance she received about the Islamic faith:

> When you enter into a new faith it is like being reborn. There is a lot of euphoria and excitement all around you and people encouraging you and helping you and trying to guide you but over time you begin to realize that some of that guidance is also laced with culture and that based on the culture it can influence the guidance that you are receiving.

Her struggles, both in her marriage to her first husband and in her marriage to her current one (still intact), taught her the importance of being financially independent and self-sufficient. She advises, "Even if a woman had everything, she should never give up her education so she can stand on her own feet and never be in trouble."

Participant 6 - Sakina

Sakina married a man who matched her in his level of education and his well-to-do family background. Her husband was brought up abroad while she was raised in the U.S.. His job required a great deal of travel, while she served her family as a homemaker and was never employed. She considers herself blessed because her husband has been an excellent provider for her and their children, always fulfilling all their needs and wants. The *mahr* specified in the marriage contract was a small and symbolic amount, but the bride received the *mahr* immediately, without any deferment. Once married, the husband moved his new wife into a well-furnished home that was commensurate with the lifestyle she had been accustomed to prior to marriage. Likewise, he tended to food, clothing, and all her personal needs to her satisfaction. Sakina had only one complaint – her total loss of privacy, as her mother-in-law lived with them from day one of the marriage until today.

Sakina has taken care of her mother-in-law all her married life. Out of courtesy, she has never pressed her husband for hired help to assist in the care of her mother-in-law, and her husband has never taken the initiative to offer. He has always alleged that prior to the couple's marriage, Sakina's mother agreed to his mother residing with them, and her family simply never informed Sakina of this arrangement. Their living situation and the stress of having to serve as the full-time caregiver to an elderly person has created some resentment. She feels coerced by her husband into a life-long responsibility that is not hers to carry, one that has left her unable to spend as much time as she would like with her children and husband or take part of social and religious events in her community. Although her four children were well-aware of their mother's bitterness at having to care for their grandmother, Sakina did not want to take her frustrations out on them, so she would inevitably lash out at her partner for his lack of understanding. Ironically, although her husband showed a lack of empathy for how trying it has been for Sakina to share her home with her mother-in-law, when their only daughter received a marriage proposal from a gentleman who had everything to offer, except that he requested for his mother to reside with them after marriage, Sakina's husband swiftly and firmly refused the proposal. For the first time, Sakina felt validated. It seemed that her husband finally recognized that "My wife was someone's daughter too."

Sakina suspects that her patience and forbearance in this situation may be the reason behind her husband spending so liberally on her and their children – it has been his way of repaying her. Although her husband has always shouldered the full responsibility of providing for the family, when Sakina inherited a substantial amount of money upon the death of a parent, her husband would at times borrow from the separate joint account in which this inheritance was kept. He did recognize that this wealth belonged to his wife and would always pay her back when able to do so. Sakina's reasoning behind giving her husband access to the account was that if she was ever to fall ill or pass away, he and their children could take out this large sum.

Participant 7 - Sophia

Sophia was a Christian woman who married a Muslim man from another country. He had come to the States a couple of years prior to their marriage. She came from a very wealthy family whereas his had limited financial means. He held a bachelor's degree, while she was three-quarters through hers upon marriage. After the marriage, upon her insistence, she did complete her bachelor's while he pursued his graduate studies and other certifications. Being ambitious, she hoped to further her education, but he would never allow it.

A civil marriage took place along with an Islamic contractual ceremony, known as the *nikāḥ*, and although Sophia knew next to nothing about the requirements of a Muslim marriage or the rights and responsibilities of each partner in a Muslim marriage, she recalls having two witnesses but not a *walī* – a representative or guardian who advocates for the bride's rights and gives her away. She also recounts that the marriage contract did not specify a *mahr*, and it was only upon her conversion to Islam two years later that she inquired about this financial right, and her husband answered that the diamond ring he gifted her prior to the marriage constituted her *mahr*. The most disturbing part about the nature of her marriage was its secrecy, especially from the people she loved most, her parents:

> The way in which we got married was very disgusting and absolutely not Islamic. I was very innocent and he was looking for his citizenship. He convinced me to marry him behind my parents back because I told him my parents would not agree, but he twisted my arm and made me fear that he would leave the country if I didn't marry him and at the time, I thought I loved him and didn't want him to leave…so I married him and he did that without asking my father or my mother for permission.

Although Sophia came from an affluent family, she worked full-time and did not rely on her parents for financial assistance. Her husband also proved to be a hardworking man, simultaneously holding down three jobs to provide for his wife and children. Both their earnings were of relatively equal value and placed in a joint account. They used this account to pay for any living expenses, including rent, groceries, and utilities, as well as to, at the husband's insistence, regularly send some portion of their savings overseas to his parents and siblings, both those married and those single. Sophia did not mind assisting her in-laws but felt resentful when her husband prioritized his overseas relatives over his own household in the U.S., because she felt her and their children's needs ought to be met before tending to her in-laws. His favoritism continued even when it came time for their children to attend college. Sophia hoped her husband would chip in and help pay for their college loans in order to shield them from paying high interest rates, but he declined to support his children, saying they must take responsibility for their own loans because his parents and siblings are more deserving of his savings. Sophia also recalls times when she wanted to buy gifts for her own parents and extended family or even make a charitable donation, but her husband would be adamant that their savings were reserved for his relatives. Over time, Sophia gave up asking or arguing and instead would tuck away any money her parents gifted her and surreptitiously spend it on herself, her children or charitable causes.

It seemed that her husband also expected her to clear any purchases with him ahead of time while he felt free to spend as he saw fit. She recalls one instance in which she bought a fifty-dollar dress for a formal event without her husband's approval;

when he discovered the dress, he was furious. Sophia felt she certainly deserved this purchase, not only because she was working at the time, but also because, she said, "He [bought] things every day without discussing with me." The inequity of her husband's expectations and the subsequent lack of communication were the sorts of incidents that created a rift between the two.

Her husband's thwarting of any attempts Sophia made to separate her wealth from his or use her earnings as she wished only deepened this rift. For example, she encouraged him to open IRA accounts – a retirement savings accounts that offers tax advantages – to better secure their financial future. He took his wife's advice but opened only one account in his name, with a share of her earnings being deposited into this account. When, after some time had passed and she had learned enough about her financial rights in Islam to build up the courage to suggest opening an account separate from their joint one in which to deposit *her* earnings, he immediately threatened that if she followed through on this idea, he would give her neither any portion of his IRA account later nor of their home equity, even though the deed of their home was in both their names. Her husband's curtailing of her financial rights both confuses and saddens Sophia. She has only ever supported her husband's career and financial wellbeing, yet he persistently behaves in a way that leaves her feeling financially insecure, and she tolerates the mistreatment to keep the peace.

In recent years, Sophia has noticed that her husband frequently speculates how much she will inherit when her now elderly parents pass away, and even accuses her of gleefully waiting for their impending deaths. "I just can't even fathom how he could say this to me. It's so hurtful and disgusting. I love and adore my parents and pray they live the longest life *inshā'Allāh*. I feel he says this to me because he can't stand the thought of me having my own money which he can't control." Sophia went on to say that if ever such thoughts came to her mind, her husband can take full credit for her anxiously anticipating her inheritance because he is the one who has always usurped her personal wealth and fostered a feeling of financial dependency in her.

The lowest point came when the couple moved overseas to a country similar in culture to his country of origin. In the years prior to the move, Sophia had stepped away from her job to become a full-time homemaker and mother to her young children, but now that her children no longer needed her on a daily basis coupled with the isolation she felt in a new, unfamiliar country, she resumed working. However, this time around, her paycheck was not directly deposited into a joint account, but rather into an account solely in her husband's name. She had zero access to the money and was left entirely dependent on her husband. At this time (while living abroad), Sophia's husband flatly refused to pay for their child's college tuition in the U.S. (Sophia suspects that her husband's repudiation was a ploy to pressure their child to move abroad and attend college near the parents). Sophia proposed she use her earnings to subsidize their child's tuition, but her husband's responded with intimidation once again. "He tells me if I were to route my paycheck to my own account, he will make my life hell: "he will cancel my visa, cancel my insurance, take my car and hold me responsible to pay half of our bills and I would get nothing of 'his' retirement nest egg."

She was miserable in the marriage and considered divorce. Upon asking to spend the summer in the United States with her children, her husband refused unless she signed a document agreeing that if they are not to come back by the end of the summer, she gives up her rights to equity in their home and of any portion of their retirement, income, future child support or alimony. She signed just to be able to leave but prayed to God that it would not hold up in a court of law in the United States. Once back to the States, she filed for divorce. Upon presenting this document during their court hearing, the judge told him to his face that this is domestic violence and that the contract he made her sign was meaningless.

Her divorce journey, she explains, was a hard one. His rage upon being informed about her filing for divorce left her in a bad place without money or a place to live. Besides stopping all her money sources, he would not even allow her and the children to remain in their home in the U.S., which was at the time under lease, since they lived overseas. "I asked renters who were on a month-to-month lease to leave our house so I would have a place to live, but behind my back, he gave them a new one-year lease. This left the kids and me living temporarily with my adult daughter in her studio apartment." Under these cramped living conditions, Sophia considered the purchase of a home of her own but that route was shut in her face since she had no bank account and her work experience for the past years was overseas and not in the U.S., which disqualified her for a bank loan. She then assisted her daughter to apply and, given that she was a college graduate and got her first job, she was approved and was able to purchase a two bedroom condominium for them to live in. Sophia, left without transportation to even make job interviews, asked her husband to send her the money for her car that she left overseas, but he refused. She spent about two months without any financial assistance from her husband and if it wasn't for her husband's interest to legally re-marry, he would not have bent to her attorney's pressure to send her and their children a temporary amount until the divorce took place. When the judge ordered both of them to turn over their bank statements, she discovered there was $225,000 in cash withdrawals made by him in just the last two years during which she earned a good income overseas but never kept her earnings. Upon this being disclosed, his attorney offered only $50,000 as a settlement and because she wanted out of the marriage, she accepted. Her attorney fees alone are $40,000, yet to be paid.

Through all her trials, she remains hopeful that one day, if not in this life, then in the next, God will reward her for her patience and compensate her for the denial of her financial rights as a Muslim. Her main focus now is to ensure that her daughters marry men who encourage financial independence and security for their wives.

Participant 8 - Farida

At less than 40 years of age, Farida is one of the two youngest of all the participants in this study. She was born and raised in the U.S. and when she was a mere 17-years-old, her parents took her back to their native country to get married. Her parents' country was almost foreign to her, as she could not even speak the language. When her marriage was being contracted, the groom recorded a *mahr* amount of approximately one hundred and sixty-six dollars. It was customary for the *mahr* to be regarded as symbolic, so neither she nor her parents disputed the value, especially since the groom was family and had limited financial resources at the time of marriage. She did receive the *mahr* and used it to purchase a ring for herself.

The groom's family belonged to what would be considered the middle-class in his native country, with his mother owning her own business and him being a college graduate with a good income; in the U.S., however, his family would fall below the working-class income bracket. Farida's family, on the other hand, was far more affluent; Farida held an associate degree and although she chose to work, she had the luxury of spending her earnings on whatever she wished because her parents took care of all her financial needs. As one might anticipate, the chasm between the couple's economic backgrounds created problems from the start. After the wedding, Farida remained in her new husband's home country and quickly found that her quality of life as a married woman was a far cry from her pampered lifestyle in the U.S.. She and her husband lived in a home that did not have what most Americans would consider the bare necessities – a freezer to store groceries, air-conditioning, a leak-free roof, hot water, or even clean drinking water. Her complaints fell on deaf ears, as her in-laws did not understand or empathize with the disparity between the lifestyle to which she had been accustomed and the one she now found herself enduring. She did feel that, at the very beginning of the marriage, her husband, recognizing the comfortable life she had left behind in America, made an effort to accommodate some of her needs. Soon, however, he followed his mother's example, shaming her for any requests or purchases that he and his family considered extravagant – like bottled water – but for Farida, were the most basic essentials.

Aside from the absence of amenities, Farida also lacked privacy in her new home. Once the couple had found a modest place to rent, the husband's parents and brother immediately moved in with them. From day one, her husband, without question, took on financial responsibility for his parents and siblings, and although he had a well-paying job, this additional financially responsibility severely curtailed what he was able to spend on his own wife and children. Farida was never asked if she felt comfortable with this living arrangement and she understood that to object would be tantamount to being labeled "a bad wife." She resigned herself to the loss of privacy and, because of the constant presence of her father and brother-in-law in her home, to the discomfort of having to wear a *hijab* at all times.[19] She could not turn to her parents in the U.S. for support because the only phone in her home was located in her mother-in-law's room, a part of the house to which Farida did not have easy access.

After living in his home country for two years, the couple moved abroad. To help advance his career, Farida's parents had covered the cost for their son-in-law to complete an expensive course in his field, and it was this certification that landed him a higher-paying job in a foreign country. Farida hoped this would be a turning point. Instead, for nearly eight years, the couple and their children ping-ponged back and forth between his home country and the one where he worked. Meaning, he would work abroad for a year of two, then surprise her with the decision of them moving back to his home country. Her in-laws would demand that their son and his family return to live with them and Farida's husband would acquiesce, hastily moving his family back to his home country, only to pack them up some time later and shift back abroad.

His wife never had a say in whether or when they moved, she was expected to just obey and described herself as feeling "broken, with no identity and no money" as a result of these constant displacements. She now reflects, "Isn't Islam about practicing *shūrā*?" (that is, for spouses to consult with one another about their life decisions.)[20] With every haphazard move, their belongings would be sold at a cheap price in a hurry, and then purchased again upon their return to another country. This wasteful spending led to Farida's husband becoming quite miserly toward his wife and children, and this is about when the physical abuse began. He was under great financial stress, since he was expected to keep sending money home to his parents and save to pay for his brother's wedding. His ongoing physical and mental abuse eventually led her to a severe state of depression.

She was rarely permitted to buy new clothes or indulge in foods she liked, even during pregnancy cravings. She had hoped that being in a foreign country where its customary for women to drive, he may allow her to drive like she used to in the U.S. prior to marrying him, but that was out of the question given the price of a car, gas, and insurance. The only consolation was that her husband met all her medical needs, but only because the government offered free health care in the country where he worked. Upon their final move back to his home country for his brother's wedding, which he fully paid for, she noticed her brother-in-law's bride received lavish gifts and generous amounts of gold jewelry, tokens her husband never thought to give his own wife.

After eight years of seesaw moves, Farida's husband received a good job offer in the U.S. and the couple and their children moved back. Now that the burden of having to constantly save for his brother's wedding was lifted, Farida observed an incremental improvement in her husband's tight-fisted attitude. Her monthly allowance rose by fifty dollars, from $150 to $200 a month. After some time, her husband secured another job with a much higher salary – $100,000 a year – and this time the family would relocate to the same state in which Farida's parents resided. Despite living closer to her parents, their marriage continued to deteriorate. The physical abuse had continued through their many moves until one day they fought so intensely that he abruptly dropped his wife and children at his in-laws' home and disappeared. He cut off all financial support and Farida was left in possession of a single credit card with a small limit reserved for emergencies. She and her children spent the next year living with her parents, who took care of all their financial needs. During this time, Farida realized she needed to complete her college education in order to have any success in finding work, so with her parents paying her tuition, she enrolled in college.

As the months passed, she felt increasingly heartbroken that her children were growing up without a father and with two years left until her college graduation, she agreed to return to her estranged husband. They bought a single-family home but within days of settling into their new place, a dozen of his family members, including his mother, arrived for a month-long visit. Farida was at their beck and call for the next thirty days, cooking for them and chauffeuring them. To keep the peace in her newly renewed relationship, she remained silent, and when she would work up the nerve to ask for house help, her husband would reply, "This is your job!" She felt he even managed to convince her children not to help their mother. Her husband's relatives finally departed, but his mother remained and continued living with them permanently. Farida dutifully served her mother-in-law, but even then her husband showed no appreciation and made her feel unworthy by excluding her when he took his mother out for a meal or an outing of some sort. Farida poured her energy into completing her undergraduate degree and soon thereafter began working. She felt a sense of accomplishment and independence, knowing that she was earning her own money for the first time in her marriage.

The marriage ultimately disintegrated after some time, with Farida's husband divorcing her. During her waiting period (*ʿiddah*), he offered to reconcile, but upon the condition that she financially contribute to the household. At the time he made this offer, he was earning approximately $250,000 a year while her salary was only $40,000. She countered by requesting that if she contributed to their mortgage payments, he must add her name to the house's deed, but he rejected her proposal. She asked if he would be willing to pay for house help or even help her himself with day-to-day chores, and he retorted, "If you want me to help you with the dishes, then contribute financially in the household." She marveled at his unyielding attitude, "He had so much money, but this is his ego!" For the past year, she has been awaiting judgment from the American court system, and while she languishes in this limbo, her husband has not financially supported her and their children in any way. During this time she discovered that he placed a substantial amount of money into his mother's bank account. She also found out that he hid much of his wealth in his native country which made him appear less wealthy before the judge during the divorce proceedings. The final verdict was odd and not to her favor. Instead of her gaining custody for her teen child and child support, the matter flip-flopped and the judge ruled that her husband would be given custody and that she would have to pay him $1000 child support. Greedy for more, her husband asked the judge to include in the marital fund to be split between them her valuables including jewelry and purses which she purchased from her earnings, but this he was denied.

She feels her only survival tool thus far has been the college degree she obtained near the end of her marriage and, of course, her faith in God.

Participant 9 – Nermin

Nermin's marriage is another matrimony between two Muslim Americans from different cultural backgrounds. Both have a college education, but the wife holds a much higher professional degree over his. The wife's family was slightly more educated and affluent than the husband's family. To guarantee his daughter's security, the father of the bride asked for a large *mahr* of $100,025, and the groom agreed to pay twenty-five dollars (*muqaddam*) upon the signing of the marriage contract, but deferred the remaining $100,000 (*mu'akhkhar*) to a later date when he could afford the sum.[21] Approximately a year after the couple had married and consummated the union, the husband expressed concern over the large amount of money he still owed his wife, saying he did not believe he could ever manage to pay it. Nermin decided to relieve her partner from this duty altogether, especially because she was under the misconception that a husband is not obliged to pay the *mahr* except upon divorce, and she did not want her husband to feel compelled to remain in a marriage due to what he owes.

After the couple married, it was Nermin who provided, with her parents' help, a fully-furnished apartment for the newlyweds. Her husband quickly found work and began earning a shade more than she did at her part-time position. They opened a joint account through which they paid, and continue to pay, for all their living expenses – rent, groceries, clothing, medical needs and maid service. However, from early on in the marriage Nermin had set the condition that one-third of her salary would always go to her own separate account for her personal use. Her husband agreed. To this day, she feels this was one of the wisest decisions she made to protect her financial security and psychological peace, especially since over time she transitioned to working full-time and began to earn much more than her husband.

She does however have one regret: when Nermin's father gifted her with a substantial amount of money, she shared the news with her husband and he expected her to put it towards purchasing a house. She obliged and they bought a new home in both their names. She understood that from an Islamic point-of-view, this sum of money was hers alone to do with as she pleased, but she said she felt a pressure to fulfill her husband's expectations. "It just seemed like the right thing to do." She wishes she had either not capitulated when her husband suggested buying a house in both their names or that she had simply kept this money aside in her private account without her partner's knowledge to use for her personal needs. Soon after they shifted into the house, Nermin's in-laws began to visit any time they wished without prior notice. She was not comfortable with or accustomed to this open-door policy because she cherished her privacy, but when she expressed her disquietude to her husband, he argued that this was his house as much as it was hers, and so his parents could come and go as they pleased. She felt forced to remind him, much to his chagrin, that even though both their names are on the house's deed, the property belongs more to her and her parents than to him because of how much she paid into it with the gift her father gave her. Her in-laws now no longer drop in without a call.

Nermin is grateful to God for her education and financial independence, as it not only allows her a feeling of security, but also has enabled her to assert herself in her marriage in times when she felt slighted. Based on these past lessons, she disclosed that when her parents pass away and she inherits an abundance of wealth, she would like to place the amount she inherits in her personal account. Nermin remains married to her husband today.

Participant 10 – Layla

Layla is a Muslim American who first married a Muslim man from one continent and, once this marriage came to an end, remarried – this time to another Muslim man from a different continent and culture. Both her first and second husband did not share her cultural background. With respect to her background, Layla had been raised in a comfortable, middle-income family, but when her father remarried after his wife's passing, Layla and her siblings were pushed to leave home, find jobs, and live on their own. She and her first husband came from comparable economic backgrounds and both held a graduate university degree and a well-paying position.

Layla and her first husband signed their marriage contract in the U.S., and a *mahr* of $3,500 was recorded. The couple agreed that half would be paid right away (*muqaddam*) and the other half at a later time (*mu'akhkhar*). However, the groom failed to produce the initial amount, assuring his new bride that she would receive her gift once the two had shifted to his home country in the coming months. He did not fulfill his promise. Once they arrived in his native country, the marriage had to be registered at the government's local Islamic office, at which time the *mahr* amount that was agreed upon in the U.S. was freshly recorded. This second documentation worked to Layla's advantage, because when, upon divorce, her husband tried to renege on his Islamic obligation, his government intervened and issued an ultimatum that he either pay the *mahr* or they would garnish his earnings. Her *mahr* was therefore paid in full.

For most of their marriage, Layla and her husband lived overseas, residing in the U.S. for only a brief time. Regardless of the culture or country in which they lived, he behaved in a possessive and controlling manner when it came to their finances. He had a vengeful nature to the point that, when his mother once complained about her, he cut all her houseplants (which he knew she loved), took her phone, hid her passport and locked her up in the house for three months. She managed to get a hold of the key and would, when it seemed secure, go get food while he was at work. He did provide her with a reasonably comfortable home that met all her basic needs, but he would not budge on the issue of domestic help even though hiring housemaids were customary in the country in which they resided. She had absolutely no say in any household spending, a disenfranchisement that left her feeling impotent. Even once they had children, Layla was simply handed a monthly allowance of a paltry eighty-five dollars to suffice for both her and the children's needs. She tolerated her husband's frugal behavior until the day he falsely accused her of cheating on him. This was the last straw and she decided she no longer wanted to carry on this marriage. His accusation also explained why he stopped spending on her before the divorce (since such an accusation, if true, would make her a *nāshiz* wife disentitled to financial maintenance according to some scholars), something she never understood until this day. She then initiated the divorce but before she left her husband, he contemptuously spit out, "I hate every penny I had to spend on you!" He soon regretted his baseless accusation and tried to reconcile, but Layla had no interest in returning to the marriage. Once they divorced, he refused to pay her any child support or *mut'ah* or her due right to breastfeeding wages even though she was still nursing his child at the time. She suspects he withheld the *mut'ah* as a means of coercing her into remarrying him, but his ploy was ineffective. Layla returned to the U.S. with their children and began working towards her graduate degree to better support her family. For several years, her ex-husband did not send a penny towards providing for his children, until one day he returned to the U.S., reestablished contact and began showering Layla and their children with gifts. His apparent intention was to reconcile, but at this point she had lost all respect for him as a father and husband and she firmly refused to do so.

Many years later, after her children had grown into adulthood and moved out, Layla accepted a new marriage proposal. At this stage in life, she was financially secure and only requested a Qur'an as her *mahr*, but upon seeing that the groom was a wealthy man, the imam conducting the *nikah* insisted that a $2,000 *mahr* be specified in the marriage contract. The imam also had Layla's new husband pay her the *mahr* in full prior to consummation, and even though, after the marriage, her husband hinted that it was customary for her to return the *mahr* back to him. Layla knew her financial rights and refused.

Her husband provided her with a satisfactory furnished home and, in contrast to her first husband, would occasionally seek Layla's advice and input on their finances. Unfortunately, she quickly noted his tightfisted attitude towards spending; for example, he limited how much she ate by taking count of how much she consumed, flatly refused to spend on any domestic help and resisted buying her certain health-related products that were of higher quality because they were also more expensive. Layla was working at the time and she would deposit her earnings into a separate personal account, and although her husband seemed to resent her having money of her own, he ultimately told her to use her earnings to purchase her clothes and personal care items, saying "That's all you deserve, a home and food, that's it!"

Her second husband's verbal abuse, his temper and his penny-pinching ways changed her love for him to deep acrimony. She dreaded the shouting and interrogation over every line of each monthly statement, especially since she would take care to buy only the absolute necessities like groceries and material for home repair projects that she took on herself. To eschew arguments, she would tackle the work normally delegated to a carpenter, painter and handyman. She sanded, spackled, caulked, primed and pressure washed just to save money, but it was never good enough. "Who knows how much it would have costed to pay someone to do those projects?" she says in frustration.

Not only would her husband count every penny spent, he also assumed that Layla's personal wealth was his. When she inherited a sizable chunk of wealth from a loved one who had passed away, her husband insisted that she hand it over to him to invest, but she refused.

When she earned money by selling gifts her son had given her which she did not have use for, her husband would demand that she hand over the money to him but she kept her stance, saying "It's mine, you have no right to it." When she would refuse, saying it was hers to keep, he would become enraged.

Over time, his anger and miserliness led to Layla distancing herself from her husband. She did not have extended family living close by and could not look to her in-laws for support, as they too mistreated her. Instead, she leaned on her children, her friends in the community and her relationship with God to fill the emotional chasm. Despite her two unhappy marriages, her second marriage still stands as she feels certain that Allah will take care of her and reward her the hardship and injustice she endured, in this life and in the Hereafter.

Participant 11 – Rahma

Rahma married a man who shared her cultural background, but while he was born and raised in the U.S., she grew up overseas in the country of both their parents' origin. His family was slightly more well-off than her parents, but at the time of marriage, she had already completed her graduate and professional degree from a distinguished university in the U.S. and her husband was in the process of pursuing the same degree through a university overseas. Rahma's husband had been interested in another young woman, but his parents pressured him into marrying her instead because they believed that, given her exceptional academic record, she could reign in his remiss temperament and help him complete his studies.

A *mahr* amount of $1,000 was agreed upon and recorded in the marriage contract, but the bride never received any portion of it. The groom's parents provided a fully furnished home for the couple with the hope that their son would soon graduate and begin earning. The couple lived overseas for a year and a half, during which time Rahma did her best to help her husband with his courses, but he languished in his studies, complaining that he disliked living outside the U.S.. The couple shifted to the U.S. where he resumed classes, but he dawdled away the years, failing to secure a degree. He also fell seriously ill and received treatment for nearly a year. For the first nine years of their marriage, Rahma's husband remained a jobless student and his parents financially supported their son, his wife and their new baby. Rahma felt unhappy at their dependence on her in-laws and although she could not land a job in her field until she first passed a set of professional exams, she began working a minimum wage job that allowed her to feel a modicum of independence. When the couple moved to another state near Rahma's brother-in-law, he took on the responsibility for caring for her and her husband's family.

Her brother-in-law purchased a fully-furnished condominium for her and her husband's family and even paid for a babysitter. Rahma recounts, "[My husband's] family was always compensating for him to make sure the marriage stayed intact." Her husband did not appear to feel any sense of shame or remorse that his parents and siblings had adopted financial responsibility for his family, but it very much bothered Rahma.

She finally persuaded her husband to begin working; his first job brought in a decent income and by that time she too had completed all her exams and was earning $120,000 a year. However, because Rahma was bringing in a good income, her husband would spend nothing from his own salary on the household or children. She said, "He felt the money he earned was [reserved] just for himself." Asking him to contribute only led to arguments, so Rahma resigned herself to her role as the breadwinner and to the stress that came with shouldering this burden alone. "I had no choice, since he never wanted the responsibility," she said. The one consolation was that he wanted no part of the decision making related to household expenses and gave her complete reign in this area. Still, she recounted, "I felt good that I had the freedom to buy whatever for the house and children by my choice, but I always felt the lack of connection or interest from my husband's side – in any matters of daily life, be it with the children or the home."

Once Rahma's in-laws passed away, her husband bluntly told her that he wanted out of the marriage. He dismissed it as a phony union because he said he had never wanted to marry Rahma in the first place and only agreed in order to placate his parents. Ultimately, they did not divorce, but instead decided to separate due to the cost and split the expenses for the children's needs. However, he never fulfilled his part of the agreement to divide expenses and although he and Rahma have been living apart for four years now, he has spent nothing on his children, some of whom are now in college, and instead simply sees them twice a week for fun visitations. If they were to divorce, Rahma knows that her husband, who does not consider religion a priority, and has demonstrated generally selfish behavior, will not abide by any Islamic financial laws not enforced in the U.S..

Participant 12 – Jenna

Jenna is an American convert to Islam. She converted long before her marriage to her Muslim husband. From age 10 she had been searching for the true faith. Her husband, on the other hand, originally came from a country that restricted its citizens from practicing Islam, so although he was born Muslim, he knew little about the religion. His family lived in extreme poverty and his culture dictated that he, as the eldest of nearly a dozen siblings, was to provide for all his siblings throughout his life no matter their ability to work and earn for themselves. A hardworking man, he worked his way to the U.S. where he met Jenna and the two soon married. The bride's *walī*, who also happened to be an Islamic scholar, had the groom gift Jenna as her *mahr* all that he possessed at the time, which was $200, and made sure the amount was paid to her in full before consummation. Jenna herself came from a low-income family, but her parents' economic background was still more robust than her husband's, and her parents did not approve of the marriage, fearing that this young man with a low-paying job could not adequately provide for their daughter.

Their apprehension proved reasonable when their son-in-law lost his job, along with many subsequent ones because the recession hit and he did not yet have a green card. Jenna did not have a college education; she had started working at the age of ten, initially as a babysitter to help support her fledgling family. Despite this, she had a strong work ethic and once married became the breadwinner. For the first two years of the marriage, her income paid for the rent, groceries, transportation, medical insurance, as well as her husband's visit to his home country to see his family. She opened two bank accounts: one that was hers alone, in which a very small part of her income went into for personal needs, and the other, a joint account that listed her as the primary account holder and her husband as the secondary, through which all bills were paid. Doing this, however, never changed his frugal nature.

By the third year of marriage, her husband secured a reasonably well-paying job and assumed responsibility for a little over half of the couple's expenses. He followed his wife's lead and opened two bank accounts – a private one for himself and a joint account that recorded him as the primary account holder and Jenna as the secondary. From the start, her husband made clear that as long as she worked, Jenna was to pay for all her personal needs, including clothing and toiletries. In reality, she found herself spending on much more than just her personal care needs; her husband regularly sent money to his family overseas and he withdrew the amount from their joint account (in which she was the primary account holder) where both their monthly paychecks were deposited. She tolerated this arrangement for the sake of keeping the peace.

Jenna had been raised with the understanding that the husband and father should shoulder the financial responsibility for the family and when she converted to Islam, she found that her new faith also echoed this outlook. However, her Muslim husband seemed to feel that because she was an American convert, accustomed to working hard and earning, she somehow did not deserve or qualify for this right. Jenna resented this unjust attitude and felt exceedingly taken advantage of, but bore the family's financial burden in order to keep the marriage intact. She held two jobs all her life, clocking in even through each pregnancy, while he worked one. All the while, she managed the house without any help: "I did all my own cleaning and cooking and brought weekly laundry to an outside Laundromat. It was like I was a co-worker or roommate rather than a wife and lover."

Jenna felt drained, and when the grind would catch up to her, she would broach her husband with the possibility of taking a break from working outside the home, but her request would be met with an argument followed by a warning, "If you do so, you will live as a beggar." She did not take the threat as a hollow one, as she knew her husband was a miserly man who did not even like to spend on himself; for any formal events during the last 40 years, she had seen him pull out the same well-worn suit that he had donned on his wedding day. To preserve her and her children's quality of life and, more importantly, to continue to pay for her children's costly Islamic education, Jenna would retreat. Her resentment quietly burgeoned over the decades until she lost all respect and love for her husband and the two rarely communicated.

Their financial situation did not improve with time. Some years ago, her husband had an accident that left him severely injured, but qualifying for disability assistance from the government proved difficult. Her husband now relies even more heavily on his wife's earnings than before, and Jenna, although she is in her sixties, has had to delay her retirement. Even when her father passed away and she inherited $45,000, a cushion that could have lessened the financial burden, she used the money to pay off $20,000 worth of her son's college loans. Her greatest comfort and source of pride is that the Islamic education she gave her children has led to her sons taking complete financial responsibility for their wives and children.

Participant 13 – Suraya

Suraya and her husband came from the same economic background, but she grew up in a blue-collar family in the U.S. while he only arrived in the U.S. after marriage. During a visit to her home country, Suraya, a deeply religious Muslim, met her husband and felt it was best to marry young in order to protect her faith. The bride's father wanted to request a large *mahr* for his daughter's benefit, but Suraya asked that she receive an amount in line with women during the life of the Prophet ﷺ, as is the Sunnah. The amount they settled on was $2,500, and the groom, who was of little financial means at the time the marriage was contracted, gifted his wife the *mahr* when he was financially able, but only when his wife pressured him to give it.

At the time of the marriage, the bride had not yet completed high school and the groom had only recently graduated from high school. From the start, his family disapproved of the union, possibly because she was raised in the U.S. and adapted to its culture. They refused to financially assist their son, leaving the bride's parents to cover the cost of the couple's rent and living expenses. Shortly after the wedding, the newlyweds shifted to the U.S. and began living with the bride's parents, until, through his in-laws' help, the husband found work and the couple moved into a rental accommodation. They initially used empty cardboard boxes as tables because they did not have the means to buy furniture pieces, but once the bank approved her husband for a credit card, he purchased a bedroom set. Without a college degree, her husband had no choice but to work low-income jobs until one day he landed a job as a salesman in a liquor store. She could not bear the thought of being nourished from an unlawful (*haram*) avenue. Ironically, the singular condition Suraya had stated in their marriage contract was that her partner would never come near alcoholic drinks. The two had a huge argument, and although she knew that violating her condition was grounds for annulment of the marriage contract, she remained in the marriage out of financial necessity.

Suraya recognized the value of education and re-enrolled in high school soon after the couple married, and although she became pregnant within a few months of resuming her education, she persisted and ultimately earned her high school diploma. She wanted to pursue an undergraduate degree, or, at the very least, begin working to help supplement her husband's income, but he would not allow it. She said, "he wanted to control everything." Not only did he insist she remain at home, but he also refused to give her access to his bank accounts, remaining secretive about money matters. As their family quickly grew, their economic situation proportionately deteriorated. One of the couple's children was born handicapped, and a friend advised Suraya to apply for government assistance. This surreptitious stream of money gave her the freedom to purchase what she and the children needed, allowing her to provide her children with an Islamic education through the community *masjid* without having to turn to her husband. When her husband discovered Suraya was receiving assistance and tried to usurp control of the money, she refused. She stood her ground for the sake of her children, despite his temper and physical and verbal abuse.

Suraya encouraged her husband to earn a college degree in order to better provide for their children, but each time he would enroll only to drop out soon after. She also urged him to leave his job at the liquor store and buy his own business, one that would be compliant with Islamic law. Once again, he repeatedly failed, abandoning one business after another because he was unable to generate a profit. By now years had passed, and her parents have become too elderly and depleted to continue to help Suraya. Facing financial collapse, the family shifted to their home country, where her husband began working small day-to-day jobs. Because they did not have access to proper medical care for their disabled child in their native country, the father placed Suraya and their children in the home and care of his unmarried brother, while he flew with their handicapped daughter back to the U.S., allegedly to seek treatment. Their stay alone with his brother was a horrible experience as she watched him try to enter her daughter's room during the night and fought to protect her. In the meantime, unbeknownst to Suraya, her husband gave away their daughter away through some illegal means while in the U.S. in order to relieve himself from her medical costs. Suraya of course was horrified when he returned without their child, and her shock was only compounded when she learned that he had plans to marry a second wife. Her husband then callously moved Suraya and their remaining children to a dilapidated rental so shabby that her bed was outdoors on the porch. Penniless and heartbroken, she sold what little gold jewelry she had in her possession to feed her children.

She decided to file a petition in the country they were in to remove herself (*khulʿ*) from the marriage. When he found out, he took her to the community shaykh (religious leader) and planned to divorce her, possibly since culturally, it is somewhat offensive for a man to lose control over divorcing his wife himself and be forced by her out of matrimony. However, after coming to realize that her practice of *khulʿ* would be financially to his favor, he backed off, so that she had to proceed with removing herself from the marriage. The marriage ended and when Suraya tried to enter her former home to gather her valuables and clothes, her ex-husband barred her from stepping foot into what had been her house. He also gained custody of the children and would not permit her to see them – including the youngest who was still nursing – even once. It seemed he sought revenge for her daring to remove herself (*khulʿ*) from the marriage. He remarried and she found herself homeless. Suraya found refuge in her mother's home for some time, but soon her stepfather, who considered her a financial burden, told her to leave. Evicted, first from her husband's home and then her mother's, Suraya returned to the U.S.. Once in the U.S., her other former brother-in-law accepted to take her in temporarily until she got back on her feet. He was well off but offered the bare minimum in hopes that she would soon leave. She sought help from the community mosque but found that they had no programs in place to train or assist women in finding employment.

"It's a terrible system," she lamented. Destitute and having zero work experience, Suraya resorted to cleaning homes, which she did not enjoy doing. Still, even while away from her children, she held fast to her hope of one day completing college – a goal she did ultimately realize.

For the next six years, Suraya did not see her children, while her ex-husband had re-married for the third time. However she was grateful to God to find her handicapped child in the U.S. and got her back. It was only when a relative in the U.S. convinced her ex-husband to allow the children to visit their mother that he paid for their plane tickets and sent them to the U.S.. Once there, the children refused to return home to their verbally and physically abusive father, and thankfully he did not fight to bring them back. Suraya worked tirelessly to provide for her children and, most importantly, give them all college educations. Once their father learned that his adult children were earning well, he came to the U.S. to threaten them for handouts. He was successful in wrangling money from his children, who complied knowing his abusive nature, but when he tried to move into their mother's home, they wouldn't allow it. His avariciousness even affected his daughter's marriage prospects because he would demand unreasonably high *mahr* amounts from suitors with plans of snatching a share of the *mahr* for himself. His daughter remains unmarried to this day.

Although Suraya successfully rebuilt her life after ending her abusive marriage, the trauma of those years continues to haunt her – "It's been years, but still I am a prisoner." She cannot erase from memory the beatings, the hunger, or the many times he threw her out of her home, spitting on her and shouting, "Go kill yourself! No one wants you. I will take care of the kids!" She recounts, "He drove me to feel less than human [so that] I hated myself." Her lingering anxiety has led her to distrust people, and she tends to isolate herself from society. After divorce she asked for financial assistance from her local *masjid,* feeling eligible to a portion of the *zakāt*, but no one would help. Even as she acknowledges the few who stood by her during her financial hardships, she cannot forget the absence of compassion and respect from the majority. And even the well-intentioned individuals in her local *masjid* who helped her would give her charity, or *ṣadaqah,* in open view of others rather than respecting her sense of dignity. "It hurt because I didn't have the privilege of privacy. We should not treat people poorly just because they are poor." These exchanges would leave her feeling deeply ashamed when, in fact, she was a victim who fell into the hands of a cruel and greedy husband who failed to honor his basic Islamic duties to his wife. In the interview and post-interview questions, her repeating of *Alḥamdulillāh,* despite her monumental hardships, was striking. Both her trust in people and her confidence in herself has been broken, but her faith in God remains intact.

Participant 14 – Amani

Amani and her husband shared the same culture, but he came to the U.S. in his early twenties, while she was born overseas to a wealthier family and arrived to the U.S. upon marriage. The couple met in a summer school program overseas. The two quickly became engaged, at which point Amani observed a few odd behaviors; for example, when she let her friend borrow an expensive piece of jewelry she owned, her fiancé and his family expressed annoyance and complained as if the jewelry now belonged to them. This possessive behavior was a harbinger of things to come. Also, Amani's elder sister was told by his family that they had family members and friends who frequently traveled to the U.S. who could deliver money to her sister in the U.S. if she wanted to send her money. Upon hearing this, Amani's sister was puzzled and replied, "Why would I need to send money to my sister?"

Amani faced a number of problems from very early on in her marriage. First, the *mahr* specified in the contract was part monetary ($10,000) and part jewelry (a diamond necklace). Amani received only the jewelry at the time of marriage, but the couple agreed that the cash would be deferred to a later date – after the consummation of the marriage and once the husband felt financially able to offer the full cash amount. That time never came. The husband also set some money-related conditions in the marriage contract, one of which included the stipulation that any money earned by either spouse prior to the marriage belonged only to that individual, while any earnings thereafter would be split between the two partners. Amani agreed and signed the document. This clause would go on to create disagreements between the two for the remainder of their marriage, as they would interminably argue about who owned the home in which they lived; Amani's husband came into the marriage with the home legally under his name, but at this point he had only paid off a scant amount of its mortgage, most of which was actually paid off during the marriage using a combination of the husband's earnings and the wife's personal wealth. When Amani dared to seek divorce, her partner threatened that she would be in the street, since she had no legal rights to the home in which the couple lived. This fear was enough to keep Amani locked in the marriage.

Amani came from an affluent family that enjoyed live-in domestic help. Before she married and moved to the U.S., her father had passed away, leaving his wife and four children with a substantial amount of wealth. Amani did bring a small amount of cash (from what she inherited in her native country) back to the U.S. and opened a private account for her personal spending needs. Her husband was aware of this, although it did not please him. Her husband enjoyed a high-paying career. He had been previously married and had a child from his first union, whereas this was Amani's first marriage. She moved from her country of origin to the U.S. and into the home that her husband's first wife inhabited. The home was adequate but had shabby and damaged furniture pieces. When she requested at the very least a new mattress to replace the sunken, old one in the couple's bedroom, her husband harshly refused. Even when Amani developed severe backaches during her pregnancy, to the point that she had to sleep on the bedroom floor for months, her husband remained unmoved, dismissively telling her it was not a priority. When she gave in and offered to buy it herself he refused because he told her she should not spend her own money on household items. She tried to comply with this demand for a short time but being so deprived, she was left with no option but to discreetly spend from her private account to meet her basic needs. She felt that he did not want her to have any freedom to spend money whatsoever, even from her own money. At times, Amani's older sister would transfer money to her to help her. Eventually, Amani's husband came to realize the extent of her cash accessibility and started to straight out tell her to spend from her money when she needed something.

Along with the run-down furnishings in her new home, Amani also faced a shortage of food. Her husband gave her the absolute minimum dollar amount to spend on weekly groceries, so much so that at times she and their children found themselves living on milk and cereal. Despite his miserly attitude towards his new family, he spent generously on his child from his previous marriage. In fact, Amani's children looked forward to their half-sibling's visits, because they knew their father would allow them to come along to the expensive restaurants where he took his child from his first wife. He showed the same generosity to his parents and siblings, going so far as to curtail Amani's weekly household allowance – including the meager grocery budget – when his family visited. He would often use her monetary allowance as a weapon, taking back the amount if she argued with him. Amani would then have to resort to paying from her own pocket (wealth that she happened to inherit from her father). At times she would beseech him out of dire need to purchase basic necessities, even though she felt certain the answer would be no. At other times she did not ask, simply to avoid the harassment that would inevitably follow. This then led to silence and a lack of communication in their relationship.

Given that she was young and inexperienced when she married her husband, in the early years of the marriage Amani wavered between confusion and tolerance of her partner's behavior. She neither had a solid understanding of her financial rights in Islam nor a sense of how a healthy, respectful relationship between husband and wife should look. Once she had children, they began to complain of the deprivation in their home, especially after visiting friends and seeing their well-stocked pantries, refrigerators and wardrobes. It was then that Amani fully realized that her gut feelings were right – she was not being treated as the wife of a Muslim husband should be treated. Resentment replaced her confusion as she noticed that her children did not have warm clothes to wear during the winters (at times Amani was forced to accept hand-me-down coats and sweaters from others, even though accepting charity felt deeply degrading to her personally) and that, even while indoors in very cold weather, her husband would not raise the home's thermostat above 60 degrees, only fully warming up the home if his child from his first marriage, his parents, or his siblings visited. Over the years, Amani realized that she and her children were treated like second-class citizens in their own home, and that this was simply wrong. Still, she felt powerless in the face of this injustice.

Once their children were in their teens and twenties and required more expensive necessities like transportation for college, Amani's husband did fulfill those needs. However, he also took on the responsibility of supplying those same provisions to his siblings' children (including those siblings who were financially robust), using money that could have otherwise gone towards providing basic necessities, like winter clothing or a stocked refrigerator, to his own children. So, strangely enough, while Amani's husband did come through for his children when it came to their education or any recreational activities, he failed to meet their most basic needs.

Amani's husband showed some measure of care for his children, but throughout their marriage he remained callous and dismissive towards her needs. Whether she requested money to travel overseas to visit her elderly mother, or when she herself fell ill and needed to see a doctor during periods in which she had no health insurance, he would not budge and left the burden of payment on Amani. There were times when she was desperate for physical therapy, but his cold-hearted reply was always, "You just need attention!" Over the course of their married life, she exhausted most of her inheritance (by selling one property after another) and even her mother's wealth to care for herself, her children and their home – she estimates she has spent nearly $500,000 – until she reached a financial breaking point and resorted to borrowing money from friends and relatives. Today all that is left of her personal wealth is one piece of property in her home country that she must soon sell to cover her cost of living. Amani found this particularly degrading, recalling, "It has been such a bitter taste [having to borrow money]...especially [since] it [could have been] avoided without significant difficulty." Her acrimony is further compounded by the fact that the very man who would not spend on her and their children had borrowed over $100,000 of her personal wealth and, to this day, has not repaid it. She explained that from early on in the marriage, he asked her for money knowing that after her father's death she inherited a substantial amount of wealth. He said he would invest this money for her and give her a share of the profit. She voluntarily accepted for several reasons. First, she felt bad about the large amount of interest he paid on their home equity loan and because of the child support amount he paid every month from his past marriage. And second, in hopes that by doing this, he would become closer to her and be more generous to her. She said for a number of years, he did give her some profit for investing her money (a few hundred dollars a month) but then stopped with the excuse that she spent too much money on credit cards, and therefore, concluding that he owed her nothing.

During a particularly financially difficult time in her marriage, Amani would work up the courage to demand at least a portion of her deferred *mahr*, even just $500, but this strategy would backfire because her husband would tauntingly reply that he will only give her the remaining *mahr* upon divorce. Amani would desist out of fear of what would happen to her children's well-being if she and her husband divorced. On the occasions that she dared to challenge him and herself mention divorce, her husband would threaten that if she ended the marriage, he would retire and the judge would force Amani to work and pay *him* child support. She believed her husband because she was unfamiliar with the court system in the U.S..

At times she would try another avenue of improving her and her children's quality of life; she would try to pursue higher education in the U.S. in hopes that she might work outside the home and earn her own money. Her husband continually demoralized her, insisting that she was not capable of earning a degree. He would also use the children to guilt her into remaining at home. Yet even after their children grew up, Amani's husband gave her no time to seek a higher education, keeping her busy day and night doing chores and working as his personal assistant in his business – without pay. In this way she remained dependent on him. "He want[ed] me under his full control without a penny."

Over the decades, Amani's husband's behavior bred a mixture of negative feelings in her heart toward him – from disappointment, to frustration, to anger. She ultimately lost respect for the man and over time this disdain turned to resentment. She essentially felt debased by him, reflecting, "I used to be, by the grace of Allah, a princess, then I became a peasant, *Alḥamdulillāh*."

Amani has lived her entire married life victimized by financial abuse. This relentless mistreatment inevitably took a toll on her health; she has been diagnosed with depression, anxiety, an eating disorder, and severe sleep apnea. She says, "My physical, emotional, as well as mental health is pretty bad; anxiety, however, hit me more than depression." She has sought treatment, paying for any health care herself of course because her husband remains disinterested and unsympathetic. Given that her husband is the source of the financial abuse, she now feels anxiety when physically near him, so much so that she looks forward to his work trips so she can feel at ease, even if temporarily. Amani's husband's behavior not only left her with emotional and psychological damage, but also affected her children, all of whom suffer from depression and anxiety. She speculates that the financial abuse they endured in their younger years might be an underlying cause for two of her kids to marry only to divorce shortly thereafter. She is desperate to bring positive change in her life, but thus far she has not been able to climb out from under the decades of damage her husband wrought. Her healing process may take a very long time.

Participant 15 – Suzzanne

Suzzanne met and married her husband, who had been raised in the U.S., when he visited her country. The groom paid all wedding costs, as was customary in their homeland. They were both college-educated and came from fairly well-to-do families. As was the custom in their hometown, the marriage contract stated that the groom pay a *mahr* of three dollars at the time of the wedding and then a deferred *mahr* (*mu'akhkhar*) of $30,000. Suzzanne did not receive the remaining *mahr* after consummation, or even upon the later death of her husband.

Suzzanne was an assertive, self-reliant personality, and so upon arriving in the U.S., she immediately opened a private bank account and deposited the $10,000 in savings that she had brought from her home country. She had worked prior to marriage and made it clear to her husband that she wanted to continue working outside the home now that she had become wife, and that she expected her earnings would be hers alone. He agreed and, as an owner of more than one business, her husband encouraged that she works and placed her in charge of managing one of his businesses. While Suzzanne never received wages for her work for her husband, she was able to create her own private business, in which she bought and sold merchandise and earned good money. She used her earnings to pay for her personal needs, including her and her children's clothes, home repairs and trips of any kind. Her husband, meanwhile, paid for the family's furnished home, health insurance, groceries and transportation. Although Suzzanne had access to her husband's savings account, she proudly noted, "[My husband] never spent a dollar on me…I never allowed myself to ask." Her father had instilled the value of self-reliance in her when she was only ten, warning her never to depend on anyone but herself. Suzzanne appreciated that not only did her husband respect that her earnings were hers to do with as she pleased, but he also did not interfere with or encroach upon her right to any wealth her family sent her way. During the marriage, she lost her father and inherited a large sum of money; having a keen business mind, she purchased a home and rented it out as an investment property. Suzzanne ascribed her happiness in her marriage to her financial independence and to her husband giving her the time and freedom to pursue her humanitarian work with refugees and the impoverished.

Her husband was nearly twenty years older than Suzzanne and retired only five years into their marriage. His many businesses continued to generate a profit and the family lived well. When, a few years ago, her husband passed away, Suzzanne received all of the money in his savings account. Her daughters gave up their inheritance share to their widowed mother out of compassion, and her brother in law too decided to forgo his share, as it was customary in their culture that a brother gift his inheritance to female family members who did not have sons. Suzzanne was, therefore, well taken care of after the passing of her husband and was able to raise her children and pay for their college tuitions and weddings. Her husband did have another private account which he did not account for in his will, so state probate laws blocked Suzzanne from receiving funds from it for many years.

Participant 16 – Malak

Malak is a woman who lost her husband at a young age and was left with many children to support. She and her husband grew up overseas and came from a middle-class background, both holding Bachelor's degrees from universities in their homeland. She married her husband in their native country and their marriage contract recorded a *mahr* of approximately $300, which was deferred but never paid because, as she explained, a bride's right to *mahr* was given no importance in her culture and dismissed largely as symbolic. They came to the U.S. after marriage.

Malak recounted that her husband had taken care of her and the children to the best of his ability, providing them with a home, food, clothing, transportation and medical care. He gave Malak an allowance for her personal needs and she generally felt content with their quality of life. Unfortunately, her husband unexpectedly fell seriously ill and ultimately passed away, and as a wife, who had been accustomed to being a homemaker and mother but not an earner, she was left feeling alone and unmoored. Both she and her husband co-owned the family home and he had stated in his will that when he passed away, his share would be hers. She used the settlement from the life insurance her husband had purchased to pay off the house, but since the couple had no other property or investments and had depleted their savings paying for the husband's costly treatments, Malak had to start anew.

Malak had never worked before and without a resume of any kind, she was relegated to finding random part-time jobs to support her children. She was desperate for assistance, yet no male family members stepped up to help. Her father had passed away years earlier; her only brother, who lived overseas and was earning a good income, did not offer to help; and her brother-in-law did not even bother to contact Malak once she became a widow. In deep financial trouble, Malak reached out to her community *masjid* for a lifeline, hoping that perhaps the leadership could help her secure a job or offer some sort of funding, but to her astonishment, even this avenue came up empty. She turned to the government as her last resort, and it was there that Malak found she qualified for assistance for her youngest child. She began to receive $500 a month, which, while not a large sum, certainly eased her financial strain. She also sought help from United Health Care, but the organization redirected her to her place of worship for assistance. When Malak explained that her *masjid* had turned her away, United Health Care itself called and prodded the *masjid* to offer financial assistance to its community member in distress. The *masjid* grudgingly obliged, but only assisted her for one month before discontinuing it.

Abandoned by her fellow Muslims and local Islamic organizations, from that point on Malak did whatever work she could find to make ends meet. The years were long and her financial state precarious, but she managed to scrape by and successfully raised children who appreciate all their mother endured to support them. Despite the uphill slog, Malak held on to her faith and is deeply grateful to Allah for her sons, daughters, and even sons-in-law who now lovingly care for her.

Participant 17 – Fareeha

Fareeha and her husband shared the same cultural and economic background, but he had arrived in the U.S. from their homeland as a teenager while she moved to the U.S. in her late twenties. She held a Bachelor's degree from her home country while he had completed his graduate studies in the U.S.. Their marriage took place in the U.S. and the marriage contract specified the *mahr* as the cost the couple performing the pilgrimage (Hajj) to Mecca, as well as the cost of traveling to visit other holy sites in the Middle East. Her husband never gifted Fareeha her *mahr* until this day.

Prior to marriage, Fareeha had owned and lived in a fully furnished condominium; she worked full-time while pursuing her graduate studies. Once the couple married, her new husband shifted into her home for a few months until Fareeha sold her condo, using the money to pay off outstanding loans. Her husband purchased a new house with both their names on its title; the couple settled into their new home, and each added the other to his/her bank account. However, Fareeha recounted that her husband insisted that all payments for their household spending come out of his account, and if he ever discovered that she had dipped into her account to cover their needs, he would transfer the exact amount back into her account.

Immediately after marriage, Fareeha quit her job and focused full-time on pursuing her studies for the next three years. Her husband was employed as a salesman but being laid off time after time made him decide to run his own business. While the downside of his self-employment was that he did not get health insurance benefits for the family, he was a good provider for their growing family. Once she had graduated, Fareeha wished she could remain at home with her two small children, but she felt compelled to work in order to put her degree into practice, to pay off the $40,000 debt in student loans she had accrued, and most importantly, to secure health insurance for the family. Her husband gave her the space and freedom to make household decisions independently, such as hiring a cleaning service or buying appliances for their home. While she enjoyed taking charge to some degree, she would have liked for her husband to have been more involved, especially when it came to making expensive home purchases. However, she described him as an easy-going man who, while not miserly, had an unmaterialistic approach to life. Over the years, his contentment with the simple things in life rubbed off on her, and she tried to pass this attitude on to their children. Today her children are in their teens and although she still wishes to be a homemaker and mother, her husband encourages her to work and hold on to her earnings as a form of security for herself and their children in the event that something happens to him. It seems that the lack of guarantee of the success of his business, plus the risk of being terminated from his employment, were added reasons for her to have no option but to always remain employed. She does enjoy one particular benefit of earning her own money – being able to generously give charity from her personal wealth as a way of investing in her Hereafter.

Participant 18 – Tanya

Tanya is an American woman whose parents divorced and both remarried, and whose father had reverted to Islam. When she met her husband, who had been born overseas but who moved to the U.S. as a young boy, she learned that he too had accepted Islam some years earlier. She began to study the faith herself and embraced Islam one year before she married her Muslim husband. Following the marriage (*nikāḥ*), the imam who performed the ceremony produced a marriage contract for the couple. However, the bride said it was not documented in contractual form with room for conditions or a *mahr* specification. New to the Islamic faith, the bride was not aware of her Islamic rights, particularly those related to finances, and the imam performing the *nikah* did not explain these rights to her. Nevertheless, her right to a marital gift of value (*mahr*) was verbally-specified during the contractual agreement as a serge that she requested, which the groom honored and presented to her prior to consummation. Tanya, at the time of the *nikah,* knew her husband did not make much money while she was well off, so she chose something simple that she needed and was content with.

At the time of their marriage, Tanya held both an Associate and a Bachelor's degree in different fields, while her husband had an Associate degree. She was a well-established professional who owned and lived in her fully furnished condominium. Her husband, who had been living with his mother, moved into her place for the first year of their marriage, and the two began splitting the living expenses between them, but continued to maintain separate bank accounts. Once Tanya became pregnant, she left her job to care for their baby, and the couple, needing more space to accommodate their growing family, moved into a larger apartment. Tanya used the money from the sale of her condo to pay off college loans and credit card debt. From this point forward, her husband took on two jobs to compensate for his wife being a mother and homemaker, and he covered the cost of nearly all their living expenses – rent, groceries, medical care – while Tanya used her savings to pay for clothing and other personal items. A second baby soon followed their first-born, but along with this good news came a difficult diagnosis – Tanya's mother fell ill with terminal cancer. Tanya took in her teen half-sister, who had already lost her father and was now coping with her mother's passing, and with two new family members in their home, Tanya rejoined the work force for a few months to supplement her husband's income.

Within a few months of the birth of her second baby, Tanya decided to return to college to earn a second Bachelor's degree in science. She successfully juggled both caring for her children and completing her schoolwork by taking courses online and on the weekends. Once she graduated, she began working part-time, but kept her earnings for herself; however, once she resumed working full-time, her husband instinctively expected her to pay half the rent and some portion of their more expensive household purchases, such as appliances. Tanya obliged, but inwardly felt her husband took her assistance for granted.

In recent years, she and her husband met with an imam they both respected and the subject of a wife's role in helping to provide for the family came up. Their imam informed the couple that according to Islamic law, a wife's earnings, or wealth of any kind, is hers alone and it is her Muslim husband's religious duty to fully cover the cost of the family's needs. After this eye-opening conversation, both Tanya and her husband understood for the first time a wife's power and position of privilege in Islam when it comes to finances, and Tanya began to keep her paycheck entirely for herself:

> Since then, I have been able to purchase the car I wanted and have taken two international trips over the past year. I feel liberated keeping all of my own money. However, I still [choose to] contribute to groceries; It makes me feel good that I am in a position to help.

Tanya also likes to contribute to a monthly charity her husband set up for orphans. The difference between paying for household expenses all her life because she believed she *had* to compared with contributing because she *wants* to, is the difference between feeling powerless and powerful, she explained. In fact, Tanya recounted that in the past, when she would work rather than remain at home with her children, only to then see most of her earnings eaten up by household expenses, she felt less financially secure than when she was a homemaker, "I felt poorer!"

Tanya has continued striving to earn higher degrees and climb upwards in her career. She recently began pursuing graduate studies and, as a result of her hectic schedule, decided to use some of her earnings to hire house help. Her driving motivation behind building her career is a desire for her and her family to have the same quality of life – in terms of dining out, hosting friends and family, taking vacations and indulging in expensive purchases now and again – that she enjoyed while single. Her husband has proven a good provider, giving them all he can within his means, and Tanya has been able to step up and cover their needs in times of crisis; for instance, when her husband's company slashed his earnings during the pandemic, Tanya picked up the cost of the groceries and their children's Islamic education. Tanya has always felt happy in her marriage, but the contentment born of freedom that she felt once she was able to keep all her earnings cannot be compared to any other time: "Since exerting my financial freedom a year or so ago, I have never been happier."

Participant 19 – Maysa

Maysa and her husband were raised in different countries. At the time of their marriage, the bride was a high school graduate and the groom, having completed his Bachelor's degree, was pursuing a professional degree.

Maysa, along with her three sisters, did not grow up in the most loving home environment. In fact, when Maysa was young, her father quickly arranged a marital match for her. Her father's choice of a spouse for her did not practice Islam. Still a naïve adolescent with scant understanding of Islam, Maysa consented to the marriage and, with her paternal uncle as her *walī*, signed the marriage contract. The contract recorded the *mahr* amounts to approximately a few dimes and nickels, and the bride's uncle (*walī*) received this sum before consummation but never handed it to the bride. Maysa carelessly referred to the amount as being, "Worthless then and worthless now," insinuating that it deserves no mention. However, Maysa recounted that prior to marriage she was also promised a diamond ring once her husband could afford to buy her one, and although she remains unclear as to whether this piece of jewelry constituted part of her *mahr* or represented a separate present, many years have passed and her husband is doing well financially, but she has yet to receive the ring.

Because her husband was a full-time student abroad at the time of their marriage, the couple initially lived in his native country, and shifted into his parents' home. Maysa promptly discovered that her in-laws regarded her as akin to a housemaid and expected her to cook, clean and wash laundry for the entire family as a way of earning her keep – a jarring change in circumstance for a girl who had been accustomed to having house help when she lived in her parents' home. Maysa dreamed of pursuing a higher education and registered for college, but, since her husband was not working and her father declined to send her money to pay her tuition, she sought refuge from her home life through work as a photographer. She used her earnings to support both herself and her husband through his years of study, since his parents only gave him a small allowance to meet his own leisurely needs. She would return home from work each day to a small plate of dinner leftovers and a sink piled with crusty dishes waiting to be washed. Thankfully, once Maysa became pregnant in their fourth year of marriage, the couple moved into an apartment, but her reprieve from his family's abuse proved short-lived because, 12 months later, when Maysa could no longer afford to pay the rent, they returned to her in-laws' home. After some time, Maysa had managed to set aside enough from her meager income to pay for classes at a local college. Once she earned her college degree and landed a well-paying job, she hired a cook for the family to relieve her of some of her workload.

Several years into their marriage, her husband finally completed his studies abroad, after which he took on low-paying jobs for a few years. Three years later, Maysa applied for his green card, purchased their tickets back to the U.S. – paying for them herself, of course – and at long last, they arrived in the U.S.. They stayed with her sister for one month, sharing all expenses, before moving into their own place. She began working immediately, while he attended graduate school in the U.S.. Even when he began working, she was still making more money than him and continued to make all the financial decisions. Their family grew and Maysa diligently strove to tuck away savings from both their earnings, hoping to own their own home one day. Her dream took a hit when her husband, who did not himself have the funds to bring his parents to the U.S., asked that she break into her 401k retirement fund – the only money she had set aside for her own security – to finance her in-laws' visit which lasted for an entire year. He assured her he would pay her back, but never did.

After some time, Maysa decided to become a full-time homemaker and mother because her husband had reached a stage where he could finally take on the role of the sole breadwinner. She noticed that in his new role, her husband displayed quite self-centered decision making. For example, when Maysa had been the earner, she had bought a car for the family in both their names, yet her husband now purchased an incredibly expensive car and registered the vehicle under his name only. Similarly, when she had been the provider for the family, she and her husband shared a joint bank account, but now he had opened a private account in which to squirrel away his money. She felt shocked and hurt at his selfish attitude and she repeatedly reminded him, "No one will take anything with them to their grave," but her words fell on deaf ears.

Over the years, Maysa observed that her husband had begun to return home late into the night, sometimes spending entire nights away from home. She suspected infidelity on his part, but it wasn't until the matter was verified and when she developed precancerous cells that develop from sexually transmitted diseases that she knew he had been committing adultery. She was gravely ill and required immediate surgery, but her husband refused to pay for treatment and denied any responsibility. It was only because she became pregnant right around this time that she made a full recovery; the pregnancy miraculously eradicated the pre-cancerous cells. After regaining her health, Maysa turned to a religious scholar for guidance on how to handle her adulterous husband; he advised her that since intimacy with her partner could jeopardize her health, she should leave town until her husband comes to his senses. She did as the scholar had suggested, but this course of action only emboldened her husband. He had more freedom than ever before to carry out his lascivious behaviors, and it was much more difficult for his wife and children, to demand money. She never anticipated this happening to her – otherwise, she would have tried to put aside some of her lifelong earnings that were spent on him and their children, for a day like this. Divorce was not realistic for her, since doing so would jeopardize any chance of him paying for the kids' education, which was her priority.

While separated, Maysa and her children borrowed money to survive, and it was only after begging her husband for help, that he gave her access to a minimal amount of money through a bank account he kept. To survive and plan for her children's future, she suggested investing on his behalf and because of her business-oriented mind and talent in the field, he agreed and started to send money to that account as needed. She put all her effort into investing in business endeavors in his name, which was his condition. He allowed her to take the profits from these business ventures so she pursued these various projects to guarantee some income for her and the children. Eventually, she and the children returned to the marital home. Her husband, who at this stage had an excellent income and had amassed a fair amount of wealth, resented the return of his family, and in order to drive them to leave again, set them up in an almost unlivable home. When Maysa complained that she and their children were sleeping on the floor, her husband snapped, "You're the one who chose to come!" Fed up with her husband treating his own family like derelicts and forcing them to live under such restrictive conditions, Maysa threatened to end the marriage, at which point her husband agreed to buy the family a proper home in which to live.

It is unclear why he gave in upon hearing that his wife shall pursue divorce. Given the amount he may have to pay for both child and spousal support if they were to get divorced in the U.S., the avenue of providing them with a decent home probably appeared to be a better option to him.

Although Maysa had successfully pressured her husband into buying his family a suitable home, he persisted in his licentious lifestyle and continued to financially torment his wife and children. He hid his money, denied Maysa access to his bank account, and refused to include her as a beneficiary on his Social Security so that she would receive this income stream in her old age. He also refused to assist his children when they asked him to help pay for their college tuitions, making it difficult for them to both hold jobs and continue through their schooling when they didn't qualify for funding. They eventually separated again. Maysa managed to carve out a life for herself and her children, continuing to negotiate with her husband to secure some financial assistance. Living in a spacious home without basic living expenses, the children would say they felt simultaneously rich and poor. Maysa worked hard to manage various business ventures on behalf of her husband to provide her and her children a comfortable lifestyle.

Maysa reflected on how she financially supported her husband for almost 16 years, yet when it came time to return the favor, he turned his back on her and their children. Today, none of the children, now independent college graduates with careers, harbor respect or affection for their father and they would do anything before asking him for financial help.

Participant 20 – Ranya

Ranya, one of my youngest participants, was born and raised in the U.S. and, while visiting her parents' native country, met and married her husband. Both Ranya and her husband came from middle-class families and had successfully earned their Bachelor's degrees. The bride's father paid for an extravagant wedding and the *mahr* agreed upon in the marriage contract was a symbolic $10 based on the currency of their native country although it was never paid.

The newlyweds comfortably lived in a property owned by the groom's sister, and after one year, shifted into a condominium the groom had bought for the couple. Ranya's husband paid for the home's appliances and her parents for the furniture, but it was as this point that their financial situation deteriorated; Ranya noted that her husband lacked drive and would drift from one job to the next. After some time, he launched a business of his own but even this failed due to his indolent work habits. They took a significant loss as a result of their business folding and this financial hit, coupled with her husband's excessive spending, forced them to sell property he owned. When even this did not cover their cost of living, Ranya's husband began to borrow money and fell into a great deal of debt. By now, the young couple had a child and Ranya began working to meet their growing family's needs. Her parents, seeing the mounting debts the newlyweds were facing and their son-in-law's lackadaisical attitude, stepped in and helped pay off their credit card bill.

Frustrated with her husband's behavior and worried that he would continue to waste away time visiting family and going out with friends, Ranya convinced her husband to apply for U.S. residency and the family relocated to America. They lived in her parents' home and relied on them financially during their first year in the U.S.. Once Ranya and her husband had both secured jobs, with her earning $30,000 a year and him $40,000, they moved into an apartment. Only his job (not hers) provided medical insurance for the family at this time. The couple opened a joint account, sharing all living expenses, and continued to expand their family. After some time, they bought a home, and, with the help of Ranya's father, managed to make a large down payment thereby trimming their mortgage to only $500 a month. Soon, however, Ranya's husband resumed old habits and began aimlessly drifting from one job to the next, sometimes choosing to leave a place of employment and at other times being let go. After three different jobs, he never again had steady employment; he tried his hand at running small side businesses from home, but they all quickly fizzled. Because the mortgage payment was so low, he managed to take care of it, while Ranya covered the cost of all other living expenses using her income. To his credit, her husband never asked her to give any portion of her earnings to him, but it distressed and embarrassed Ranya to see him continually borrowing from relatives and friends. She explained, "The debt and financial issues have caused me much anxiety. I feel like [my husband] doesn't listen to me when I do talk, so I stopped trying to communicate."

Without a steady job to keep him in the U.S., Ranya's husband would pass the time chatting on the phone with his family overseas or going out with local friends. He often made spontaneous travel plans to his home country to visit relatives, sometimes lingering there for months at a time. He seemed unconcerned about his family and complacent due to his belief that his in-laws would take care of his wife and children in his absence. As a result, Ranya's parents grew to resent their son-in-law. Still, out of love for their daughter they would invariably fill the gap he left behind; for example, her father bought a home and rented it out, giving Ranya the rental income of almost $1,500 to supplement her own earnings.

Things got even worse when her husband developed serious illnesses that made him temporarily disabled. They went through hard times, especially since they had no health insurance. She felt she had to do something to bring in income and pursued her studies for a certification that gained her a stable job.

In recent years, the family's precarious financial state worsened when Ranya's husband survived a major accident which left him handicapped. The surgeries he required caused the family to spiral deeper into debt. After he sought treatment and recovered, he fell back into his lazy lifestyle. Ranya continues to tend to the children and household chores while working a full-time job. Her husband's inability, or perhaps unwillingness, to fulfill her financial rights placed a deep strain on their marriage, but when Ranya contemplated ending the marriage, she pulled back for fear of a divorce negatively impacting their children. Eventually, when she came to realize that the situation would not change and that she would always carry the financial burden for herself, her children, and him, she built up the courage to file for divorce. The journey was not, by any means, an easy one, as he began to physically abuse her and the children to get them to leave their home since he claimed it was his home. She moved into her parent's home for some time while awaiting divorce proceedings in which he would not agree to let them move back into their home unless he was paid $180,000. When she informed him of not having any money to give him, he told her to take it out of her IRA and the mutual funds her dad purchased in her name when she was born. He also suggested she goes to live in the home her father invested in that provided her some rental income (which she used to pay her and the children's living expenses) but she replied that the home was not hers, and that it was her father's. He bargained that she could move back into their home only if she removed her name from the title upon which he would pay for their living expenses, but she knew well of his unemployment history and tendencies. Eventually, Ranya's parents paid him $140,000 so that ownership could be transferred to their daughter so that they could live comfortably. They also spent $20,000 on attorney fees. Once a settlement and a court date was set, his claim of poverty to the judge got him to only order $700 in child support per-month, which is insufficient for her children's needs Her ex-husband often fails to pay even that amount.

Participant 21 – Nadia

Nadia is from a predominantly Muslim country and met her husband while she and her family were residing in Europe.[22] They met one another while he was working towards his Bachelor's degree and she was earning an Associate degree. She came from a significantly wealthier family than her husband, and being an only child, was especially pampered by her parents. Nadia's parents disapproved of her marrying a young man who was neither Muslim nor from their cultural background, but her father, anxious that his only daughter would resent him if he restricted her from marrying the man she loved, acquiesced. The groom's own father warned Nadia the day before the wedding's civil ceremony not to marry his son because of the young man's ill temperament, but the bride, to her own peril, dismissed her future father-in-law's exhortation.

At the time of the marriage, Nadia and her husband were both full-time college students and neither was earning an income. It was not the norm in the groom's native country and culture for his parents to financially assist the newlyweds, so the bride's family stepped up, renting a place for the couple and covering all their living expenses. A few months later Nadia's parents bought a condominium in both their daughter and son-in-law's names and the pair settled into their new fully paid home. After one year of marriage, Nadia's husband's employer laid him off from his part-time job and the couple decided to move to the U.S. to pursue their studies there, but when they both applied for green cards upon arrival in the U.S., her native country's embassy would not allow them to apply as spouses unless he converted to Islam. They located a small Islamic center where Nadia's husband pronounced the testimony of faith (*shahādah*) and the man in charge at this center then married the couple Islamically (*nikāḥ*). A few men who happened to be at the center served as their witnesses, but Nadia did not have a guardian present, as she was unaware of this obligation according to at least three classical schools of thought. She was also unaware of her financial rights as the wife of a Muslim husband, and was taken by surprise when the representative who married the pair asked what *mahr* she required from the groom. She felt embarrassed to ask for anything directly in front of her husband, so she simply requested a Qur'an. Once he became Muslim, her husband did show an interest in learning more about the faith, but without any religious support system, such as a local Muslim community, in place, he never practiced. By the time they moved to the U.S., Nadia had seen her husband's selfish and cruel nature. Although she realized why his own father had cautioned her not to marry him, she left her parents behind and was now in an unfamiliar country with her new husband, feeling there was no way for her to turn back.

Her husband managed to find part-time employment with a firm that agreed to finance his college tuition, but his income was not substantial, and Nadia's father paid for most of the couple's living expenses, including rent, clothing and at times even groceries. Her husband paid the gas and electric bills and bought a portion of their groceries, but he meticulously accounted for every penny she spent, giving her a tight weekly allowance that did not even cover her basic needs; if she exceeded the allowance limit on her credit card, even by the cost of a bottle of Tylenol, he would shave off the exact amount from the next week's allowance. There were weeks when she had spent her allotted amount and had no money left for food, but his curt response would be, "Not my problem." Nadia would resort to asking her father for money in order to eat, but felt humiliated, as though she had been reduced to a beggar. She doesn't remember asking for anything when her husband's reply was anything other than, "I can't afford it." Matters only worsened once the couple had children and, although parenthood brought with it rising expenses, Nadia's husband continued to give her a paltry weekly allowance. There were times when she was given only $100 per week to cover the cost of gas, groceries, school supplies and household items for the entire family. Throughout her entire life, Nadia was employed only three times, each for just a few months, during which her husband would confiscate her income. And although for almost the entirety of their marriage, she had no income, when their children enrolled in colleges (prior to their later divorce), her husband forced Nadia to sign the financial loan papers instead of him so he would not bear any responsibility.

Her father always sensed how shabbily Nadia's husband treated her, so he financially supported his daughter, in one form or another, throughout her marriage. For example, when her husband, who kept a reliable vehicle for himself, left Nadia stranded in the middle of the road in her dilapidated, second-hand car, refusing to give her a ride home, it was Nadia's father who immediately sent her $30,000 to purchase a new car. When the couple wanted to buy a home in the U.S. for their growing family, they sold the condominium Nadia's father had purchased for them in her husband's home country to finance their new house, but still fell short; again, Nadia's father gifted them $120,000 so they would have enough funds to buy their dream home. Her father was always her sanctuary and he spent on his daughter and grandchildren until he, quite literally, had nothing left to give. It was because of his constant financial support to his daughter that, when he died, her father had no estate left for her to inherit.

Nadia explained that she kowtowed to her husband's demands in part because he was an abusive man – both verbally and physically. She lived in terror of his tirades and beatings, as did the children, who would at times wonder if they had done something to deserve such terrible treatment. As their mother, she would assure them they had done nothing wrong. She desperately wanted out of the marriage, but she had no access to money and feared her husband's retaliation against both her and their children. Her husband, meanwhile, seemed aware of his family's aversion for him because he hid all their passports so they could not flee the country without him. Over the decades, the abuse caught up with Nadia until one day her health deteriorated to the point that she could not stand due to the pain. Her husband grudgingly drove her to the hospital, but only after he saw she was planning to ask their neighbor to take her. The hospital staff gave her heavy doses of pain medication, yet when she felt well enough go home, Nadia was puzzled to find that the doctors and nurses would not discharge her. After three days, she learned that her husband had lied to the staff, telling them that she had tried to commit suicide and was mentally unstable. When she refuted having attempted suicide and revealed how truly abusive her husband was, they agreed to release her, but insisted she set up appointments with a psychiatrist before leaving. It was at this juncture that Nadia made up her mind to leave her husband. Her opportunity came when he booked an international vacation for the family. When she cited her poor health as the reason for her inability to travel and the children also offered up last-minute excuses, her husband furiously left for the trip on his own. In his absence, Nadia hired a lawyer to file an order of protection against him. When he returned home a week later, the police met him at his home and, to his complete shock, informed him that his wife had filed a restraining order against him. Nadia recalled, "A part of me hated divorce. I was dreaming of growing old with a man I loved and had married. And the other part of me hated what he had reduced me to."

The order of protection was the start of a sordid and expensive divorce that stretched out for years and drained both sides of hundreds of thousands of dollars before a settlement was reached. Interestingly, Nadia's husband tried to employ Islamic law in the U.S. court in order to gain custody of the children, but his own father foiled his strategy by serving as a witness on Nadia's behalf and requesting that the judge deny his son custody. Nadia was awarded custody of their children, along with monthly spousal support for the remainder of her life due to her poor health, old age, and her lack of work experience. The settlement did not last however; today Nadia's ex-husband is taking her back to court, claiming that he is unable to afford the alimony payment because he lost his job. Once again, Nadia finds herself in a place of financial insecurity.

The many forms of abuse – financial, verbal, and physical – that Nadia experienced at the hands of her ex-husband have left her with multiple chronic diseases that constantly lead to her being hospitalized. Along with the physical injury and sickness she experiences, she carries psychological trauma from her life with her ex-husband: she is under the care of psychiatrists and is dependent on antidepressants and anxiety medications. After sharing her life story in bits and pieces over the course of multiple interviews, Nadia concluded by saying, "This isn't even a fraction of what happened to me." Still, she remains grateful to God for her children. She managed to raise them well, and they are a source of comfort for her.

CHAPTER FIVE

Islamic Compliance in Muslim Households: An Analysis

In this chapter, I delve further into the 21 case studies to examine the extent to which the financial rights of the women I interviewed, based on Islamic principles, were enjoyed or violated. I assess the magnitude of any such violations, explore potential underlying causes for such violations, and highlight the resultant physical, mental, and social ramifications of such deprivations. Furthermore, I examine how the rampant financial abuse we find in marriages today are not only in direct conflict with Islamic law, but at times stemming from patriarchal biases and/or selective reliance on textual misinterpretations.

Violations of Financial Rights

To begin, I must emphasize that women married to Muslim men who live in a non-Muslim country should still enjoy all the financial rights they would have under Islamic Law. I asked each of the 21 study participants about whether or not and how certain indisputable financial rights, rooted in the Qur'an and Prophetic traditions, were granted to them throughout their marriages, including but not limited to (1) the right to a wedding reception (*walīmah*) in which the marriage is made public, (2) the right to the marital gift (*mahr*), (3) the right to manage her own personal wealth, (4) and the right to financial support throughout the marriage or *nafaqah*, which covers residence, nourishment, clothing, and hired domestic help. It is important to note that there does exist some disagreement on whether or not the husband has the religious obligation within *nafaqah* to pay for his wife's medical expenses. However, as I explained in Chapter Three, according to the majority of today's scholars, based on the Qur'an and Prophetic traditions, a wife has an unequivocal right to receive support for medical expenses from her husband.

An analysis of the 21 study participants' responses revealed a stark and disheartening reality: it appears that many Muslim men living in the U.S. today do not adhere to the example of the Prophet ﷺ when it comes to upholding the financial rights of their wives. The 21 study participants and their marriages notably exhibited diverse backgrounds in terms of the couples' cultural backgrounds, level of education, economic status and more. However, the consistent thread running through the lives of the majority of these wives, divorcées, and widows of American Muslim husbands was that of financial abuse.

Violations Related to the Mahr

17 of the 21 study participants, in other words 80% of participants, experienced violations of their basic Islamic right to receive a *mahr*. Of this 80%, the vast majority (14 of the 17 wives) never received a *mahr* at all – not even upon divorce or the death of their husband. In 10 of the 14 cases, the marriage contract did specify a *mahr*, either immediate or deferred, but the wives never received the specified amount. For example, Nadia did not know what *mahr* was and when the person marrying the couple took her by surprise by asking what *mahr* she

wanted, she was too embarrassed to ask for anything and only asked for a Qur'an but never received it. Fareeha's *mahr* to perform Hajj and visit holy sites in the Middle East was left unfulfilled. Maysa's recorded portion of her *mahr* of dimes and nickels was handed to her guardian and never given to her. She was also verbally promised a diamond ring once her husband was financially able but never received that either.

In the remaining 4 of the 14 women who did not receive *mahr*, there was no mention of the *mahr* at all, and these four women did not receive any *mahr al-mithl*—which is normally provided when no *mahr* is specified— either.

Only four study participants reported that their husbands did, in fact, fulfill their right to *mahr* without the wife having to ask for it.[1] In Suraya's situation, the immediate *mahr* was not paid upon marriage and the husband was silent on the matter; however, later in the marriage when she learned of her rights and demanded the *mahr*, he paid it.

The majority of the 21 study participants either had a partial understanding of their right to *mahr* or had an active misconception of this right when they married their husbands. For example, in instances where the marriage contract specified a deferred *mahr*, most wives were not clear on *when* precisely this delayed marital gift was due to them. According to scholars of *fiqh*, a Muslim husband must normally gift his wife the *mahr* once the marriage is contracted and prior to consummation, but some permit the couple to agree to defer part of the *mahr*. Some jurists ruled that the parties can agree to defer *mahr* to a set time after consummation; others place restrictions on how delayed that time could be.[2] Some jurists (like the Hanbalis and Ḥanafis, in certain instances) permit deferring the *mahr* to divorce or death, while others (like the Mālikis and Shāfiʿīs) do not permit a delay unless the specific deferment date or event is clearly indicated in the marriage contract.[3] The marriage contracts of 6 of the 21 study participants specified the *mahr* amount as deferred. In the case of Amani, her husband refused to pay off the deferred portion, asserting that *mahr* was only due upon divorce; Amani, after making repeated requests, did not pursue the matter. Nermin's groom agreed to pay $25 upon signing the contract and deferred $100,000 to a later date. Approximately a year after consummation, he expressed anxiety about the size of the deferred amount and said he did not believe he could ever afford to pay it. Despite the various opinions and nuances, Nermin incorrectly assumed that her husband owed her the full *mahr* only in the case of divorce, and not wanting him to feel forced to remain in the marriage, she relieved him from the burden. Layla (a former Christian who converted to Islam prior to her marriage) married twice, and, at the time of her first marriage, her marriage contract indicated that half of the *mahr* amount would be paid upfront and half would be deferred. However, her husband failed to pay either portion until the couple divorced, at which time he tried to renege on his Islamic obligation. The government of the Muslim country where they resided intervened and issued an ultimatum that he either pay Layla the *mahr* or the government would garnish his earnings. Interestingly, when Layla remarried, the imam who performed the ceremony insisted that the groom pay the *mahr* in full prior to consummation, and when, after consummation, Layla's husband hinted to his wife that cultural custom dictated she return the bridal gift to him, she knew her financial rights and flatly refused. In the examples of Suzzanne and Malak, the deferred *mahr* was never paid. Some of these wives did not know to advocate for their right to *mahr* because they did not fully understand this right or were manipulated out of their right to one.

Similar to the confusion surrounding deferred *mahr*, study participants demonstrated a lack of understanding when it came to *mahr al-mithl* (*mahr* of her equal). As mentioned earlier, 14 of the 21 study participants did not, at any point, either during the marriage or upon divorce or the death of the husband, receive *mahr*. In 2 of these 14 cases, Dana and Sophia, there was no mention of the *mahr* either by verbal agreement or in the written contract. It is not Islamically acceptable that the husbands of these women maneuver around this fact by suggesting a gift that suits them to be the actual *mahr* at a later date or upon divorce. In other words, the *mahr* cannot be hidden from the brides to be; it is their full right to be consulted about the gift. This is particularly important when women do not have a *walī* whose responsibility is to inform them of their rights and protect them. In instances where *mahr* is not specified, Islamic law dictates that the brides receive *mahr al-mithl* (*mahr* of her equal). However, these two study participants, whose right to *mahr* went unfulfilled, were unaware that they deserved *mahr al-mithl*. In fact, they did not even know of the concept or term itself and had simply assumed that they were not due a bridal gift.

In 7 of the 21 study participants, *mahr* was specified but *not* identified as *deferred*, but the husbands did not pay it, suggesting either that they expected the *mahr* was deferred or that they simply had no intention of paying it.[4]

The actions of certain Muslim husbands could be attributed to their lack of knowledge about the significance of the marital gift in Islam. There are, of course, some husbands that adopt the view (supported by some scholars) that *mahr* may be deferred until the time of divorce or even death, but that holding only applies when a couple agrees to the *mahr* being deferred *prior* to consummation.[5]

Dana and Sara never received the *mahr*, even upon divorce – so what legal authority do these husbands cite to justify their actions?

Nine participants stated that they had contracted a *mahr* that was symbolic in nature due to cultural custom, or very small due to the husband's financial circumstances. Considering the husband's financial circumstances is not only acceptable according to Islamic law but also a commendable act on the part of the bride-to-be.[6] However, in today's society, many women receiving a symbolic *mahr* or a very small *mahr* from financially able and even wealthy men find themselves in trouble and without any form of security in the event of divorce or the death of their spouse. Surprisingly, Aya's parents brought harm to their own child when they deprived her from her Islamic right to a marital gift by asking for a symbolic amount that amounts to nothing, then, in addition, coercing her to forgive it.

In four of these (nine) participants whose *mahr* was symbolic in nature, the *mahr* was paid immediately. With one participant, the symbolic *mahr* was never paid, and the remaining one was paid upon divorce. Table 2 gives a precise count of the situation of these wives with regards to their *mahr* rights:

In keeping with this trend of women not fully understanding their financial right to *mahr*, we see that among the 21 participants, 8 explicitly complained of their own ignorance. 5 of the 8 were either not Muslim (before matrimony) or Muslim converts (before or after matrimony). These five women were understandably not initially well-versed in Islamic law, and the imams performing their marriage ceremonies failed to inform these brides of their right to *mahr* and a *walī* to advocate on their behalf for their financial rights.[7] For example, Dana, an American convert to Islam, had no

Table 2: Payment of *Mahr* Received by Study Participants

Participant	Marital Status Married (M), Divorced (D), or Widowed (W)	Was *Mahr* Mentioned in Contract? (Y/N)	Was *Mahr al Mithl* Applied? (Y/N or N/A)	Was *Mahr* (Prompt Portion) paid upon marriage? (Y/N)	Was *Mahr* (Deferred) portion paid durinssg marriage? (Y/N)	Was *Mahr* (Deferred) portion or *Mahr al-mithl* paid at/after divorce? (Y/N)	Was *Mahr* Relieved by the Wife? (Y/N)	If applicable, Was *Mahr* paid from the estate of deceased husband? (Y/N or N/A)
1 Dana	D	N	N	N	N	N	N	N/A
2 Sara	D	Y	N/A	N	N	N	N	N/A
3 (1st) Nabila	D	Y	N/A	N	N	N	N	N/A
3 (2nd) Nabila	M	Y	N/A	N	N	N	N	N/A
4 Aya	M-In Process of D	Y	N/A	N	N	N/A	Y	N/A
5 Jasmine	M	Y	N/A	N	N	N/A	N	N/A
6 Sakina	M	Y	N/A	Y	N/A	N/A	N/A	N/A
7 Sophia	D	N	N	N/A	N/A	N	N	N/A
8 Farida	D	Y	N/A	Y	N/A	N/A	N/A	N/A
9 Nermin	M	Y	N/A	Y	N/A	N/A	Y	N/A

Participant	**Marital Status Married (M), Divorced (D), or Widowed (W)**	**Was *Mahr* Mentioned in Contract? (Y/N)**	**Was *Mahr al Mithl* Applied? (Y/N or N/A)**	**Was *Mahr* (Prompt Portion) paid upon marriage? (Y/N)**	**Was *Mahr* (Deferred) portion paid durinssg marriage? (Y/N)**	**Was *Mahr* (Deferred) portion or *Mahr al-mithl* paid at/after divorce? (Y/N)**	**Was *Mahr* Relieved by the Wife? (Y/N)**	**If applicable, Was *Mahr* paid from the estate of deceased husband? (Y/N or N/A)**
10 (1st) Layla	D	Y	N/A	N	N	Y	N/A	N/A
10 (2nd) Layla	M	Y	N/A	Y	N/A	N/A	N/A	N/A
11 Rahma	M	Y	N/A	N	N	N/A	N/A	N/A
12 Jenna	M	Y	N/A	Y	N/A	N/A	N/A	N/A
13 Suraya	M	Y	N/A	N	Y	N/A	N/A	N/A
14 Amani	M	Y	N/A	Y	N	N	N	N/A
15 Suzzanne	W	Y	N/A	N	N	N	N	N
16 Malak	W	Y	N/A	N	N	N/A	N	N
17 Fareeha	M	Y	N/A	N	N	N/A	N/A	N/A
18 Tanya	M	Y	N/A	Y	N/A	N/A	N/A	N/A
19 Maysa	M	Y	N/A	Y&N	N	N/A	N/A	N/A
20 Ranya	D	Y	N/A	N	N/A	N/A	N	N/A
21 Nadia	D	Y	N/A	N	N	N	N	N/A

idea of the concept of *mahr* and did not learn that this right had, in fact, been written into her marriage contract until she and her husband divorced, at which time she learned the *mahr* due to her was a paltry 25 cents – a *mahr* she never agreed to. Similarly, Sophia never knew she was entitled a *mahr* and there was no mention of it in her marriage contract or by the imam who married them. After she converted to Islam two years later, she discovered this right and upon questioning her husband about it, was told her *mahr* was the ring he gave her—failing to recognize the agency she might have had in determining the value of her *mahr*. In the case of Tanya, another convert to Islam, the imam performing the marriage produced a marriage certificate, but there was no room to specify a *mahr.* When she later, after matrimony, learned more about Islam and questioned the imam about why her *mahr* and other financial rights were not explained or specified in the contract, he apologized and informed her that her verbal request for a serge constituted her *mahr*.

Of the eight who expressed regret for not fully understanding their financial rights in Islam, including the right to *mahr*, three were women born into Islam but just not properly educated about their financial rights.[8] These three study participants, Jenna, Maysa and Nadia, also happened to marry men who were not actively practicing Islam.

Violations Related to Nafaqah

Islamic law squarely places the responsibility of providing for women on the shoulders of men – it requires Muslim men to finance all the necessities of a woman's life including residence, food and drink, clothing, and—as most scholars rule today—medical needs.[9]

It is the religious obligation of a Muslim husband to guarantee this support, termed *nafaqah*, to his wife so long as the two are married, and in the case of women who are unmarried, this obligation of *nafaqah* falls upon a male family member, such as a father, brother or uncle.[10] If a woman (Muslim, Christian or Jewish) does not have a provider – a father, a brother, a husband etc. – the Islamic state should by default take over the responsibility of financially supporting her using its *zakāt* funds or funds from the state's treasury box (*bayt al-māl*).[11]

A wife divorced through a revocable divorce is also entitled to receive *nafaqah* up to the end of her three-month waiting period, at which point the couple may reconcile.[12] The *nafaqah* a man owes his wife, followed by the support he owes his children, takes precedence over *nafaqah* for all other family members, including a man's parents.

Keeping in mind the emphasis placed within Islamic law on this particular financial right of a wife, it is more than a little distressing to see that the majority of study participants reported that their husbands spectacularly failed to provide *nafaqah*. 15 of the 21 study participants found themselves spending either their parents' money or their own personal wealth – be it earnings, inheritance or some other source of wealth – to pay for housing, groceries, clothes, transportation, or medical needs for many years of married life. And in many of these cases, when the wives had exhausted all sources of wealth in an effort to cover their own living expenses, they had to borrow money to survive. The women in this study appeared to be no more aware of/educated about their financial right to *nafaqah* than they seem to have been of their right to *mahr*. The women I interviewed reported that the neglect of their right to *nafaqah* directly led them to experience stress, and,

Table 3: Payment of Nafaqah Received by Study Participants

Participant	Provision of Food to Standards (Y/N)	Provision of Clothing to Standards (Y/N)	Provision of House Help to Standards (Y/N)	Provision of Personal Hygiene Products to Standards (Y/N)	Provision of Medical Care to Standards (Y/N)	Provision of Transportation to Standards (Y/N)	Provision of Residence to Standards (Y/N)
1 Dana	N	N	N	Y	N	N	N
2 Sara	N	N	N	N	N	N	N
3 (1st) Nabila	N	N	N	Y	Y	N	Y
3 (2nd) Nabila	Y	N	N	N	Y	Y	Y
4 Aya	N	N	N	N	N	N	N
5 Jasmine	N	N	N	N	N	N	N
6 Sakina	Y	Y	N	Y	Y	Y	Y
7 Sophia	N	N	N	Y	Y	Y	Y
8 Farida	N	N	N		N	Y	N
9 Nermin	N	N	N	Y	N	N	N
10 (1st) Layla	Y	Y	N	Y	Y	Y	Y
10 (2nd) Layla	Y	Y	N	Y	Y	Y	Y

Participant	Provision of Food to Standards (Y/N)	Provision of Clothing to Standards (Y/N)	Provision of House Help to Standards (Y/N)	Provision of Personal Hygiene Products to Standards (Y/N)	Provision of Medical Care to Standards (Y/N)	Provision of Transportation to Standards (Y/N)	Provision of Residence to Standards (Y/N)
11 Rahma	N	N	N	N	N	N	Y
12 Jenna	N	N	N	Y	N	N	N
13 Suraya	Y	Y	N	Y	N	N	N
14 Amani	N	N	N	N	N	N	N
15 Suzzanne	N	N	N	N	Y	N	Y
16 Malak	Y	Y	Y	Y	Y	N	Y
17 Fareeha	Y	Y	Y	Y	Y	Y	Y
18 Tanya	N	N	N	Y	N	N	N
19 Maysa	Y	Y	N	N	N	Y	N
20 Ranya	N	N	N	N	N	N	N
21 Nadia	N	N	N	Y	Y	Y	Y

in some instances, even physical illness. Table 3 demonstrates the situation of these wives with regards to their *nafaqah* rights:

Food

15 of the total number of 21 study participants, astonishingly enough, reported that their husbands did not adequately provide food for them. For example, Amani recalled times when she and her children did not have enough food in the fridge or pantry to last even one full day and would subsist on "milk and cereal." Nabila recalls how penny-pinching her husband was when it came to food. The ways in which these women's husbands denied them this particular category of *nafaqah* and the excuses they offered for the neglect varied. Sara explained that her husband selected all the food for the household and did not permit her to request anything. "I cooked whatever he brought," she said. Nadia, on the other hand, recalled that her weekly allowance was too meager to meet her and her children's nutritional needs, but when she asked her husband to increase her allowance, he would curtly reply, "Not my problem." Farida was deprived of the bare necessity of drinking clean water and even shamed for asking this while residing in her husband's home country. She also reported craving foods during her many pregnancies that she had been accustomed to eating while living in the U.S. before marriage, her husband again and again refusing to purchase these foods because he deemed them too expensive. Jenna's husband cited her weight as being the reason why he curtailed her intake. When Suraya felt desperate for sufficient nourishment during her pregnancy, she often went to her parents' home to eat meals. The behavior of some of these

husbands and their actions depriving their wives of this type *nafaqah* becomes even more puzzling when they deprive their wives of using funds they themselves earned to buy food, as in Sara's and Jenna's case. Other wives, like Jasmine, always expected they would need to buy their own food. Across the board, we see that the men who failed to fulfill their wives' right to *nafaqah* generally nearly always failed to fulfill their right to adequate nourishment.

Residence

According to Islamic law, a husband is religiously mandated to provide financial support to his wife in the form of a safe, private and furnished residence that is comparable to the lifestyle to which she had been accustomed prior to marriage. While 72% of the study participants reported that their husbands, in one form or another, neglected the wives' right to *nafaqah*, 57%, or 12 of the 21 women, said their husbands specifically failed to provide adequate housing for them. The majority of this percentage, or 9 of the 12 women, recounted that either they or their parents partially or fully financed the couple's housing after marriage. For example, at the start of her marriage, Amani paid a significant amount (over $100,000) towards her new husband's house debt to protect him from having to pay interest. Nermin also dipped into her personal wealth, a large sum of money gifted to her by her father, to buy a home for her and her spouse, with her husband asking to ensure that the title of the house was in both their names. Nadia's father, seeing that his son-in-law, still a student, would not be able to give his daughter the sort of comfortable home she was accustomed to, bought the couple a condominium in both their names a few months into their marriage.

While some of these nine women found themselves or their parents financing the couples' home at the start of the marriage, others reported that even once their husbands began to earn enough to fully support the family, they still failed to provide a home for their wives. They would either allow their wives to languish in inadequate living conditions or pressure them to financially contribute to the cost of the home. In the case of Suraya, the newlyweds settled into the bride's parents' home after marriage, and when Suraya's husband did shift them into a rental apartment, he said he could not afford to furnish it, so the pair used empty, upturned cardboard boxes as tables and chairs. She recalled that she regularly escaped to her parents' home as a respite from the austere living conditions. Tanya experienced a similar disappointment. After their wedding, the couple moved into a condominium she had purchased prior to marriage. Once they began to grow their family and shifted into a larger apartment, her husband took care of all living expenses, including rent, but when Tanya began working full-time, he demanded that she chip in for half the rent. This arrangement persisted until an imam advised Tanya of her Islamic right to keep all her earnings for herself and her right over her husband that he be the one to fully finance their home.

Of the 52% of study participants whose husbands did not fulfill the wives' right to adequate housing, 5 women reported that their husbands neglected this right by not providing them with a private residence separate from either their husbands' families or from their own.[13] For example, after their wedding, Sakina's husband moved his new wife into a well-furnished home that was commensurate with the lifestyle she had been accustomed to prior to marriage, but she was taken aback to learn that her husband's mother was moving in with them from day one. In the case of Aya, once she had finally persuaded her husband that they should move out of her parents' home and into their own place, her mother-in-law immediately moved in with the couple without Aya's consent. Soon after, her husband's five siblings each took turns visiting the couple with their families in tow for two-month stretches, one coming after the other all year long. Rahma lost her Islamic right to privacy not because her husband insisted his family live with them, but rather because the couple was forced to reside with her husband's parents for most of the marriage. Her husband never managed to hold a steady job and to compensate for their son's laziness, his parents took on all financial responsibility for Rahma and the grandchildren. As for Amani, it is true that none of her husband's family lived with them but one can say her home was an open house, in which her husband's family felt free, by his consent, to drop in spontaneously and without notice; this left Amani with no privacy and continually exhausted.

There is yet another category of study participants who, because they had been employed and living independently prior to marriage, found that, in the eyes of their new husbands, this self-reliance seemed to negate their Islamic right to *nafaqah*, specifically housing. Of the two participants that experienced this happening to them upon marriage were two converts, Sara and Jasmine. In both cases, the husbands moved to America from overseas finding the convenience of an already established home along with provisions provided for them by their wives. Can the action of these husbands be defined as taking advantage of women of other faiths that were unaware of their *nafaqah* rights under Islam or was this just a coincidence? And if it was a coincidence, why did the situation of these women as the breadwinners not change for a long time after matrimony?

These women's status change from single to married did not in any way ease their financial burden, but rather they only saw their financial responsibilities burgeon once they became wives. In these cases, the husbands conveniently took the initiative to simply settle into their wives' established homes. For example, Jasmine's husband quickly moved into his new wife's fully-furnished home after marriage and thereby freed himself from the responsibility of providing a comfortable residence for his wife. It was almost as though he took it upon himself to switch the gender roles and their accompanying responsibilities set by Islamic law. Similarly, after marriage, Sara's husband automatically shifted into the house she had bought while single, and she continued to pay the mortgage and taxes for the home. In fact, even though he paid no portion of the home's monthly payments, he relentlessly pressured her to add his name to the house title and she ultimately capitulated.

Domestic Services

The Prophet ﷺ often performed daily household chores right alongside his wives. His wife ʿĀ'ishah ؓ recalled, "He ﷺ used to keep himself busy serving his family." She also recounted, "He ﷺ was like any human being, patching his garments, milking his sheep, and serving his own self."[14] Although it is a Sunnah, it is not mandatory for a Muslim husband to take on housework, and I found that nearly all the study participants' husbands did not. However, it *is* a Muslim husband's religious obligation – and thereby his wife's Islamic right – to provide his wife with domestic help. According to Islamic law, it is not her duty to cook, clean and serve her husband, and most scholars agree that if a wife does so, it is essentially a voluntary act of good will.[15] In fact, Musa Furber, a prominent contemporary Shāfiʿī scholar who delivers legal edicts (*fatwas*) explains, "The wife is entitled to wages for doing house chores – if she decides not to do [the chores] as an act of charity. Her refusal to do so is not an act of disobedience and he cannot withhold her [financial] support if she refuses."[16] When Fāṭimah ﵂, the daughter of the Prophet ﷺ, would take care of her home and husband out of a sense of love and appreciation, her father never defined this as Fāṭimah ﵂ performing a religious responsibility owed to her husband according to the Mālikī scholar Imam Ibn Baṭṭāl ﵀.[17] The Prophet ﷺ himself at times gifted women in the community with domestic help who would manage or assist in managing the household's day-to-day housework, and he encouraged his Companions to do the same.[18] The Islamic schools of jurisprudence point to such examples as evidence that a wife is not religiously mandated to cook, clean and perform household chores, and that she is entitled domestic assistance if she (1) is accustomed to receiving help, (2) when her husband can afford it, (3) and/or when his wife is in bad health; other scholars, such as Imam Ibn Ḥazm ﵀, ruled that a wife deserves house help as part of her *nafaqah* in all circumstances, even if, for instance she was never accustomed to it.[19] With respect to the scholars who rule that a wife should receive assistance at home in certain circumstances (such as when she was accustomed previously), the Ḥanafī, Shāfiʿī and Ḥanbalī schools agree that, generally, the wife is entitled to one assistant, while Imam Malik declared that if she is in need of more to relieve her burden, then more should be hired by her husband. Followers of these schools of thought such as the scholar Imam Abū Thawr ﷺ (170 AH), who belonged to the Shāfiʿī school of thought, and Imam Abū Yūsuf ﷺ (113 AH-182 AH), who belonged to the Ḥanafī school, ruled that the wife of a husband who has the means is entitled to not only one assistant or domestic helper but two, one to meet her indoor needs and one for outdoor chores.[20]

If applying Imam Ibn Ḥazm's ruling requiring a husband to hire domestic help to alleviate the burden sure to fall on a woman's shoulders, all 21 of the study participants were denied *nafaqah* in the form of domestic help. If the wives persisted in their requests for some form of help with the housework, the husbands often shamed them, disparaging them for shirking what the husbands considered were their wifely duties. Some women, such as Layla, took on carpentry and plumbing-related tasks, as their husbands refused to hire a professional to do the work. Even if we apply the more conservative legal opinion held by the majority of scholars, the women who were accustomed to having house help prior to marriage and whose husbands had the means to provide it, still did not receive this form of *nafaqah*. Of the 21 women, 11 would have been entitled to receive *nafaqah* under the more conservative and conditional rulings, yet their husbands still failed to provide the domestic support these women were unequivocally entitled to by any of the traditional scholars' standards. For example, prior to marriage, Sara held a job that paid a good salary, and lived in a spacious home with her children from her first marriage where she had house help. Despite knowing the comfortable lifestyle his wife had been accustomed to enjoying before they married, and possessing a fair amount of wealth himself (which she discovered later because he deliberately did not disclose his financial status to his wife), Sara's second husband still refused to pay for a nanny or cleaning service. Farida serves as another example. She came from an affluent family, but even once her husband began to make good money, he avoided hiring household help. His relatives stayed with the couple most of the year and his mother permanently lived with them, so when Farida, overwhelmed by the housework, requested that her husband, at the very least, ease her burden by sharing in the chores, he callously retorted, "This is your job." Years into the marriage, Farida's husband initiated divorce, but then offered reconciliation during the three-month waiting period. She accepted on condition that moving forward he assist her with housework, but despite his $250,000 salary at the time, he replied that she had to financially contribute to the household if he wanted her to help him with the dishes. At the time, Farida earned a fifth of his salary.

Out of the 21 wives (and 23 marriages since two participants married twice) only 6 were never employed during their entire marriage. 17 (81%) were employed, either full-time or part-time, during their married life. More specifically, in nine of the marriages, the wives worked full-time during the entire marriage. In four of the other marriages, the wives worked full-time during *most* of the marriages. In three of the marriages, the wives worked full-time during part of the marriage (e.g. Nabila's first marriage). Consequently, the majority of women I interviewed not only managed the cooking, cleaning, laundry, child care, and all other such household tasks, but they also either worked part-time or full-time outside of the home, as is common nowadays in the U.S. and other western countries. Additionally, some of these women fulfilled these demands within their marriages even while ill, as exemplified by Dana, a condition that all scholars agree warrants domestic assistance for the wife.[21] These women bore the weight of household duties twofold: by day, they shouldered the stress and responsibility of employment, only to return home in the evening to tend to domestic tasks— neither of which are mandated by Islamic law for wives. The mother's role as primary nurturer of her children is unquestionable according to Islamic law, as is her responsibility to safeguard her husband's belongings and meet his intimate needs when able (actually, a mutual right of both spouses towards one another), but 90% study participants reported that their husbands, whether religious or not, believed it was their wives' duty to cook, clean, and serve.[22] In fact, in addition, some of the husbands expected their wives to be in service of their mothers (as in Sakina's example) and of their entire families (as in the examples of Maysa, Aya and Amani).

Although cultural norms and traditions as well as more selfish exploitative tendencies are partly to blame for misconceptions about a wife's role, it is important to note that misinformation about Islam in Western countries is also a culprit.[23] For example, a widely-used manual written by Muslim scholars, translated and published in South Asian communities in the U.S. teaches that Islam requires a wife to take care of all household chores.[24] Note the following excerpt:

> The house should be kept neat and tidy. All bedding and laundry should be regularly cleaned and replaced in their pre-arranged places. To act only when he [the husband] comments is no big achievement. Success is to organize all domestic chores upon one's initiative without him hav-

> ing to prompt you. By relieving the husband from domestic worries, his heart and mind will become content and forever indebted to you.[25]

Haqqani, an academic researcher goes to explain why certain Muslim scholars teach such concept when it has no basis in Islamic texts and is not by any means truly Islamic:

> These differing views on the wife's roles and obligations according to male Muslim scholars can be attributed to the social and historical contexts in which these manuals were originally produced. They are clearly written for South Asian readers – wives – in that they address social phenomena, practices, and customs that are prevalent in South Asian cultures.[26]

Clothing and Personal Needs

Part of a Muslim husband's religious obligation to his wife when it comes to *nafaqah* is to provide her with adequate clothing and personal care items that meet the standard she was accustomed to enjoying before marriage. Of the 21 study participants, 16 wives, or 76%, did not receive their Islamic right to reasonable, adequate clothing. For instance, Amani reported that neither she nor her children had enough warm clothing to withstand the frigid winter weather. Farida, who had been accustomed to buying her wardrobe from higher-end boutiques, found that her husband would give her just enough to afford clothes from discount stores like Wal-Mart. Suzzanne also bought her and her children's clothing with her own earnings, noting, "[My husband] never spent a dollar on me," and adding, "I never allowed myself to ask."

But does she need to ask? She is entitled this right even in cases where she is able and willing to the cover the cost herself; rather, it is her husband's religious duty to step in and cover these costs. Disappointingly, the husbands of four other women demanded that their wives pay for their clothing out of their own incomes, sometimes as a condition for allowing these women to work. Of course, this is an evasion of the husbands' clear religious responsibility to provide for their wives' clothing needs.

When it came to providing their wives with sufficient personal care items (other than clothes such as hygiene products), 62% of the study participants, or 13 women out of the 21, reported that their husbands expected them to cover the costs from their own resources. These women used their earnings, inheritance, or whatever other source of personal wealth they could tap into, to tend to their hair care, skin care and hygiene needs. Once again, this arrangement violates Islamic law and is an eschewal of the Muslim husband's responsibility to his wife.

Medical Needs

While there does exist some disagreement on whether or not the husband has the religious obligation within *nafaqah* to pay for his wife's medical expenses, the majority of contemporary scholars rule that, based on the Qur'an and Prophetic traditions, this is, in fact, a wife's right upon her husband. 9 study participants, which constitutes 43% of the total 21 participants, partially paid for their medical care, and 4, or 19%, fully paid for their own medical expenses. Amani suffered from severe medical issues, yet despite her pain, her husband treated her dismissively and refused to pay for her treatment. Dana similarly recalled how she was in great pain after the birth of her first child as a result of TMJ (temporomandibular joint syndrome), but because her insurance did not cover the treatment for this rather serious condition, her husband downplayed her symptoms to save money until she finally collapsed. Even then, he left her to borrow thousands of dollars to pay for her recovery and, to add insult to injury, resented her for falling sick and not completing her work as his assistant. She said, "I felt abandoned, unloved, and mistreated." Maysa's husband showed no less of a callous attitude to his wife falling ill; when she developed a life threatening illness as a result of his infidelity and required surgery, he refused to pay for it.

Transportation

A vehicle is a necessary asset for both Americans and those living in most developed countries today. However, of the 21 study participants, 14 could not rely on their husbands for their transportation needs and had to purchase their own cars and/or fuel. This 66% figure includes women who paid entirely for their own car and gas bills, as well as women whose husbands had them share in the cost of their vehicles. Fareeda, accustomed to having her own car in the U.S. found herself car-less when she married and moved to her husband's home country. Asking for a car was out of the question, even when her family was stranded with no one to drive her anywhere, and despite him being able to afford it. Nadia's husband, who owned for himself an expensive and reliable vehicle, left his wife stranded in the middle of the road in her run-down car, refusing to give her a ride home— triggering Nadia's father to immediately send her $30,000 to purchase a new car.

Wives who are Pressured or Forced to Serve as Breadwinners

9 of the 21 women who participated in this study reported that their husbands either strongly encouraged or pushed or explicitly forced them to work outside the home during their marriages. These 43% of women were then required to cover their general living expenses. For instance, Sara earned nearly double what her husband did and he cited the disparity in their salaries as justification for his insistence that she serve as the main breadwinner for the household throughout the entire marriage. He set this as a ground rule from day one of the marriage, and to keep up with all the bills, Sara took on part-time work in addition to her full-time job. Jenna also found herself holding down two jobs to meet their living costs, but when she complained of exhaustion and suggested being a homemaker, her husband would threaten, "If you do, you will live as a beggar!" Dana's husband used his wife's strong organizational and administrative skill to benefit his work and forced her to work as his personal assistant without pay throughout their marriage. Amani, similarly, had no choice but to take care of her husband's business needs for no pay. Aya said, "He actually wanted me to work to bring home money." Suzzanne's husband encouraged her to work based on her interest; however, he assumed that she would use her money to spend on herself and his children. Three of the study participants reported that their husbands demanded they earn a paycheck even while pregnant to cover the additional costs of healthcare.

Of the 21 women participants, 71%, or 15 women in all, were either sole breadwinners or equal breadwinners alongside their husbands throughout their marriages. Some were in this position out of necessity; Rahma's husband was without a job for the first nine years of their marriage, and Maysa's husband did not serve as breadwinner while he sought an education and career. 4 women out of this 71% majority stood alongside their husbands as equal breadwinners in their households. However, they ultimately felt that because they were contributing just as much income to the home, their husbands should have consulted with them when spending large sums of money. Jenna said in frustration, "I want my spouse to consult with me as a respectful courtesy, or simply advise me if he is spending or gifting a very large amount of money, but as a rule he does not do this, so that causes mistrust as well as resentment." In Islam, a woman is regarded as an independent legal entity whose financial independence should be secured outside as well as inside matrimony. Therefore, when her paycheck is being spent from, it should be with her consent.[27] If her husband is struggling financially, it is her prerogative to assist him from her earnings as a form of charity (according to most scholars [but with conditions] with the exception of Imam Abū Ḥanīfah), or even as a portion of her *zakāt* if her spouse falls under the categories whom *zakāt* is due to.[28] If she had no choice but to spend from her earnings (as the sole or equal provider) while neither were her desire, then what she spent becomes a debt owed to her by her husband during his life or after he passes (separate from her inheritance portion).[29]

Interestingly, Rahma, the only woman who did not report living through significant financial insecurities during her married life, was the sole breadwinner for her family.

Wives not Given Highest Priority for Nafaqah

Islamic law prioritizes the *nafaqah* due to one's wife to such a degree that this financial support, followed by the support a man owes his children, takes precedence over *nafaqah* to all other family members, including a man's parents. 8 study participants, or 38% of the women in this study, reported that their husbands prioritized *nafaqah* for their parents, siblings, and children from previous marriages over *nafaqah* for the participants and their children – a behavior that is contrary to Islamic law. These wives unanimously felt both frustrated and diminished by always falling last in line when it came to financial support. For instance, Amani's husband would spend generously on his parents and siblings, but would neglect Amani and their children altogether, depriving them of food, clothing, house help, medical care, and college tuition. Farida's husband traveled for work for many years, exhausting himself to make money that would then fund his parents' living expenses and fund his brother's lavish wedding. Meanwhile, his wife and children would be left home penniless and having to fend for themselves. Farida said, "I felt my and my children's comfort did not matter. [The] priority was to save up for his family's needs." In quite a few cases, the study participants noted that their husbands would channel money to family living overseas and use what was left over to care for their immediate family. In fact, Sophia and Jenna were forced to send a portion of *their* own personal earnings to finance their husbands' parents and siblings' lifestyles.

Wives whose Husbands were Miserly or Frugal

When reflecting on their husbands' spending tendencies, many wives used one of two terms: miserly or frugal. Some added the qualifier "very" along with the term frugal.

Islam is a religion that places emphasis on the principle of balance in all aspects of life, including money matters and how to economically behave in the proper manner.[30] Overspending as well as underspending are both rejected in the Qur'an and Prophetic traditions. Either route can bring harm to its doer and those under his or her care. Unfortunately, a person who is frugal – as in, a simple person who deprives himself from life's pleasures – can sometimes fall on a spectrum that leans towards miserliness.

Those wives who uttered the term "miserly" about their husbands described penny-pinching behavior as in the example of Nabila who felt traumatized from having to beg for small things like fries from McDonald's every now and then. Descriptions of their husband's behavior indicated miserliness, as in the example of Sara, who, on her honeymoon, refused to buy her a bottle of water in the scorching heat, or, later, would remove the meat out of the sandwiches in the lunchboxes of her children from her first marriage and eat it himself.

9 of the 21 study participants— 43% — were married to husbands who were frugal to the point of being miserly toward their wives or children. For example, Jasmine reported that her husband typically wore the same thing over and over again, and would

not allow her to buy clothing unless she pressed him for it. Jenna mentioned that her husband still wore the suit he wore at their wedding 40 years ago to every formal evening event today, saying that his miserly ways made her lose respect and love toward him. Nadia said that if she were to purchase even a bottle of Tylenol and it went above her weekly allowance, its cost was taken out of her next week's allowance. She barely had enough to support her and her children.

Husbands who Claimed Poverty to Avoid Paying Nafaqah

3 of the 21 study participants, or 14%, reported that their husbands claimed poverty to avoid paying *nafaqah*. For example, Aya's husband was a college-educated business owner who earned an income comparable to that of his new wife's family income, but once his immigration documents were finalized, and he moved to the United States and into her parents' home, he alleged he was penniless. She was aware that he sold his business before shifting to the U.S., but did not know if, or why, he did not bring any of the profit from the sale with him. Aya provided for the family for many years while her husband had only occasional work in fast-food restaurants. In the case of Suraya, her husband always kept his money hidden from her and contributed the bare minimum required to support them during hard times. From day one of the marriage, his parents, out of disapproval of his choice of a bride, would not offer financial support, forcing her family to provide for the both of them abroad and in the U.S.. He took full advantage of this and kept any money from his petty jobs to himself so that his in-laws would cover their expenses. Upon finding out that his wife received a monthly check from the U.S. government

for her handicapped child, he tried to take the money, but she refused. He withheld her *nafaqah* money to pressure her to spend on the household using the child's disability income. Interestingly enough, Suraya's husband—who claimed he was impoverished—managed to marry not once or twice, but three times in his lifetime.

Wives Pressured to File a Khulʿ to Relinquish their Mahr and Nafaqah Rights

Two of the study participants' husbands refused to divorce them and instead pressured these women to file a *khulʿ*– in other words, to remove themselves from the marriage, and thereby, in keeping with Islamic law, relinquish their rights to *mahr* or some type of monetary amount. In the case of Sara, her husband returned from his native country with a new bride but refused to grant Sara an Islamic divorce. She would not allow her husband to hold her hostage in the marriage, however. She presented proof to the community imam of her earnings and explained how she had essentially been the provider for the family from the very beginning of the marriage. Seeing that Sara's husband had failed to fulfill her right to *nafaqah*, the imam granted her a divorce, not a *khulʿ*, and judged that her husband owed her $250,000 as compensation for the neglected *nafaqah*. Suraya put *khulʿ* into practice when she discovered that her husband was about to remarry. When her husband found out of her petition to remove herself from the marriage, he took it as a form of disgrace within his social setting overseas and was about to initiate a divorce himself. But he quickly backed off and let her pursue *khul'* after considering his retention of the *mahr* he gifted her.

Wives Treated as Nāshiz

It appears that three of the participants were presumed to be treated as *nāshiz* by their husbands at certain points in their marriages, a term some scholars interpret as meaning that she is so defiant that she loses her right to *nafaqah*. During these times, their husbands deprived them of financial support without offering any explanation, despite being obliged to do so based on the command in verse 4:34 of the Qur'an to, "advise them." If Amani disagreed with her husband, he accused her of being disobedient (which some might translate as being *nushūz*), subsequently restricting or withholding his wife's weekly allowance, including a meager grocery budget, as punishment. Amani did not realize the purpose behind his label, but repeatedly said, "He seems to be punishing me for answering back" or "He's not pleased with how my mother raised me so it appears that he intends to raise me all over again!" Layla's first husband similarly used her *nafaqah* as a weapon, but in her case, he identified her as *nāshiz* because he accused her of committing what we previously discussed as acts of "pre-adultery." She, like Amani, would not be told the reason for her denial of *nafaqah*. Layla's first husband's accusation was based on pure suspicion, but he stopped providing her with any financial support altogether. This was, of course, the last straw for her—she had tolerated her husband's miserly behavior until the day he falsely and without any evidence or basis accused her of cheating on him, and it was at this point that she decided she no longer wanted to carry on this marriage. Aya, unaware of why her husband refrained from intimate relations with her for years, was apparently treated as *nāshiz* for daring to refuse to relinquish her right to her property when the two were estate-planning and creating a will. Of course, even by the standards of those scholars who recognize *nāshiz,* a wife's disagreements with her husband or a man's mere baseless suspicion could not rise to the level of threatening the harmony or stability of the marriage. As previously discussed, many prominent scholars do not interpret primary texts to mean a man can withhold his fundamental marital job of financially providing for his wife at any point in time during a marriage—regardless of any perceived defiance in the union.

Violations Related to Making the Marriage Public: Payment for the Wedding Party (*Walīmah*)

According to Islamic law, the groom bears responsibility for the cost of the wedding party or *walīmah* that takes place following the contractual marital agreement and different from *nafaqah* obligation. However, in 6 of the 21 cases, or 29% of the studies, the wives or their parents fully paid for the wedding *walīmah* or shared the cost with the groom. For example, Ranya's father fully paid for an extravagant wedding party. When Nabila married for the first time, her father foot the bill for all wedding party expenses. When it came to her second marriage, she and her husband split the costs equally. 14% of study participants (as in the example Sophia) were deprived of any kind of wedding party (*walīmah*) for the purpose of secrecy or to avoid the expense, both of which contradict the Sunnah of the Prophet ﷺ. In addition to payment for the wedding *walīmah*, these participants were deprived of the Sunnah of having their marriage made public in accordance with the Shariah.

Violations Related to Wives' Personal Wealth

Islamic law grants women the right to keep and fully control their own wealth – be it in the form of income, inheritance, gifts, or property.[31] However, this study revealed that the majority of husbands, whether out of ignorance, avarice or a desire for control, failed to honor this basic right of their wives. One of the ways in which the husbands would trample upon this right would be to pressure or manipulate their wives into handing over a large chunk of their personal wealth during their marriages. 4 of the 21 study participants reported that their husbands employed this tactic. For example, Amani was pressured to let her husband attain over $100,000 from her inheritance money to pay off his house debt. Sara capitulated to her husband's relentless demands that she add his name to the title of the home she fully owned in order to placate her husband and avoid the constant arguments he would instigate on the matter. Aya recounted a similar experience. Her income had paid for the lion's share of the home the couple had bought, and she took on sole responsibility for the mortgage, also giving in to her husband's relentless pressure to include both their names on the house title. Years later, when they sold the home to fund the launch of a family business, she discovered that her husband had declared himself the sole owner of the business, leaving her out entirely. Nermin's parents gifted her with a substantial amount of money, and when she shared the news with her husband, he expected her to put the sum towards purchasing a house for the couple in both their names. She obliged out of a misplaced sense of duty to her husband.

Along with usurping control of their wives' personal wealth through pressure and emotional manipulation, husbands would encroach on their wives' wealth through the use of joint accounts. Many husbands would insist that the couple place their earnings in a joint account, which is an account that allows multiple account holders to claim its full ownership and have total control over it. Account holders can pay bills, spend, withdraw, or deposit without the consent of their partner or partners. Similarly, they can obtain a checkbook and debit card to access money as needed.[32] It is an account especially convenient for people who share living expenses such as a home mortgage, rent, groceries, clothing, car expenses and all general bills. What is problematic in this partnership, based on the stories of the women in this study, is that the husband— even when not raised Muslim— tends to exert ultimate control over the account. The wives in the stories I uncovered had to get permission or account for the money they spent, despite using their own income, inheritance, or gifted wealth, which was deposited into the joint account they also fully owned. Those who voiced objections or refused to comply were met with a range of threats, including divorce.

A joint account, practically speaking, functions differently in a Muslim household than other American ones. In more mainstream American culture, it is the norm for spouses to have joint accounts and for the wife's personal income to be spent on the household in a way equal to her spouse's. In Islam, however, a woman is never required to contribute her personal income or wealth to living expenses, and her husband bears complete responsibility for household expenses.

Several working women in this study indicated that their paychecks were directly deposited into a joint checking account from which they could only spend with their husband's permission. As quoted by Sophia:

> He tells me if I were to route my paycheck to my own account, he will hold me responsible to pay half of our bills and I would get nothing of "his" retirement nest egg... I don't have control over the money I make. It goes into an account that he has control of. I don't have access to it. I'm simply a depositor. I feel such shame that I allow myself to be manipulated like this, but his threats to me keep me from doing anything about it.

In Sara's case, she was highly educated, holding a high-paying position managing hundreds of employees. Yet while honored at her workplace, she was financially humiliated in her home – to the point where she was unable to spend from her own paycheck on her children from a previous marriage. She had no control over her paycheck, which the husband required to be directly deposited into their joint account from which she was not permitted to spend except for a small allowance he gave her. When Nabila's children grew up, her husband finally accepted her ongoing request to work but on one condition – that her paycheck be directly deposited into their joint account.

Another example is Dana, who reports that she was not permitted to keep any of the money she earned. In her own words, "I was shamed into sharing it from the very beginning of our marriage." In Nabila, Rahma and Jenna's cases, their husbands informed them that if they worked, they would have to pay for their own clothing and personal needs. As Rahma stated, "….it was my responsibility" because "[h]e felt I was making so much money."

Violations Related to Education

Women in this study who did not have a college degree upon marriage struggled to get back on their feet when financial problems occurred in the marriage and even more so after its dissolution. They shared with me that they felt worthless, unable to feed themselves or their children, such that their only outlet was to go back to school to guarantee financial security for themselves and their children. Five participants went back to college and/or completed their college educations or studied for certifications (as in Ranya's example) during their marriages to guarantee support and more comfortable lives for themselves and their children. For instance, Rahma completed certain licensing exams that extensively increased her earning potential.

But the road to continuing their education was, to say the least, not an easy one. Suraya fought her husband to complete high school after marriage and managed to do so, but when she tried to pursue an undergraduate degree, her husband would not allow it. She said, "He wanted to control everything." Maysa, who carried the burden of being the provider for her family while her husband was studying for a higher degree, dreamt of pursuing higher education and registered for college before she had to withdraw after receiving no support from her husband and father. When she finally made a meager income to pay for classes at a local college, she did so—earning a college degree and landing a well-paying job.

Others less fortunate were sternly discouraged, as in the example of Amani, who had struggled to obtain spousal support to continue her graduate studies in the U.S., her husband constantly making her feel incompetent, and keeping her busy serving him at home and abroad with no time to study. She said: "He wants[ed] me under his full control without a penny."

Violations of Inheritance Rights

Another major finding I've made pertains to the study participants' right to inheritance – particularly their husbands violation of these women's right to hold onto and use this money as they wanted. This study revealed that some husbands either coerced their wives into relinquishing control of their inheritance or into having to dip into their inheritance because their husbands failed to adequately provide for them. For example, Amani reported that her husband knew she came from a wealthy family and, by refusing to spend on even the most basic essentials – like winter clothes or a comfortable mattress – her husband forced her to use her inheritance for basic living expenses. Over the many decades of their married life, she exhausted all her family had given her, spending nearly $500,000 to provide for herself and her children until she had nothing left and resorted to borrowing money from friends and relatives. After Layla received inheritance, her husband insisted that she give him the money to invest for her but she pushed back, telling him he had no right to it.

Jenna, although in her sixties and desperate to retire with a cushion to lessen her financial burden, spent $20,000 from the $45,000 she inherited from her father on her son's college loans. When her mother died, Dana inherited $5,000, but her husband coerced her into depositing it into their joint account and then spent the entire sum to purchase an ostentatious handmade rug she was not interested in purchasing. Women who suffered a loss of their inheritance at the hands of their husbands said that moving forward they would place any inheritance or gifts given to them by family into private accounts and keep it for themselves.

Violations During and Following Divorce

Of the 21 women in this study, 8 were divorced and one was in the process of divorce. Most of the study participants whose marriages ended in divorce found that just as their financial rights under Islamic law had been violated during the course of the marriage, their financial rights upon divorce were also neglected. For example, when Sophia filed for divorce, she found herself and her young children empty-handed without any source of money, living in the streets when her husband, without her knowledge, leased their home out to others for a year to keep them out. Heartsick, Sophia said, "I was left feeling completely broken and scared. It was terrifying to feel I was starting my life completely over at nearly 50 years old." The moment Suraya was divorced while in her husband's home country, she lost access to her home and was unable to even pack up her clothes and valuables. She was traumatized from not being able to see her children again, including a baby who was still nursing.

To summarize, a woman married to a Muslim man has the following rights upon divorce: if not an owner or partial owner of their home, to remain in the marital home during the three month waiting period; to receive financial support (*nafaqah*) for the length of the three-month divorce waiting period; if pregnant at the time of a revocable or irrevocable divorce, she is to remain in her home and receive financial support until she gives birth; to receive monetary compensation for breastfeeding any babies from the marriage; to receive a permanent home for her and her children if unable to afford one for herself (according to the Ḥanafī and Mālikī schools of thought); to receive any deferred *mahr* or a *mahr* of her equal (*mahr al-mithl*) that has not yet been paid; to receive *mutʿah* or alimony (according to most scholars); to receive *nafaqat al-walad* or child support; to receive a separate *ujrat al-ḥaḍānah* or childcare expenses (according to some scholars); and to receive *kadd and siʿāyah* or a marital property settlement when entitled (according to the Mālikī school of thought).

In addition to not receiving their Islamic right to alimony, all participating divorcees did not receive their due right to some of the marital property (*kadd and siʿāyah*) as defined by scholars.[33] Of course, these *kadd and siʿāyah* payments are intended to compensate these wives for surpassing their prescribed roles in Islam when they contributed so substantially to their households and in support of their husband's career growth.[34] Other services provided by these wives included contributing all their wealth, as in the cases of Sara and Sophia, to their households. Farida's parents invested a substantial amount of money towards their son-in-law's training to complete an important program in his field, earning him a high salary. Dana worked as her husband's personal career assistant from day one of their marriage; not only did she prepare and/or take care of his work memoranda, bookkeeping, and accounting, but she mentored him while he prepared his work presentations and for meetings, assisting him tirelessly until he attained one of the highest-paying positions in his field, earning around $250,000 annually.

Four of the divorcées never received their deferred *mahr* upon divorce. Ranya never received her three-month divorce waiting period *nafaqah* or child support, or childcare for her children for an entire year until the civil divorce took place. Five divorcees in this study neither received their three-month divorce waiting period *nafaqah, nafaqah* for their children, or childcare expenses. Those amongst them who did not have a secure job prior to the divorce resorted to working any job they could find or asking their parents or adult employed children for money to help them pay basic living expenses. Nor did these women receive compensation for childcare or breastfeeding their babies post-divorce, as in the case of Layla's separation from her first husband. Although Ranya did receive some *nafaqah* support for her and her children when an Islamic divorce took place abroad, she received no marital or child support for the entire prior year while her legal divorce was pending in the U.S.— a time period that was never accounted for in the quasi-Islamic court. As for the child support the U.S. court ordered, it was only paid for a few months before her husband claimed he did not have the money to pay it.

It is important to note that the study participants who had been completely dependent on their husbands while married found themselves deeply financially insecure once the marriage ended, in part because of the prohibitive cost of divorce and in part due to their ex-husbands failing to fulfill their Islamic rights post-divorce. There is no denying that those who had been working while married fared better.

Farida's case yielded some unusual findings. The judge in the U.S. court granted her husband custody for her older son and, because her income was high, ruled that she pay her husband $1,000 a month for child support, a ruling that in every way violates a divorcee's Islamic financial rights because Islam places the burden of financially supporting the children on the father— regardless of how much a woman makes. Further, the husband appealed, asking that the court grant him all her valuable jewelry as he had been paying *zakāt* for it while married. He also asked the judge to include in the division of marital funds certain valuable purses she had recently purchased out of her own personal income, again contravening Islamic law since Islam would not consider such property marital.

In Layla's situation, after her divorce from her first husband, she returned to the U.S. with her children but did not receive child support for many years. As for Nadia, her alimony has been halted because her ex-husband filed a petition claiming poverty. She ultimately received no financial support post-divorce, neither child support, childcare or *mutʿah*. Unfortunately, it appears she will live the rest of her life in hundreds of thousands of dollars of debt to divorce attorneys. Ranya's ex-husband similarly claimed poverty to their U.S. judge, reducing her child support payment to $700 a month for all her children, leaving her with no alternative but to take on two jobs to make ends meet. Were it not for her parent's support to pay off her ex-husband the $140,000 that he bargained to transfer the marital home to her name, she and her children would not have had a home to return to.

Violations regarding Wives Not Born Muslim

Some non-Muslim born convert wives felt that when it came to finances, they were taken advantage of because they were not born Muslim. When Jenna converted to Islam, for instance, she found that her new faith echoed her understanding that the financial responsibility should be on the head of the household – either the father or husband. However, being born and raised American, her husband did not feel she was entitled instead to this right. Jenna resented this unjust attitude and felt exceedingly taken advantage of, being forced into a situation in which she bore the family's financial burden in order to keep the marriage intact:

> It was a big burden on me and still is stress on me, especially now that I would love to not work and enjoy my grandchildren, retire early, or just retire; I have been working very hard my whole life and feel that my heart and my persona or soul had been suffering from it for many years.

Similarly, Sophia felt cheated from the financial rights she had when marrying a Muslim man. Nothing was explained to her prior to the marriage, neither her rights nor his obligations towards her and her children to come. Once married, she was expected to just hand over her money to her husband and pay the bills. At first, and after learning bits and pieces about Islam, she thought this could be because she wasn't Muslim, but after she converted, nothing changed and she came to realize, "It was because I was American" (her husband was American through immigration, but not born and raised in the U.S.). She said, "Even after I converted, he never corrected the financial situation between us and continued to take my money." Sophia, throughout her entire married life, felt that not only she, but his own children, were treated as though the rights that Muslim children had did not apply to them. After their divorce was finalized and he was about to remarry a wife who was born Muslim from his hometown, he harshly told his small children that he didn't need them and that he was going to get remarried and have new children to replace them.

Islam requires Muslim men who marry women who are Christian or Jewish or converts to treat them with no less generosity than wives born into Islam. There are a growing number of Muslim reverts in western countries, and a violation of this kind is extremely serious and needs to be addressed by Muslim scholars today so that they educate and reprimand Muslim men who behave in this un-Islamic manner.

Understanding the Physical, Psychological and Social Ramifications of Financial Rights Violations for Women

Islam elevates marriage and the role of a wife to a position of dignity. It is therefore understandable that when a woman's financial rights as a wife are violated, the aftereffects she experiences can be deep and life-altering. This study revealed that these ripple effects span her physical health, her psychological well-being and her social status. Table 4 provides a detailed breakdown of the impact of financial deprivation on these wives, based on both their reported experiences and beliefs:

Table 4. Impact of Financial Deprivation on Study Wives

1 Dana	Y	Y	Y	N	N
2 Sara	Y	Y	Y	Y	Y
3 Nabila (1)	N	Y	Y	Y	Y
4 Aya	N	Y	Y	Y	Y
5 Jasmine	N	N	N	N	N
6 Sakina	N	Y	Y	Y	Y
7 Sophia	N	Y	Y	Y	Y
8 Farida	Y	Y	Y	Y	Y
9 Nermin	N	N	N	Y	N
10 Layla (1)	Y	Y	Y	Y	Y

10 Layla (2)	N	N	N	N	N
11 Rahma	N	N	N	N	N
12 Jenna	Y	Y	Y	Y	Y
13 Suraya	Y	Y	N	Y	N
14 Amani	Y	Y	Y	Y	Y
15 Suzzanne	N	N	N	N	Y
16 Malak	N	N	N	N	Y
17 Fareeha	Y	N	Y	Y	Y
18 Tanya	N	N	N	Y	N
19 Maysa	Y	Y	Y	Y	Y
20 Ranya	N	Y	N	N	N
21 Nadia	Y	Y	Y	Y	Y

Physical Effects

9 of the 21 study participants, or 43%, reported that the neglect of their financial rights within their marriages directly damaged their physical health.[35] Amani's husband forced her to sleep on a sunken mattress or on the floor, neither of which offered her proper lumbar support, leaving her with severe backaches. Later when she had a serious injury that required an MRI, her husband expected her to pay for it, knowing full well she had no income stream. Another example is that of Sara; during their honeymoon (which she paid for), he denied her even a bottle of water to quench her thirst, despite the soaring high temperatures, having her resort to sucking on water wipes to quench her thirst. Layla's second husband provided her with food and drink, but curtailed how much she consumed; in fact, when his mother complained about her, he locked his wife in the house for three months with hardly any food to eat, leaving her hungry and fatigued. Similarly, Suraya, deprived of food while pregnant, often had to visit her parents' home for nourishment. Upon the birth of her child, Dana, who was denied house help during her final weeks of pregnancy, was diagnosed with a stress-induced joint disorder that caused her chronic pain.

Physical Effects Stemming from Exterior Responsibilities

According to Islamic law, it is improper for a husband to ask his wife to perform outdoor labor, such as mowing the lawn, gardening, or snow blowing. Some traditions indicate that upon marrying his daughter Fāṭimah to Ali, the Prophet ﷺ divided the duties between Fāṭimah and Ali, ensuring Ali was doing the exterior work.[36] Jurist Al-Kāsānī clarified that this did not mean that

Fāṭimah was obligated to take on cooking and housework duties. To clarify the type of work Fāṭimah ﷺ would have taken on, a wife shouldered the responsibility to raise her children as good Muslims, a duty that requires time and much endurance on her part. As for other duties, the classical schools of thought, with some conditions, considered domestic chores voluntary, based on the Words of Allah, "Live with them [your wives] in kindness."[37] It is also important to recall Imam Ibn Ḥazm's statement emphasizing the wife's role as her husband's companion rather than a household servant—a perception that regrettably prevails in contemporary times. When some Muslim men object to scholars that many of the female Companions did serve their husbands, these scholars clarified that such actions were voluntary choices made by those women, not obligations imposed by Islam.[38]

7 of the 21 study participants reported that their husbands had them doing yard work, shoveling snow, or completing tasks related to carpentry or mechanics. Nermin for instance was expected to shovel snow on their property while pregnant. Layla and Maysa both took on the role of being a handyman in their homes, taking on different tasks like renovating the floors or serving as carpenters, mechanics, and plumbers, since their husbands refused to hire professionals. These chores took a toll on the physical health of these women.

Psychological Outcomes

Psychological damage is often more lasting and insidious than physical pain. 14 of the 21 participants, or 67%, reported experiencing post-traumatic stress disorder (PTSD), anxiety, and debilitating depression as a consequence of their loss of *nafaqah*.[39] Amani, summed up her state as follows, "My physical, emotional, as well as mental health, is pretty bad. Anxiety, however, hit me more than depression." She also reported that her children, who witnessed and themselves experienced their father's financial abuse, also battle with depression and anxiety.

When she tried to improve the quality of her and her children's life by pursuing higher education hoping that she may someday work outside the home and earn her own money, she was demoralized by her husband's persistence that she was unqualified to earn a degree.

Sara's intelligence was ridiculed when she was brainwashed to feel unfit to wisely spend from her own earnings, and thus lost that privilege, being called "stupid" by her husband until she lost confidence and started to believe it, despite being a reputable leader at work. Nabila, deprived from any domestic help, took on the role of a housemaid for her husband and children, cleaning, doing laundry, and cooking with minimal groceries, only to hear belittling remarks when he returned from work such as, "What have you been doing all day – nothing!" Nabila described the miserliness of her first husband as making her life a "living hell" over the course of their marriage. However, she considers the most devastating emotional blow to be when her husband deprived her of having custody of her young children when he took them, all of whom were under 11-years-old, back to his native country, Nabila then not seeing them until years later when they had reached adulthood. Sakina's courteous nature never allowed her to ask her husband to hire help to care for his elderly mother, but her ongoing cries to him from the workload she shouldered never caused him to offer this as an outlet to relieve her grievance and anxiety. As for Sophia, after the divorce, she still seeks therapy to heal from what she endured. She said, "The financial abuse – part of the overall abuse – made me feel incredibly anxious. The effects of living in a marriage like this are precisely the same as someone who suffered long term trauma from a war. You go through a similar PTSD."

Examples of the psychological battering that these women endured are abundant. Nadia lived in fear of her husband's retaliation, both in the form of verbal and physical abuse, if she ever upset him by confronting him over his lack of financial support. These decades of abuse have left Nadia under the care of psychiatrists, dependent on antidepressants and anxiety medication—despite not having a prior or family history of anxiety or depression. Suraya's husband also left behind a deeply traumatized woman in the wake of his financial neglect. She cannot erase from memory the hunger pains or the many times he threw her out of the house. He decimated her confidence and sense of self-worth, "He drove me to feel less than human, I hated myself." Her lingering anxiety has led her to distrust people, and she tends to isolate herself from society. "It's been years, but still I am a prisoner," she says. During the final weeks of her pregnancy, Dana, under stress to perform her expected routine duties, pleaded with her husband to hire house help, but since the matter had to do with money, she was left unheard and upon delivery of her child, she was diagnosed with temporomandibular joint disorder, a condition that left her in chronic pain for the rest of her life. Dana tried to cope with the damage her husband's financial abuse has wrought on her psyche and personality by spending tens of thousands of dollars of her own money on therapy. She would sneak out surreptitiously to meet with her counselor because if her husband discovered she was spending money on her healing, he would have been enraged.

Seven of these wives said they experienced financial humiliation during marriage. For example, during disagreements or fights, Amani's husband threatened to withhold her weekly spending money and take her credit cards.[40] Layla, in her first marriage, was given $85 to spend for an entire month while living in a foreign country. She reports feeling unworthy, saying that she was told, "That's all you deserve, a home and food, that's it!"

On the flip side, study participants who were able to gain some financial independence freed themselves to some degree from their husband's financial abuse, reporting feeling liberated, as though a crushing weight had been lifted off of their minds and spirits. Tanya expressed that she had never felt happier than when she achieved her own financial freedom by working and asserting her right to keep her paychecks for herself.

Relationship Outcomes

It seems inevitable that if a violation of a woman's financial rights would precipitate psychological damage, it would also impair the relationship between husband and wife, as well as between her and her spouse and their children. Of the 21 study participants, 15, or 71%, indicated that the lack of financial security impacted their internal familial relationships.[41] For example, Sakina's husband denied her right to a private home – a right that falls under the umbrella of *nafaqah* – by having his mother live with them from day one of the marriage. Sakina reports that she served her mother-in-law all her married life without any choice in the matter, which fostered feelings of resentment towards her husband. The bitterness manifested itself in angry, abrasive communication between the couple. The lack of privacy also resulted in a diminished quality time between Sakina and her husband, as well as between the parents and their children. Another example is that of Amina, whose long-life financial deprivation and humiliation tore apart the unity of her family and created distance, not only between her and her husband, but—as she reports— between her and her own children. As for Nabila, her (first) husband's parsimonious quality of holding back from spending money on her and her children made her lose respect and any love she had towards him, such that she was willing to do anything to be relieved from her marriage, going so far as to sign away all of her financial rights and, ultimately, lose custody of her children.

Studies by a Rutgers University research team on violence against women and children revealed that wives who bore and raised children while living in an economically abusive relationship have a negative effect on their children by the age of five. Associate Professor Postmus said, "It's possible that having a partner control access to money or preventing independence through work or school may have a lasting impact on women's mental health, and feelings of disempowerment may force mothers to resort to spanking as a parenting tactic."[42] Ranya appears to serve as an example of this dynamic. She played the role of the breadwinner, as well as homemaker for the family, and these demands exhausted her patience so that she found herself often shouting at her children. She reflects that her children, especially her teenaged son, in turn, often reciprocated with disrespect. Amani, on the other hand, felt humiliated in front of her children as a result of the financial abuse. From a young age, her children witnessed their mother begging their father for dire necessities like food, clothing or medical treatment; at times, he handed over the household allowance to the children, leaving her to ask them for money which she felt belittled her in their eyes.

Study participants Amani and Aya, who had the courage to stand up for their financial rights, were labeled greedy and money hungry by both their husbands and in-laws. They reported that their children lost respect for them after repeatedly hearing consistent derogatory accusations against their mother's characters.

12 of the 21 total participants, or 57%, reported that the neglect of their financial rights created significant communication gaps between themselves and their spouses. Layla said that the mental pressure her first husband put her through was so bad that to get away from him, she would at times go into a dark room to hide and read. Layla also noted that the very frugal nature of her second husband changed how much she was willing to do for him.

Separation and Divorce

Out of the 21 wives interviewed including 2 married twice, 8 of them were divorced; 2 separated, and 1 in the process of divorce.[43] Rahma is only separated, yet carries the sole responsibility of financially providing for herself and her children; the father's role is limited to making friendly visitations to his children twice a week. When these participants were asked the primary reason for their separation or divorce, all 10 women cited financial abuse as the culprit.

Decision-Making

5 of the 21 study participants were not allowed to make any financial decisions whatsoever in their households, and 3 were limited to making minor financial decisions such as the purchase of groceries, children's clothing and house supplies. Only 2 study participants were given the agency to make major household financial decisions such as purchasing appliances or furniture, one being the sole breadwinner. Interestingly, the participant who was the sole breadwinner reported that it was her husband who wanted her to carry all the responsibility and although she felt empowered, she wished he would help sometimes.

Social Outcomes

12 (57%) of the 21 participants stated that financial abuse and insecurity affected their ability to be socially active or contribute to society.[44] For instance, Amani explained that the deprivation and poverty she experienced in her marriage kept her in a state of social paralysis. The chronic physical illnesses and the psychological trauma engendered by what she deemed as financial abuse barred her from taking on many social service projects she hoped to pursue, like opening an Islamic school for children and teaching proper Qur'an recitation (*tajwīd*) at religious centers in her community. Aya's added responsibility to care for her mother-in-law reduced her opportunities to be involved in the community. Sara distanced herself from friends because she was unable to

spend on the social outings and gifts that normally anchor these relationships. Instead, she focused her energy on volunteering at her children's school and other social activities that did not require her to spend money. Layla also distanced herself from friends, but she cited the depression triggered by the financial abuse as the catalyst for her social isolation. "I kept up with close friends on the phone, but didn't feel like going out." Suraya said the lingering anxiety from the financial abuse she endured led her to distrust people, and she tends to isolate herself from society. And while Sakina was well provided for, her coerced, unpaid burden to be the caretaker of her mother in law throughout her entire married life eliminated any chance of her being socially active in her community, a matter that could have been avoided if her husband hired a cleaning service and homecare for his elderly mother.

Several study participants reported that financial abuse resulted in yet another kind of limitation to their social life and contribution. If a Muslim husband fails to financially support his wife and meet her needs, she—according to scholars— has every right to step out of the home and earn a living. However, many of the study participants' husbands, who did not honor their wives' right to *nafaqah*, explicitly prohibited their wives from working, even after their children had become independent. In doing so, they not only barred their wives from earning a living, but also from using their education and/or skill to add value to society and cultivate relationships outside of the home.

Yet another social consequence of the financial abuse was that the study participants felt unable to support charitable causes of their choosing. For example, whenever Sophia wanted to make a charitable donation, her husband would be adamant that their savings were reserved for his relatives overseas. "There were many times I wanted to give to people in need, but he would always say no, as that would be charity or *ṣadaqah* we could give his family. He controlled all of those decisions."

Shortcomings of Islamic Institutions in Providing Assistance

This study revealed a persistent failure of *masjids* and other Islamic organizations to step up and support women who sought help for the financial abuse they endured at the hands of their husbands. Echoing the findings of other studies, here too we see that in instances where the study participants were seeking a divorce on the basis of a violation of their financial rights, they found many imams particularly unhelpful.[45] Dana, desperate for assistance upon divorce, went to the community imam and told him her story and the financial torture she endured from her husband, but found he was not trained to address women going through a trauma of this kind. She said, "They only know about their culture but nothing about mainstream Islam in America." She felt divorce to them was "like dirty water." Suraya, after facing financial difficulties and unbearable living conditions throughout her married life, found herself penniless with no education nor work experience to find a decent job upon divorce. When she reached out to her community *masjid* thinking she might be eligible for portion of *zakāt*, they could not offer her much help. "It's a terrible system," she said, "They should help women become independent – for instance, offer women ways to generate income; ways to become interns in a business – but they don't do any of that!"

It's a shame that when Malak (a widow with small children) contacted United Health Care for assistance, they redirected her back to her local mosque. When she explained that they could not help, they took it upon themselves to contact the mosque, urging them to stand by those in need in their own communities. Only then did the mosque offer her assistance, which only lasted for one month.

Wives who Were Content in Matrimony

A balanced discussion requires that we mention the study participants who experienced happiness within matrimony. Of the 21 women, 8 reported being content with their married lives. 2 wives were unhappy, and 13 reported not merely being unhappy, but suffering deeply. It is important to note that the women who felt content had some form of financial security; they were not completely financially dependent on their husbands. But rather had an independent source of wealth, either through employment, parental assistance, or inheritance (of note, *mahr* did not appear to play a role in the financial security of these independent women).

Among the study participants, Suzzanne appeared most content. She took a proactive approach to financial matters in her marriage, establishing a separate bank account at the beginning of her marriage and setting ground rules that aligned with her rights under Islamic law. She also specified in her marriage contract that she would have the freedom to work full-time and use her earnings as she wished, which, once again, is her right in line with Islamic doctrine. Her husband agreed and even assisted her by employing her in his business. Her husband gave her space to fulfill her professional goals, as well as her charitable work, and did not monitor how she spent her personal wealth. On her own accord she insisted on using her own money to buy her clothes and personal care items but acknowledged that had she asked her husband to pay for these expenses, he would have agreed. Suzzanne is now a widow, but is financially secure and managing her own business, which her husband helped her build from the start of the marriage. Her strong physical and mental health appears to be a reflection of her happiness with her husband and in her marriage.

Another wife who reported being content with her marriage is Fareeha. She too worked and enjoyed a separate bank account. Her husband paid for all living expenses, and if he ever discovered that she had dipped into her own account to cover their needs, he would transfer the exact dollar amount back into her account. Her single complaint was that she wishes she could simply be a homemaker, but felt compelled to work in order to secure health insurance for the family. Her husband also encourages her to work and hold on to her earnings as a form of security for herself and their children in the event that something happens to him.

Notably, the three wives in this study who set financial conditions in their marital contracts, similar to the requirements delineated in what is called a prenuptial agreement in the U.S., found that spelling out these prerequisites worked in their favor. While most of the the requirements these women established in their marriage contracts are their God-given financial rights according to Islamic law, it seems that making it a point to specifically articulate them in the marriage contract helped to assure that certain particular rights would not be violated. Although she suffered in other financial aspects of her marriage, Sara's guardian set a condition that guaranteed all wealth the bride had accumulated prior to the marriage would remain hers alone. Nermin's father set the condition in the marriage contract that one-third of his daughter's paycheck would be placed in her private bank account and she could do with it as she pleased. Suzzanne set the condition in her contract to have the freedom to work full-time and that the money she earns was hers alone.

The Women's Financial State Compared with the Wives of the Prophet ﷺ

In describing the Prophet ﷺ, the Companion Ibn ʿAbbās ﵄ said, "Allah's Messenger ﷺ was the most generous person, even more generous than the strong uncontrollable wind (in readiness and haste to do charitable deeds)."[46] So then how did the study participants' financial conditions compare with those of the wives of a man who was the paragon of generosity and charity?

Based on the findings and the reports of the women I studied, only a few Muslim-American husbands ultimately adhered to the example of the Prophet ﷺ with regard to honoring and protecting the financial rights of their wives. On the contrary, most husbands actively stripped away many of those rights. For example, the wives of the Prophet ﷺ saw their right to *mahr* treated with the utmost priority and expediency. Each received a *mahr* amount that was considered generous during the time of the Prophet ﷺ.[47] When he married older women, widows or women with children from previous marriages, as in the cases of Umm Salamah ﵂ and

Umm Ḥabībah ﷺ, he gave them a *mahr* no less than those who had never been married.[48] Meanwhile certain study participants, such as Jasmine, who were older than the men they married or who had children from a prior marriage, were made to feel ashamed to even ask for their marital gift. Similarly when Sara entered matrimony with children from a previous marriage, her husband shamed her, offering her only 25 cents.

Each of the wives of the Prophet ﷺ received her *mahr* prior to moving into her husband's home or prior to consummation; thus, the marital gift fulfilled its objective of honoring and providing the wives with financial security from the start of the union. Most study participants, on the other hand, found that their husbands grossly neglected their right to *mahr*. In many cases the husbands knowingly offered a paltry *mahr* that was more symbolic than sincere. They merely satisfied custom by verbally settling upon an amount or recording the value in the contract, but unless the imam performing the ceremony pressed for the *mahr* to be paid right then or at a designated later date, the matter was oftentimes brushed under the rug with husbands bristling at their wives bringing it up during their married life. Other study participants' husbands pledged, at the time of marriage, a *mahr* amount beyond their means, and subsequently pressured their wives to relieve them from the obligation. The Prophet ﷺ forbade this practice, requiring every man stand by his covenant. In fact, on one occasion a man who promised an Anṣārī woman a larger *mahr* than he could deliver asked for the assistance of the Prophet ﷺ in paying it off.[49] The Prophet ﷺ gently reprimanded him for exaggerating his means and then sent him on a mission that would help him earn what he needed to meet the *mahr* amount he had promised.[50]

Interestingly, although the four *awāqs* this man had agreed to give his wife proved a burdensome amount for him, the Prophet ﷺ actually gifted his wives up to 12.5 *awāqs*, but it was an amount he could afford.[51] The example set by the Prophet ﷺ thus illustrates that a husband must always be generous but never promise beyond his means.

Most study participants' husband also failed to adhere to the example of the Prophet ﷺ when it came to respecting their wives' personal wealth. He never interfered in how his wives managed their possessions; in fact, oftentimes they would dispense of their jewelry or clothing and he would find out after the fact. Those who had their own businesses, such as his first wife Khadījah ؓ, kept their earnings entirely for themselves.[52] Meanwhile, most husbands of the study's participants usurped or in some way controlled their partner's inheritance, paychecks, possessions, or gifts from family. They demanded that if their wives were employed, they would spend on the household – whether on the mortgage, rent, utilities, groceries, clothes, travel expenses, or medical needs. Some even expected that wives take charge of all the expenses related to the children's needs, such as school supplies and activities. These women did not have the option of holding on to their compensation from work and leaning on the income as a form of security during hard times or to use towards leisure and pleasure. Some historians erroneously presume that Khadījah ؓ – the wife of the Prophet ﷺ – used her ample wealth to take care of household expenses.[53] However, this is incorrect and baseless; the Messenger ﷺ was indeed the *qawwām* of his home, and neither Khadījah ؓ nor any of his other wives ever spent their personal wealth on living expenses.[54]

As demonstrated by Hadith, when it came to *nafaqah*, the Prophet ﷺ spent his own personal earnings on a wedding party (*walīmah*), private residence, and living expenses for each of his wives. He ﷺ purchased the property on which his mosque (*masjid*) was built and designated separate portions of it for each of his wives' living quarters. He even gave each wife's home to her.[55] He furnished their homes in an appropriate manner and provided them with all necessary supplies, and he himself would assist in household chores. The Prophet ﷺ used profits from the ongoing sale of palm trees on his properties to ensure that every wife received a satisfactory amount of financial support for the entire year.[56] His wives enjoyed a comfortable, safe, and private lifestyle where all their needs were met, so that they never ran in desperation to their parents for relief or aid.[57] In comparison, many men in this study failed, as a result of miserliness or indolence, to fulfill the various elements of the *nafaqah* owed to their wives, denying their partners the right to a private home, a home that met their standards, proper furniture, security, house help, adequate clothing, proper nourishment, and even medical care.[58]

The majority of study participants' husbands did not spend on their wives' personal essentials, especially if their wives were employed, as in the examples of Nabila, Rahma and Jenna. Amani, who was not earning an income, was accustomed in her native country to having regular appointments at the hair salon, but after marriage, her husband, even though he could easily afford it, labeled this an unnecessary extravagance. In contrast, tradition shows the wives of the Prophet ﷺ enjoyed having their hair styled professionally. In 7th Century Arabia, his ﷺ wife Umm Salamah ؓ began relaying a Hadith by recounting when her hair was being brushed by a servant.[59]

The financial support of the Prophet ﷺ extended beyond his wives to their previously conceived children as in the examples of Umm Salamah ﷺ who had previously been widowed with four children and Umm Ḥabībah ﷺ whom upon marrying the Messenger ﷺ, had one child. He once singled out Abū Zarʿ as being among the best of husbands because of his generosity to his wife and her two children from a previous marriage.[60] Some study participants, on the other hand, lamented that their husbands inflicted their miserliness onto their stepchildren, depriving them of essentials like food, drink, clothing, a warm home when it was cold outside and even hot water for bathing. Some study participants' husbands not only withheld *nafaqah* from their wives and children, but redirected it towards their parents and siblings, when the example set by the Prophet ﷺ was to always give first priority to his wives and children over any extended family or friends.[61] The Prophet ﷺ warned, "It is enough sin for a person to hold back what's due for the one whose provision is in his hand."[62] In fact, he ﷺ took great measures to guarantee his wives and children financial protection not only during his life, but even after his death.[63] When he died, the Prophet ﷺ left his wives and children farmland in a form of a *waqf*, meaning the property could never be sold, and each wife would continually receive from its produce her entire life.[64]

If we consider the way in which the wives of the Prophet ﷺ poured their energy into benefiting their communities, it becomes evident that it was, in part, their financial security that gave them the means and self-confidence to do so. As the select few who experienced married life with the Prophet ﷺ and were in closest proximity to him in his day-to-day life, it was his wives who taught the people a large portion of the Sunnah of the Prophet ﷺ.[65] They participated in elections, politics, and even battles. They joined in the communal and funeral prayers in the Mosque of the Prophet ﷺ, devoted time to worshiping in seclusion during the last 10 days and nights of the holy month of Ramadan, made the pilgrimage to the House of God along with countless other Muslim men and women, and joined in the community's wedding celebrations and Eid festivities.[66] In fact, ʿĀ'ishah ؓ used to lend a beautiful but expensive party dress of hers to women for such special events.[67] Along with rejoicing on these happy occasions with their community members, the wives of the Prophet ﷺ who possessed substantial personal wealth channeled this wealth towards providing social services, such as treating the ill or housing guests visiting the city.[68] One cannot compare this level of participation and service to the wives in this study, many of whom felt cut off from their communities due to their financial insecurity, unable to use their time, energy and potential to contribute to society. Amani, for example, was proficient in the Qur'an and Prophetic traditions, and aspired to open an Islamic school, but the financial abuse she endured robbed her of her health, confidence, and ambition.

Perhaps the most heartbreaking case illustrating the consequences of abuse – financial, verbal, and physical – is that of Dana. Her Muslim husband's violation of nearly all her rights as a wife traumatized her to such a degree that she abandoned Islam altogether. Failing to fulfill the God-given rights of one's fellow man or woman is to commit a sin against that soul, and invariably each human will have to answer for the ways in which he oppressed others.

Reasons for Financial Abuse

After examining the various ways in which so many of the study participants' husbands neglected their wives' financial rights, the obvious question arises – what are the reasons for this failure?

First, it appears that some men used Islam to subordinate their wives, either by claiming that they were following the Shariah or by citing Qur'anic verses and Prophetic traditions, when in truth these men were acting upon personal whim, cultural beliefs and customs incompatible with Islam.[69] Aya's story offers an example of one such instance. Her earnings had paid for the purchase of the family business; to her surprise, her husband declared that he was going to follow the Sunnah of the Prophet ﷺ when drawing up a will. Aya quickly discovered that he intended to use the will to name himself as the sole owner of all the family's wealth, including the business her earnings financed. The will was her husband's attempt to manipulate a Sunnah to oust his wife from her rightful share of the family wealth.

This study revealed that in many of the instances where husbands oppressed the participants, these men would trot out certain words or verses from the Qur'an to justify the abuse. The words *ṭāʿah* (obedience) and *qawwām* (protector and provider), which appear in the Qur'anic verse 4:34, were often cited and misused by some of the men in this study to financially abuse their wives. Husbands would claim that because they are leaders of the household to whom wives must show blind "obedience," their wives must do as they are told without question or argument. In Sara's case, this involved her depositing her paycheck into a bank account she was not permitted to access without her husband's permission. Her husband convinced her that in order to be a good and loving Muslim wife, she must relinquish all control over her earnings to him. Similarly, Nabila's husband made her put her earnings in a joint bank account and informed her that he was in charge of all finances. Amina's husband refused to buy her a new mattress to alleviate her severe back pain during her first pregnancy and would not allow her to purchase one herself, because he claimed that she was not supposed to purchase items for the house. Sophia was forced to put her paychecks into her husband's bank account, and if she showed discomfort or was opposed to obeying him, she said he would "stonewall, degrade, berate and bully me into compliance, saying 'I am the man of the house and this is how it's going to be.'" Suraya's husband would not permit her to leave the home and earn a living to feed herself and her children, even though he was not adequately providing for them. According to scholars of *fiqh*, once a man proves unable to support his wife, Islamic law allows her to provide for herself and she does not require the permission of her husband to do so. These men expected complete obedience to be their right, without recognizing that Allah ﷻ set limitations and conditions to what a husband can demand of his wife. For example, a husband's leadership role as the *qawwām* in the marriage is conditional upon him fulfilling his responsibilities to his wife and children; if he fails to do so, he is no longer in a position to demand anything, including the deference, of his wife. Relevantly, and with respect to the husbands who demanded that their wives hand over or share their personal wealth and income, an overarching principle in Islam is encapsulated in the following quotation by the Prophet ﷺ, "There is no obedience to anyone if it is in disobedience to Allah. Verily, obedience is only in good conduct."[70] In other words, if abiding by or complying with what someone demands of you sits in opposition to what Allah asks of you, you must obey Allah and not that person.

Amani's husband was among the men in the study who would misuse the word *qawwām*. When his wife disagreed with him in some way, he would utter "I [as the husband] am in charge [*qawwām*]!" Being well versed in the Qur'an, Amani would reply by reciting the complete Qur'anic verse. "Men are in charge of women [*qawwāmūn*] by [right of] … what they spend [for maintenance] from their wealth." Ignoring the full Qur'anic verse, Amani's husband would hasten to place her into the category of a *nāshiz* or defiant or disobedient wife whenever her point of view clashed with his and would either curtail or stop spending on her in retaliation. Similarly, he would misuse another Hadith to justify his miserliness. When Amani questioned why he treated his relatives so generously, yet behaved in a miserly fashion towards her, he would reply with the words of the Prophet ﷺ, "The best of you are those who are best to your family." If one takes a look at the larger context in which the Prophet ﷺ made this statement, it becomes obvious that he was referring specifically to wives when he used the word "family" (In fact, this Hadith is often found under chapters pertaining to marriage or the treatment of wives in Islam). So, while this Hadith serves as evidence in favor of a Muslim husband behaving generously towards his wife, Amani's husband would apply it incorrectly to justify the very opposite – financial neglect and preferential treatment for more family members outside of his nuclear household.

Psychologist, scientist, and professor of mental health at Lebanon University, Dr. Mustafa Hijazi opines that this behavior, which he terms "social backwardness," developed unconsciously in countries that live under colonization or dictatorship.[71] He explains that oppression and loss of economic rights leads the populace to treat the most vulnerable and dependent segments of their society with the same type of oppression they themselves are experiencing – and as a demographic who are globally devalued and often viewed as property, none are more susceptible to this kind of tyranny than women.[72] Men whose fathers came from such societies or who themselves have emigrated from countries with such cultures are entrenched in these values, and even after having moved to a liberal, democratic society – in this case, the U.S. – they may carry these values with them and inflict them upon their wives.[73]

So, if we apply the "social backwardness" theory, it seems that religiosity has little to do with the financial abuse of the study participants. This aligns with the study findings, which revealed that some husbands who violated their wives' Islamic financial rights had scant knowledge about Islamic law, while others who engaged in precisely the same sort of abuse considered themselves pious. Whether their husbands were well-versed in Islamic law or not, the study participants almost unanimously echo the broader literature on the subject of abuse in their testimonies: the purpose of abuse is to control, and in this study, the financial abuse Muslim husbands inflicted upon their wives was with the aim of asserting control.

Another related question: how do wives fall into the cycle of financial abuse? This study revealed that the single greatest catalyst, behaviorally speaking, that appeared to facilitate a cycle of financial abuse is for a wife to fully combine all of her money, regardless of whether the source of her money is earnings, inheritance, or gifts, with that of her husband's, into one account, even if jointly owned. Study participants who did so effectively and wholly lost control of their personal wealth. Even those who voluntarily shared their wealth came to regret it, reporting that giving their spouses total access to their money strained the couple's relationship, creating feelings of distrust and resentment.

Unexpected Findings

The study yielded a few unexpected findings that do not neatly fit into the above major categories related to violations of the wives' financial rights. Those findings are briefly summarized in this section.

Malak's case revealed a unique point of discussion. When her husband died, he left behind no wealth for his family to inherit, but during his lifetime he had bought a life insurance policy that saved Malak from bankruptcy. She used it to pay off her home in one full swoop, thereby avoiding mortgage payments and guaranteeing a place of residence for her and her children for the rest of their lives. Some contemporary scholars permit this type of life insurance agreement in situations where its benefits override its drawbacks. Their view is founded in Ḥanafī jurisprudence, who consider business transactions to be generally made out of necessity.[74]

Rahma's case offered another interesting anomaly. Although her in-laws financially provided for her in order to compensate for their indolent son, she remained unsatisfied. She had difficulty respecting her shiftless husband for not taking responsibility for his family, and felt humiliated when her in-laws had to step in and provide financial assistance. Her response reflects the words of the Sayyid Qutb, who said that a woman in such a situation naturally feels "deprived, less than others, worried and unhappy."[75]

Summary

My interviews with 21 women revealed a pattern where Muslim men consistently violated the Islamic financial rights of their wives. These basic deprivations in the relationship came with consequences. Not only did this undermine the relationship as a whole, but it ate away at these women's physical and psychological health in a myriad of ways, and, importantly, impacted their participation and contribution to their communities. Significantly, the financial conditions of these women looked drastically different than the financial stability and independence the wives of the Prophet ﷺ enjoyed.

The study findings suggest that we, as a community, need to educate our communities about the Islamic financial rights of women, and that we additionally need to re-open *fiqh* practices to ensure that Islamic rulings appropriately address and protect a Muslim woman's basic Islamic financial rights in today's context.

Rulings derived in the far past may not necessarily apply to women navigating modern-day society. The sixth and final chapter will offer some suggestions and recommendations for action to address some of the issues presented in this book.

CHAPTER SIX

Recommendations and Conclusions

The results of this study are disheartening to say the least. This collection of study participants unambiguously reveals that a diverse group of American women married to Muslim men in the U.S. have, for the most part, not received their most basic financial rights according to the Shariah. The women in these marriages were rarely treated in a fashion that even remotely resembled the financial stability and independence the Prophet ﷺ granted his own wives. What's more is that these women have been deprived of these rights to the obvious and often severe detriment of their physical, psychological, and social well-being.

What do we do with this wealth of information? As I see it, there are three ways in which we can make changes to help married women safeguard their financial rights as given to them by Islamic law, and thereby strengthen their marriages and protect their physical and mental well-being. First, we will look at the first-hand recommendations that many of the 21 study participants themselves give to other women who are either in similar positions or who are single and contemplating marriage in the U.S.. Their advice is invaluable as it comes from their decades-long lived experiences. Second, I will advocate that today's scholars reopen the practice of *fiqh* when it comes to women's financial rights in Islam with the purpose of re-examining the rulings on the rights of married women in the U.S. so that these rulings—while consistent with Islamic principals and laws— are also consistent with the lifestyle, education, intellect, and family status of Muslim-Americans today. Third, I will recommend practical and feasible actions women in America can take today to protect their God-given financial rights.

Recommendations from the Women in this Study

After detailing their personal, often harrowing life stories, the women in this study offered their best, most pertinent advice to help other women make choices that would lead to prosperous, healthy marriages with their current or prospective spouses. Their advice boils down to the following four prescriptions for women: to do everything in your power to attain a college degree; to educate yourself on your specific financial rights within Islam and then vigorously assert the fulfilment of those rights; to choose a partner who is compatible with you in terms of faith, culture, and personality; and finally, to reach an agreement with your husband prior to or at the very beginning of marriage regarding your personal earnings.

Education

Several of the women echoed one another in saying that education is the foundation of financial independence within matrimony. Jasmine explained that all else of monetary value that a woman might own –inheritance, a business, or jewelry – can be taken from her, but her education will endure, never to be diminished in any way. Tanya concurred with Aya and Farida on education being the antidote to financial dependence on one's husband, but further added that a college degree liberates a woman psychologically. She explained that knowing she, through her intellect and hard work, earned a college degree which could never be taken from her and could potentially open new sources of income, raised her self-esteem exponentially. She felt capable and resilient. Tanya added that when her husband uttered "divorce," her education was her saving grace and lifelong security.

Suraya pointed out that while a woman should do all she can to prioritize attaining an education – put in the time, dig up the drive, and exhaust whatever resources are available to her – her efforts would be made infinitely easier if Islamic organizations stepped up to help. If the mosques (*masjids*) and other Muslim civil society organizations offered help in the form of – for example – academic scholarships, career counseling, or computer classes, they would make the path to attaining a college degree and ultimately a job more accessible for these women. They would help these women and wives to, as Suraya said, "learn how to break through [into the academic and professional world]."

Women Knowing their Financial Rights

Several women strongly recommended that one of the best ways a woman can protect her financial rights, as granted to her by the Shariah, is to educate herself on what precisely those rights are *before* she enters marriage. In fact, Jasmine advised that both the man and woman who plan to marry educate themselves not only on their own respective rights, but also the rights and obligations due to one another, according to Islamic law. Amani took it a step further by counseling women to relay to their children what they have learned about their financial rights so the cycle of education and self- protection continues. And Layla pointed out that culture and Islam are often conflated, muddling and negating women's financial rights, "Know the difference between the customs of certain countries and what is actually Islamic," she cautioned.

Several study participants underscored that if a woman knows her rights, she will be less likely to allow anyone, namely the husband-to-be, to use her circumstances to shame her into relinquishing any part of her rights. As Jasmine emphatically said, "No matter if the wife is divorced, older in age [than the husband] or has children from a previous marriage, she has a right to all financial provisions set for her by Shariah." She should not feel any reticence in advocating for herself and asserting that her age, marital history, personal wealth, or anything else does not debar her from her God-given rights to *mahr, nafaqah,* or having complete control over her personal earnings.

Sophia and Nadia also pointed out that, along with knowing and advocating for one's rights of oneself, it is also incredibly beneficial to have a strong *walī* present at the time the marriage is contracted who will represent the woman's interests. This is especially important if the woman is Christian, Jewish, or a convert to Islam, Sophia added, because she may not be fully aware of the financial protections Islam affords her as a woman and wife; her *walī* can step in and help her establish a fair and thorough marriage contract that delineates her rights in writing. Similarly, Layla advised that all women, especially those new to Islam, seek a *walī* who is both well-versed in the rights Islam grants women and assertive in personality in order to ensure that "He will have no qualms about bringing up any subject having to do with your rights, financial or otherwise."

Several of the women encouraged the imams and religious leaders who perform marriage ceremonies to take responsibility to guarantee that the bride's rights are understood by all parties and are clearly articulated in the marriage contract. Sara said the following:

> Imams performing marriages in the U.S. must be required to document whether a *mahr* will be paid immediately or deferred. If not deferred, they are responsible [for] making sure the *mahr* is paid to the wife prior to the consummation of the marriage. Financial matters are very sensitive topics and frequently the parents of the girl or the wife [herself] are embarrassed to make the request, thus it is crucial for the matter to be handled by the imam performing the marriage.

Nermin takes this advice a step farther by suggesting that the financial responsibility of the husband not only needs to be clarified by a scholar at the time of the *nikāḥ* but that the imam performing the marriage ceremony should add into the marriage contract that the husband *must* have a job in order to consummate the marriage. This recommendation is a practical way of addressing how so many men are unaware of their key religious responsibility as husbands to financially provide for their wives.

Compatibility

Many study participants strongly cautioned women to choose their spouses wisely, selecting men with whom they are compatible – religiously, culturally, intellectually, and personally. Two participants underscored religious values as being essential to a successful marriage. Sara emphasized that Christian and Jewish women who marry Muslim men must look to see if the men merely identify as Muslim in name or if they, in fact, display a "pious and God-fearing" character. Suraya echoed her peer's sentiment, pointing out that women should choose a Muslim man who is a "practicing Muslim," and who truly tries to live out the spirit and principles of Islam – compassion, justice, and generosity, to name a few.

Other womens' advice focused on cultural compatibility. Aya, who was born and raised in the U.S. while her husband grew up abroad, urged women to marry men who share the woman's birthplace and upbringing in order to avoid a cultural divide and the conflicting expectations it creates. Farida advised women to partner with men whose outlook, intellect, and goals align with their own because such a person "will help you to move forward educationally, financially, and socially, and add value to your life."

The study participants offered two ways to determine whether a prospective spouse would make for a suitable partner. Sakina recommended that women seek out "premarital counseling with a qualified therapist, so [this professional] can evaluate the [couple's] compatibility before marriage." For those who do not have access to or cannot afford counseling, Layla offered the following sage yet practical advice:

Discuss what your suitor's expectations are of you as a wife. Does he expect you to work? Do you want to work but he expects you to stay home? Does he expect you to do all the housework, even if you're working? Does he expect you to do everything related to raising children or does he want to share with you? How many children does he want? How many children do you want? These are important issues that should be discussed and agreed upon before marriage.

What are the "deal breakers?" What are the non-negotiables for each of you? For example, do you have children from a previous marriage? Does he accept them? How does he feel about supporting them? Do his parents live with him and will you be living all together?

I advise "wives-to-be" to write everything down for both of you. It's easy in the initial stages of love and hope to overlook things that later become points of contention, points that can leave you with a broken heart and a broken marriage. This is your responsibility to discuss these things in an open and honest fashion now before the actual legal bond takes place.

Finally, remember Allah ﷻ has put *raḥmah* (mercy) and *mawaddah* (love) between the spouses. A bit of compassion and forgiveness can go a long way towards healing hearts as long as both are willing to give a little.

If, after having a frank and candid discussion like the one above, a woman senses that the man she is contemplating marrying is not a like-minded person, Nadia exhorted women not to dismiss these red flags. She lamented, "We as women, especially when we are in love, tend to be forgiving of [men's] flaws and think we can change them after the marriage. This is the biggest mistake." She cautioned women to evaluate a man for who he is in the present and not allow their empathy or passion override obvious signs of incompatibility.

Agreement Regarding the Wife's Earnings

The final, and most often repeated, recommendation the women in this study gave pertained to the wife's earnings. Suzzanne, who appeared to have been the most content with her degree of financial security and independence in her marriage, offered this advice:

> It is important to set rules from [the] beginning of marriage that what [the wife] earns is hers alone. A key to happiness for every wife is that her husband does not interfere in her personal money or earnings. [Financial] independence is power.

Suzzanne laid out the ground rules at the beginning of her own marriage. She opened a personal bank account where she deposited the money she had earned prior to marriage. She kept her earnings after marriage separate as well. Other participants also agreed, adding that a woman's right to keep and spend her personal wealth and earnings as she sees fit is an Islamic right so important that it should be specifically articulated in the marriage contract (even more so if the wife has a profession in which her income will likely exceed that of her partner, cautioned Maysa). As Nermin explained:

> There should be a condition in the [marriage] contract that the salary or a good portion of the wife's salary [is] to

> be placed into her personal account. Establishing this early prevents financial arguments later in the marriage.

Her own father insisted that his daughter's contract state that one-third of her salary will always be placed into her personal and separate account – a decision Nermin says was her saving grace. Nermin also recommended that during the marriage ceremony, the imam presiding over the ceremony or a Muslim scholar should speak about the wife's right to her own earnings. While this is a God-given right and no woman should feel guilty in asserting this protection, a religious leader pointedly stating this right during the ceremony will ensure that the wife feels confident once married to insist upon this right.

Maysa advised that if the wife plans to use her earnings to pay for some household expenses, this too should be clearly laid out in the marriage contract – who will assume responsibility for which family expense and what portion or percentage of their respective incomes they will contribute:

> If he is materialistic and the plan is for both to spend on the house mortgage, rent, etc., there needs to be an agreement as to how much he will put in and how much she will [contribute] from the beginning of the marriage.

Even if the couple agrees to share expenses, Jenna advised that women set aside a chunk of their earnings in case the spouse becomes physically or emotionally abusive. She suggested that the wife keep a portion of her money in a separate account, but also have a trusted friend or family member safeguard some money as a backup in the event of an emergency.

The study participants recognized that not all women will want to work or feel able to work outside the home. If the couple plans for the husband to be the sole breadwinner, Maysa suggested that this too must be stipulated in the marriage contract, along with what percentage of the husband's income the wife will receive in pocket money.

And as a woman may have sources of wealth apart from job earnings, such as inherited wealth, Sophia suggested that the marriage contract should also state that a wife's personal inheritance is hers alone to keep and spend as she pleases, as is her right within Islam. Specific to her own situation, Sophia said:

> If I ever receive a substantial inheritance some day and I can keep it in my account, it would feel like I have a safety net for the first time in my married life. I would feel that I could survive without being at the mercy of this man. It would feel like peace.

It should be reiterated that while Islam indisputably grants women total control over their personal wealth – be it earnings, inheritance, or any other form of income – the study participants felt that a marriage contract must painstakingly delineate these rights to ensure that there exists a written, binding document that will protect the woman from potential injustice and abuse.

Recommendations for Jurisprudence Review

Drawing on their own deeply personal and painful lived experiences, the women in this study offered invaluable practical advice on how to protect married women's financial rights. This is an excellent start. However, their recommendations must be supplemented with today's scholars reopening the practice of *fiqh* when it comes to women's financial rights in Islam. *Fiqh* is the practice of studying the Qur'an and Hadith to derive rulings on all varieties of issues and, unlike the Shariah, it is neither immutable nor complete.[1] In fact, it is a dynamic, ongoing endeavor that factors the customs and needs of current society into its decision-making, provided of course that no ruling transgresses the parameters set by the Shariah. Therefore, it is the duty of today's Islamic scholars to recommence *fiqh* with the purpose of re-examining and revising the rulings on the financial rights of married women in Western societies so that these laws are reflective of the evolving needs and realities of Muslims living in these contexts today. This update requires a working knowledge of western culture and of how finances are usually handled within matrimony today, something which Muslim scholars of past ages and places obviously did not have. Present-day scholars must find Shariah-compliant solutions based on today's family structure and contemporary gender roles through the reapplication of the five major rules of jurisprudence derived from the Qur'an and authentic Prophetic traditions that must be applied when considering each potential ruling:[2]

1. Certainty prevails over doubt.
2. Difficulty is met with leniency.
3. Harm must be removed.
4. Custom is to be enforced.
5. Matters are based on intention.

The 20th century heralded significant gains for women when it came to earning a higher education and participating in the workforce. This progress naturally led to a more equitable sharing of earned income between spouses, as well as greater financial independence and decision-making power for wives.[3]

Yet the studies above reveal that women married to Muslim husbands continued to experience financial oppression, despite specific Islamic financial protections not typically seen in even western culture. This oppression, as detailed at length in earlier chapters, came in many forms. Whether it was wives who did not work outside the home but fulfilled the many responsibilities of being homemakers, yet whose husbands refused to provide household help; or wives who were employed and forced to pay for household expenses, yet denied control over their own earnings; or wives who could not spend money without their husbands' permission and if the husbands arbitrarily deemed the wives disobedient or argumentative in some way, they would curtail their meager allowances even further – these are each examples of denials of a woman's financial rights within Islam.

These acts of injustice do not align with the husband's religious obligation to act as the *qawwām*, or leader of his household who provides for his wife (and children) and protects them from any harm.[4] They are in defiance of the command of Allah ﷻ, "*wa ʿāshirūhunna bilmaʿrūf,*" meaning "to never insult [one's wife] and preserve her honor."[5] They certainly do not emulate the lived example of the Prophet ﷺ or comply with his advice on how to treat women: "The most complete of the believers in faith is the one with the best character among them and the best of you are those who are best to their family [wives]."[6] Similarly, these acts do not align with the practice of *shūrā* in this contractual partnership.[7]

Evolving Understandings: Revisiting Traditional Interpretations of Certain Texts

Solutions aimed at curbing the financial abuse suffered by so many women today who are married to Muslim men will require a serious re-evaluation of past scholars' *fiqh* rulings and interpretations. It must be both male and *female* scholars and jurists who come together to derive new rulings that adhere to the Shariah and reflect the needs and customs of our current society, because, after all, it is women who will experience the outcomes of these rulings. Even during the lifetime of the Companions, male religious leaders sometimes decided matters that specifically affected women. However, in these instances, female scholars, such as ʿĀʾishah ﷜ the wife of the Prophet ﷺ, intervened and corrected any misruling that, although well-meaning, did not take a woman's circumstances fully into account. In one instance, a Companion named ʿAbdullāh ibn ʿAmr ibn al-ʿĀṣ ﷜ was teaching women how to purify themselves after menstruation and childbirth. These women kept their hair braided as this was the custom of the time, and he made the religious ruling that they must unbraid their plaits during the ritual bath. Upon hearing this, ʿĀʾishah ﷜, who recognized that unbraiding and washing their hair would be an inconvenience for women because of the scarcity of water and cleaning products, intervened, saying:

> What a strange position from the son of ʿAmr. Shouldn't he require them also to shave their heads? When I used to perform *ghusl* with the Prophet [ﷺ] from a single vessel, I simply poured water on my head three times.[8]

When deriving laws that govern the lives of women married to Muslim men it is incumbent on scholars to start by re-examining the Qur'an, the Sunnah, and the objectives behind the Shariah. This involves distinguishing between revelation (Qur'an verses and Prophetic traditions), interpretation, and application.[9] In his book *Islamic Law, Understanding Juristic Differences*, Dr. Ahmad Zaki Hammad emphasizes the absolute nature of the first, the speculative nature of the second, and the practical nature of the third, which then become laws and ultimately "a way of life."[10] The Qur'an is, of course, immutable but its interpretations may vary based on the *fiqh* principles scholars use and the particular exegesis they use as a reference. Therefore, the interpretation and application of the Qur'an and Hadith remain open and malleable. However, Dr. Hammad, while residing in the U.S., observed:

> Some zealous students in the United States and Canada, unwittingly, but nevertheless rigidly, hold the opinions of leading imams and scholars – i.e., their understanding and *ijtihad* – as equal to the Book of Allah and the *Sunnah* of his Messenger. So, when one expresses a dissenting opinion unknown to them or offers an original understanding based on a comprehensive survey of the Islamic texts or credible Islamic experience, he or she is easily charged with altering religion.[11]

Many contemporary scholars make this very mistake when they advocate adherence to the unchanged *fiqh* as if it were the fixed divine Shariah of Allah.[12] As Dr. Hammad explains, "They often cite political, social, moral, or economic practices in 'this' or 'that' time, within a particular society, as defining Islam itself."[13] When male and *female* scholars and jurists come together to derive new rulings on women's financial rights that adhere to Shariah but reflect the needs and customs of our current American society, they must remember to make this distinction between revelation and their human interpretation and application.

Chapter Three highlights various controversial primary texts that I strongly believe should be re-examined by *fiqh* scholars given the contextual considerations past scholars applied when issuing specific rulings. The following are just a few examples of texts and issues raised in this publication that I believe merit further analysis by contemporary *fiqh* and *tafsīr* scholars:

Recommended Reinterpretation of the Meaning of Qawwāmmūn in Chapter [4:34] of the Qur'an

ٱلرِّجَالُ قَوَّٰمُونَ عَلَى ٱلنِّسَآءِ بِمَا فَضَّلَ ٱللَّهُ بَعْضَهُمْ عَلَىٰ بَعْضٍ وَبِمَآ أَنفَقُوا۟ مِنْ
أَمْوَٰلِهِمْ ۚ فَٱلصَّٰلِحَٰتُ قَٰنِتَٰتٌ حَٰفِظَٰتٌ لِّلْغَيْبِ بِمَا حَفِظَ ٱللَّهُ ۚ وَٱلَّٰتِى تَخَافُونَ
نُشُوزَهُنَّ فَعِظُوهُنَّ وَٱهْجُرُوهُنَّ فِى ٱلْمَضَاجِعِ وَٱضْرِبُوهُنَّ ۖ فَإِنْ
أَطَعْنَكُمْ فَلَا تَبْغُوا۟ عَلَيْهِنَّ سَبِيلًا ۗ إِنَّ ٱللَّهَ كَانَ عَلِيًّا كَبِيرًا ﴿٣٤﴾

Men are the *protectors and maintainers* [*qawwāmūn*] of women, because Allah has made the one [or some] of them to excel the other, and because they spend (to support the women) from their means...[14]

According to the women in this study, many men today appear to misunderstand the meaning of their role as the *qawwām* (singular form of *qawwāmūn*) of women and use the verse above to abuse and subjugate their wives. It seems that some men fixate on memorizing this particular verse from the Qur'an, while neglecting the innumerable ones that warn men not to treat their wives unjustly.[15] This problem is due in part to misinterpretations and, at times, inaccurate translations by prominent exegesis scholars whose works are found in Arabic, Urdu, or English, the three languages most widely read in Western Muslim households.

There exists a group of scholars who approaches the verse from the perspective that men are the providers and protectors of their wives. For example, Amin Ahsan Islahi argues that "*qawwām*" refers to the guardian of the family, while Abul Kalam Azad unpacks this word's meaning as "the head of the family or a person who manages the affairs of the family."[16] Umar Ahmad Usmani interprets "*qawwām*" as the provider of the family and takes it a step further by claiming that the term refers to "the act of providing supplies [for one's wife and children]."[17] Apart from these scholars, two of the most widely-read English translators of the Qur'an – Yusuf Ali and Marmaduke Pickthall – share the understanding that the verse does not grant men total control over their wives. Ali translates the word "*qawwāmūn*" as "protectors" in his Qur'anic translation, while Pickthall translates the term as "the ones who are in charge."[18] Predictably, most of the Muslims who read these contemporary scholars' translations of the Qur'an are either reverts to Islam or Muslims born and raised in the United States, whereas Muslims who migrated to America as adults have often been raised with the translations and commentaries of more traditional scholars.[19]

A second group of scholars translate the word *qawwāmūn* to mean that men are the absolute masters of their wives; a translation that is narrow given the linguistic dimensions of the Arabic language and inconsistent with the Prophetic tradition. Ibn Kathīr ﵀ (565-737CE), for example, whose exegesis gained popularity in North America and is among the few classical works that has been translated into the English language, describes the word *qawwām,* in his Arabic commentary of *Tafsīr al-Qur'ān al-ʿAẓīm,* as a word that carries several varied meanings, but ones that include the words "master, king and ruler."[20] Ibn Kathīr ﵀ adds that the *qawwām* is the one who disciplines the wife when she deviates, and categorically states men are the more superior gender, a meaning that is found on many English websites.[21] Shaykh Muhammad Shafīʿ ﵀, a twentieth-century Sunni scholar from Pakistan, echoes Ibn Kathīr's point of view and specifically translated the word *qawwām* to mean that a man is his wife's master.[22] Abū al-Farash ʿAbd al-Raḥmān ibn ʿAlī ibn Muḥammad Ibn al-Jawzī ﵀, a well-known 12th century scholar of Qur'anic interpretation (*tafsīr*) and *fiqh*, noted in his book *Aḥkām al-Nisā'* that "a woman…is the owned property of her husband."[23] A particularly influential Pakistani interpreter, al-Maududi ﵀, who wrote the popular English exegesis *The Meaning of the Qur'an,* uses the word 'superior' to describe men's roles *vis*-à-*vis* their wives. One famous Urdu translation of the Qur'an is "*Tafsīr Bayān al-Qur'ān*" by Ashraf Ali Thanwi ﵀, a translation that is commonly seen amongst south Asian communities in America.[24] The translation of *qawwām* as an authoritative ruler (*ḥākim*) is one interpretation that has been clearly indicated in Thanwi's marriage manuals, where he writes the following advice for every wife:

> To try to think of him as one's equal is a grave mistake…
>
> Remember well, Allah has created men as dominating. (Women) cannot overcome him by pressure or force. To confront him by displaying anger is the height of folly.
>
> Whenever your husband becomes displeased or angry with you, for whatever reason, irrespective of who is at fault, never sulk, display anger, let loose a mouthful or withdraw. Adopt humility and apologize, even when he is clearly at fault.
>
> Never ever ask him to physically serve you. Even if he should lovingly come and massage your head and feet... politely, ask him not to take the trouble...Why? Because would you prefer your father to physically serve you? Do remember a husband's rank is higher than one's father.[25]

Thanwi's words suggest a superior nature of the husband and inferior nature of the wife. Thanwi's recommendations, however, clearly conflict with the Prophetic tradition where he ﷺ routinely served and assisted his wives. When his wife ʿĀ'ishah (raḍiya Allāhu ʿanhā) was asked about what he ﷺ used to do in his household, her reply was "He was serving his family" and in another tradition, "He was a human like all humans, he used to sow his cloth, and milk his sheep and serve his own self."[26] In fact, similar traditions are found in al-Bukhārī's book of *nafaqah* under a chapter entitled "the man serving his family (pertaining to wife)." And in response to a general question about the person who Islamically deserves the highest level of respect, he ﷺ said: "your mother…your mother…your mother" and last, "your father," with no reference to a woman's husband.[27]

These translations and interpretations that describe the word *qawwāmūn* to mean protectors, guardians, providers, and the like seem more accurate, particularly when one examines the verse in its entirety. In the second half of the verse, God describes men as the ones who spend from their earnings to financially support their wives. This is the duty of a provider or protector, rather than an authoritarian ruler. If the verse intended to convey the leadership of the male gender over the female, it is not due to the latter's inadequacy, but rather for the sake of designating men as bearing greater responsibility. Abū Ḥayyān al-Andalusī ﵀, in his work *Tafsīr al-Baḥr al-Muḥīt*, pointed out that Imam al-Qurṭubī ﵀ warned that a husband who does not satisfy the key condition of this leadership role by failing to financially provide for his wife cannot be called a "*qawwām*."[28] Interestingly, the verse (4:32) which appears shortly before this verse grants women the right to earn a living and use their wealth as they wish – a right which belies the superiority of a man over a woman. One Qur'anic exegete suggested that verse 4:32 is directed toward ignorant societies who "may deprive women of some of their rights for economic reasons, such as giving a woman a lesser wage than a man who does the same job, or giving her a smaller share of inheritance or depriving her of the right to manage her own property."[29] And if we take a step back and consider the broader context of the verse including the chapter and book as a whole, we see that this contentious verse cannot be translated to mean that one gender is the master of the other, because such an interpretation would contradict several other verses in the Qur'an that grant women a variety of rights, protections, and privileges over men.

Since it appears that the "*qawwām*" is the provider for – and thereby the leader of – the household, and yet we see that among the majority of married couples living in the U.S. today both husband and wife act as breadwinners, the scholar Nasr Hamid Abu Zayd posits:[30]

> The man who sees that a woman's only possible job, is to care for the children and do housework has an extremely limited view of life because women today proved their proficiency in every work field, thus in line of such progression, the *qiwāmah* becomes a matter that is shared between the man and the woman."[31]

Tunisia stands as a present-day example of a Muslim country that has instituted this fact in its civil law code. Specifically, one family law designates the husband who supports his family as the head of the household but does not prescribe obedience (on the woman's part), but rather requires both partners to equally respect and cooperate with one another within matrimony.[32] The new code appears to have stabilized marriages and decreased the divorce rate in Tunisia, since past family laws brought about much financial repercussions for women. The country received pushback from those who argued that this law goes against verse 34 of Sūrah al-Nisā', but contemporary scholars rebutted those claims stating the gender equality principals in Qur'an 5:45 and 9:71, including, "The believing men and believing women are allies of one another," and by giving reference to a Prophetic tradition that indicates equality between genders prior to the revelation of verse 34 of Sūrah al-Nisā'.[33] When a woman complained to the Prophet ﷺ that her husband assaulted her, his ﷺ reply was "eye for an eye." After his judgment, verse 34 was revealed describing the general and complementary roles of the husband and wife within the broader marital framework. The women at the time of the revelation did not enjoy all the rights they should have as 'Umar ibn al-Khaṭṭāb ؓ said, "By Allah, in the pre-Islamic era, we did not value women whatsoever until Islam came and God mentioned them, causing us to realize that they have rights over us."[34] In fact, the Meccan men were known to be harsh with women. Despite women not typically taking on warrior roles at the time, scholars cite the unique example of female Companions such as Hind bint 'Utbah who played a crucial role on the battlefield. Hind was the wife of the Companion Abū Sufyān ؓ, who took on a leadership role in her household in many instances. In fact, at times she challenged her husband on his shortcomings as a provider and protector.[35] *Fiqh* scholars and organizations in the U.S. have an opportunity to review the Qur'an and Hadith and derive rulings that both comply with divine law and address the needs of present-day society.

A Muslim husband's Islamic duty to honor his wife's financial rights is not dependent on his wife's religion, cultural background, employment status, or socioeconomic class. If women living in the U.S. or the West and married to Muslim men want to see their financial rights safeguarded, they need the Muslim scholarly community to reevaluate the true meaning of *qiwāmah* and religious leaders must educate both men and women through weekly Friday sermons (*khuṭbahs*) and wedding ceremonies on the accurate definition of *qawwām* as the protector and provider of a husband's wife and family. Misinterpreting the concept of *qiwāmah* to control, undermine, and erase a woman's identity paves the way to psychological, physical, and/or financial abuse.

Recommended Reinterpretation of the Meaning of Nushūz: The Qur'an 4:34

Another contentious word that appears in the Qur'an and is sometimes wielded by husbands as justification for refusing to financially support their wives is the term *nushūz (nushūzuhuna sing. nushūz).* We find this word in verse 34 of Sūrah al-Nisā', and it is translated by some scholars as "recalcitrant." However my research posits that "*nushūz*" is not referring to a recalcitrant wife, but rather a wife who wants out of the marriage. There are a number of reasons – relating to context, human psychology, and the example of the Prophet ﷺ, all explained at length in Chapter Two of this book – why this study arrives at the conclusion that the word *nushūz* refers to a wife who wishes to be relieved of the marriage and not a wife who is defiant or disobedient. Other suggested meanings, "refusal of intimacy" or "leaving the household without the husband's permission," are based purely on scholars' independent reasoning, or *ijtihād*, and are not contextualized. Further, an important note is that the traditional scholars who consider a *nāshiz* wife (based on how each define it) to not be entitled *nafaqah* consider the marriage contract similar to a business transaction in which matrimony becomes an exchange of financial support for intimacy, which does not reflect the much higher objectives of marriage in Islam based on the Qur'an and the Sunnah of the Prophet ﷺ.[36] However, regardless of how one understands the meaning of "*nushūz*," the Qur'an 4:34 instructs husbands to address any marital discord through a series of measures, none of which involve neglecting their financial responsibilities towards their wives. Because men will at times point to the interpretations of the word *nushūz* that are mentioned above as justifying why they have deprived their wives of *nafaqah* (financial maintenance) or other financial rights, contemporary scholars must reassess the varied interpretations derived by past scholars ensuring their appropriate application in the current context.

Even if we are to say that a wife's *nushūz* refers to her refusal to have intimate relations with her spouse while physically able to and in the absence of a legitimate reason such as sickness, exhaustion, menstruation, nursing, abuse (mental, verbal or physical) or old age, and we say that those who suggest that a husband is then within his rights to withhold her *nafaqah* are correct, would doing so be in line with the words of God in the Qur'an, verse 19, "and live with them in kindness"? And would this apply to a woman who had been loyal and dutifully cared for her husband and children for years? Given that Islam intends to prevent harm based on the tradition "*lā ḍarar wa lā ḍirār* (no harm to oneself nor to others)," a main principle of *fiqh* followed by all *fiqh* scholars, wouldn't this be disproportionately detrimental to her well-being, especially if she's financially dependent on her husband?[37] What if she refuses intimacy with her husband in *response* to his failure to provide for her – is she then guilty of *nushūz*? What can a woman do when the blanket reply of the scholars is always the same: "… the *nafaqah* for the wife is the responsibility of her husband…as long as she is not *nāshiz*"?[38]

Nushūz Interpreted as Disobedience or Arrogance

As for the specific suggestion that *nushūz* means disobedience, one wonders how this applies to women living in societies where women are educated and where marriage is viewed as a partnership. In this context, the view of Imam Ibn Ḥazm ﷺ might be appropriate: "Once the marriage is contracted, the husband cannot withhold from his wife her *nafaqah* (including the purchase of clothing and provision of residence), regardless of her age, marital status, being obedient or disobedient, *nāshiz,* or not *nāshiz*!"[39] Furthermore, men and women are created from the same soul and both are equally human in their emotions; just like her husband, a wife will, at times, feel frustrated with her partner and be defiant and disagreeable. This basic understanding of human psychology makes clear that it is both unreasonable and unjust to claim that a wife who disagrees with her husband now automatically loses her entitlement to financial maintenance.

Author's Practical Recommendations

Taking into account the suggestions from the study participants based on their lived experiences along with the recommendations for jurisprudence review, I have a few further recommendations for women entering into marriages with Muslim husbands in the modern societies.

Fostering Women's Awareness of their Islamic Financial Rights as Wives, Divorcées, and Widows

Allah ﷻ said in the Qur'an:

ذَٰلِكَ بِأَنَّ ٱللَّهَ لَمْ يَكُ مُغَيِّرًا نِّعْمَةً أَنْعَمَهَا عَلَىٰ قَوْمٍ حَتَّىٰ يُغَيِّرُوا۟ مَا بِأَنفُسِهِمْ ۙ وَأَنَّ ٱللَّهَ
سَمِيعٌ عَلِيمٌ ﴿٥٣﴾

That is because Allah would not change a favor which He had bestowed upon a people until they change what is within themselves. And indeed, Allah is Hearing and Knowing.[40]

Some women refused to take part in this study because they believed that their husbands had the right, within Islam, to treat them in the despotic ways that they did. They accepted the abuse because they did not recognize it was a violation of their Islamic rights. Others declined to participate in the study because although they felt their husbands had financially oppressed them, they were reticent to voice their grievances for fear that this would qualify as a kind of defiance of their husbands and would compromise their Hereafter. The first step toward change is awareness. A wife, divorcée, or widow needs to know her rights to avoid financial abuse. The most concrete way to achieve this is through a variety of means: Islamic online education, Islamic seminars and pre-marital counseling, to name a few.

Pre-Marital Islamic Counseling on Spousal Financial Rights

Studies show a divorce rate of 31 percent in American Muslim households today. One of the most common reasons behind divorces around the world and across faiths is financial problems.[41] A possible remedy for this problem is premarital counseling with the express purpose of educating both the man and woman about their respective financial rights and obligations to one another. For example, a woman entering into matrimony with a Muslim husband should be aware of her right to live in a private residence without having to share her home with her husband's relatives except with her permission, which she then has the right to retract if her decision brings her harm. This sort of detailed understanding of one's financial rights as a spouse would go a long way toward heading off financial neglect and abuse.

Building Support Programs

Muslim leadership, such as psychologists and imams, needs to develop support groups for women who are currently enduring financial abuse at the hands of husbands or ex-husbands, as well as support groups for divorced or widowed women who spent years being financially dependent on their spouses and are now trying to build independent lives for themselves. Such programs have been successful when launched in predominantly Muslim countries and have helped participants build self-confidence, communication skills, and stress management skills.[42] Group therapy not only educates but also provides emotional support to women in what is often an incredibly isolating time in their lives, emboldening them to speak up and insist upon their financial rights within Islam. These sorts of forums find precedent 14 centuries ago, when groups of women would gather in the presence of ʿĀ'ishah ﵂ and find a safe space to break their silence about their relationships.

Establishing a Prenuptial Agreement

A prenuptial agreement is another safeguard against financial abuse. A woman married to a Muslim man should insist upon a prenuptial agreement that guarantees she will remain the sole owner of her personal wealth, as well as any future income, during the marriage. Such a provision would, in fact, be consistent with both Islamic law and American laws. Islamically, the prenuptial agreement is permissible and recommended by *fiqh* scholars today; this recommendation is included in the Assembly of Muslim Jurists of America Family Codes, Article 14 (see appendix E). It is particularly important in the West to preserve one's Shariah rights. The making of prenuptial agreements is evident from the saying of the Prophet ﷺ, "The condition which most deserves to be fulfilled is that by means of which intimacy becomes permissible for you."[43] Prenuptial agreements are well recognized and applied in the U.S. and other nations worldwide.

A recent phenomenon in American divorce courts is Muslim husbands making the misleading and self-serving claim that the *mahr* agreement is tantamount to a prenuptial agreement. *Mahr* is a gift of value that Islamic law obligates every Muslim husband to give his wife upon contracting their marriage; it is a gesture to prove his intention to commit to and financially care for this woman. A prenuptial agreement, on the other hand, lays outs conditions (financial or otherwise) by which the husband and wife must abide during the marriage and upon its dissolution. So, the two are not equivalent and conflating them may result in the wife being deprived of certain financial rights and benefits.[44] Different courts in the U.S. sanction a Shariah-based agreement signed in the couple's native country differently; some see it as a mere marriage certificate whose intent is to only identify both parties to be wed while others view it as a pre-nuptial agreement that addresses post-divorce financial support, which can leave a divorced wife destitute. Both concepts differ, as the *mahr* contained in a marriage contract is a marital gift to the wife, whereas a pre-nuptial agreement is a way to protect and divide the properties of both husband and wife upon divorce. Living in the West makes a prenuptial agreement a vital addition to the marriage contract, ensuring certain rights are recognized in non-Muslim courts in case of death or divorce. Attorney Abed Awad of New Jersey, a litigation expert, encourages Muslim couples in the U.S. to have both a marriage contract as well as a pre-nuptial contract so that the *mahr* in a marriage contract is not interpreted as limiting a wife's right to seek post-divorce support, but just viewed as a simple contractual gift:

> Awad argues for defining the Islamic marriage contract as a simple enforceable contract to ensure that additional rights that the wife may have, such as alimony, inheritance, community property, and equitable distribution of property, are not bargained away. In recent years Islamic marriage contracts are increasingly having greater success being enforced as simple contracts rather than prenuptial agreements.[45]

Compatibility

Islam considers shared faith and morality the most important measures of compatibility, but recognizes that congruency when it comes to education and socioeconomic status also increases the chances of a marriage succeeding and decreases the probability of financial abuse.[46] Communities during the lifetime of the Prophet ﷺ were more devoted to the principles of Islam and more homogeneous in their composition; both characteristics made selecting one's partner a simpler, safer process. Today's women do not have these advantages, and therefore I advise them to practice great caution when choosing whom to marry because, as these participants have shown, a lack of compatibility – be it religious, cultural, socio-economic or intellectual in nature – is often a harbinger of financial abuse and possibly divorce. Part of the reason why compatibility in education levels and socioeconomic background is key is that all the schools of jurisprudence base their legal rulings regarding how a husband ought to provide for his wife on the lifestyle the wife was accustomed to enjoying prior to marriage. If the husband comes from a dramatically different culture and economic background, he will be less willing and able to care for the wife in the way to which Islam entitles her.[47]

Considering Mahr a Form of Social Security

The Qur'an clearly indicates that there are no limits to the amount of *mahr* a bride may receive, and the Prophet ﷺ of course was always generous with the bridal gifts he presented to his wives. The study participants' experiences presented men who did not appear to be concerned about their Islamic duty to provide their wives with certain post-divorce support. Thus while *mahr* may have —at times— been a symbolic, rather than practical, token during an age of pious, honorable Muslim men during the Prophet's era, today this bridal gift can function as a necessary source of financial security for women in case of divorce or widowhood. This is especially true for women living in the U.S., in which studies show wives tolerate more abuse from their spouses than those living in their native countries; it is a society in which women often live far away from their parents, making it difficult for the mother and father to support their daughters financially or even to be fully aware of their financial distress.[48] Therefore, it is essential that both the bride-to-be and her parents do not shy away from advocating for a generous *mahr*. Furthermore, because of various societal, cultural, or religious pressures, women today, whether living in the U.S. or elsewhere in the world, will often conceal their problems to maintain family integrity and honor.[49] Studies indicate the cultural pressure as follows:

> The concepts of shame (*ayb*) and honor (*sharaf*) are at the core of the family structure, therefore all members are called to protect family integrity and respectability. In this view, family needs should precede individual needs and women in particular are the ones who have the responsibility of keeping the family together, maintaining harmony, solidarity and loyalty between members. Privacy and the family integrity should be preserved, even at the sake of the happiness of their individual members. The utmost importance of privacy and honor can prevent abused immigrant women from seeking help for fear of being judged or even stigmatized by friends and relatives. On a similar

> note, divorce is disregarded and considered to put shame on the family, therefore spouses are advised to stay together even if they are unhappy with their marriage. Women wishing to divorce their husbands (a practice called *khula*) are generally stigmatized and socially disapproved.[50]

This way of thinking often leads to women, and wives in particular, to conceal financial abuse from family and friends and is all the more reason for a bride-to-be and her parents to treat *mahr* as a form of social security.

The Deferred Mahr

Scholars of *fiqh* agree that a husband is religiously obligated to pay the *mahr* to the bride before the consummation of the marriage, but — according to many — if the couple agrees upon a deferred *mahr* – one specified to be paid at a later date – only then may the husband delay gifting his wife her *mahr* until after consummation. Some scholars rule that the deferred *mahr* must be paid to the wife by a date agreed upon by the bride and groom, while others leave the matter an open debt until death or divorce. Based on the study results, I recommend that a couple adopt the former approach. None of the study participants received any *mahr* upon divorce, nor was the subject of deferred *mahr* addressed upon widowhood. Therefore, I advise women in the West to protect this critical financial right by, first, having the imam who is performing the marriage ceremony record an agreed-upon *mahr* amount in the marriage contract itself. Second, if the wife has acquiesced to a deferred *mahr*, then the imam should make sure that a deferred *mahr* is clearly recorded and a payment date is set. If the husband follows the school of jurisprudence that allows *mahr* to be deferred until divorce, he should voice this request or have it written in the contract to give the bride and her *walī* a chance to agree or disagree. Since *mahr* is a Shariah-based requirement of the marriage, and any permitted deferral is *fiqh*-based, it is essential to stipulate that any deferred *mahr* shall become immediately payable upon the wife's demand. These safeguards will ensure that a husband does not shirk this religious duty.

Trained Imams

The imams certified to perform Muslim marriage ceremonies in the U.S. should be required to adhere to a set of clear guidelines pertaining to the information they must include in the marriage contract to ensure that financial rights are not overlooked and unwritten. *Fiqh* organizations such as the Assembly of Muslim Jurists of America (AMJA) should hold yearly training conferences mandated for imams to keep their certifications active. Furthermore, either before or after a marriage ceremony, trained imams should deliver a lecture on the financial rights of the wife.

I base these recommendations on recent studies that revealed that most imams in the U.S. migrated to this country after receiving their training overseas, and therefore do not fully understand the customs and needs of the people they are serving.[51] Studies also suggest that the few who do train in American institutions, such as seminaries, often do not graduate with the proper Islamic education:

The curriculums of overseas universities are not established for graduating imams who can serve specifically in American society. Moreover, the study in the American universities is not sufficient for the same reason to graduate imams for serving Muslim communities. Therefore, the study suggests inaugurating a new school in America that takes the responsibility of educating, preparing, training students to graduate as qualified imams for serving Muslim communities in America based on the findings of this study.[52]

Nafaqah Due upon Contractual ('Aqd) Agreement

Among the study participants, there were women who were left without financial support for a lengthy time following the marriage having been contracted, and in some cases, even consummated. I recommend that Islamic *fiqh* organizations in North America collectively adopt Imam Ibn Ḥazm's ruling, which states that *nafaqah* is promptly due to the wife once the marriage is contracted. Countries like Iraq did adopt this view as part of their family code laws.[53] The code makes a wife entitled to *nafaqah* even if she is living in a different home (with her parents), city, or country, unless she refuses to move into her husband's home, which meets all Shariah requirements. Although Islamic *fiqh* organizations cannot legally enforce their rulings in the United States and other Western countries, by holding one consistent viewpoint in the U.S. or the U.K., for instance, on this stance through seminars and annual conventions, they will, in due time, succeed to educate Muslim men of this responsibility.

Best Approaches when Wives Desire to Share their Wealth with Spouses

Based on the study participants experiences, I recommend that the best approach for a wife who would like to loan but not gift a large amount of her money to her husband, as in Amani's example, would be to dispense the money through a formal loan – one that is recorded in writing and overseen by a lawyer.[54] Amani handed over $100,000 to her husband out of good will when he asked for it and assured her that the money would be invested such that she will receive its profit every month. However, this only happened for a few months, after which he started giving one excuse after another, until one day he told her that he did not owe her anything additional because of how she allegedly overspends. To avoid such injustice, Allah ﷻ Himself advised to take the following approach in verse 282 of Sūrah al-Baqarah, the longest verse of the entire Qur'an:

> *O you who have believed, when you contract a debt for a specified term, write it down.* And let a scribe write [it] between you in justice. Let no scribe refuse to write as Allah has taught him. So let him write and let the one who has the obligation dictate. And let him fear Allah, his Lord, and not leave anything out of it. But if the one who has the obligation is of limited understanding or weak or unable to dictate himself, then let his guardian dictate in justice. And bring to witness two *witnesses* from among your men… And if there are not two men [available], then a man and two women from those whom you accept as witnesses - so that if one of the women errs, then the other can remind

> her. And let not the witnesses refuse when they are called upon. *And do not be [too] weary to write it, whether it is small or large, for its [specified] term.* That is more just in the sight of Allah and stronger as evidence and more likely to prevent doubt between you, except when it is an immediate transaction which you conduct among yourselves. For [then] there is no blame upon you if you do not write it. *And take witnesses when you conclude a contract.* Let no scribe be harmed or any witness. For if you do so, indeed, it is [grave] disobedience in you. And fear Allah. And Allah teaches you. And Allah is Knowing of all things.

A formal loan with witnesses guarantees that the husband will have to pay back his wife her money and will protect the wife's right to her personal wealth, avoiding any ambiguity or subsequent resentment between the couple.

Regarding Women's Financial Rights in the Event of Divorce: Mutʿah

According to the Shariah, as established in Qur'anic verses 236, 237, and 241 of Sūrah al-Baqarah and verse 28 of Sūrah al-Aḥzāb, a Muslim husband who divorces his wife owes her *mutʿah,* which is essentially what is known in the American legal system as spousal support or alimony. Scholars held differences on whether the *mutʿah* is owed to an ex-wife only if the marriage was not consummated and no *mahr* was established or for every divorcee, before or after consummation. *Mutʿah* can be monetary or in the form of services. For example, classical scholars such as Imams Ibn Ḥazm, Aḥmad ibn Ḥanbal, and al-Shāfiʿī ﷫ adopted the view of the Companion Ibn 'Abbās 🕮, who considered gifting the divorced wife with lifetime maid service (*khādim*) to be a good *mut'ah* from a financially well-off husband.[55] How much and for how long a divorced woman deserves this form of financial security or *mut'ah* is a *fiqh*-based matter that should align with the social conditions and times.

Many scholars today conclude that the amount the ex-wife receives should allow her a reasonably comfortable lifestyle for the remainder of her lifetime and can be paid in monthly installments or in a lump sum. Scholars rule that the amount the couple settles on should reflect the husband's means and the norms of the time and place in which they live, and so I recommend that the ex-wife should receive a value of *mut'ah* that aligns with her needs based on what is customary in the West.[56]

With regard to *mut'ah*, I recommend that the *fiqh* organizations in the West look to and adopt the Tunisian family laws on divorce.[57] Tunisian courts grant every female divorcee the right to a residence and *mut'ah*; the courts mandate that the *mut'ah* should cover the ex-wife's living expenses for the remainder of her life, and she can choose to receive the money in a lump sum or as a monthly payment based on the cost of living.[58] The only exception to this compensation is if the woman's social and economic status changes through remarriage. In Muslim nations where courts have legislated, based on their *fiqh* scholars' rulings, that the divorcee receives only one year's worth of *mut'ah*, many women were left lost after the marriage and resorted to borrowing and begging in order to survive.[59]

In fact, the U.S. Library of Congress in 2006 recognized the Tunisian marriage and divorce laws as the best model of gender legislation to honor the rights of women in the Muslim world.[60] This code of laws is rooted in some of the secondary *fiqh* sources adopted by the schools of thought on particular issues as that of keeping the welfare of the general public (*al-maṣāliḥ al-mursalah*) in mind and on warding off corruption (*sadd al-dharā'iʿ*).[61]

Despite the *fiqh* principles in which this Tunisian legal code is grounded, contemporary scholars refute some of these laws, saying they are not in compliance with the Shariah. I, however, would argue that *fiqh* organizations in Western societies should adopt the Tunisian laws regarding marriage and divorce because they fully apply the two Qur'an-based *fiqh* principals – "Custom is to be enforced" and "Harm must be removed", and because Islamic law does not need to be applied in a rigid and literal manner. Our own history teaches us that Muslim leaders would consider context and nuance when implementing Shariah. For example, no one rebutted Caliph ʿUmar ibn al-Khaṭṭāb ﵁ when he did not apply word-for-word the Qur'anic verse that calls for punishing a thief by cutting off his or her hand. Instead, he ﵁ would simply threaten those who stole to instill fear in their hearts, that if they were to repeat their crime, he would take this action. He determined that it would be neither just nor merciful to enforce this law during a year of famine (18 AH), called ʿĀm al-Ramādah, when the inhabitants of Medina were quite literally starving to death.[62] Similarly, during his Caliphate, ʿUmar ﵁ temporarily forbade Muslim men from marrying Christian or Jewish women, a matter clearly made permissible in verse five of Sūrah al-Mā'idah in the Qur'an. Upon hearing that the Companion Ḥudhayfah 🕮 married a Jewish woman, 'Umar 🕮 commanded that he divorce her so others would not follow Ḥudhayfah's example. Although Allah had granted Muslim men permission to marry Christian or Jewish women, the aim of 'Umar 🕮 at that specific time and place was to implement the broader ideals behind the Shariah, specifically the principal that holds one should strive to prevent harm (sadd al-dharā'i'); he noted that if the Muslim men who were then currently traveling to and settling in non-Muslim lands married Christian and Jewish women of these nations, the Muslim women who had also migrated to these lands, and who, according to Islamic law, could only marry Muslim men, would be left with no one to marry.[63] Another example is during the Caliphate of Abū Bakr 🕮, when one of the categories of zakāt-eligible recipients listed in verse 60 of sūrah nine ("those whose hearts are to be reconciled) was discontinued because of the Muslims' growth and self-sufficiency.[64] That category of individuals used to receive zakat because they were either skeptical towards Islam or had the potential to cause harm to the Muslim community, but who were considered susceptible of being won over or pacified through acts of kindness or assistance like through charity or zakāt. When the Prophet 🕮 died and Islam spread and became more powerful, these specific individuals who historically received zakāt requested their share, but the head of the treasury department, 'Umar ibn al-Khaṭṭāb 🕮, with the approval of Caliph Abū Bakr, rejected their request.[65] Just as 'Umar 🕮 showed flexibility and sensitivity in the application of Islamic law, considering what would minimize harm and amplify benefit to the vulnerable, so too should fiqh scholars and institutions in the U.S. and Western societies.

Kadd and Si'āyah or Post-divorce Right to Marital Property Settlement

Kadd and si'āyah refers to a woman's right to a share of the wealth, including property, that the couple earned as a unit while married – a pension, so to speak.[66] This financial right finds its basis in Islamic law only in the Mālikī jurisprudence.[67] I strongly recommend that we adopt the Mālikī allocation of *kadd and si'āyah* so that divorced women in our communities are not left disadvantaged after years of investing into the success of their homes and families. It only seems fair for female divorcees, who do not carry an obligation to financially provide for their families, to receive a share of accumulated marital wealth proportionate to their overall and sometimes more discreet contribution to the financial well-being of the family— managing childcare, schooling, household activities, and other household tasks, for instance, so that their husbands could go to school or advance their careers. It would be unjust for a woman who, during her marriage, earned an income, worked as the primary caregiver of the children, or took on the role of homemaker to then watch her ex-husband walk away in possession of nearly every penny accumulated during their life together. The concept of *kadd* and *si'āyah* prevents this inequity, and for this reason I suggest that *fiqh* organizations in Western societies such as the U.S. adopt the rulings found in several Muslim countries, such as Morocco, declaring that upon divorce a wife's Islamic right to *kadd and si'āyah* must be fulfilled. Interestingly enough, family law courts across the U.S. often use the same concepts described by the Mālikī school in making determinations about the division of marital property (or in granting alimony) after a long marriage between a homemaker and her professionally accomplished and high-earning husband: in many courts, a homemaker's hard work is recognized as contributing to the overall wellness and financial success of the family. One ruling provided by the Assembly of Muslim Jurists of America (AMJA), to some degree, recognizes this right to compensation but I believe there is room to take it a step further so that it recognizes the often overlooked invisible labor women undertake on a day-to-day basis:

> **Article 67:** If the wife shares in her husband's work, or business investments, with her skills, then she is entitled to a share of his resources that is proportionate to her contribution in this work. Estimating this share should be referred back to the experts, and the two spouses should negotiate in good will concerning that and should agree from the start on clear terms in order to prevent dispute.[68]

Heeding Islamic Law Despite the U.S. Legal System

While Muslims living in non-Muslim countries are obligated to follow local laws and can seek rulings from courts of those nations, a Muslim husband's religious duties regarding his wife's financial rights, both during marriage and in divorce, remain clear. He should not use the legal system of a country to bypass or neglect these responsibilities to his wife or ex-wife. For example, a Muslim husband should not use the U.S. legal system to avoid the following requirements of Islamic law: (1) he should pay his divorced wife the *mahr* he never paid her (without claiming such gift amounts to a comprehensive prenuptial agreement meant to address post-divorce financial arrangements so as to deprive her of other post-divorce support); (2) he should not hide his wealth or transfer it to his native country to claim poverty to the judge in order to avoid paying the court's equivalent of *nafaqah* (post-divorce financial support), *mut'ah* (alimony), *kadd and si'āyah* (post-divorce right to marital property settlement), childcare and child support required of him under Islamic law; (3) he should not try to take possession of her precious jewelry and valuable personal items upon divorce; and (4) he should not accept child support, even if the children live with him and his ex-wife earns an income. Muslims cannot exploit the legal system of the non-Muslim country to neglect one another's Islamic rights. If he uses the American court's ruling to shirk his religious responsibilities, he is committing a sin. The post-divorce ethics mandated in the following Qur'anic verses and Prophetic tradition must be abided and applied by Muslim husbands toward their wives in the U.S. and abroad:

وَكَيْفَ تَأْخُذُونَهُۥ وَقَدْ أَفْضَىٰ بَعْضُكُمْ إِلَىٰ بَعْضٍ وَأَخَذْنَ مِنكُم
مِّيثَٰقًا غَلِيظًا ﴿٢١﴾

And how could you take it (*mahr, gifts*) while you have gone in unto each other and they [your wives] have taken from you a solemn covenant?[69]

*

وَإِنْ أَرَدتُّمُ ٱسْتِبْدَالَ زَوْجٍ مَّكَانَ زَوْجٍ وَءَاتَيْتُمْ إِحْدَىٰهُنَّ قِنطَارًا فَلَا
تَأْخُذُوا۟ مِنْهُ شَيْـًٔا ۚ أَتَأْخُذُونَهُۥ بُهْتَٰنًا وَإِثْمًا مُّبِينًا ﴿٢٠﴾

But if you want to replace one wife with another and you have given one of them a great amount [in gifts], *do not take [back] from it anything*. Would you take it in injustice and manifest sin?[70]

*

۞ وَالْوَالِدَاتُ يُرْضِعْنَ أَوْلَادَهُنَّ حَوْلَيْنِ كَامِلَيْنِ ۖ لِمَنْ أَرَادَ أَنْ يُتِمَّ الرَّضَاعَةَ ۚ وَعَلَى الْمَوْلُودِ
لَهُ رِزْقُهُنَّ وَكِسْوَتُهُنَّ بِالْمَعْرُوفِ ۚ لَا تُكَلَّفُ نَفْسٌ إِلَّا وُسْعَهَا ۚ لَا تُضَارَّ وَالِدَةٌ بِوَلَدِهَا وَلَا
مَوْلُودٌ لَهُ بِوَلَدِهِ ۚ وَعَلَى الْوَارِثِ مِثْلُ ذَٰلِكَ ۗ فَإِنْ أَرَادَا فِصَالًا عَنْ تَرَاضٍ مِنْهُمَا وَتَشَاوُرٍ فَلَا
جُنَاحَ عَلَيْهِمَا ۗ وَإِنْ أَرَدْتُمْ أَنْ تَسْتَرْضِعُوا أَوْلَادَكُمْ فَلَا جُنَاحَ عَلَيْكُمْ إِذَا سَلَّمْتُمْ مَا آتَيْتُمْ
بِالْمَعْرُوفِ ۗ وَاتَّقُوا اللَّهَ وَاعْلَمُوا أَنَّ اللَّهَ بِمَا تَعْمَلُونَ بَصِيرٌ ﴿٢٣٣﴾

… Mothers may breastfeed their children two complete years for whoever wishes to complete the nursing [period]. Upon the father is the mothers' (and his children's') provision and their clothing according to what is acceptable. No person is charged with more than his capacity. No mother should be harmed through her child, and no father through his child. And upon the [father's] heir is [a duty] like that [of the father] And if they both desire weaning through mutual consent from both of them and consultation, there is no blame upon either of them. And if you wish to have your children nursed by a substitute, there is no blame upon you as long as you give payment according to what is acceptable. And fear Allah and know that Allah is Seeing of what you do.[71]

*

لَا جُنَاحَ عَلَيْكُمْ إِنْ طَلَّقْتُمُ النِّسَاءَ مَا لَمْ تَمَسُّوهُنَّ أَوْ تَفْرِضُوا لَهُنَّ فَرِيضَةً ۚ وَمَتِّعُوهُنَّ عَلَى
الْمُوسِعِ قَدَرُهُ وَعَلَى الْمُقْتِرِ قَدَرُهُ مَتَاعًا بِالْمَعْرُوفِ ۖ حَقًّا عَلَى الْمُحْسِنِينَ ﴿٢٣٦﴾

There is no blame upon you if you divorce women, you have not touched nor specified for them an obligation. *But* [*matti'ūhunna*] *give them* [*a gift of*] *compensation* [*mut'ah* in addition to *mahr*] – the wealthy according to his capability and

> the poor according to his capability – a provision according to what is acceptable, a duty upon the doers of good.[72]

Doing otherwise, as seen in some of the stories of the divorced participants in this study, would not coincide with the final words of the Prophet ﷺ during his final sermon: "Fear Allah in your dealings with women for you have taken them as your wives under Allah's trust and consummated the marriage by His permission…"[73]

Legal Guidelines in non-Muslim Countries

In 2010, the Assembly of Muslim Jurists of America (AMJA) printed a family code for Muslims residing in Western countries.[74] The code is a great start, although I recommend that AMJA reviews Tunisian family laws, for instance, to further revise the existing guidelines. The scholars who drafted this set of guidelines underscored that the rulings within this code are the result of their reasoning and interpretive efforts (*ijtihād*) and therefore fall under the category of *fiqh*, which is not the immutable, timeless Islamic law. They organized these rulings into a format that resembles modern-day legal codes, addressing the possible stages of marriage and the different circumstances surrounding marriage – from marrying outside the faith, raising a family, and maintaining the household, to divorce, spousal support, and child custody.[75] Muslim couples can use these guidelines to navigate marital disputes in a way that aligns with Islamic principles and ensures that each party's God-given financial rights are fulfilled.[76] However, the AMJA does point out that as Muslim jurists based in non-Muslim countries, the scholars who drafted this code of conduct cannot enforce its rulings, only recommend them. Their actual implementation is contingent on the couples themselves mutually accepting and abiding by the rulings. In 2004 the AMJA declared that women who do not receive their financial legal rights in accordance with the Shariah are permitted to use the American legal system instead: since they reside in the U.S., they can abide by their laws.[77]

Although the AMJA cannot enforce its codes as law, I recommend that its members introduce these thoughtful rulings at annual conferences, such as the ones hosted by the Islamic Society of North America (ISNA) and the Islamic Circle of North America (ICNA). Scholars and jurists can prepare lectures that review these codes with Muslim American audiences in simple terms so that both men and women are aware of their financial rights over one another. Audiences will leave armed with knowledge, and the follow-up questions these lectures will generate will help jurists derive new rulings that better cater to Muslim Americans' evolving needs.

Recommendations on Khulʿ

Some study participants' husbands refused to divorce them and instead pressured the wives to initiate *khulʿ*, and in this way tried to shirk the financial obligations they would have towards their ex-wives in the case of the more traditional male-led or court-imposed divorce. To avoid such manipulation, I recommend that wives include a condition in the marriage contract providing that she can end the marriage without the consent of her husband. Given the different opinions on *khul'*, this is a simple precaution that scholars agree constitutes a valid divorce that would guarantee her the full financial security and rights she would enjoy if her husband had been the one to initiate the divorce, without any question of having to relinquish any sort of gift, item, or portion of wealth[78] Interestingly, a ruling established by AMJA, article 148, gives wives who were coerced by their husbands to initiate *khulʿ* to be given back any valuable payment they provided in exchange for the *khul'* (see appendix E). Executive Imam and formal president of Islamic Society of North America Mohamed Majid strongly discourages *khulʿ*, "It has been the most abused form of divorce, that it puts women at a disadvantage, and that a civil divorce sufficiently dissolves the Islamic marriage contract."[79] Furthermore, in cases where a wife still chooses the route of *khulʿ*, I strongly encourage that a *khul'* contract be made legally through a third party with Islamic scholarly credentials and who is well aware of the local legal system (rather than a community mosque leader or imam who is not well-versed in the American or Western system) to guarantee that any due financial rights of the wife are appropriately retained.

Exploring Annulment as Recourse for Dissolution

The concept of annulment is recognized within Islamic law; a court can declare a Muslim marriage contract null and void, and this then is tantamount to the marriage never having taken place due to its defective nature. In the case of an annulment, the man does not have any financial obligations to the woman once they go their separate ways, because it was as though they were never husband and wife in the first place.

Annulment does *not* require the husband's consent.[80] Divorce, on the other hand, often occurs when the husband initiates the end of a marriage through the pronunciation of specific phrases that terminate the marriage contract (of course, following a divorce, Islamic law obligates a Muslim husband to follow through on certain financial responsibilities to his ex-wife). Separation through divorce does require the husband's consent unless a wife proceeds to removes herself from the marriage without his consent through *khulʿ* (or otherwise by court order).[81] Annulment, when applicable, can be useful when Muslim husbands refuse to grant their wives an Islamic divorce (by pronouncing the wife divorced Still, obtaining an Islamic divorce through a court or third party is normally preferable so that a woman is not relinquishing any of her marital financial rights). Of course, women living in non-Muslim lands must ensure their marriage is dissolved both legally and religiously. AMJA resolves that both the religious and legal divorce could, in some instances, be done at the same time: article 129 of the family law code it established provides that, in cases where a husband *does not object* to a legal divorce and willingly signs a dissolution or divorce agreement, for instance, that is enforceable in the U.S. courts, this document (upon being provided to the community mosque imam) would suffice to end the Islamic marriage and contract under Islamic law.[82]

Annulment or Divorce for Women Whose Husbands Were Dishonest About their Financial Means

Of course, in addition to a wife being able to remove herself from a marriage through *khul'*, according to many scholars, a husband's violation of his religious duty to financially provide for his wife is itself grounds for a traditional divorce for cause. I also endorse the view of Imam Ibn al-Qayyim 🙢 with regard to a man who lies to a woman about his financial well-being – concealing debt, inflating his income, holding wealth yet placing the responsibility to financially provide for the household on his wife, or whatever form the deception may take – and the wife discovers the truth after marriage while having no access to his money and no assistance from a religious leader. In such a case, the wife then has the right to seek an annulment or divorce for-cause even when her husband is simple too poor to financially support her. In such cases, the jurists rule that she can take her complaint to a Muslim judge who should grant her either an annulment or swift divorce with or without her husband's consent.[83] In the U.S. or other western countries, however, where there is no Islamic court, can the imam of her community mosque annul her marriage contract or grant her divorce? According to former president of the Fiqh council of North America, Dr. Muzammil Siddiqi, the *masjid* imam will most likely not do this until the wife files a civil divorce; once a divorce has been finalized by a U.S. civil court, the imam is to accept this document to terminate the marriage Islamically.[84]

Among many study participants, the women found themselves in marriages where they and their children were not receiving *nafaqah*, and, in some instances, had to take on the role of breadwinner themselves. A woman in the West in situations like this who seeks to dissolve her marriage should inform the community *masjid* imam to assist her in obtaining a divorce from her husband. If her husband refuses to issue a divorce, then she should file a civil divorce based on the harm she perceived and present the court-ordered divorce to the *masjid* imam so that he may religiously divorce the parties without her husband's consent.

If a woman in such a predicament seeks divorce in a U.S., Canadian, or European court, I advise her to ask for a spousal support value that reflects any portion of her personal wealth or income that she spent on her family, because under Islamic law, wives do not have to spend from their own pockets on their husbands or children. I also advise that such a woman seek compensation in the form of the spousal support for any household chores she performed while married that, according to Islamic law, were not her duty to perform. Based on some scholarly views, a woman who is denied her right to *nafaqah,* either because her husband deceived her about his financial wellbeing or because he simply refuses to provide for her, and is unable to find Muslim religious leaders to help her seek this financial right, is free to move out of the home she shares with her husband. The reasoning underpinning this view is that if her husband is not fulfilling his most basic religious obligation to her, then it is no longer incumbent upon her to meet her obligations to him.

Pushing for Contextual Legal Reform and Consistent Islamic Guidelines

In many countries today, scholars who are working to protect women's financial rights have been able to provide women with legal options that fall within the Islamic framework.[85] One author highlights how examining case law and legal practices on the ground can give practical solutions to problems women face. Studies in countries such as Malaysia, Saudi Arabia, Coastal Kenya, and Iran reveal how including stipulations in the marriage contract is both effective and in compliance with Islamic law. In Saudi Arabia, such stipulations most often concern the woman's right to an education or employment. In Iran, writing conditions into a marriage contract that strengthen the woman's position is not only permitted, but encouraged.[86] In fact, in these countries, women can print pre-written marriage contract forms that already contain such stipulations such as those establishing an obligation for the husband to pay his wife half his wealth upon divorce, or the wife's right to file for divorce if her husband was to re-marry, mistreat her, or if he does not sufficiently financially provide for her.

Still, the option to include stipulations in a marriage contract can only go so far in bringing real change if couples do not agree to include them. Many countries worldwide have taken some step towards reform to bring some financial justice to women. I recommend Muslim scholars in the U.S. and other Western countries follow their lead by issuing rulings rooted in the Islamic tradition that openly and clearly address areas of abuse:

> Algeria: If a judge finds that a man has divorced his wife in an arbitrary, unfair, or unreasonable manner, or that the wife has suffered harm during her marriage, the former husband can be ordered to compensate her for the divorce or for this harm in addition to the financial maintenance he has to pay her during the 'iddah period.
>
> Singapore: A wife will almost always receive *mut'ah* payment even if she is the party petitioning for the divorce or she has 'misconducted' herself. Arguments that a wife is 'disobedient' (*nusyuz*) [or *nushūz*] have generally not been accepted by the court to disqualify a wife from being entitled to *mut'ah* payment.
>
> Iraq, Kenya, Palestine (West Bank), Syria: If the court finds that a man has divorced his wife in an arbitrary, unfair, or unreasonable manner, the court can order him to pay

his former wife compensation for the divorce in addition to the financial maintenance he has to pay her during the *ʿiddah* period.

Tunisia: If the court finds that a wife has suffered harm during her marriage, it will award maintenance and compensation upon the pronouncement of the divorce in the form of regular monthly payments that continue until the former wife's remarriage, death, or [when] she no longer requires them. The amount awarded is based on the standard of living that the former wife was accustomed to during her marriage.

Iran: The Family Protection Act 2013 in accordance with the Civil Code enables the court to force the husband to pay the wife ujrat al-mithl ('wages in kind') for her housework during marriage based on a monetary value decided by the court.[87]

Conclusion

The main take-away of this study is that women married to Muslim men are not receiving their most basic financial rights according to the Shariah – not even those rights about which there is little or no dispute among Muslim jurists. This book has sought to educate men and women alike about Islamic laws, and lay out several practical avenues women can take to guarantee their rights at the outset of marriage and prevent financial abuse during it, as well as steps to prevent abuse in cases where the marriage is dissolved or the woman is left widowed. It is my hope that taking these practical actions may help women protect not only their financial, but ultimately their physical, mental, and spiritual well-being before, during, and after marriage.

While it is difficult to ascertain why exactly people do what they do, and whether or not culture, patriarchy, religious interpretations, or self-serving instincts are at play, there is no denying that there is room to revisit past rulings and past misinterpretations of Islamic texts that were not only made in contexts well-removed from modern societies, but more importantly, appear to be largely inconsistent with fundamental Islamic principles of justice, kindness, peace, and generosity. While many scholars firmly disagree, the view, for instance, of certain scholars that a marriage contract is a sales contract with the wife being a product of a business transaction whose right to *mahr* and *nafaqah* is based on proper fulfillment of her sexual role in the marriage wholly contradicts the Qur'an and Prophetic traditions, and gives husbands a license to abuse their wives financially and emotionally.[88] Because of such views, and in contravention of various Islamic principles, certain classical imams thereby issued rulings that denied wives the right to *nafaqah* if they, for instance, were unable to have sex.

Such ideas and their ripple effects may take ages to dissipate. They are certainly not aligned with the objective of marriage in Islam as a union built on tranquillity, love, and mercy for the purpose of companionship, procreation, and the spreading of Islam – not a union simply established for the sole cause of fulfilling one's carnal desires. This is consistent with the words of Imam Ibn Ḥazm who stated ﷺ, "Indeed the *nafaqah* (for the wife) is an exchange for marriage and not an exchange for sexual intercourse."[89] God says in Chapter 30, verse 21 of the Qur'an:

وَمِنْ ءَايَٰتِهِۦٓ أَنْ خَلَقَ لَكُم مِّنْ أَنفُسِكُمْ أَزْوَٰجًا لِّتَسْكُنُوٓا۟ إِلَيْهَا وَجَعَلَ بَيْنَكُم
مَّوَدَّةً وَرَحْمَةً ۚ إِنَّ فِى ذَٰلِكَ لَءَايَٰتٍ لِّقَوْمٍ يَتَفَكَّرُونَ ﴿٢١﴾

And of His signs is that He created for you from yourselves mates that you may find tranquility in them; and He placed between you affection and mercy. Indeed, in that are signs for a people who give thought.[90]

Not reflecting upon and adhering to these Qur'anic ideals has left gaps in the scholarly practice of *fiqh*, and these cavities are further exacerbated by longstanding patriarchal influences. While different, men and women are created to complement, rather than dominate, one another. There is no meaningful distinction between the genders in the eyes of God except in their righteousness.[91] Their human rights are equally preserved by the Shariah granting the woman – whether married, divorced or widowed – the right to think, learn, earn (when necessary), retain her earnings, and spend her money as she wishes.

Women in the West, on the other hand, are emphasized as the same as and equal to men, but from an Islamic perspective this alleged equality has burdened them with much more than is fair – they must help provide for the family, bear children, and take on the lion's share of raising the children and running the household.[92] As evident in this study, American women married to Muslim American husbands sadly still face the same financial duties and deprivations common to the broader society but with additional burdens if their husbands are also misusing religion to further denigrate them. This behavior goes against the prophetic tradition and key principles of the Islamic faith.

The intent of Islamic law, as it pertains to marriage, is to create a tranquil and fulfilling family setting in which the roles of both genders complement one another. If we look at the big picture regarding women's financial rights in Islam, we find some issues rooted in the Shariah where there is unanimous agreement, and others that are derived from the Shariah by the *ijtihād* (interpretive efforts) of scholars. Yet many women among the study participants found that they were denied even their most basic, universally agreed-upon financial rights, such as their husbands fulfilling their roles as the providers of their families.

There is no doubt that there is a need to educate both Muslim men and women about their most basic religious roles, obligations, and rights. And when there is a failure to provide for women in our communities, we do need solutions. It is, for instance, a woman's right to receive her *nafaqah* from the public treasury (*bayt al-māl*), which in the West would be defined as any charitable sources in Islamic organizations in her community. Of course, these organizations are often unable to cover these women's needs due to their own meager funds. These sorts of gaps are precisely why contemporary scholars must review and tailor some of their rulings to address the needs of today's women. This sort of re-examination is perfectly in line with Islamic law, because even the Prophet ﷺ himself used to take context – time, place, and culture – into account when providing religious rulings or opinions. For example, he recognized and highlighted that the women of Medina, unlike their more passive Meccan counterparts, were accustomed to being part of the decision-making process both within and outside of the household, and never admonished them for this. The circumstances of women living in the 1,400 years later, who are exceptionally independent and educated, deserve at least the same level of recognition and acquiescence from Muslim scholars.

I hope to emphasize through this book the need for scholars to re-evaluate Muslim jurisprudence regarding the financial rights of women, which has seen minimal change since the 10th century. Islamic thinker Jamal al-Banna grievously said, "Tens of decades have gone by while the *fiqh* of women remains as is."[93] That failure to re-examine past rulings would be tantamount to depriving people of justice and is therefore inconsistent with Islamic law. *Fiqh* scholars are responsible to re-examine the laws by reviewing the inalterable divine law derived from both the Qur'an and Prophetic tradition (Sunnah) to derive new rulings that apply to our societies today. Contemporary female scholars must be a part of this re-evaluation, working hand-in-hand with their male counterparts, because women best understand the difficulties and injustices women in their communities face when it comes to marriage and family life. As seen in examples of rulings made by the Companions of the Prophet, I would argue that Islamic law does not need to be applied in a rigidly literal sense when its effects will not accomplish important Islamic ideals.

I also believe there's a need for additional research on married, divorced, or widowed women in Muslim communities, as well as research examining past cases in U.S. courts that addressed Islamic laws, contracts, and conflicts, since the data and analysis of such subjects is scant. Alongside such research, we need to focus on education. Muslim scholars need to educate both men and women in Muslim communities as well as judges, lawyers, accountants, and other professionals about Islamic law to enable them to understand and implement the rights of women in Muslim households, and to provide resources when conflicts arise. To this end, I recommend that trained imams hold frequent Friday sermons about the financial rights of women during and after matrimony, while *fiqh* organizations, like AMJA, should conduct annual, mandatory training conferences for these imams. Such conferences could include basic education and perhaps result in certifications that would ensure these imams have the necessary knowledge and skillset to effectively and confidently address their communities' needs.

I sincerely hope this work will raise greater awareness about the financial rights of women in Islam, and will encourage scholars to reopen *fiqh* practice to re-examine and revise rulings of jurisprudence in a way that protects women in Muslim communities from financial abuse and its damaging psychological and spiritual effects. I will conclude this book with an essential verse from the Qur'an, emphasizing the importance of God-consciousness and reminding us of our accountability for our behavior with others:

يَٰٓأَيُّهَا ٱلنَّاسُ ٱتَّقُوا۟ رَبَّكُمُ ٱلَّذِى خَلَقَكُم مِّن نَّفْسٍ وَٰحِدَةٍ وَخَلَقَ مِنْهَا زَوْجَهَا وَبَثَّ مِنْهُمَا رِجَالًا كَثِيرًا
وَنِسَآءً ۚ وَٱتَّقُوا۟ ٱللَّهَ ٱلَّذِى تَسَآءَلُونَ بِهِۦ وَٱلْأَرْحَامَ ۚ إِنَّ ٱللَّهَ كَانَ عَلَيْكُمْ رَقِيبًا ﴿١﴾

O mankind, fear your Lord, who created you from one soul and created from it its mate and dispersed from both of them many men and women. And fear Allah, through what you ask one another, and [honor] the wombs [family ties]. Indeed, Allah is ever, over you, an Observer.[94]

Endnotes

Chapter One

1. References to "American women" in this book are references to women who live in the United States.
2. The Chancellor, Masters and Scholars of the University of Cambridge, *The Encyclopedia Britannica*, s.v. "Women," 11th edition, Volume 28 (Cambridge, England, the University Press, 1911), https://archive.org/details/Encyclopaedia-bri28chisrich_201303/page/n815/mode/1up, 782.
3. Britannica, "Women," 782.
4. Ibid.
5. Ibid.
6. Sir Henry Sumner Maine, Lectures on the Early History of Institutions, 7th edition (London, John Murray, 1914), Lecture XI. The Early History of the Settled Property of Married Women, https://oll.libertyfund.org/titles/maine-lectures-on-the-early-history-of-institutions, 124-37.
7. Glanville L. Williams, The Legal Unity of Husband and Wife, *Modern Law Review*, Vol. 1, Issue 1(1947), https://onlinelibrary.wiley.com/doi/pdf/10.1111/j.1468-2230.1947.tb00034.x, 17-18.
8. Gerda Lerner, *The Creation of Patriarchy*, Volume One (New York, Oxford, Oxford University Press, 1986), https://gepacf.wordpress.com/wp-content/uploads/2015/03/women-and-history_-v-1-gerda-lerner-the-creation-of-patriarchy-oxford-university-press-1987.pdf, 216-18; Maine, Lectures on the Early History of Institutions, 124-37.

9. Maine, Lectures on the Early History of Institutions, 124-37, https://ia801600.us.archive.org/6/items/earlyhistoryofpr00main/earlyhistoryofpr00main.pdf, 5.

10. Ibid, 126.

11. Britannica, T. Editors of Encyclopedia. "Married Women's Property Acts." *Encyclopedia Britannica,* September 8, 2010. https://www.britannica.com/event/Married-Womens-Property-Acts-United-States-1839; Lewis, A. D.E., Kiralfy, Albert Roland and Glendon, Mary Ann. "Common law." Encyclopedia Britannica, October 30, 2020. https://www.britannica.com/topic/common-law.

12. Britannica, T. Editors of Encyclopedia. "Custom." *Encyclopedia Britannica,* February 4, 2018. https://www.britannica.com/topic/custom-English-law.

13. Britannica, T. Editors of Encyclopedia. "Coverture." *Encyclopedia Britannica,* October 8, 2007. https://www.britannica.com/topic/coverture.

14. Britannica, "Coverture."

15. Ibid.

16. Mohammad Ali Syed, *The Position of Women in Islam: A Progressive View* (Albany, NY: State University of New York Press, 2004).

17. John Esposito, "Women's Rights in Islam." *Islamic Studies* 14, no. 2 (1975): 99-111, http://www.jstor.org/stable/20846947.

18. Abu Ameenah Bilal Philips, *The Evolution of Fiqh* (Riyadh, Saudi Arabia: International Islamic Publishing House, 1995), 2.

19. Esposito, "Women's Rights in Islam."

20. Muṣṭafā al-Sibāʿī, *Al-Mar'ah bayn al-Fiqh wa al-Qānūn* (Cairo, Egypt: Dār Al-Salām for Printing and Publications and Distribution and Translation), 17-18.

21. Ibid Al-Sibāʿī, *Al-Mar'ah bayn al-Fiqh wa al-Qānūn*, 21-23.
22. ʿAbd al-Ḥalīm Muhammad Abū Shuqqah, *Tahrīr al-Mar'ah fī ʿAsr al-Risālah: Part 1-2* (Cairo, Egypt: Dār Al-Qalam Publications and Distribution, 2011), 301-05; See details of Sūrahs al-Nisā' and al-Ṭalāq in Chapters 1, 2.
23. Abū Shuqqah, *Tahrīr al-Mar'ah fī ʿAsr al-Risālah.*
24. ʿAbd al-Karīm Zaydān, *Al-Jāmiʿ fī al-Fiqh al-Islāmī al-Mufaṣṣal fī Aḥkām al-Mar'ah wa al-Bayt al-Muslim* (Beirut, Lebanon: al-Risālah Publications, 1993), Volume 10, 334, Net Library E-Book Retrieved from https://waqfeya.net/book.php?bid=2676.
25. Zaydān, *Al-Jāmiʿ fī al-Fiqh al-Islāmī*; Wahbah al-Zuḥaylī, *Al Wajiz Fi al-Fiqh al-Islami* (Beirut, Lebanon: Dār Al-Khair Publications and Distribution, 2006), Volume 1, 492, Net E-Book Library Retrieved from https://ia601302.us.archive.org/14/items/FP87019/01_87018.pdf.
26. Ibid, Volume 10, 334-35.
27. Ibid, Volume 4, 289, 290.
28. Ibid, Volume 4, 291-92.
29. Al-Sibāʿī, *Al-Mar'ah bayn al-Fiqh wa al-Qānūn*, 24-26.
30. Ibid.
31. Sayyid Qutb, *Fī Ẓilāl Al-Qur'ān* (Cairo, Egypt: Dār al-Shurūq, 1972), Volume 2, 615.
32. Shihāb al-Dīn Maḥmūd al-Ālūsī, *Tafsīr Ruḥ al-Maʿānī* (Maghribi, Pakistan: Maktaba Imdadiah Miltan, n.d.), Volume 27, 128.
33. Syed, *The Position of Women in Islam.*
34. Arianne Renan Barzilay, Power in the Age of in/Equality: Economic Abuse, Masculinities, and the Long Road to Marriage Equality (January 29, 2018). Akron law Review,

Vol. 52, 2018, Available at SSRN: https://ssrn.com/abstract=3117817; https://www.researchgate.net/publication/323080748_Power_in_the_Age_of_InEquality Economic_Abuse_Masculinities_and_the_Long_Road_to_Marriage_Equality, 227-29.

35. Barzilay, Power in the Age of in/Equality, 229.
36. Olufunmilayo I. Fawole, Economic violence to women and girls: Is it receiving the necessary attention? *Trauma, Violence, & Abuse*, 9:3, 167-77.
37. Barzilay, Power in the Age of in/Equality, 222, 230.
38. Ibid, 235.
39. Ibid, 226.
40. Ibid.
41. Jacquette M. Timmons, *Financial Intimacy* (Chicago, Illinois: Chicago Review Press, 2010), 73.
42. Timmons, *Financial Intimacy*, 78.
43. Sadaf Farooqi, "The Economic Dynamic of a Muslim Marriage," *AboutIslam* (2019). https://aboutislam.net/family-life/laying-foundations/in-marriage-money-does-matter/.
44. Azizah Y. Hibri, "Muslim Women's Rights in The Global Village Challenges and Opportunities," Law Faculty Publications 15 J. L. & Religion 37 (2000), https://scholarship.richmond.edu/cgi/viewcontent.cgi?article=1162&context=law-faculty-publications, 54.
45. Hibri, "Muslim Women's Rights," 41, 54.
46. Ibid.
47. ʿĀbidah al-Mu'ayyad al-Aẓam, *Sunnah al-Tafāḍul* (Beirut, Lebanon: Dār Ibn Ḥazm for Printing & Publication & Distribution, 2000), https://ia903400.us.archive.org/17/items/women00000/Women01365.pdf, 97; ʿĀbidah al-Mu'ayyad

al-Aẓam, *Mā Ḥudūd Ṭā'at al-Zawj?* https://abidaazem.com/ حدود-طاعة-الزوج/, 8.

48. Al-Aẓam, *Sunnah al-Tafāḍul*, 47.
49. See Qur'an 4:34.
50. Muhammad ibn Yūsuf ibn ʿAlī ibn Yūsuf ibn Ḥayyān, *Tafsīr al-Baḥr al-Muḥīt* (Beirut, Lebanon: Dār Iḥyā' al-Turāth al-ʿArabī, 2002), Volume 3, 335.
51. Ibn Ḥayyān, *Tafsīr al-Baḥr al-Muḥīt*, 335.
52. Ibid, 336.
53. Azizah Y. Hibri, "Muslim Women's Rights in The Global Village Challenges and Opportunites," Law Faculty Publications 15 J. L. & Religion 37 (2000), https://scholarship.richmond.edu/cgi/viewcontent.cgi?article=1162&context=law-faculty-publications, 46-47.
54. Sonia D. Galloway, "The Impact of Islam as a Religion and Muslim Women on Gender Equality: A Phenomenological Research Study." Doctoral dissertation. Nova Southeastern University. Retrieved from NSUWorks, Graduate School of Humanities and Social Sciences. (14), https://nsuworks.nova.edu/shss_dcar_etd/14, 141.

Chapter Two

1. Al-Ḥāfiẓ Aḥmad ibn ʿAlī ibn Ḥajar al-ʿAsqalānī, *Fatḥ al-Bārī* (Cairo, Egypt: Dār al-Ḥadīth, 1998).
2. Adil Salahi, "Imam Ali ibn Hazm" (Muslim Heritage, visited 2020), http://www.muslimheritage.com/article/imam-ali-ibn-hazm; Abū Muhammad ʿAlī ibn Aḥmad ibn Saʿīd ibn Ḥazm, *Al-Muḥallā fī Sharḥ al-Mujallā bi al-Ḥujaj wa al-Āthār* (Amman, Jordan: International Idea Home, n.d.), 7; Ibn Ḥazm al-Ẓāhirī (384 AH- 456 AH): One of the most prom-

inent scholars of Hadith and *fiqh* (jurisprudence) known in history.

3. ʿĀbidah al-Mu'ayyad al-Aẓam is the grandchild of prominent jurist ʿAlī al-Ṭanṭāwī, She is an Islamic thinker and Shariah professor who authored 16 books on women related matters and human rights; https://abidaazem.com/مثال-على-صفحة/.
4. Sayyid Qutb, *Fī Ẓilāl Al-Qur'ān* (Cairo, Egypt: Dār al-Shurūq, 1972), Volume 2, 574, 615; Muhammad Fakhr al-Dīn al-Rāzī, *Tafsīr al-Fakhr al-Rāzī* (Beirut, Lebanon: Dār al-Fikr Printing and Publication), Volume 2, 574, 615, https://ia904709.us.archive.org/8/items/FPtrazitrazi/trazi02.pdf.
5. Qutb, *Fī Ẓilāl Al-Qur'ān*, Volume 1, 575.
6. Sahih International; *The Qur'an, The Quranic Arabic Corpus*, (Kais Dukes, 2009-2017), https://corpus.quran.com; Italics or brackets are often added for emphasis and clarity for Qur'anic English translations.
7. Ibn Ḥajar al-ʿAsqalānī, *Fatḥ al-Bārī*, Volume 9, 227.
8. The Qur'an 4:2.
9. The Qur'an 4:3.
10. Yūsuf al-Qaraḍāwī, *The Status of Women in Islam* (Cairo, Egypt: Islamic INC Publishing & Distribution, 1997), 90-91.
11. Qutb, *Fī Ẓilāl Al-Qur'ān*, 577; Fakhr al-Dīn al-Rāzī, *Tafsīr al-Fakhr al-Rāzī*, Volume 9, 177. Italics or brackets are often added for emphasis and clarity for the Hadith English translations or quotes in this book.
12. Fakhr al-Dīn al-Rāzī, *Tafsīr al-Fakhr al-Rāzī*, Volume 9, 177.
13. Abū al-Fiḍā' Ibn Kathīr, *Mukhtaṣar Tafsīr Ibn Kathīr*, ed. Muhammad ʿAlī al-Ṣābūnī, (Beirut, Lebanon: Dār al-Qur'ān al-Karīm, 1981), Volume 1, 355-56.

14. Abū ʿAbdullāh Muhammad ibn Aḥmad al-Anṣārī al-Qurṭubī, *al-Jāmiʿ li Aḥkām al-Qur'ān* (Dār ʿUlūm Al-Qur'ān), Volume 5-6, 10.
15. Fakhr al-Dīn al-Rāzī, *Tafsīr al-Fakhr al-Rāzī*, 178.
16. Ibid.
17. Al-Qurṭubī, *al-Jāmiʿ li Aḥkām al-Qur'ān*, 14.
18. Rahmin Hussain, Arifuddin Aḥmad, Kara Siti and Zulfahmi Alwi, "Polygamy in the Perspective of hadith", *Madania Jurnal Kajian Keislaman*, 10.29300/madania.v23.1954:95, https://www.researchgate.net/publication/335221025_Polygamy_in_the_Perspective_of_hadith_Justice_and_Equality_among_Wives_in_A_Polygamy_Practice.
19. Abū Jaʿfar Muhammad ibn Jarīr al-Ṭabarī, *Jāmiʿ al-Bayān ʿan Ta'wīl āy al-Qur'ān* (Beirut, Lebanon: Mu'assasah al-Risālah Printing and Publications, 1994), Volume 2, 389.
20. ʿAlā' al-Dīn Abū Bakr ibn Masʿūd al-Kāsānī, *Al-Badā'iʿ al-Ṣanā'iʿ fī Tartīb al-Sharā'iʿ*, (Beirut, Lebanon: Dār al-Kutub al-ʿIlmīyyah, 2003), Volume 3, 610, https://ia801201.us.archive.org/11/items/waq75041/03_75043.pdf.
21. Fakhr al-Dīn al-Rāzī, *Tafsīr al-Fakhr al-Rāzī*, Volume 9, 201.
22. Ibid.
23. The Qur'an 4:7.
24. Ibn Kathīr, *Mukhtaṣar Tafsīr Ibn Kathīr*, 368.
25. The Qur'an 4:19.
26. Qutb, *Fī Ẓilāl al-Qur'ān*, Volume 1, 604.
27. Fakhr al-Dīn al-Rāzī, *Tafsīr al-Fakhr al-Rāzī*, 11.
28. The Qur'an 4:19.
29. ʿĀtikah al-Būrīnī, "Mā Hiya Sūrah al-Farā'iḍ" (Mawḍūʿ, 2019), https://mawdoo3.com/ما_هي_سورة_الفرائض.

30. The Qur'an 4:32.
31. Qutb, *Fī Ẓilāl al-Qur'ān*, Volume 1, 557.
32. 'Abd al-Karīm Zaydān, *Al-Jāmi' fī al-Fiqh al-Islāmī al-Mufaṣṣal fī Aḥkām al-Mar'ah wa al-Bayt al-Muslim* (Beirut, Lebanon: al-Risālah Publications, 1993), Volume 7, 50, Net E-book Library Retrieved from https://waqfeya.net/book.php?bid=2676.
33. Wahbah al-Zuḥaylī, *al-Fiqh al-Islāmī wa Adillatuhu* (Beirut, Lebanon: Dār al-Fikr, 2014), Volume 7, 249.
34. The Qur'an 4:4.
35. Zaydān, *Al-Jāmi' fī al-Fiqh al-Islāmī*, Volume 7, 7, 50, 53.
36. Ibid, Volume 7, 48-53.
37. The Qur'an 2:236.
38. Al-Zuḥaylī, *al-Fiqh al-Islāmī wa Adillatuhu*, Volume 7, 249-50; *Mahr al-Mithl*: A stipulated mahr set according to what other female family members were gifted upon marriage.
39. Ibid, Volume 7, 250; 'Abd al-Raḥmān al-Jazīrī, *Kitāb al-Fiqh 'alā al-Madhāhib al-Arba'ah* (Beirut, Lebanon: Dār al-Fikr, 1986), Volume 4, 128-130.
40. Ibid.
41. 'Abd al-Raḥmān al-Jazīrī, *Kitāb al-Fiqh 'alā al-Madhāhib al-Arba'ah*, Volume 4, 128-130.
42. Al-Jazīrī, *Kitāb al-Fiqh 'alā al-Madhāhib al-Arba'ah,* Volume 4, 175.
43. Zaydān, *Al-Jāmi' fī al-Fiqh al-Islāmī*, Volume 7, 323, 325-26.
44. Ibn Ḥajar al-'Asqalānī, *Fatḥ al-Bārī*, Volume 9, 522-23; *Li'ān*: An oath taken by both the husband and wife if the husband accuses his wife of committing adultery while being the only witness. It results in their eternal separation.
45. Ibid.
46. The Qur'an 4:4.
47. Ibid.

48. Shams al-Dīn Muhammad ibn Muhammad al-Khaṭīb al-Shirbīnī, *Mughnī al-Muḥtāj* (Cairo, Egypt: Dar al-Ḥadīth Publications, Printing and Distribution, 2006), Volume 5, 149.
49. Zaydān, *Al-Jāmiʿ fī al-Fiqh al-Islāmī*, Volume 7, 50-51.
50. The Qur'an 2:272.
51. ʿAbd al-ʿAzīz ibn Muhammad al-ʿAqīl, "Al-Ḥathth ʿalā al-Nafaqah fī al-Khayr [Advocacy Towards Good Spending]" (*al-Alūkah al-Sharīʿah*, 2014), https://www.alukah.net/sharia/0/78965/.
52. Al-ʿAqīl, "Al-Ḥathth ʿalā al-Nafaqah fī al-Khayr."
53. Ibid.
54. Abū al-Ḥasan ʿAlī ibn Muhammad ibn Ḥabīb al-Māwardī, *Kitāb al-Nafaqāt* (Beirut, Lebanon: Dar Ibn Ḥazm Publications, 1998), 29, 30.
55. Ibn Ḥajar al-ʿAsqalānī, *Fatḥ al-Bārī*, Volume 9, 570-71.
56. The Qur'an 34:39.
57. Al-Māwardī, *Kitāb al-Nafaqāt*, 2.
58. Ibid.
59. Al-Khaṭīb al-Shirbīnī, *Mughnī al-Muḥtāj*, Volume 5, 149.
60. Yūsuf Qāsim, "Ḥuqūq al-Usrah fī al-Fiqh al-Islāmī (The Family Rights Within Islamic Derived Laws)" (*al-Alūkah al-Sharīʿah*, 2010), https://www.alukah.net/sharia/0/23148/.
61. Qāsim, "Ḥuqūq al-Usrah fī al-Fiqh al-Islāmī."
62. Ibid.
63. Al-Jazīrī, *Kitāb al-Fiqh ʿalā al-Madhāhib al-Arbaʿah*, Volume 4, 589.
64. Al-Khaṭīb al-Shirbīnī, *Mughnī al-Muḥtāj*, Volume 5, 149.
65. Ibid.
66. Ibid, Volume 5, 182-83; Qāsim, "Ḥuqūq al-Usrah fī al-Fiqh al-Islāmī."
67. Ibid, Volume 5, 149.

68. Muhammad ibn ʿAlī ibn Muhammad al-Shawkānī, *Nayl al-Awṭār* (Beirut, Lebanon: Dār al-Maʿrifah, 2002), Volume 2, 1460.
69. Al-Shawkānī, *Nayl al-Awṭār*, Volume 2, 1460; Abū Muhammad ʿAlī ibn Aḥmad ibn Saʿīd ibn Ḥazm, *Al-Muḥallā bi al-Āthār* (Beirut, Lebanon: Dār al-Kutub al-ʿIlmiyyah, 2003), Volume 9, 59, Net E-Book Library Retrieved from https://archive.org/details/FP74771/09_74779/page/n58/mode/1up?view=theater; Zaydān, *Al-Jāmiʿ fī al-Fiqh al-Islāmī*, Volume 10, 225.
70. Fayṣal Mubārak, "Ḥukm al-Nafaqah ʿalā al-Zawjah [The Legal Ruling of Maintenance for the Wife]" (*al-Alūkah al-Sharīʿah*, 2017), https://www.alukah.net/sharia/0/112941/.
71. Zaydān, *Al-Jāmiʿ fī al-Fiqh al-Islāmī al-Mufaṣṣal fī Aḥkām al-Marʾah wa al-Bayt al-Muslim*, Volume 7, 181-83.
72. Ibid, Volume 7, 183.
73. Ibid, Volume 10, 225.
74. Muhammad ibn Idrīs al-Shāfiʿī, *Al-Umm* (Cairo, Egypt: Dār al-Ḥadīth, 2008), Volume 6, 202.
75. Al-Shāfiʿī, *Al-Umm,* Volume 6, 202.
76. Al-Jazīrī, *Kitāb al-Fiqh ʿalā al-Madhāhib al-Arbaʿah*, Volume 4, 157-162.
77. Al-Khaṭīb al-Shirbīnī, *Mughnī al-Muḥtāj*, Volume 5, 149.
78. Muhammad ibn ʿAlī ibn Muhammad al-Shawkānī, *Nayl al-Awṭār* (Beirut, Lebanon: Dār al-Maʿrifah, 2002), Volume 2, 36.
79. Zaydān, *Al-Jāmiʿ fī al-Fiqh al-Islāmī*, Volume 7, 153.
80. Ibid.
81. Ibid.
82. Ibid, Volume 7, 180-81.
83. The Qur'an 65:6.
84. The Qur'an 2:233.
85. Ibn Ḥazm, *Al-Muḥallā bi al-Āthār*, Volume 9, 228-29.

86. Zaydān, *Al-Jāmiʿ fī al-Fiqh al-Islāmī*, Volume 7, 196.
87. Ibid, Volume 7, 195-96.
88. Ibid, Volume 7, 195.
89. Al-Khaṭīb al-Shirbīnī, *Mughnī al-Muḥtāj*, Volume 5, 183.
90. The Qur'an 2:233.
91. Zaydān, *Al-Jāmiʿ fī al-Fiqh al-Islāmī*, Volume 10, 162.
92. Ibid, Volume 10, 160.
93. Ibid, Volume 10, 158; Volume 7, 201.
94. Zaydān, *Al-Jāmiʿ fī al-Fiqh al-Islāmī*, Volume 10, 158; Ibn al-Mundhir: "He is Abū Bakr Muhammad ibn Ibrāhīm ibn al-Mundhir al-Naysābūrī. He died 318 AD/930 AD. He learned under one of Imam al-Shāfiʿī's students."
95. Al-Jazīrī, *Kitāb al-Fiqh ʿalā al-Madhāhib al-Arbaʿah*, 585.
96. Ibn Taymiyyah al-Ḥarrānī, *Al-La'āli al-Lāmiʿāt fī Aḥkām al-Muʿāmalāt* (Beirut, Lebanon, Sharikah Binā' Sharīf al-Anṣārī for Printing and Publication and Distribution, 2011), 1059; Ibn Jarīr al-Ṭabarī, *Jāmiʿ al-Bayān ʿan Ta'wīl āy al-Qur'ān*, Volume 2.
97. Ibn Jarīr al-Ṭabarī, *Jāmiʿ al-Bayān ʿan Ta'wīl āy al-Qur'ān*, Volume 2, 62.
98. The Qur'an 4:23.
99. The Qur'an 86:7.
100. Zaydān, *Al-Jāmiʿ fī al-Fiqh al-Islāmī*, Volume 10, 159.
101. Ibid, Volume 10, 162.
102. Ibid, Volume 10, 171.
103. Mustafa al-Adawy, *Jami' Ahkam Al-Nisaa'*, Volume 2 (Cairo, Egypt, Dar Ibn Affan, 1999), 171.
104. Zaydān, *Al-Jāmiʿ fī al-Fiqh al-Islāmī*, Volume 7, 201, 218-19; ʿAbdullāh ibn ʿAbd al-Muḥsin al-Tarīqī, "Al-Nafaqah al-Wājibah ʿalā al-Mar'ah li Ḥaqq al-Ghayr" (*al-Alūkah al-Sharīʿah*, 2007), http://cp.alukah.net/web/turaiqi/0/363/.

105. Al-ʿAdawī, *Jāmiʿ Aḥkām al-Nisāʾ*, Volume 2, 99-101.
106. Ibid, Volume 2, 94-99; Alāʾ Jarrār, "Waṣiyyah al-Rasūl ilā al-Nisā" [The Bequest of the Messenger Regarding Women] (*Mawḍūʿ*, 2021), https://mawdoo3.com/وصية_الرسول_بالنساء.
107. Zaydān, *Al-Jāmiʿ fī al-Fiqh al-Islāmī*, Volume 10, 183-84.
108. The Qur'an 2:83.
109. Al-Zuḥaylī, *al-Fiqh al-Islāmī wa Adillatuhu*, Volume 7, 782
110. The Qur'an 31:15.
111. Al-Zuḥaylī, *al-Fiqh al-Islāmī wa Adillatuhu*, Volume 7, 782
112. Ibid.
113. The Qur'an 65:6.
114. Qutb, *Fī Ẓilāl al-Qur'ān*, Volume 6, 3593; Zaydān, *Al-Jāmiʿ fī al-Fiqh al-Islāmī*, Volume 9, 248.
115. Ibid, Volume 6, 3593; Ibid, Volume 9, 240-43.
116. Ibid, Volume 6, 3594; Zaydān, *Al-Jāmiʿ fī al-Fiqh al-Islāmī*, Volume 9, 255.
117. The Qur'an 65:6.
118. Zaydān, *Al-Jāmiʿ fī al-Fiqh al-Islāmī*, Volume 9, 249-50.
119. Qutb, *Fī Ẓilāl al-Qur'ān*, Volume 6, 3594
120. Zaydān, *Al-Jāmiʿ fī al-Fiqh al-Islāmī*, Volume 9, 248.
121. Ibid, Volume 9, 248, 250-51.
122. Ibid, Volume 9, 252-53.
123. Ibid, Volume 9, 255.
124. Ibid, Volume 8, 126.
125. Ibid, Volume 8, 126, 130.
126. Ibid, Volume 8, 126.
127. Ibid, Volume 8, 227-28, 115.
128. Ibid, Volume 8, 320.
129. Ibid, Volume 8, 321-22, 397.
130. The Qur'an 24:4.

131. The Qur'an 24:6
132. The Qur'an 24:7.
133. Zaydān, *Al-Jāmiʿ fī al-Fiqh al-Islāmī*, Volume 7, 103.
134. The Qur'an 2:237.
135. Al-Jazīrī, *Kitāb al-Fiqh ʿalā al-Madhāhib al-Arbaʿah*, Volume 4, 131.
136. The Qur'an 2:241.
137. Al-Jazīrī, *Kitāb al-Fiqh ʿalā al-Madhāhib al-Arbaʿah*, Volume 4, 602-03; The Qur'an 2:236.
138. Zaydān, *Al-Jāmiʿ fī al-Fiqh al-Islāmī*, Volume 9, 255.
139. The Qur'an 2:233.
140. Al-Jazīrī, *Kitāb al-Fiqh ʿalā al-Madhāhib al-Arbaʿah*, Volume 4, 602-03; Zaydān, *Al-Jāmiʿ fī al-Fiqh al-Islāmī*, Volume 8, 200.
141. The Qur'an 2:233.
142. The Qur'an 65:6.
143. Al-Jazīrī, *Kitāb al-Fiqh ʿalā al-Madhāhib al-Arbaʿah*, Volume 4, 602.
144. Al-Khaṭīb al-Shirbīnī, *Mughnī al-Muḥtāj*, Volume 4, 9.
145. Ibid, Volume 4, 9-10.
146. Zaydān, *Al-Jāmiʿ fī al-Fiqh al-Islāmī*, Volume 11, 268; Al-Shāfiʿī, *Al-Umm*, Volume 4, 473.
147. The Qur'an 4:12.
148. Zaydān, *Al-Jāmiʿ fī al-Fiqh al-Islāmī*, Volume 11, 268.
149. Ibid, Volume 11, 268-69; Al-Adawy, *Jami' Ahkam Al-Nisaa'*, Volume 4, 659.
150. Ibid, Volume 11, 269.
151. Muṣṭafā al-Sibāʿī, *Al-Mar'ah bayn al-Fiqh wa al-Qānūn* (Cairo, Egypt: Dār al-Salām for Printing and Publications and Distribution and Translation), 25.
152. The Qur'an 4:11.

153. Mālik ibn Anas, *Muwaṭṭa' li Imām Mālik* (Shubra, Egypt: Al-Andalus al-Jadīdah for Publications and Distributions, 2009), 361.
154. *Yaḥjub*: The literal meaning of *al-ḥajb* in the Arabic language is to deprive. Its meaning, according to the Shariah, however, is to specifically deprive someone from all or some of his or her inheritance due to the existence of another person more deserving of it. There are two types of *ḥajb* (blockage): one called *ḥajb ḥirmān* (blockage of complete deprivation), while the other is termed *ḥajb naqṣān* (blockage that partly deprives). The daughter falls only under being partly deprived, since no one is able to completely deprive her of her inheritance rights but based on other family members that are alive, her share maybe reduced.
155. Al-Shāfi'ī, *Al-Umm*, Volume 4, 473.
156. Zaydān, *Al-Jāmi' fī al-Fiqh al-Islāmī*, Volume 11, 280-82.
157. The Qur'an 4:12.
158. Zaydān, *Al-Jāmi' fī al-Fiqh al-Islāmī*, Volume 11, 300-01.
159. Mālik ibn Anas, *Muwaṭṭa' li Imām Mālik*, 363.
160. Ibid, 362-63.
161. Zaydān, *Al-Jāmi' fī al-Fiqh al-Islāmī*, Volume 4, 282-83.
162. Ibn Ḥazm, *Al-Muḥallā bi al-Āthār*, Volume 10, 381.
163. Ibn Kathīr, *Mukhtaṣar Tafsīr Ibn Kathīr*, Volume 1, 157.
164. The Qur'an 4:12.
165. Mālik ibn Anas, *Muwaṭṭa' li Imām Mālik*, 558.
166. Ibid, 558-59.
167. Ibid.
168. Zaydān, *Al-Jāmi' fī al-Fiqh al-Islāmī*, Volume 1, 345.
169. Ibid, Volume 1, 343.
170. Ibid, Volume 4, 282.

171. Ibid, Volume 4, 284.
172. Ibid.
173. Ibid, Volume 4, 283.
174. The Qur'an 9:60.
175. Al-Shāfiʿī, *Al-Umm*, Volume 4, 445.
176. Ibid.
177. The Qur'an 33:35.
178. The Qur'an 2:215.
179. Zaydān, *Al-Jāmiʿ fī al-Fiqh al-Islāmī*, Volume 1, 455.
180. Ibid.
181. Al-Shawkānī, *Nayl al-Awṭār*, Volume 2, 1230-32.
182. Zaydān, *Al-Jāmiʿ fī al-Fiqh al-Islāmī*, Volume 10, 421.
183. Ibid.
184. Al-Shāfiʿī, *Al-Umm*, Volume 8, 402; my translation.
185. The Qur'an 5:89.
186. Ibn Kathīr, *Mukhtaṣar Tafsīr Ibn Kathīr*, Volume 3, 459.
187. The Qur'an 58:2.
188. Zaydān, *Al-Jāmiʿ fī al-Fiqh al-Islāmī*, Volume 2, 431.
189. Ibid, Volume 2, 430.
190. Ibid, Volume 2, 429.
191. Ibid, Volume 2, 329.
192. Ibid, Volume 2, 437-38; my translation.
193. Ibid, Volume 2, 436.
194. Ibid, Volume 2, 446-50; The Qur'an 108:2.
195. Zaydān, *Al-Jāmiʿ fī al-Fiqh al-Islāmī*, Volume 4, 287.
196. Ibid, Volume 4, 263.
197. Ibid, Volume 4, 265.
198. Ibid.
199. The Qur'an 4:32.
200. Zaydān, *Al-Jāmiʿ fī al-Fiqh al-Islāmī*, Volume 10, 335-36.

201. The Qur'an 2:233.
202. Zaydān, *Al-Jāmiʿ fī al-Fiqh al-Islāmī*, Volume 10, 335.
203. Ibid, Volume 10, 337.
204. Ibid.
205. Al-Shāfiʿī, *Al-Umm*, Volume 8, 581.
206. Ibid.
207. The Qur'an 5:45.
208. The Qur'an 4:92.
209. Ibn Kathīr, *Mukhtaṣar Tafsīr Ibn Kathīr*, Volume 1, 520.

Chapter Three

1. ʿAbd al-Karīm Zaydān, *Al-Jāmiʿ fī al-Fiqh al-Islāmī al-Mufaṣṣal fī Aḥkām al-Mar'ah wa al-Bayt al-Muslim* (Beirut, Lebanon: al-Risālah Publications, 1993), Volume 7, 50.
2. The Qur'an 4:4.
3. Zaydān, *Al-Jāmiʿ fī al-Fiqh al-Islāmī*, Volume 7, 50, 52-53; Wahbah al-Zuḥaylī, *al-Fiqh al-Islāmī wa Adillatuhu* (Beirut, Lebanon: Dār al-Fikr, 2014), Volume 7, 247; Aḥmad al-Ḥijī al-Kurdī, "Al-Mahr", (Shabakat al-Fatāwā al-Sharīʿah, 2020), http://www.islamic-fatwa.com/library/book/8/136; ʿĀrif al-Shaykh, "Hal al-Mahr Sharṭ fī Ṣiḥḥah al-Nikāḥ [Is the Mahr a Condition for the Validity of the Marriage Contract?]" (*al-Khalīj*, 2020), https://www.alkhaleej.ae/-عالم متجدد/هل-المهر-شرط-في-صحة-النكاح؟.
4. Zaydān, *Al-Jāmiʿ fī al-Fiqh al-Islāmī*, Volume 7, 50-52.
5. Al-Zuhaily, *Al-Fiqh Al-Islami wa-Adilatuhu*, Volume 7, 247; ʿĀrif al-Shaykh, "Hal al-Mahr Sharṭ fī Ṣiḥḥah al-Nikāḥ.
6. Zaydān, *Al-Jāmiʿ fī al-Fiqh al-Islāmī*, Volume 7, 52; ʿĀbidah al-Mu'ayyad al-Aẓam, *Mā Ḥudūd Ṭāʿah al-Zawj?* https://abidaazem.com/حدود-طاعة-الزوج/, 18.

7. The Qur'an 4:21; The Qur'an 2:187.
8. Ḥasan al-Ṣaffār, "Al-Ṣadāq" (Maktab Samāḥah al-Shaykh Ḥasan al-Ṣaffār, 2001), https://www.saffar.org/?act=artc&id=957; Wahbah al-Zuḥaylī, *al-Fiqh al-Islāmī wa Adillatuhu*, Volume 7, 247.
9. Al-Zuḥaylī, *al-Fiqh al-Islāmī wa Adillatuhu*, Volume 7, 248.
10. Zaydān, *Al-Jāmiʿ fī al-Fiqh al-Islāmī*, Volume 7, 51; Muhammad Fakhr al-Dīn al-Rāzī, *Tafsīr al-Fakhr al-Rāzī* (Beirut, Lebanon: Dār al-Fikr Printing and Publication), Volume 9, 186.
11. The Qur'an 4:24.
12. Zaydān, *Al-Jāmiʿ fī al-Fiqh al-Islāmī*, Volume 7, 7, 50, 53.
13. Ibid, Volume 7, 48-53.
14. The Qur'an 2:236.
15. ʿAbd al-Raḥmān al-Jazīrī, *Kitāb al-Fiqh ʿalā al-Madhāhib al-Arbaʿah* (Beirut, Lebanon: Dār al-Fikr, 1986), Volume 4, 157-162. Net Library E-Book Retrieved from https://ia601608.us.archive.org/12/items/waq78101/04_78104.pdf.
16. Al-Jazīrī, *Kitāb al-Fiqh ʿalā al-Madhāhib al-Arbaʿah* , Volume 4, 158, 160,162.
17. ʿAlāʾ al-Dīn Abū Bakr ibn Masʿūd al-Kāsānī, *Al-Badāʾiʿ al-Ṣanāʾiʿ fī Tartīb al-Sharāʾiʿ*, (Beirut, Lebanon: Dār al-Kutub al-ʿIlmīyyah, 2003), Volume 3, 515, Net Library E-Book Retrieved from https://ia801201.us.archive.org/11/items/waq75041/03_75043.pdf.
18. Al-Jazīrī, *Kitāb al-Fiqh ʿalā al-Madhāhib al-Arbaʿah*, Volume 4, 157-62.
19. *Mu'ajjal: A mu'akhkhar mahr* is one that is specified in the marriage contract without any mention of it being expedited or deferred. Based on some schools of thought (Abū Ḥanīfah), the husband is required to immediately pay it off to his wife

and, in the event of non-payment, he loses rights over her while expected to provide for her.

20. Ibn Rushd, *The Distinguished Jurist's Primer*, trans. Imran Ahsan Khan Nyazee, Volume II (Reading, United Kingdom: Garnet Publishing Limited, 1996), 25.
21. Ibn Rushd, *The Distinguished Jurist's Primer*, 25.
22. Zaydān, *Al-Jāmiʿ fī al-Fiqh al-Islāmī*, Volume 8, 502.
23. Ibid, Volume 8, 501.
24. Ibid, Volume 8, 501-02.
25. Ibid, Volume 8, 501.
26. Ibid, Volume 8, 502.
27. The Qur'an 4:21.
28. Al-Jazīrī, *Kitāb al-Fiqh ʿalā al-Madhāhib al-Arbaʿah*, Volume 4, 128-30.
29. Ibid, Volume 4, 131; Zaydān, *Al-Jāmiʿ fī al-Fiqh al-Islāmī*, Volume 7, 51, 125.
30. Ibid, Volume 4, 128-130; Zaydān, *Al-Jāmiʿ fī al-Fiqh al-Islāmī*, Volume 7, 50-52.
31. Al-Jazīrī, *Kitāb al-Fiqh ʿalā al-Madhāhib al-Arbaʿah*, Volume 4, 128-30.
32. Ibid, 130; my translation.
33. Ibid, 128-30; *Fāsid*: A *fāsid* contract is one that is corrupt, meaning that there is something incorrect about the contract. One example is if a female is married with a *walī* but no witnesses. The reason that this contract is *fāsid* but not invalid is due to differences between the schools of thought. Abū ʿAbd al-Raḥmān Ayman Ismāʿīl, "Al-ʿAqd al-Bāṭil wa al-ʿAqd al-Fāsid" (*al-Alūkah al-Sharīʿah*, 2020), https://www.alukah.net/sharia/0/138890/.

34. Al-Jazīrī, *Kitāb al-Fiqh ʿalā al-Madhāhib al-Arbaʿah*, Volume 4, 130.
35. Zaydān, *Al-Jāmiʿ fī al-Fiqh al-Islāmī*, Volume 7, 51.
36. Al-Zuḥaylī, *al-Fiqh al-Islāmī wa Adillatuhu*, Volume 7, 260.
37. Zaydān, *Al-Jāmiʿ fī al-Fiqh al-Islāmī*, Volume 7, 51.
38. Ibid, 51.
39. Al-Jazīrī, *Kitāb al-Fiqh ʿalā al-Madhāhib al-Arbaʿah*, Volume 4, 96.
40. Al-Zuḥaylī, *al-Fiqh al-Islāmī wa Adillatuhu*, Volume 7, 253; Abu Salma Muhammad Aydeed and Abul Abbas Naveed Ayaaz, "How Much Was the Prophetic Dowry in Today's Economy" (Madeena, 2019), https://www.madeenah.com/wp-content/uploads/how-much-was-the-prophetic-dowry-in-todays-economy.pdf, 11-12.
41. Zaydān, *Al-Jāmiʿ fī al-Fiqh al-Islāmī*, Volume 7, 61, 54.
42. Abū Bakr Jābir al-Jazā'irī, *Minhāj al-Muslim* (Riyadh, Saudi Arabia: Darussalam Global Leader in Islamic Books, 2001), Volume 2, 325-26.
43. Zaydān, *Al-Jāmiʿ fī al-Fiqh al-Islāmī*, Volume 7, 103-04.
44. The Qur'an 2:237.
45. Abū ʿAbdullāh Muhammad ibn Aḥmad al-Anṣārī al-Qurṭubī, *al-Jāmiʿ li Aḥkām al-Qur'ān* (Dār 'Ulūm Al-Qur'ān), Volume 3-4, 74; *Īlā'*: The linguistic meaning of *īlā'* is a general oath of any kind. From the Islamic legal perspective (*sharʿan*), it stands for a vow of continence in which the husband abstains from having intercourse with his wife. It is conditioned that he utters that he will not have an intimate relation with her forever or for four or more months; The Qur'an 2:226; Al-Jazīrī, *Kitāb al-Fiqh ʿalā al-Madhāhib al-Arbaʿah*, Volume 4, 463.

46. The Qur'an 2:226.
47. Zaydān, *Al-Jāmiʿ fī al-Fiqh al-Islāmī*, Volume 7, 104; *Liʿān*: This is a course of action that is taken if a man accuses his wife of adultery while being unable to provide four witnesses. According to the Qur'an 24:6-9, imprecation (*liʿān*) is a type of oath that requires the accuser to swear four times that he speaks the truth followed by a fifth accepting the curse of Allah to befall him if he is not truthful. His wife would follow by also swearing four times that she speaks the truth and a fifth accepting Allah's anger if she lies. Once the procedure comes to an end, both spouses are separated and the marriage comes to an end. Ibn Rushd, *The Distinguished Jurist's Primer*, 585.
48. ʿAbdullāh ibn Mubārak ʿAlī Sayf, "Min Aḥkām al-Liʿān fī al-Fiqh al-Islāmī [Amongst the Legal Rulings Regarding Imprecation Within Islamic Fiqh]" (*al-Alūkah al-Sharīʿah*, 2014), https://www.alukah.net/web/abdullah-ibn-mubarak/0/76957/#_ftnref2.
49. Zaydān, *Al-Jāmiʿ fī al-Fiqh al-Islāmī*, Volume 7, 104.
50. Ibid.
51. Fakhr al-Dīn al-Rāzī, *Tafsīr al-Fakhr al-Rāzī*, Volume 9, 189; Shurayḥ: "His name is Shurayḥ ibn Qays ibn Ḥārith and was the first Muslim judge (*qāḍī*) of Kufa (Iraq). He remained in this position during the Caliphate of ʿUmar ibn al-Khaṭṭāb and ʿUthmān ibnʿAffān. He was removed during the Caliphate of ʿAlī and re-instated during the Caliphate of Muʿāwiyah". Rāghib al-Sirjānī, "Shurayḥ al-Qāḍī (Qiṣṣah al-Islām, 2019), https://islamstory.com/ar/artical/3408542/شريح-القاضي.
52. ʿAbd al-Malik ibn Marwān: The fifth Umayyad Caliph and one of the most prominent scholars of Dimashq (Syria). He was

born in the year 26 AH and passed away 86 AH. Razān Ṣalāḥ, "Ma'lūmāt 'an 'Abd al-Malik ibn Marwān" (Mawḍū', 2019), https://mawdoo3.com/معلومات_عن_عبد_الملك_بن_مروان.

53. Fakhr al-Dīn al-Rāzī, *Tafsīr al-Fakhr al-Rāzī*, Volume 9, 189.
54. The Qur'an, 4:20.
55. Fakhr al-Dīn al-Rāzī, *Tafsīr al-Fakhr al-Rāzī*, Volume 9, 189.
56. Muhammad ibn Idrīs al-Shāfi'ī, *Al-Umm* (Cairo, Egypt: Dār al-Ḥadīth, 2008), Volume 8, 507; my translation.
57. Muṣṭafā al-'Adawī, *Jāmi' Aḥkām al-Nisā'* (Cairo, Egypt: Dār Ibn 'Affān, 1999), Volume 5, 222-23.
58. Al-'Adawī, *Jāmi' Aḥkām al-Nisā'*, Volume 5, 223.
59. Ibid, Volume 5, 171.
60. Zaydān, *Al-Jāmi' fī al-Fiqh al-Islāmī*, Volume 7, 201'Abdullāh ibn 'Abd al-Muḥsin al-Tarīqī, "Al-Nafaqah al-Wājibah 'alā al-Mar'ah li Ḥaqq al-Ghayr" (*al-Alūkah al-Sharī'ah*, 2007), http://cp.alukah.net/web/turaiqi/0/363/.
61. Ibn Qudāmah, *Al-Mughnī* (Riyadh, Saudi Arabia: Dār 'Aalam al-Kutub'Publications, 1986), Volume 4, 100-02, https://ia801609.us.archive.org/23/items/WAQmogni/mogni04.pdf; Ibn al-Hamam, Fath al-Qadeer (Beirut, Lebanon: Dār al-Kutub al-'Ilmiyyah, 2003), Volume 2, 275, https://ia802801.us.archive.org/22/items/waq72501/02_72502.pdf; Mustafa al-Adawy, *Jami' Ahkam Al-Nisaa'*, Volume 2, Net Library E-Book Retrieved from https://archive.org/details/jami-3-ahkam-nissa-e/202%ج20%النساء20%أحكام20%جامع/page/n96/mode/1up?view=theater, 97.
62. Ibn Qudāmah, *Al-Mughnī*, Volume 4, 101-02.
63. Zaydān, *Al-Jāmi' fī al-Fiqh al-Islāmī*, Volume 10, 224.
64. Ibid, Volume 10, 227.
65. Ibid, Volume 10, 228.

66. Ibid, Volume 10, 227.
67. Ibid, Volume 7, 158.
68. Ibid, Volume 7, 154-59.
69. Ibid, Volume 7, 158.
70. Ibid, Volume 7, 158-59, 197-98.
71. Ibid, Volume 7, 199.
72. Ibid, Volume 7, 198-99.
73. Al-Shāfiʿī, *Al-Umm*, Volume 6, 202; Zaydān, *Al-Jāmiʿ fī al-Fiqh al-Islāmī*, Volume 7, 181-82.
74. The Qur'an 4:19.
75. Zaydān, *Al-Jāmiʿ fī al-Fiqh al-Islāmī*, Volume 7, 182.
76. Abū Muhammad ʿAlī ibn Aḥmad ibn Saʿīd ibn Ḥazm, *Al-Muḥallā bi al-Āthār* (Beirut, Lebanon: Dār al-Kutub al-ʿIlmiyyah, 2003), Volume 9, 227, https://archive.org/details/FP74771/09_74779/page/n227/mode/2up?view=theater; my translation.
77. Ibn Ḥazm, *Al-Muḥallā bi al-Āthār*, Volume 9, 227-29; Al-ʿAdawī, *Jāmiʿ Aḥkām al-Nisā'*, Volume 2, 199-202; ʿAbd al-Halīm Abū Shaqqah, *Taḥrīr al-Mar'ah fī ʿAṣr Al-Risālah* (Kuwait, Dar al-Qalam li al-Nashr wa al-Tawzīʿ, 1990), Volume 5-6, 127-29.
78. Zaydān, *Al-Jāmiʿ fī al-Fiqh al-Islāmī*, Volume 7, 195-96.
79. Ibid, Volume 7, 185.
80. Ibid.
81. Ibid; the Qur'an 4:19.
82. ʿĀbidah al-Mu'ayyad al-Aẓam, *Mā Ḥudūd Ṭāʿah al-Zawj?* https://abidaazem.com/حدود-طاعة-الزوج/, 10.
83. The Qur'an 30:21.
84. Al-Jazīrī, *Kitāb al-Fiqh ʿalā al-Madhāhib al-Arbaʿah*, Volume 4, 558.
85. Ibid.
86. Ibid, Volume 4, 557.

87. Zaydān, *Al-Jāmi' fī al-Fiqh al-Islāmī*, Volume 7, 185; Abbas Sofwan Matlail Fajar, "Criticism of Gender Mainstreaming According to Abdul Karim Zaidan in 'Al-Mufassol Fi Ahkam Al-Mar'ah wa Bayt Al-Muslim'," AHKAM Jurnal Ilmu Syariah 19(2) DOI: 10.15408/aiis v19i2.10852 (2019), https://www.researchgate.net/publication/338259095_Criticism_of_Gender_Mainstreaming_according_to_Abdul_Karim_Zaidan_in_Al-Mufassol_Fi_Ahkam_Al-Mar'ah_wa_Bayt_Al-Muslim/link/5e0eb1b74585159aa4adb897/download, 271.
88. Al-Jazīrī, *Kitāb al-Fiqh 'alā al-Madhāhib al-Arba'ah*, Volume 4, 557.
89. 'Ābidah al-Mu'ayyad al-Aẓm, *Mā Ḥudūd Ṭā'ah al-Zawj?* 10.
90. The Qur'an 4:34. Note: *Sahih International* defines *nushuz* as arrogance, which, as described in this book, is a translation some scholars disagree with. It is worth noting that, later in this verse, the translation of the word ""*wa-ḍribūhunna*"" is also subject to some disagreement. While many translate this word as "strike them" or "strike them lightly," some translate the word as "go away from them," for instance.
91. Abū al-Faḍl Jamāl al-Dīn Muhammad ibn Mukarram Ibn Manẓūr, *Lisān al-'Arab* (Beirut, Lebanon: Dar Ṣādir), Volume 12, 497-99.
92. Sahih International, *The Qur'an*, "Verse (4:34)- English Translation," *The Quranic Arabic Corpus*, (Kais Dukes, 2009-2017), https://corpus.quran.com/translation.jsp?chapter=4&verse=34.
93. Ibn Manẓūr, *Lisān al-'Arab*, Volume 12, 325-26.
94. Azizah Y. Hibri, "Muslim Women's Rights in The Global Village Challenges and Opportunities," Law Faculty Publications 15 J. L. & Religion 37 (2000), https://scholarship.

richmond.edu/cgi/viewcontent.cgi?article=1162&context=law-faculty-publications, 51.

95. See Chapter 2.
96. Al-Khaṭīb al-Shirbīnī, *Mughnī al-Muḥtāj*, Volume 5, 165.
97. Abū al-Ḥasan ʿAlī ibn Muhammad ibn Ḥabīb al-Māwardī, *Kitāb al-Nafaqāt* (Beirut, Lebanon: Dār Ibn Ḥazm Publications, 1998) 31- 32; The Qur'an 2:233.
98. Al-Jazīrī, *Kitāb al-Fiqh ʿalā al-Madhāhib al-Arbaʿah*, Volume 4, 566.
99. Al-Māwardī, *Kitāb al-Nafaqāt*, 101.
100. Zaydān, *Al-Jāmiʿ fī al-Fiqh al-Islāmī*, Volume 7, 173.
101. Ibid, Volume 7, 173.
102. Al-Khaṭīb al-Shirbīnī, *Mughnī al-Muḥtāj*, Volume 5, 165.
103. Al-Kāsānī, *Al-Badāʾiʿ al-Ṣanāʾiʿ fī Tartīb al-Sharāʾiʿ*, Volume 5, 129.
104. Zaydān, *Al-Jāmiʿ fī al-Fiqh al-Islāmī*, Volume 7, 158.
105. Ibid, Volume 7, 163.
106. Ibid, Volume 7, 161, 310.
107. Ibid.
108. Al-Jazīrī, *Kitāb al-Fiqh ʿalā al-Madhāhib al-Arbaʿah*, Volume 4, 565.
109. Jamal al-Banna, *Al-Mar'ah al-Muslimah bayn Taḥrīr al-Qur'ān wa Taqyīd al-Fuqahā'* (Cairo, Egypt: Dār al-Shurūq, 2007), 187.
110. The Qur'an 4:128.
111. Abū Jaʿfar Muhammad ibn Jarīr al-Ṭabarī, *Jāmiʿ al-Bayān ʿan Ta'wīl āy al-Qur'ān* (Beirut, Lebanon: Mu'assasah al-Risālah Printing and Publications, 1994), Volume 7, 548.
112. Abū al-Fiḍā' Ibn Kathīr, *Tafsīr al-Qur'ān al-ʿAẓīm* (Riyadh, Saudi Arabia: Dār Ṭaybah Publications, 1997), Volume 2, 426,

https://ia802808.us.archive.org/29/items/43005PDF/tqa2.pdf.

113. Ibn Kathīr, *Tafsīr al-Qur'ān al-'Aẓīm*, Volume 2, 428.
114. Muhammad Bakr Ismā'īl, *Al-Fiqh al-Wāḍiḥ* (Cairo, Egypt, Dār al-Manār Publications, 1997), Volume 2, 97.
115. Al-Kāsānī, *Al-Badā'i' al-Ṣanā'i' fī Tartīb al-Sharā'i'*, Volume 3, 611; Muhammad Saalih al-Munajjid, "The Reasons Mentioned in Sawda's Gift of Her Night to Aisha and an Explanation of the Most Correct of Them" (Islam Question and Answer, 2019), https://islamqa-info.translate.goog/ar/answers/127828/الاسباب-الواردة-في-هبة-سودة-ليلتها-لعايشة-وبيان-الراجح-منها?_x_tr_sl=ar&_x_tr_tl=en&_x_tr_hl=en&_x_tr_pto=sc; Zaydān, *Al-Jāmi' fī al-Fiqh al-Islāmī*, Volume 9, 218-19.
116. Mannā' al-Qa ṭṭān, *Mabāḥith fī 'Ulūm al-Qur'ān* (Cairo, Egypt: Maktabah Wahbah, 2000), 321.
117. Faḍl Ḥasan 'Abbās, *Al-Tafsīr wa al-Mufassirūn* (Amman, Jordon: Dār al-Nafā'is for Publications and Distributions, 2016), 645.
118. Ibn Ḥazm, *Al-Muḥallā bi al-Āthār*, Volume 9, 249.
119. 'Ābidah al-Mu'ayyad al-Aẓam, *Sunnah al-Tafāḍul* (Beirut, Lebanon: Dār Ibn Ḥazm for Printing & Publication & Distribution, 2000), Net Library E-Book Retrieved from https://ia601509.us.archive.org/32/items/wom-en00000/Women01365.pdf, 217.
120. 'Ābidah al-Mu'ayyad al-Aẓam, *Mā Ḥudūd Ṭā'ah al-Zawj?*, 12, 13; Saḥar Fīdah, "Shakṣiyyah Mulhimah" (*Sayyidaty*, 2016), https://www.sayidaty.net/node/442021/أسرة-ومجتمع/شخصية-اليوم/عابدة-العظم-سليلة-العثمانيين-وحفيدة-الطنطاوي#photo/1.

121. Ṣafī al-Raḥmān al-Mubārakfūrī, *Al-Raḥīq al-Makhtūm* (Al-Mansura, Egypt: Dār al-Wafā' for Printing, Publications and Distribution, 1999), 462.
122. Mukamaleen TV, "Ḍarb al-Zawj li al-Zawjah lā Yakun il fī Muqaddimāt al-Zinā", Guest Speaker 'Ābidah al-Mu'ayyad al-Aẓam (2016), https://www.youtube.com/watch?v=CIYGkHN8vyk.
123. Al-Aẓam, *Sunnah al-Tafāḍul*, 217-18.
124. Abū Shaqqah, *Taḥrīr al-Mar'ah fī 'Aṣr Al-Risālah*, 234; Mālik ibn Anas, "*Al-Mudawwanah al-Kubrā*". The Hadith is narrated in *Ṣaḥīḥ al-Bukhārī*, Chapter 8, 230.
125. Muhammad Ṣāliḥ al-Munajjid, "Did the Prophet (saw) Ever Hit His Wife Aa'isha," Islam Question & Answer, Question 164216 Publication: 06-12-2013, https://islamqa.info/en/answers/164216/did-the-prophet-blessings-and-peace-of-allah-be-upon-him-ever-hit-his-wife-aaishah-may-allah-be-pleased-with-her; Hadith narrated by Aḥmad in *al-Musnad*, 30/341-342. The commentators said, "Its *isnād* is *ṣaḥīḥ* according to the conditions of Imam Muslim."
126. Abū Shaqqah, *Taḥrīr al-Mar'ah fī 'Aṣr Al-Risālah*, 235; Ibn Ḥajar al-'Asqalānī, *Fatḥ al-Bārī*, Volume 9, 318.
127. Zaydān, *Al-Jāmi' fī al-Fiqh al-Islāmī*, Volume 7, 350, 354.
128. The Qur'an 58:11.
129. Shihāb al-Dīn Maḥmūd al-Ālūsī, *Tafsīr Ruḥ al-Ma'ānī* (Beirut, Lebanon: Idārah al-Ṭibā'ah al-Munīriyyah) Volume 28.
130. Ibn Ḥajar al-'Asqalānī, *Fatḥ al-Bārī*, Volume 9, 386.
131. Zaydān, *Al-Jāmi' fī al-Fiqh al-Islāmī*, Volume 7, 162.
132. Ibid, Volume 7, 166.
133. Ibid, Volume 7, 162, 164-65.
134. Ibid, Volume 7, 165.

135. Ibid, Volume 7, 164-65.
136. Dār Al-Iftā' al-Miṣriyyah, "The Obligation for a Woman to Obtain Her Husband's Permission to Travel for Hajj" (22 October 2020), https://www.dar-alifta.org/Foreign/ViewFatwa.aspx?ID=8119.
137. 'Ābidah al-Mu'ayyad al-Aẓam, *Mā Ḥudūd Ṭā'ah al-Zawj?*, 11.
138. Ibid, 11; my translation.
139. Ibn Ḥazm, *Al-Muḥallā bi al-Āthār*, Volume 9, 250.
140. Al-Māwardī, *Kitāb al-Nafaqāt*, 120.
141. Zaydān, *Al-Jāmi' fī al-Fiqh al-Islāmī*, Volume 7, 162.
142. Ibid, Volume 7, 161-63.
143. Ibid, Volume 7, 161-62.
144. Al-Jazīrī, *Kitāb al-Fiqh 'alā al-Madhāhib al-Arba'ah,* Volume 4, 566, Net Library, Volume 4, 143-44; Zaydān, *Al-Jāmi' fī al-Fiqh al-Islāmī*, Volume 7, 162.
145. Al-Jazīrī, *Kitāb al-Fiqh 'alā al-Madhāhib al-Arba'ah*, Volume 4, 566.
146. Ibn Ḥazm, *Al-Muḥallā bi al-Āthār*, Volume 9, 249.
147. Ibid, Volume 9, 112-13.
148. Ibid, Volume 9, 249.
149. Ibid, Volume 9, 250.
150. Ibid, Volume 9, 249-50.
151. Ibid, Volume 9, 250.
152. The Qur'an 30:21.
153. Mukamaleen TV, "Ḍarb al-Zawj li al-Zawjah lā Yakun il fī Muqaddimāt al-Zinā".
154. Ibn Shihāb al-Zuhrī, *Al-Nāsikh wa al-Mansūkh fī al-Qur'ān al-Karīm* (Cairo, Egypt: Dar Ibn 'Affān li-Nashr wa al-Tawzī', 2008), 67.

155. Ibn Rushd, *The Distinguished Jurist's Primer*, trans. Imran Ahsan Khan Nyazee, Volume II (UK, Garnet Publishing Limited, 1996), 63.
156. Al-Khaṭīb al-Shirbīnī, *Mughnī al-Muḥtāj*, Volume 5, 150.
157. Muhammad Saalih al-Munajjid, "Islamic Weights and Measures and Their Modern Equivalents" (Islam Question and Answer, 2019), https://islamqa.info/en/answers/154588/islamic-weights-and-measures-and-their-modern-equivalents; Moosaa Richardson "Zakaat al-Fitr Measurment One Sa'=3 Litre, One Mud=. 75L" (Bakkah Publications, 2012), https://www.bakkah.net/en/zakat-fitr-measurements-saa-three-litres-mudd.htm.
158. Al-Shāfiʿī, *Al-Umm*, Volume 6, 206.
159. Zaydān, *Al-Jāmiʿ fī al-Fiqh al-Islāmī*, Volume 7, 190-91, 194-96.
160. Ibid, Volume 7, 211.
161. Ibn Rushd, *The Distinguished Jurist's Primer*, 63.
162. Zaydān, *Al-Jāmiʿ fī al-Fiqh al-Islāmī*, Volume 7, 201.
163. Ibid.
164. Ibid, Volume 7, 200-02.
165. Al-ʿAdawī, *Jāmiʿ Aḥkām al-Nisā'*, Volume 3, 555-56.
166. Ibid, Volume, 3, 555.
167. Zaydān, *Al-Jāmiʿ fī al-Fiqh al-Islāmī*, Volume 8, 480-481; Rīnād al-Ṣabāḥ, "*Ma Huwa Faskh Al-Nikāḥ* [What is the Invalidation of the Marriage Contract]" (2020), https://mawdoo3.com/ما_هو_فسخ_النكاح.
168. Zaydān, *Al-Jāmiʿ fī al-Fiqh al-Islāmī*, Volume 8, 479.
169. Ibid, Volume 8, 472, Volume 7, 218-19.
170. Ibid, Volume 8, 473.
171. Ibid, 472-73.

172. The Qur'an 2:280.
173. Zaydān, *Al-Jāmiʿ fī al-Fiqh al-Islāmī*, Volume 8, 475.
174. Ibid.
175. Ibid, Volume 8, 476, 480-81.
176. Ibid, Volume 8, 674; Fayṣal ibn ʿAbd al-ʿAzīz Āl Mubārak, "Iʿsār Al-Zawj [The Withholding of the Husband]" (*al-Alūkah al-Sharīʿah*, 2017), https://www.alukah.net/sharia/0/113501/.
177. Zaydān, *Al-Jāmiʿ fī al-Fiqh al-Islāmī*, Volume 8, 481.
178. Ibid, Volume 8, 476; my translation.
179. The Qur'an 2:229.
180. Zaydān, *Al-Jāmiʿ fī al-Fiqh al-Islāmī*, Volume 8, 477.
181. Ibid, Volume 8, 478.
182. Ibid, Volume 8, 481, 482; ʿĀbidah al-Mu'ayyad al-Aẓam, *Sunnah al-Tafāḍul*, 225.
183. Al-Jazīrī, *Kitāb al-Fiqh ʿalā al-Madhāhib al-Arbaʿah*, Volume 4, 580; Al-Khaṭīb al-Shirbīnī, *Mughnī al-Muḥtāj*, Volume 5, 165.
184. Al-Jazīrī, *Kitāb al-Fiqh ʿalā al-Madhāhib al-Arbaʿah*, Volume 4, 577-78.
185. Ibid, Volume 4, 577-78.
186. Ibid, Volume 4, 578; my translation.
187. Ibid, Volume 4, 579-80.
188. Jamaal Zarabozo, "Fiqh of Marriage," (2013), http://www.smahate.com/islamic-classes/2013-winter/fiqh-of-marriage.
189. Zarabozo, "Fiqh of Marriage."
190. Ibid; Al-Māwardī, *Kitāb al-Nafaqāt*, 150.
191. The Qur'an 65:6.
192. The Qur'an 65:7.
193. The Qur'an 2:233.

194. Al-Māwardī, *Kitāb al-Nafaqāt,* 31; Ibn Taymiyyah al-Ḥarrānī, *Al-La'āli al-Lāmi'āt fī Aḥkām al-Mu'āmalāt* (Beirut, Lebanon, Sharikah Binā' Sharīf al-Anṣārī for Printing and Publication and Distribution, 2011), 1055.
195. Al-Māwardī, *Kitāb al-Nafaqāt,* 31; Al-Ḥarrānī, *Al-La'āli al-Lāmi'āt fī Aḥkām al-Mu'āmalāt,* 1055, 1058.
196. Ibid.
197. Zaydān, *Al-Jāmi' fī al-Fiqh al-Islāmī,* Volume 10, 159, 160.
198. Ibid, Volume 10, 164.
199. Ibid, Volume 10, 165.
200. Ibid, Volume 10, 165-66.
201. Ibid, Volume 10, 166.
202. Ibid, Volume 10, 168.
203. Ibid, Volume 10, 162-63.
204. Ibid, Volume 10, 168.
205. Ibid, Volume 10, 169.
206. Ibid, Volume 10, 166-67.
207. Ibid, Volume 10, 167.
208. Ibid, Volume 9, 245.
209. Muhammad 'Uqlah al-Ḥasan al-'Alī, "'Iddah al-Wafāh: Mafhūmuhā wa Aḥkāmuhā fī al-Sharī'ah al-Islāmiyyah [The Waiting Period for the Widow and its Meaning and Rulings]" (Bingol Universities, 2015), https://dergipark.org.tr/tr/download/article-file/206271, 86.
210. Zaydān, *Al-Jāmi' fī al-Fiqh al-Islāmī,* Volume 9, 245.
211. Kecia Ali, *Muslim Sexual Ethics: Triple Repudiation* (Brandeis University, 2003).
212. Ismā'īl, *Al-Fiqh al-Wāḍiḥ,* 129; Ibn Taymiyyah al-Ḥarrānī, *Al-La'āli al-Lāmi'āt fī Aḥkām al-Mu'āmalāt,* 1059-60.

213. ʿAlī ibn al-Ḥusnī al-ʿIlmī, *Kitāb al-Nawāzil* (Rabat, Morocco: Wizārah al-Awqāf fi Al-Shu'ūn al-Islāmiyyah, 1983), Volume 1, 279.
214. Ismāʿīl, *Al-Fiqh al-Wāḍiḥ*, Volume 2, 129; Zaydān, *Al-Jāmiʿ fī al-Fiqh al-Islāmī*, Volume 9, 243; The Qur'an 65:1.
215. Al-Shāfiʿī, *Al-Umm*, Volume 6, 221.
216. Maḥmūd Maḥmūd al-Najīrī, "Tanāzuʿ al-Zawjayn fī Matāʿ al-Bayt" (Al-Multaqā al-Fiqhī, 2008), https://feqhweb.com/vb/threads/796.تنازع-الزوجين-في-متاع-البيت/.
217. Al-Shāfiʿī, *Al-Umm*, Volume 6, 220.
218. Ibid, 220, Volume 6, 221.
219. Ibid, Volume 6, 220; my translation.
220. Zaydān, *Al-Jāmiʿ fī al-Fiqh al-Islāmī*, Volume 8, 227-28.
221. Ibid, Volume 8, 228; Abū Muhammad ʿAlī ibn Aḥmad ibn Saʿīd ibn Ḥazm, *Al-Muḥallā bi al-Āthār*, Volume 9, 225.
222. Ibid, Volume 9, 514; Musawah: For Equality in the Family, "Positive Developments in Muslim Family Laws," (2019), https://www.musawah.org/wp-content/uploads/2019/02/Positive-Developments-Table-2019_EN.pdf, 13-14; Saʿīd Ḥijāzī and ʿAbd al-Wahhāb ʿĪsā, "Al-Azhar: Ṭalab al-Khulʿ la Yatawaqqaf ʿalā Riḍā al-Zawj [The Request of Khulʿ Is not Based on the Husband's Consent], https://www.elwatannews.com/news/details/2990337.
223. Zaydān, *Al-Jāmiʿ fī al-Fiqh al-Islāmī*, Volume 8, 212-15, 173; Ibn Ḥazm, *Al-Muḥallā bi al-Āthār,* Volume 9, 518-19.
224. Ibid, Volume 8, 126, 172-73.
225. Ibid, Volume 8, 201-02.
226. Ibid, Volume 8, 201.

227. Sāmiḥ ʿAbd al-Salām Muhammad, "Al-Khulʿ ʿalā Baʿḍ al-Manāfiʿ wa al-Ḥuqūq" (2015), https://www.alukah.net/sharia/0/85169/.
228. Ibid.
229. Ismāʿīl, *Al-Fiqh al-Wāḍiḥ*, Volume 2, 135.
230. Zaydān, *Al-Jāmiʿ fī al-Fiqh al-Islāmī*, Volume 8, 176.
231. Ibid, Volume 8, 177.
232. The Qur'an 4:19.
233. Abū al-Fiḍā' Ibn Kathīr, *Mukhtaṣar Tafsīr Ibn Kathīr*, ed. Muhammad ʿAlī al-Ṣābūnī, (Beirut, Lebanon: Dār al-Qur'ān al-Karīm, 1981), Volume 1, 221.
234. Ibn Jarīr al-Ṭabarī, *Jāmiʿ al-Bayān ʿan Ta'wīl āy al-Qur'ān*, Volume 7, 80.
235. The Qur'an 2:241.
236. Ibn Jarīr al-Ṭabarī, *Jāmiʿ al-Bayān ʿan Ta'wīl āy al-Qur'ān*, Volume 7, 80-81.
237. Ibn Ḥazm, *Al-Muḥallā bi al-Āthār*, Volume 10, 3; my translation.
238. Mālik ibn Anas, *Muwaṭṭa' li Imām Mālik*, 415.
239. Ibid.
240. Ibid; Zaydān, *Al-Jāmiʿ fī al-Fiqh al-Islāmī*, Volume 7, 138.
241. Ibn Ḥazm, *Al-Muḥallā bi al-Āthār*, Volume 10, 4.
242. Ibid.
243. Sayyid Mubārak, "Ṣadāq al-Zawjayn bayn al-ʿUrf wal-Sharʿ" (*al-Alūkah al-Sharīʿah*, 2018), https://www.alukah.net/social/0/132617/.
244. Mubārak, "Ṣadāq al-Zawjayn bayn al-ʿUrf wal-Sharʿ."
245. Karamah Muslim Women Lawyers for Human Rights, "Ask Zahra" (Ask Zahra Advice Column, 2015), https://karamah.org/wp-content/uploads/2020/07/Answer-to-alimony-question.pdf, 3.

246. Ibid.
247. The Qur'an 53:39.
248. The Qur'an 53:41.
249. Karamah Muslim Women Lawyers for Human Rights, "Ask Zahra", 3.
250. Al-Ḥasan al-ʿAbbādī, *Kitāb al-Nawāzil fī Sūs* (Casablanca, Morocco: Maṭbaʿah al-Najāḥ al-Jadīdah, 1999), 12.
251. Karamah Muslim Women Lawyers for Human Rights, "Ask Zahra", 4.
252. Ibid.
253. Zaydān, *Al-Jāmiʿ fī al-Fiqh al-Islāmī*, Volume 9, 484-89; my translation.
254. Ibid, Volume 9, 285.
255. Al-Jazīrī, *Kitāb al-Fiqh ʿalā al-Madhāhib al-Arbaʿah,* Volume 4, 602.
256. Al-Jazīrī, *Kitāb al-Fiqh ʿalā al-Madhāhib al-Arbaʿah*, Volume 4, 602-03; ʿAbd al-Raḥmān Al-Jazīrī, *Kitāb al-Fiqh ʿalā al-Madhāhib al-Arbaʿah*, Volume 4, 527-28, https://ia601608.us.archive.org/12/items/waq78101/04_78104.pdf, 527-28.
257. Ibid, Volume 4, 527-28.
258. Ibid.
259. Zaydān, *Al-Jāmiʿ fī al-Fiqh al-Islāmī*, Volume 8, 200.
260. Ibid, Volume 8, 404.
261. Muhammad Jabr al-Alfī, "Ithbat al-Nasab wa Nafyihi bi al-Baṣmah al-Wirāthiyyah [Proof of Paternity and Rejecting it Through DNA]" (*Al-Muslim*, 2015) https://almoslim.net/node/250399.
262. Zaydān, *Al-Jāmiʿ fī al-Fiqh al-Islāmī*, Volume 8, 327.
263. Ibid.
264. Ibid, 323.

265. Ibid, 327.
266. Ismāʿīl, *Al-Fiqh al-Wāḍiḥ*, Volume 2, 153.
267. Al-Shāfiʿī, *Al-Umm*, Volume 4, 474-75.
268. Zaydān, *Al-Jāmiʿ fī al-Fiqh al-Islāmī*, Volume 11, 253.
269. Ibid, Volume 11, 254.
270. Ibid.
271. Al-Shāfiʿī, *Al-Umm*, Volume 4, 476.
272. Ibid, Volume 4, 473.
273. Mālik ibn Anas, *Muwaṭṭaʾ li Imām Mālik*, 365.
274. Ibid.
275. Ibid, 367-68.
276. Zaydān, *Al-Jāmiʿ fī al-Fiqh al-Islāmī*, Volume 11, 297.
277. The Qur'an 4:176.
278. Al-Shāfiʿī, *Al-Umm*, Volume 4, 485.
279. Mālik ibn Anas, *Muwaṭṭaʾ li Imām Mālik*, 559; Mālik ibn Anas, *Muwaṭṭaʾ of Imām Mālik ibn Anas The First Formulation of Islamic Law*, Translated by Aisha Bewley (Norwich, UK, Diwan Press Ltd, 1982), 565-66, https://ia903201.us.archive.org/22/items/al-muwatta-of-imam-malik/Al-Muwatta%20of%20Imam%20Malik.pdf.
280. Zaydān, *Al-Jāmiʿ fī al-Fiqh al-Islāmī*, Volume 10, 382.
281. Ibid, Volume 10, 401.
282. Mālik ibn Anas, *Muwaṭṭaʾ li Imām Mālik*, 559.
283. Zaydān, *Al-Jāmiʿ fī al-Fiqh al-Islāmī*, Volume 10, 401.
284. Ibid, Volume 1, 415-16.
285. Ibid, Volume 4, 282-83.
286. Ibid, Volume 4, 280-83.
287. Ibid, Volume 1, 426-27.
288. Ibid, Volume 1, 421.

289. Ibid, Volume 1, 422.
290. Al-ʿAdawī, *Jāmiʿ Aḥkām al-Nisā'*, Volume 5, 174.
291. Ibid, Volume 5, 175.
292. Ibn Kathīr, *Mukhtaṣar Tafsīr Ibn Kathīr,* Volume 2, 151.
293. Ibid.
294. Al-ʿAdawī, *Jāmiʿ Aḥkām al-Nisā'*, Volume 5, 175.
295. Zaydān, *Al-Jāmiʿ fī al-Fiqh al-Islāmī*, Volume 4, 285-86.
296. Ibid, Volume 4, 284-86.
297. Al-ʿAdawī, *Jāmiʿ Aḥkām al-Nisā'*, Volume 5, 173-74 or Net Library E-Book Retrieved from https://archive.org/details/jami-3-ahkam-nissa-e/205%ج20%النساء20%أحكام20%جامع/page/n163/mode/1up?view=theater, 164; *Al-Umm, Kitab Al-Nafaqat*, Volume 2, 478; Zaydān, *Al-Jāmiʿ fī al-Fiqh al-Islāmī*, Volume 4, 285-86; my translation.
298. Al-Madinah News, "Taqrīr: Thulthay Fuqarā' al-ʿĀlam min al-Nisā' [Report: One Third of the Poor in the World are Women]" (Al-Madīnah al-Ikhbāriyyah, October 17, 2018), https://www.almadenahnews.com/article/701459--تقرير-ثلثي-فقراء-العالم-من-النساء.
299. Jamāl Muhammad ʿUbaydāt, "Ta'nīth al-Faqr [Feminizing Poverty]" (*Al-Bayān,* 2007) https://www.albayan.ae/opinions/2007-10-10-1.797670; Al-Madinah News, "Taqrīr: Thulthay Fuqarā' al-ʿĀlam min al-Nisā' [Report: One Third of the Poor in the World are Women]" (Al-Madīnah al-Ikhbāriyyah, October 17, 2018), https://www.almadenahnews.com/article/701459-تقرير-ثلثي-فقراء-العالم-من-النساء.
300. Muhammad Ṣāliḥ al-Munajjid, "Dafʿ al-Zakāt li al-Mar'ah al-Faqīrah Idhā Kāna Zawjuhā la Yunfiq ʿAlayhā [The Obligatory Charity for the Poor Woman When Her Hus-

band Abstains From Spending on Her]" [*Al-Islām Su'āl wa al-Jawāb*, 2007] https://islamqa.info/ar/answers/102755/دفع-الزكاة-للمراة-الفقيرة-اذا-كان-زوجها-لا-ينفق-عليها

301. Al-ʿAdawī, *Jāmiʿ Aḥkām al-Nisā'*, Volume 2, 104.
302. The Qur'an 2:43.
303. Ibn Ḥajar al-ʿAsqalānī, *Fatḥ al-Bārī*, Volume 3, 306.
304. The Qur'an 3:180.
305. Al-Mubārakfūrī, *Al-Raḥīq al-Makhtūm*, 462.
306. Abū l-Muẓaffar ʿAwn al-Dīn Yaḥyā ibn Muḥammad ibn Hubayrah, *Ijmāʿ al-A'immah al-Arbaʿah wa Ikhtilāfihum* (Cairo, Egypt: Dar al-ʿUlā, 2009), https://archive.org/stream/FP98456/01_98456#page/n267/mode/2up, 269.
307. Zaydān, *Al-Jāmiʿ fī al-Fiqh al-Islāmī*, Volume 1, 460.
308. Ibid.
309. Ibid.
310. Al-ʿAdawī, *Jāmiʿ Aḥkām al-Nisā'*, Volume 5, 176.
311. Ibid, Volume 5, 176; The Qur'an 4:19.
312. Ibid, Volume 5, 176.
313. Al-ʿAdawī, *Jāmiʿ Aḥkām al-Nisā'*, Volume 5, 176-77; Zaydān, *Al-Jāmiʿ fī al-Fiqh al-Islāmī*, Volume 10, 339, 340.
314. Ibn Rushd, *The Distinguished Jurist's Primer*, Volume II, 399.
315. Ibn Ḥajar al-ʿAsqalānī, *Fatḥ al-Bārī*, Volume 5, 241.
316. Al-Shāfiʿī, *Al-Umm*, Volume 4, 449.
317. Ibn Ḥajar al-ʿAsqalānī, *Fatḥ al-Bārī*, Volume 5, 237.
318. Ibid, Volume 5, 240.
319. Ibn Ḥazm, *Al-Muḥallā bi al-Āthār*, Volume 8, 83.
320. Zaydān, *Al-Jāmiʿ fī al-Fiqh al-Islāmī*, Volume 10, 442-43.
321. Ibid, Volume 10, 444.
322. Ibid, Volume 10, 441-42.

323. Ibid, Volume 10, 444-45.
324. Ibid, Volume 10, 443.
325. Ibid, Volume 2, 83; Al-Shāfiʿī, *Al-Umm*, Volume 8, 409.
326. Al-Shāfiʿī, *Al-Umm*, Volume 8, 409.
327. Ibid, Volume 4, 291.
328. Ibid, Volume 4, 289.
329. The Qur'an 4:32.
330. Khālid ʿAbd al-Munʿim al-Rifāʿī, "Hukm Akhdh Al-Zawj Ratib al-Zāwjah (Ruling of a Husband Taking the Wife's Paycheck)" (*Ṭarīq Al-Islam*, 2012) https://ar.islamway.net/fatwa/36835/حكم-أخذ-الزوج-راتب-الزوجة.
331. The Qur'an 92:3.
332. The Qur'an 92:4.
333. Zaydān, *Al-Jāmiʿ fī al-Fiqh al-Islāmī*, Volume 4, 268.
334. The Qur'an 28:23.
335. Zaydān, *Al-Jāmiʿ fī al-Fiqh al-Islāmī*, Volume 4, 269.
336. Ibid, Volume 4, 270.
337. Ibid.
338. Ibid.
339. Ibid, Volume 4, 273-74.
340. Ibid, Volume 4, 271.
341. Abū Shaqqah, *Taḥrīr al-Mar'ah fī ʿAṣr Al-Risālah*, 130.
342. Muhammad al-Ghazālī, *Qaḍāyā al-Mar'ah bayn al-Taqālīd al-Rākidah wa al-Wāfidah* [*Women's Issues Between Stagnant and Expatriate Traditions*] (Cairo, Egypt: Dār Al-Shurūq, 2012), 28.
343. Al-Ghazālī, *Qaḍāyā al-Mar'ah*.
344. Samiyyah Manīsī, "Ahammiyyah Taʿlīm al-Mar'ah [The Importance of Educating Women]" (*al-Alūkah al-Sharīʿah*) https://www.alukah.net/social/0/116019/.

345. Zaydān, *Al-Jāmiʿ fī al-Fiqh al-Islāmī*, Volume 4, 272-73.
346. Muhammad Farooq Khan, *Islam and Women* (Model Town, Lahore, Pakistan, Dar-Ul-Ishraq, 2002), 12-13.
347. Zaydān, *Al-Jāmiʿ fī al-Fiqh al-Islāmī*, Volume 4, 272-73.
348. Ibid, Volume 4, 273.
349. Ibn Ḥajar al-ʿAsqalānī, *Fatḥ al-Bārī*, Volume 2, 489-90.
350. Ibid, Volume 2, 489-490.
351. Khan, *Islam and Women*, 13-14.
352. Zaydān, *Al-Jāmiʿ fī al-Fiqh al-Islāmī*, Volume 4, 290-91.
353. The Qur'an 33:35.
354. Arianne Renan Barzilay, "Power in the Age of In/Equality: Economic Abuse, Masculinities, and the Long Road to Marriage Equality" (January 29, 2018). *Akron law Review*, Vol. 52, 2018, Available at SSRN: https://ssrn.com/abstract=3117817, or https://www.researchgate.net/publication/323080748_Power_in_the_Age_of_InEquality_Economic_Abuse_Masculinities_and_the_Long_Road_to_Marriage_Equality, 234-35.
355. Barzilay, "Power in the Age of In/Equality," 236.
356. Ibid, 235.
357. Ibid.
358. Al-Madinah News, "Taqrīr: Thulthay Fuqarā' al-ʿĀlam min al-Nisā'.
359. Ibid.
360. Ibid.
361. Ibn Kathīr, *Mukhtaṣar Tafsīr Ibn Kathīr*, Volume 1, 520-21.
362. The Qur'an 5:45.
363. Ibn Kathīr, *Mukhtaṣar Tafsīr Ibn Kathīr*, Volume 1,156.
364. Al-Shāfiʿī, *Al-Umm*, Volume 8, 580.
365. Ibid, Volume 8, 579.
366. Al-ʿAdawī, *Jāmiʿ Aḥkām al-Nisā'*, Volume 5, 625-26.

367. Ibn Rushd, *The Distinguished Jurist's Primer*, Volume II, 498.
368. Al-Shāfiʿī, *Al-Umm*, Volume 7, 426.
369. Ibid.
370. Ibid.
371. Saʿd al-Dīn al-Hilālī, *Al-Islām wa Insāniyyah al-Dawlah* (Cairo, Egypt: al-Hay'ah al-Miṣriyyah al-ʿĀmmah, 2012), 160.
372. Al-Hilālī, *Al-Islām wa Insāniyyah al-Dawlah*,160.
373. Ibid, 160-61.
374. Al-ʿAdawī, *Jāmiʿ Aḥkām al-Nisā'*, Volume 4 (Cairo, Egypt, Dar Ibn Affan Publication and Distribution, 1999), 613-14; al-Hilālī, *Al-Islām wa Insāniyyah al-Dawlah*, 162.
375. Saʿd al-Dīn al-Hilālī, *Al-Islām wa Insāniyyah al-Dawlah* (Cairo, Egypt: al-Hay'ah al-Miṣriyyah al-ʿĀmmah, 2012),161; Al-ʿAdawī, *Jāmiʿ Aḥkām al-Nisā'*, Volume 4, 614.
376. Al-ʿAdawī, *Jāmiʿ Aḥkām al-Nisā'*, Volume 4, 614-16.
377. Ibid.
378. Ibid.
379. Al-Shawkānī, *Nayl al-Awṭār*, Volume 2, 49.
380. Al-Kāsānī, *Al-Badā'iʿ al-Ṣanā'iʿ fī Tartīb al-Sharā'iʿ*, Volume 10, 450.
381. Ibid.
382. Al-Hilālī, *Al-Islām wa Insāniyyah al-Dawlah*, 162.
383. Ibid, 161.
384. Ibid, 161-62.
385. Ibid, 161-63.
386. Ibn Rushd, *The Distinguished Jurist's Primer*, Volume II, 513.
387. The Qur'an 5:45; The Qur'an 4:92; Saʿd al-Dīn al-Hilālī, *Al-Islām wa Insāniyyah al-Dawlah*, 161; Al-ʿAdawī, *Jāmiʿ Aḥkām al-Nisā'*, Volume 4, 614.

Chapter Four

1. Thomas Groenwald, "A Phenomenological Research Design Illustrated," *International Journal of Qualitative Methods,* 3 (1) (2004), https://journals.sagepub.com/doi/pdf/10.1177/160940690400300104, 43-44.
2. Groenwald, "A Phenomenological Research Design Illustrated," 43-47.
3. Ibid, 46.
4. Pew Research Center, "Demographic Portrait of Muslim Americans" (2017), https://www.pewforum.org/2017/07/26/demographic-portrait-of-muslim-americans/.
5. *Mahr*: In Islam, *al-mahr,* which is incorrectly translated in English as dowry, carries a totally different meaning. It is defined as an obligation of the husband toward his wife specified in the marriage contract.
6. See Chapters 3 and 4 in this study.
7. Thomas Groenwald, "A Phenomenological Research Design Illustrated," *International Journal of Qualitative Methods,* 3 (1) (2004), https://journals.sagepub.com/doi/pdf/10.1177/160940690400300104, 46.
8. Nuhā Faraj, "Al-Takāfu': Hal Yumkin al-Tanāzul ʿAnhu?" (*al-Alūkah al-Sharīʿah*, 2017) https://www.alukah.net/social/0/121128/.
9. Al-Ḥāfiẓ Aḥmad ibn ʿAlī ibn Ḥajar al-ʿAsqalānī, *Fatḥ al-Bārī* (Cairo, Egypt: Dār al-Ḥadīth, 1998), Volume 9, 316.
10. Ibid, Volume 9, 316, 291-96.
11. Hamd al-Neel Abd el-Sayed Abd el-Qadir, "Hadith Umm Zar: Dirasah fi al-Tarakeeb wadallalah," *Mugalit Kulayit al-Ulum wal-Adab bil-Ula*, Tibah University, February 2018,

https://mkda.journals.ekb.eg/article_123451_dae35f260cc11128d490c0e32c6887dd.pdf, 227-29.

12. Ibid, 10-14.
13. Ibid, 14.
14. Ibn Ḥajar al-ʿAsqalānī, *Fatḥ al-Bārī*, Volume 9, 291, 305, 316.
15. Ibid, 314.
16. Ibid, 305-14.
17. Naʿīmah ʿAbd al-Fattāḥ Nāṣif, "Umm Zarʿ: Al-Zawjah Al-Wafiyyah fī Turāthina al-Islāmī [Umm Zarʿ: the Sincere Wife in our Islamic Heritage]" (*al-Alūkah al-Sharīʿah*, 2007), https://www.alukah.net/social/0/1062/.
18. Jacquette M. Timmons, "*Financial Intimacy*" (Chicago, Illinois, Chicago Review Press, 2010), xviii.
19. *Hijab*: Islamic attire prescribed by the Shariah for females who have reached the age of puberty.
20. *Shūrā*: Consultation.
21. *Muqaddam:* The amount of *mahr* paid upfront upon the signing of the contract. *Mu'akhkhar:* The amount of *mahr* that is deferred until after consummation.
22. Western Country: For the purpose of this research and to protect the identities of various subjects, "Western Country" shall refer to North America, South America, and Western Europe.

Chapter Five

1. Sakina (6), Farida (8), Jenna (12) and Tanya (18).
2. ʿAbd al-Raḥmān al-Jazīrī, *Kitāb al-Fiqh ʿalā al-Madhāhib al-Arbaʿah* (Beirut, Lebanon: Dār al-Fikr, 1986), Volume 4, 157-162; ʿAbd al-Karīm Zaydān, *Al-Jāmiʿ fī al-Fiqh al-Islāmī al-Mufaṣṣal fī Aḥkām al-Mar'ah wa al-Bayt al-Muslim* (Beirut, Lebanon: al-Risālah Publications, 1993), Volume 7, 87-88;

Ibn Rushd, *The Distinguished Jurist's Primer*, trans. Imran Ahsan Khan Nyazee, Volume II, (UK, Garnet Publishing Limited, 1996), 25; Wahbah al-Zuḥaylī, *al-Fiqh al-Islāmī wa Adillatuhu* (Beirut, Lebanon: Dār al-Fikr, 2014), Volume 7, 271-72.

3. Wahbah al-Zuḥaylī, *al-Fiqh al-Islāmī wa Adillatuhu*, Volume 7, 271-72, Net Library E-Book Retrieved from https://ia600603.us.archive.org/19/items/WAQ7152/fia7.pdf, 278-79; ʿAbd al-Karīm Zaydān, *Al-Jāmiʿ fī al-Fiqh al-Islāmī al-Mufaṣṣal fī Aḥkām al-Mar'ah wa al-Bayt al-Muslim*, Volume 8, 502; Ibn Rushd, *The Distinguished Jurist's Primer*, trans. Imran Ahsan Khan Nyazee, Volume II, 25; ʿAbd al-Raḥmān al-Jazīrī, *Kitāb al-Fiqh ʿalā al-Madhāhib al-Arbaʿah*, Volume 4, 164, 153, Net Library E-Book Retrieved from https://ia601608.us.archive.org/12/items/waq78101/04_78104.pdf, 141.
4. The five that are still married, but have never received their *mahr:* Nabila, Jasmine, Rahma, Fareeha, Ranya.
5. Ibn Rushd, *The Distinguished Jurist's Primer*, trans. Imran Ahsan Khan Nyazee, Volume II, 25.
6. The Qur'an 4:24.
7. Sara (2), Jasmine (5), Sophia (7), Dana (1) and Tanya (18); Muhammad Ṣāliḥ al-Munajjid, "Who Decides Mahr," Islam Question & Answer, Question 224876, Publication: 21-04-2024, https://islamqa.info/en/answers/224876/who-has-the-right-to-decide-the-amount-of-mahr-to-be-given-by-the-husband-to-his-wife-how-much-is-the-mahr-supposed-to-be-is-a-marriage-valid-without-it; Abdul Karim Zaydan, *Al-Jami' Fi Al-Fiqh Al-Islami*, Volume 8 (Beirut, Al-Risala Publications, 1993), 51-52.
8. Jenna (12), Maysa (19) and Nadia (21).

9. Zaydān, *Al-Jāmiʿ fī al-Fiqh al-Islāmī al-Mufaṣṣal fī Aḥkām al-Mar'ah wa al-Bayt al-Muslim*, Volume 7, 181.
10. Ibid, Volume 4, 265.
11. Ibid, Volume 10, 280-83; Abū Jaʿfar Muhammad ibn Jarīr al-Ṭabarī, *Jāmiʿ al-Bayān ʿan Ta'wīl āy al-Qur'ān* (Beirut, Lebanon: Mu'assasah al-Risālah Printing and Publications, 1994), Volume 14, 308.
12. Zaydān, *Al-Jāmiʿ fī al-Fiqh al-Islāmī al-Mufaṣṣal fī Aḥkām al-Mar'ah wa al-Bayt al-Muslim*, Volume 9, 248.
13. Aya (4), Sakina (6), Farida (8) and Rahma (11) and Amani (14).
14. ʿAbd al-Halīm Abū Shaqqah, *Taḥrīr al-Mar'ah fī ʿAṣr Al-Risālah* (Kuwait, Dar al-Qalam li al-Nashr wa al-Tawzīʿ, 1990), 130.
15. Muṣṭafā al-ʿAdawī, *Jāmiʿ Aḥkām al-Nisā'* (Cairo, Egypt: Dār Ibn ʿAffān, 1999), Volume 2, 199-204; Abū Shaqqah, *Taḥrīr al-Mar'ah fī ʿAṣr Al-Risālah*, Volume 5-6, 127-29.
16. Rameez Abid, "Helping Your Wife with Household Chores is a Neglected Sunnah," *The Thinking Muslim* (2014), https://thethinkingmuslim.com/2014/11/01/helping-your-wife-with-household-chores-is-a-neglected-sunnah.
17. Abū Shaqqah, *Taḥrīr al-Mar'ah fī ʿAṣr Al-Risālah*, Volume 5-6, 127.
18. Zaydān, *Al-Jāmiʿ fī al-Fiqh al-Islāmī al-Mufaṣṣal fī Aḥkām al-Mar'ah wa al-Bayt al-Muslim*, Volume 4, 269.
19. Abū Muhammad ʿAlī ibn Aḥmad ibn Saʿīd ibn Ḥazm, *Al-Muḥallā bi al-Āthār* (Beirut, Lebanon: Dār al-Kutub al-ʿIlmiyyah, 2003), Volume 9, 227, https://archive.org/details/FP74771/09_74779/page/n226/mode/1up?view=theater.

20. Zaydān, *Al-Jāmiʿ fī al-Fiqh al-Islāmī al-Mufaṣṣal fī Aḥkām al-Mar'ah wa al-Bayt al-Muslim*, Volume 7, 182; Muhammad ibn Idrīs al-Shāfiʿī, *Al-Umm* (Cairo, Egypt: Dār al-Ḥadīth, 2008), Volume 6, 202; Gibril Fouad Haddad, "The Biographies of the Elite Lives of the Scholars" (Published by Zulfiqar Ayyb), https://www.google.com/books/edition/THE_BIOGRAPHIES_OF_THE_ELITE_LIVES_OF_TH/RwPnCAAAQBAJ?hl=en&gbpv=1&printsec=frontcover, 46.
21. Ibn Ḥazm, *Al-Muḥallā bi al-Āthār*, Volume 9, 228.
22. Muhammad ibn Adam, "A Wife's Right to Sexual Intimacy," Islam Question & Answer, 2011, https://islamqa.org/?p=8306; Abū Shaqqah, *Taḥrīr al-Mar'ah fī ʿAṣr Al-Risālah*, Volume 5, 196; Ibn Ḥazm, *Al-Muḥallā bi al-Āthār*, Volume 9, 227-28.
23. Shehnaz Haqqani, "Gendered Expectations, Personal Choice, and Social Compatibility in Western Muslim Marriages" (Master's Thesis, University of Texas at Austin, 2013), https://repositories.lib.utexas.edu/bitstream/handle/2152/22208/HAQQANI-THESIS-2013.pdf?sequence=1&isAllowed=y, 54-55.
24. Haqqani, "Gendered Expectations, 53-54.
25. Ibid, 55.
26. Ibid.
27. Azizah Y. Hibri, "Muslim Women's Rights in The Global Village Challenges and Opportunities," Law Faculty Publications 15 J. L. & Religion 37 (2000), https://scholarship.richmond.edu/cgi/viewcontent.cgi?article=1162&context=law-faculty-publications, 46-47.
28. Al-ʿAdawī, *Jāmiʿ Aḥkām al-Nisā'*, Volume 5, 99-101.
29. ʿAbdullāh ibn ʿAbd al-Muḥsin al-Tarīqī, "Al-Nafaqah al-Wājibah ʿalā al-Mar'ah li Ḥaqq al-Ghayr" (*al-Alūkah al-Sharīʿah*, 2007), http://cp.alukah.net/web/turaiqi/0/363/.

30. Osman Umarji, "Psychology of Wealth: An Islamic Perspective on Personal Finance," July 1, 2021. Updated March 22, 2023, https://yaqeeninstitute.org/read/paper/psychology-of-wealth-Al-islamic-perspective-on-personal-finance.
31. Zaydān, *Al-Jāmi' fī al-Fiqh al-Islāmī*, Volume 4, 335.
32. Casey Bond, "What is a Joint Account", U.S. News, August 18, 2023, https://www.usnews.com/banking/articles/what-is-a-joint-bank-account.
33. Karamah Muslim Women Lawyers for Human Rights, "Ask Zahra" (Ask Zahra Advice Column, 2015), https://karamah.org/wp-content/uploads/2020/07/Answer-to-alimony-question.pdf.
34. Ibid, 3.
35. Dana (1), Sara (2), Farida (8), Layla (10), Jenna (12), Suraya (13), Amani (14), Maysa (19) and Nadia (21).
36. Al-'Adawī, *Jāmi' Aḥkām al-Nisā'*, Volume 2, 200-202, Net Library E-Book Retrieved from https://archive.org/details/jami-3-ahkam-nissa-e/جامع%20أحكام%20النساء%20ج2/page/n201/mode/1up?view=theater; Abū Nu'aym al-Iṣfahānī, *Ḥilyah al-Awliyā' wa-Ṭabaqāt al-Asfiyā'* (Cairo, Egypt: Dār al-Fikr, 1996), Volume 6, 106; Muhammad Ṣāliḥ al-Munajjid, "Hal Yajib ala Al-Mara' Khidmat Zawjaha?" Islam Question & Answer, Question 119740, Publication: 06-28-2008, https://islamqa.info/ar/answers/119740/هل-يجب-على-المراة-خدمة-زوجها.
37. Zaydān, *Al-Jāmi' fī al-Fiqh al-Islāmī*, Volume 7, 182; Al-'Adawī, *Jāmi' Aḥkām al-Nisā'*, Volume 2, 202; The Qur'an 4:19.
38. Ibn Ḥazm, *Al-Muḥallā bi al-Āthār*, Volume 9, 227-28.
39. Dana (1), Sara (2), Nabila (3), Aya (4), Sakina (6), Sophia (7), Farida (8), Layla (10), Jenna (12), Suraya (13), Amani (14), Maysa (19), Ranya (20) and Nadia (21).

40. Sara (2), Nabila (3), Farida (8), Layla (10), Suraya (13) Amani (14) and Maysa (19).
41. Sara (2), Nabila (3), Sakina (6), Sophia (7), Farida (8), Jenna (12), Amani (14), Maysa (19), Ranya (20) and Nadia (21).
42. Rutgers University Team, "Economic Abuse Affects Maternal Mental Health, Parenting", Science Daily. https://www.sciencedaily.com/releases/2012/10/121003111359.htm (accessed June 20, 2021).
43. Eight divorced participants: Dana (1), Sara (2), Nabila (3) [from first husband], Sophia (7), Farida (8), Layla (10) [from first husband], Suraya (13), and Nadia (21). One in the process of divorce: Aya (4). Two Separated: Rahma (11) and Maysa (19). One in the process of divorce: Aya (4). Two Separated: Rahma (11) and Maysa (19).
44. Dana (1), Sara (2), Nabila (3), Aya (4), Sakina (6), Sophia (7), Farida (8), Layla (10), Suraya (13), Amani (14), Malak (16) and Nadia (21).
45. Natasha Dado, "Muslim Women Left to 'Shop' for an Imam When They Need a Religious Divorce," *New America Media* (2013), https://www.pri.org/stories/2013-09-26/muslim-women-left-shop-imam-when-they-need-religious-divorce.
46. Al-Ḥāfiẓ Aḥmad ibn ʿAlī ibn Ḥajar al-ʿAsqalānī, *Fatḥ al-Bārī* (Cairo, Egypt: Dār al-Ḥadīth, 1998), Volume 1, 38.
47. Zaydān, *Al-Jāmiʿ fī al-Fiqh al-Islāmī al-Mufaṣṣal fī Aḥkām al-Mar'ah wa al-Bayt al-Muslim*, Volume 10, 340.
48. Syed Abu Zafar Zain, *The Prophet of Islam: The Ideal Husband* (Bombay, India: Bilal Books, 1997), 51, 53.
49. ʿAbd al-Fattāḥ al-Sammān, *Nafaqāt al-Nabī Ṣallā Allāh ʿAlayhi wa Sallam ʿalā Zawjātihi fī Hayātihi wa Baʿd Mamatihi* [The Expenses of the Prophet Muhammad on His Wives

During His Life and After His Death]" (Cairo, Egypt: Dār al-Fikr, 2018), 8; https://dergipark.org.tr/tr/download/article-file/572586.

50. Al-Sammān, *Nafaqāt al-Nabī Ṣallā Allāh ʿAlayhi wa Sallam ʿalā Zawjātihi fī Hayātihi wa Baʿd Mamatihi,* 8; Ibn Ḥajar al-ʿAsqalānī, *Fatḥ al-Bārī,* Volume 16.
51. Ibid; *Awāq:* One *awāq* comprises the weight of pure silver that is equal to forty *dirhams*. https://www.dorar.net/hadith/sharh/92493.
52. Ibid, 10-11.
53. Ibid, 11.
54. Ibid.
55. Ibid, 3, 8, 11.
56. Ibn Ḥazm, *Al-Muḥallā bi al-Āthār,* Volume 9, 252; Ibn Ḥajar al-ʿAsqalānī, *Fatḥ al-Bārī* Volume 16, 342-43.
57. Ibn Ḥajar al-ʿAsqalānī, Volume 16, 342-43.
58. Participants denied the right to a private home: Sakina (6); Participants denied a home that met their standards: Participants Fareeda (8) and Amani (14).
59. Abū Shaqqah, *Taḥrīr al-Mar'ah fī ʿAṣr Al-Risālah,* Volume 1-2, 235.
60. Ibn Ḥajar al-ʿAsqalānī, Volume 9, 316.
61. Al-Sammān, *Nafaqāt al-Nabī Ṣallā Allāh ʿAlayhi wa Sallam ʿalā Zawjātihi fī Hayātihi wa Baʿd Mamatihi,* 14.
62. Yaḥyā ibn Sharaf al-Nawawī, *Riyāḍ al-Ṣāliḥīn,* https://sunnah.com/riyadussalihin: 294.
63. Al-Sammān, *Nafaqāt al-Nabī Ṣallā Allāh ʿAlayhi wa Sallam ʿalā Zawjātihi fī Hayātihi wa Baʿd Mamatihi,* 13-14.
64. Ibid, 14, 17.
65. Abū Shaqqah, *Taḥrīr al-Mar'ah fī ʿAṣr al-Risālah,* Volume 1-2, 120-24.

66. Ibid.
67. Ibid, 127-28.
68. Ibid.
69. Muṣṭafā Ḥijāzī, *Al-Takhalluf al-Ijtimāʿī: Madkhal ilā Sīkūlūjiyyah al-Insān al-Maqhūr* [*Social Backwardness: An Entrance to the Psychology of an Abused Human Being*] (Casablanca, Morocco: al-Markaz al-Thaqāfī al-ʿArabī, 2005), 105.
70. Islam Web, "Lā Ṭāʿah li Makhlūq fī Maʿṣiyah al-Khāliq [No Obedience for any of the Created When it is a Sin Against the Creator]" (*Islamweb*, 2017), https://www.islamweb.net/ar/article/213217/لا-طاعة-لمخلوق-في-معصية-الخالق; the Qur'an 4:34.
71. Ḥijāzī, *Al-Takhalluf al-Ijtimāʿī: Madkhal ilā Sīkūlūjiyyah al-Insān al-Maqhūr*, 105.
72. Ibid, 199.
73. Ibid, 83.
74. Jamaal Zarabozo, "Life Insurance and the Extent to Which it is Permitted in Case of Need," The Assembly of Muslim Jurists of America 16th Annual Imams Conference (Houston, Texas), https://www.amjaonline.org/wp-content/uploads/2019/04/Life-Insurance-and-the-Extent-to-which-it-is-Permitted-in-a-Case-of-Need-Zarabozo.pdf, 48.
75. Sayyid Qutb, *Fī Ẓilāl Al-Qur'ān* (Cairo, Egypt: Dār al-Shurūq, 1972), Volume 2, 651.

Chapter Six

1. Abu Ameenah Bilal Philips, *The Evolution of Fiqh* (Riyadh, Saudi Arabia: International Islamic Publishing House, 1995), 12.

2. Ismāʿīl ʿAbd ʿAbbas, "Anwāʿ al-Qawāʿid al-Fiqhiyyah [Types of Jurisprudential Rulings]" (*al-Alūkah al-Sharīʿah*, 2020), https://www.alukah.net/sharia/0/139783/; my translation.
3. Brady Sylva, "The Importance of Muslim Fathers in America," *Spectrum*, Vol. 8: Issue 1, Article 7 (2019), https://scholars.unh.edu/cgi/viewcontent.cgi?article=1062&context=spectrum, 3.
4. Alā' Jarrār, "Waṣiyyah al-Rasūl ilā al-Nisā'" [The Bequest of the Messenger Regarding Women] (*Mawḍūʿ*, 2021), https://mawdoo3.com/وصية_الرسول_بالنساء.
5. Jarrār, "Waṣiyyah al-Rasūl ilā al-Nisā"; Qur'an 4:19.
6. Ibid.
7. The Qur'an 2:233; Muhammad ʿAbd al-Raḥmān Ṣādiq, "Manẓūmah al-Shūrā fī al-Islām [The Shūrā System in Islam]" (*al-Alūkah al-Sharīʿah*, 2016), https://www.alukah.net/sharia/0/108384/منظومة-الشورى-في-الإسلام/; Adnan Ibrahim, "Huquq al-Mar'ah fī al-Islām [The Rights of Women in Islam]" (*Adnan Ibrahim*, 2019), http://www.adnanibrahim.net/حقوق-المرأة-في-الإسلام.
8. Ahmad Zaki Hammad, *Islamic Law, Understanding Juristic Differences* (Washington, Indianapolis: American Trust Publications & the Author, 1992), 37.
9. Hammad, *Islamic Law*, 10.
10. Ibid, 10-11.
11. Ibid, 11.
12. Saʿd al-Dīn al-Hilālī, *Al-Islām wa Insāniyyah al-Dawlah* (Cairo, Egypt: al-Hay'ah al-Miṣriyyah al-ʿĀmmah, 2012), 260.
13. Hammad, *Islamic Law*, 12.
14. The Qur'an 4:34.

15. Muhammad ʿAbd al-Maqṣūd Dāwūd, "Al-Qiwāmah ʿalā al-Mar'ah bayn al-Ḥaqā'iq al-Fiqhiyyah wa al-Mafāhīm al-Maghlūṭah", *al-Sharīʿah wa al-Qānūn*, No. 34, Part 2 (2019), https://jlr.journals.ekb.eg/article_80480_64728356f601db4917d41f278405b1d2.pdf, 76.
16. Justice Aftab Hussain, *Status of Women in Islam* (Lahore, Pakistan: Law Publishing Company, 1987), 204-05.
17. Hussain, *Status of Women in Islam,* 204-05.
18. Ibid.
19. Moeed Pirzada, "Remembering Muhammad Pickthall: Qur'an's First Credible English Translator," *Global Village Space*, May 19, 2020, https://www.printfriendly.com/p/g/mrbS2C; https://brill.com/display/book/edcoll/9789004327597/B9789004327597_001.xml?body=fullhtml-60832.
20. Abū al-Fiḍā' Ibn Kathīr, *Mukhtaṣar Tafsīr Ibn Kathīr,* ed. Muhammad ʿAlī al-Ṣābūnī, (Beirut, Lebanon: Dār al-Qur'ān al-Karīm, 1981), Volume 1, 385; Hans Wehr, *A Dictionary of Modern Written Arabic* (Spoken Language Services, Inc., Ithaca, New York, 1976), https://www.ghazali.org/books/wehr-cow-Al-76.pdf, 318; https://context.reverso.net/translation/arabic-english/%D8%B1%D8%A6%D9%8A%D8%B3.
21. Ibn Kathīr, *Mukhtaṣar Tafsīr Ibn Kathīr*, Volume 1, 385; Muhammad Ṣāliḥ al-Munajjid, "The Reason Why the Husband is Regarded as Superior and is Given the Role of Qawwam" Islam Question & Answer, Question 43252, Publication: 10-10-2003, https://islamqa.info/en/answers/43252/the-reason-why-the-husband-is-regarded-as-superior-and-is-given-the-role-of-qawwaam-protector-and-maintainer; https://www.islamweb.net/en/fatwa/381173/equality-between-men-and-women.

22. Muhammad Shafīʿ: A prominent grand *mufi* and scholar of Pakistan. Muhammad Taqī Uthmānī, "Shaykh Mufti Muhammad Shafi, The Grand Mufti of Pakistan," *Deoband*, Dec 4, 2011, http://www.deoband.org/2011/12/history/biographies-of- scholars/shaykh-muhammad-shafi%E2%80%98-the-mufti-of-pakistan/; Justice Aftab Hussain, *Status of Women in Islam* (Lahore, Pakistan: Law Publishing Company, 1987), 204.
23. Ibn al-Jawzī, *Aḥkām Al-Nisā'* [*Laws Regarding Women*] (Cairo, Egypt: Maktabah Ibn Taymiyyah, 1997), 216, Net Library E-Book Retrieved from https://archive.org/details/FP38344/page/n3/mode/1up?view=theater.
24. Ashraf Ali Thanwi, *Tafsīr Bayān al-Qur'ān* (Lahore, Pakistan: Maktaba Rehmania, n.d.) Volume 1, https://archive.org/details/TafseerEBayanUlQuran/TafseerEBayanUlQuranByMaulanaAshrafAliThanvi/page/n350/mode/1up?view=theater, 351.
25. Ashraf Ali Thanwi, *Ashraf's Blessings of Marriage* (Dewsbury, United Kingdom: Amanah Studio, 2008), https://archive.org/details/AshrafsBlessingsOfMarriage/page/201/mode/1up?view=theater, 201-207.
26. ʿAbd al-Halīm Abū Shaqqah, *Taḥrīr al-Mar'ah fī ʿAṣr Al-Risālah* (Kuwait, Dar al-Qalam li al-Nashr wa al-Tawzīʿ, 1990), Volume 5, 130; Muhammad ibn Ismāʿīl al-Bukhārī, *Ṣaḥīḥ al-Bukhārī* (Cairo, Egypt: Dar al-Ta'ṣīl, 2012), Volume 7, 181-82.
27. Shehnaz Haqqani, "Gendered Expectations, Personal Choice, and Social Compatibility in Western Muslim Marriages"(Master's Thesis, University of Texas at Austin, 2013), https://repositories.lib.utexas.edu/bitstream/

handle/2152/22208/HAQQANI-THESIS-2013.pdf?sequence=1&isAllowed=y, 58-59.

28. Muhammad ibn Yūsuf ibn ʿAlī ibn Yūsuf ibn Ḥayyān, *Tafsīr al-Baḥr al-Muḥīt* (Beirut, Lebanon: Dār Iḥyā' al-Turāth al-ʿArabī, 2002), Volume 3, 335.

29. Sayyid Qutb, *Fī Ẓilāl Al-Qur'ān* (Cairo, Egypt: Dār al-Shurūq, 1972), Volume 4, 121-22.

30. Nasr Hamid Abu Zayd, *Dawā'ir al-Khawf* (Casablanca, Morocco: al-Markaz al-Thiqāfī al-ʿArabī, 2014), 295.

31. Ibid.

32. Massan d'Almeida, "Marriage and Divorce in Tunisia" (AWID, 2010), https://www.awid.org/news-and-analysis/marriage-and-divorce-tunisia-womens-rights.

33. Azizah Yahia Al-Hibri, "Muslim Women's Rights in the Global Village: Challenges and Opportunities," https://web.archive.org/web/20101217004407id_/http://karamah.org/Portals/0/Articles/AlhibriGlobalVillage.pdf, 123.

34. Maryam Al-Dabbagh, Dr. Omar Suleiman, Roohi Tahir, and Mohammad Elshinawy, "Mā Kunnā Nu'idd li al-Nisā' Amran: Musāwah al-Jinsayn wa Buzūgh Fajr al-Islam [We Never Used to Give Women Any Value: Gender Equality and the Rise of Islam] (Yaqeen Institute, 2020), https://yaqeeninstitute.org/read/paper/ نُع-كُنَا-ما%D9%90-د للنساء%D9%90-ال-مساواة-أمرا.

35. Abu Zayd, *Dawā'ir al-Khawf*, 296.

36. Musawah: For Equality in the Family, "Policy Brief 5: Fair and Just Financial Rights Upon Divorce" (2021), https://www.musawah.org/resources/policy-brief-5-financial-rights-upon-divorce/, 1.

37. ʿAbd al-Karīm Zaydān, *Al-Jāmiʿ fī al-Fiqh al-Islāmī al-Mufaṣṣal fī Aḥkām al-Mar'ah wa al-Bayt al-Muslim* (Beirut, Lebanon: al-Risālah Publications, 1993), Volume 8, 478.
38. Islam Web, "Māhiyah al-Nafaqah ʿala al-Zawj [What is the Nafaqah Expected of the Husband]" (Islamweb, 2008),https://www.islamweb.net/ar/fatwa/113285/ماهية-النفقة-الواجبة-على-الزوج.
39. Abū Muhammad ʿAlī ibn Aḥmad ibn Saʿīd ibn Ḥazm, *Al-Muḥallā bi al-Āthār* (Beirut, Lebanon: Dār al-Kutub al-ʿIlmiyyah, 2003), Volume 8, 112-13.
40. The Qur'an 8:53.
41. Amal Killawi, Manijeh Daneshpour, Arij Elmi, Iman Dadrus and Zain Shamoon, "Community Brief: Promoting Healthy Marriages & Preventing Divorce in the American Muslim Community," (Institute for Social Policy and Understanding, 2014), https://www.ispu.org/wp-content/uploads/2016/08/ISPU_Marriage_DivorceBrief_Final.pdf.
42. Farhad Asghari, Abbas Sadeghi, Khaled Asiani, "Comparative Study of the Financial Independence, Self-Confidence and Decision-Making Power Awareness of the Social Resources and Mental Health in the Women Members of SHG and Non-Members of SHG" (Department of Counseling, University of Shahid Camran, Ahvaz, Iran. Department of Educational Sciences, University of Guilan, Rasht, Iran) DOI: 10.4236/sm.2013.31017 https://www.scirp.org/journal/paperinformation.aspx?paperid=27279, 115-18.
43. Lindsey E. Blenkhorn, "Note Islamic Marriage Contracts in American Courts: Interpreting Mahr Agreements as Prenuptials and Their Effect on Muslim Women," *Southern California Law*

Review, Vol. 76:189, 2003, 202-203, https://southerncalifornialawreview.com/wp-content/uploads/2018/01/76_189.pdf, 202-03; Muhammad Ṣāliḥ al-Munajjid, "Stipulating Conditions in Marriage Contracts in Islam, Allowed?" Islam Question and Answer, Question 173938, Publication: 02-02-2021, https://islamqa.info/en/answers/108806/stipulating-conditions-in-marriage-contracts-in-islam-allowed.

44. Blenkhorn, "Note Islamic Marriage Contracts in American Courts"; Maha al-Khateeb, "Islamic Marriage Contracts, A Resource Guide for Legal Professionals, Advocates, Imams & Communities," 2012, https://www.api-gbv.org/resources/islamic-marriage-contracts/, 27, 29.

45. Al-Khateeb, "Islamic Marriage Contracts, A Resource Guide for Legal Professionals, Advocates, Imams & Communities," 27, 29.

46. Nuhā Faraj, "Al-Takāfu': Hal Yumkin al-Tanāzul 'Anhu?" (*al-Alūkah al-Sharī'ah*, 2017), https://www.alukah.net/social/0/121128/.

47. Faraj, "Al-Takāfu'; Dana Harrington Conner, *Financial Freedom: Women, Money, and Domestic Abuse*, 20 Wm. & Mary J. Women & L. 339 (2014), https://scholarship.law.wm.edu/wmjowl/vol20/iss2/4, 394.

48. Marialuisa Gennari, Cristina Giuliani and Monica Accordini, "Muslim Immigrant Men and Women's Attitudes Towards Intimate Partners Violence". *Eur J Psychol.* 2017;13(4):688-707. Published 2017 Nov 30. doi:10.5964/ejop.v13i4.1411, https://www.ncbi.nlm.nih.gov/pmc/articles/PMC5763457/pdf/ejop-13-688.pdf, 689.

49. Gennari, Giuliani, and Accordini, 689-90.

50. Ibid.

51. Muhammad Abuelezz, "American Imams: Duties, Qualifications and Challenges A Quantitative and Religious Analysis" (Master's Thesis, University of Georgia, Athens, Georgia, 2001), https://getd.libs.uga.edu/pdfs/abuelezz_muhammad_201108_ma.pdf, 113.
52. Maḥmūd Bandar ʿAlī Muhammad, "Nafaqah al-Zawjah fī al-Sharīʿah wa al-Qānūn," Kuliyyat al-ʿUlūm Al-Islāmiyyah Magazine, 16th edition, https://www.iasj.net/iasj/download/329e2c58ffa1c074, 377.
53. Muhammad, "Nafaqah al-Zawjah fī al-Sharīʿah."
54. ʿAbd al-Fattāḥ al-Sammān, "Zawjī Hal Uqriḍuhu Mālī? [My Husband Should I Lend Him my Money?]" (2019), *Kayf Maluk TV Programme*, https://www.youtube.com/watch?v=d2F73nUPulc.
55. Zaydān, *Al-Jāmiʿ fī al-Fiqh al-Islāmī al-Mufaṣṣal fī Aḥkām al-Mar'ah wa al-Bayt al-Muslim*, Volume 7, 133-36; Abū Zayd, *Dawā'ir al-Khawf*, 296.
56. Zaydān, *Al-Jāmiʿ fī al-Fiqh al-Islāmī al-Mufaṣṣal fī Aḥkām al-Mar'ah wa al-Bayt al-Muslim.*
57. Mounira M. Charrad, "Tunisia at the Forefront of the Arab World: Two Waves of Gender Legislation," 64 WASH. & LEE L. REV. 1513 (2007), 1516; https://scholarlycommons.law.wlu.edu/wlulr/vol64/iss4/11; Abu Zayd, *Dawā'ir al-Khawf*, 296; Musawah: For Equality in the Family, "Policy Brief 5: Fair and Just Financial Rights Upon Divorce" (2021), https://www.musawah.org/resources/policy-brief-5-financial-rights-upon-divorce/.
58. Abū Zayd, *Dawā'ir al-Khawf*, 296; Musawah: For Equality in the Family, "Policy Brief 5: Fair and Just Financial Rights

Upon Divorce" (2021), https://www.musawah.org/resources/policy-brief-5-financial-rights-upon-divorce/.

59. Abū Zayd, *Dawā'ir al-Khawf.*
60. Charrad, "Tunisia at the Forefront of the Arab World: Two Waves of Gender Legislation."
61. D'Almeida, "Marriage and Divorce in Tunisia".
62. Abū Zayd, *Dawā'ir al-Khawf*, 286.
63. ʿAbdullāh al-Zāyid, "Aṭwār al-Ijtihād al-Fiqhī" (*al-Alūkah al-Sharīʿah*, 2007), https://www.alukah.net/sharia/0/423/أطوار-الاجتهاد-الفقهي/.
64. ʿAbdullāh Najīb Muhammad, "Al-ʿAmal bi Sahm al-Mu'allafah Qulūbuhum" (*al-Alūkah al-Sharīʿah*, 2015), https://www.alukah.net/sharia/0/88911/.
65. Ibid; Mannāʿ al-Qaṭṭān, *Tarīkh al-Tashrī al-Islamī* [*History of The Islamic Legislation*] (Riyadh, Saudi Arabia: Maktabah al-Maʿārif li al-Nashr wa al-Tawzīʿ, 2002), 354.
66. "Karamah Muslim Women Lawyers for Human Rights", Ask Zahra Advice Column, 07/2015, https://karamah.org/wp-content/uploads/2020/07/Answer-to-alimony-question.pdf, 3.
67. "Karamah Muslim Women Lawyers for Human Rights", Ask Zahra Advice Column.
68. Salah al-Sawy, "The Assembly's Family Code for Muslim Communities in North America," *The Assembly of Muslim Jurists of America, The Assembly's 8th Conference* (Kuwait, 2012), https://www.amjaonline.org/declaration-articles/the-assemblys-family-code-for-muslim-communities-in-north-america/.
69. The Qur'an 4:21.
70. The Qur'an 4:20
71. The Qur'an 2:233.

72. The Qur'an 2:236.
73. Al-Mubārakfūrī, *Al-Raḥīq al-Makhtūm*, 462.
74. Al-Sawy, "The Assembly's Family Code for Muslim Communities in North America."
75. Ibid; The Application of some articles regarding family laws in Muslim Marriages in the U.S. can be found in appendix E.
76. Ibid.
77. Ibid.
78. Muhammad ibn Idrīs al-Shāfiʿī, *Al-Umm* (Cairo, Egypt: Dār al-Ḥadīth, 2008), Volume 6, 265.
79. Muṣṭafā al-ʿAdawī, *Jāmiʿ Aḥkām al-Nisā'* (Cairo, Egypt: Dār Ibn ʿAffān, 1999), Volume 4, 76. Maha al-Khateeb, Islamic Marriage Contracts, A Resource Guide for Legal Professionals, Advocates, Imams & Communities, 2012, https://bwjp.org/assets/documents/pdfs/islamic_marriage_contracts_resource_guide_apiidv.pdf, 21.
80. Zaydān, *Al-Jāmiʿ fī al-Fiqh al-Islāmī al-Mufaṣṣal fī Aḥkām al-Mar'ah wa al-Bayt al-Muslim*, Volume 8, 475, 479, 482-83.
81. Muhammad Ṣāliḥ al-Munajjid, "The Difference Between Khul', Tallaq and Faskh (Ways of Ending a Marriage)" Islam Question & Answer, Question 113707, Publication: 31-03-2016, https://islamqa.info/en/answers/133859/the-difference-between-khul-talaaq-and-faskh-ways-of-ending-a-marriage.
82. Al-Sawy, "The Assembly's Family Code For Muslim Communities in North America," arts 129, 179-84.
83. Zaydān, *Al-Jāmiʿ fī al-Fiqh al-Islāmī,* Volume 8, 475; Al-Munajjid, "The Difference Between Khul', Tallaq and Faskh (Ways of Ending a Marriage)."
84. Maha al-Khateeb, Islamic Marriage Contracts, 21.

85. Priscilla Offenhauer, "Women in Islamic Societies: A Selected Review of Social Scientific Literature", The Library of Congress- Federal Research Division, Women in Islamic societies (2005), https://www.justice.gov/sites/default/files/eoir/legacy/2013/11/08/Women%20-%20Islamic_Societies.pdf, 41-44.
86. Offenhauer, "Women in Islamic Societies," 42.
87. Musawah: For Equality in the Family, "Policy Brief 5: Fair and Just Financial Rights Upon Divorce" (2021), https://www.musawah.org/wp-content/uploads/2021/08/musawah-policy-brief-5-fair-and-just-financial-rights-upon-divorce.pdf, 5.
88. Umm ʿAbd al-Raḥmān Yūsuf, "Sakan wa Mawaddah wa Rahmah" [Tranquillity, Love, and Mercy]" (*Qiṣṣah al-Islām*, 2012) https://islamstory.com/ar/artical/24806.
89. Abdul Karim Zaydan, *Al-Jami' Fi Al-Fiqh Al-Islami Al-Mufassal Fi-Ahkam Al-Maraa Wal-Bayt Al-Muslim*, Volume 7 (Beirut, Al-Risala Publications, 1993), 173; Yūsuf, "Sakan wa Mawaddah wa Rahmah."
90. The Qur'an 30:21.
91. The Qur'an 49:13; Hasan Hathut, *"Bihaza Alqa Allah"* (Kuwait, Fahad Al Marzouk Printing & Publishing Establishment), 215.
92. Abeer Idlaby, "*Al-Zawja Tas'al Wal Shar' Yujeeb*" (Dimishq, Beirut, Al-Yamamah for Printing, Publications & Distribution, 2010), 15, 16; Jane I Smith, *Islam in America* (New York, Columbia University Press, 2010), 167.
93. Jamal al-Banna, *Al-Mar'ah al-Muslimah bayn Taḥrīr al-Qur'ān wa Taqyīd al-Fuqahā'* (Cairo, Egypt: Dār al-Shurūq, 2007), 129.
94. The Qur'an 4:1.

Bibliography

Al-ʿAbbādī, al-Ḥasan. *Kitāb al-Nawāzil fī Sūs.* Casablanca, Morocco: Maṭbaʿah al-Najāḥ al-Jadīdah, 1999.

ʿAbbās, Faḍl Ḥasan. *Al-Tafsīr wa al-Mufassirūn*. Amman, Jordon: Dār al-Nafā'is for Publications and Distributions, 2016.

ʿAbbas, Ismāʿīl ʿAbd. "Anwāʿ al-Qawāʿid al-Fiqhiyyah [Types of Jurisprudential Rulings]" (*al-Alūkah al-Sharīʿah*, 2020), https://www.alukah.net/sharia/0/139783/.

Abdelhadi, Eman. "Religiosity and Muslim Women's Employment in the United States." *Socius: Sociological Research for a Dynamic World* 3 (2017): 237802311772996. https://doi.org/10.1177/2378023117729969.

Abid, Rameez. "Helping Your Wife with Household Chores Is a Neglected Sunnah." The Thinking Muslim, December 14, 2020. https://thethinkingmuslim.com/2014/11/01/helping-your-wife-with-household-chores-is-a-neglected-sunnah/.

Abidat, Gamal Muhammad, "Feminising Poverty," Al-Bayan, https://www.albayan.ae/opinions/2007-10-10-1.797670.

Abuelezz, Muhammad. "American Imams: Duties, Qualifications and Challenges A Quantitative and Religious Analysis," 2001. https://getd.libs.uga.edu/pdfs/abuelezz_muhammad_201108_ma.pdf.

Abū Nuʿaym al-Iṣfahānī, *Ḥilyah al-Awliyā' wa-Ṭabaqāt al-Aṣfiyā'*. Cairo, Egypt: Dār al-Fikr, 1996.

Abu Rahma. "Qur'anic Misconceptions Addressed: The Hadith of Women Being Created from a Rib" 2014. https://quran-answers.me/2014/12/03/the-hadith-of-woman-being-created-from-a-bent-rib/.

Abū Shaqqah, ʿAbd al-Halīm. *Taḥrīr al-Mar'ah fī ʿAṣr Al-Risālah.* Kuwait, Dar al-Qalam li al-Nashr wa al-Tawzīʿ, 1990.

Abu Zayd, Nasr Hamid. *Dawā'ir al-Khawf.* Casablanca, Morocco: al-Markaz al-Thiqāfī al-ʿArabī, 2014.

Al-ʿAdawī, Muṣṭafā. *Jāmiʿ Aḥkām al-Nisā'.* Cairo, Egypt: Dār Ibn ʿAffān, 1999.

Al-ʿAlī, Muhammad ʿUqlah al-Ḥasan. "ʿIddah al-Wafāh: Mafhūmuhā wa Aḥkāmuhā fī al-Sharīʿah al-Islāmiyyah [The Waiting Period for the Widow and its Meaning and Rulings]." (Bingol Universities, 2015), https://dergipark.org.tr/tr/download/article-file/206271.

Al-Alfī, Muhammad Jabr. "Ithbat al-Nasab wa Nafyihi bi al-Baṣmah al-Wirāthiyyah [Proof of Paternity and Rejecting it Through DNA]" (*Al-Muslim*, 2015) https://almoslim.net/node/250399.

Ali, Kacia. "The Feminist Sexual Ethics Project." Brandeis University, 2003. https://www.brandeis.edu/projects/fse/muslim/triple-repudiation.html.

Al-Ālūsī, Shihāb al-Dīn Maḥmūd. *Tafsīr Ruḥ al-Maʿānī.* Beirut, Lebanon: Idārah al-Ṭibāʿah al-Munīriyyah, n.d. Volume 28.

Al-Ālūsī, Shihāb al-Dīn Maḥmūd al-Ālūsī, *Tafsīr Ruḥ al-Maʿānī.* Maghribi, Pakistan: Maktaba Imdadiah Miltan, n.d. Volume 27.

Amir, Kia, "The Concept of Responsibility of Men and Women in Islam." *Arts & Humanities Open Access Journal* 3, no. 5 (2019). https://doi.org/10.15406/ahoaj.2019.03.00137.

Al-ʿAqīl, ʿAbd al-ʿAzīz ibn Muhammad. "Al-Ḥathth ʿalā al-Nafaqah fī al-Khayr [Advocacy Towards Good Spending]" (*al-Alūkah al-Sharīʿah*, 2014), https://www.alukah.net/sharia/0/78965/.

Al-Aṣīlī, ʿAbdullāh al-Munʿim. *Al-Furūq al-Fiqhiyyah bayn Al-Rajul wa al-Mar'ah fi al-Aḥwāl al-Shakhṣiyyah.* Amman, Jordan: Dār Al-Nafā'is for Publication & Distribution, 2011, 213.

Āl Thābit, Saʿīd ibn Muhammad. "Al-Taqwā wa Ahammiyyatuha wa Atharuha min Khilāl Sūrah al-Ṭalāq [Fearing Allah and the Effect of Sūrah al-Ṭalāq towards its Cause]" (*al-Alūkah al-Sharīʿah,* 2018), https://www.alukah.net/sharia/0/126984/.

Asghari, Farhad, Abbas Sadeghi, and Khaled Aslani. "Comparative Study of the Financial Independence, Self-Confidence and Decision-Making Power, Awareness of the Social Resources and Mental Health in the Women Members of SHG and Non-Member of SHG." *Sociology Mind* 03, no. 01 (2013): 114-17. https://doi.org/10.4236/sm.2013.31017.

"Ask Zahra Advice Column." Karamah, 2015. https://karamah.org/wp-content/uploads/2020/07/Answer-to-alimony-question.pdf; 3.

Assaad, Ragui & Nazier, Hanan & Ramadan, Racha. (2015). Empowerment Is a Community affair: Community Level Determinants of Married Women's Empowerment in Egypt. 10.13140/RG.2.1.1505.9926.

Al-ʿAsqalānī, Aḥmad ibn ʿAlī ibn Ḥajar. *Bulūgh al-Marām min Adillah al-Aḥkām.* Riyadh: Saudi Arabia: Dār al-Qabas Publications and Distribution, 2014.

Al-ʿAsqalānī, Al-Ḥāfiẓ Aḥmad ibn ʿAlī ibn Ḥajar. *Fatḥ al-Bārī.* Cairo, Egypt: Dār al-Ḥadīth, 1998.

ʿAwaḍ, ʿAbd Ḥamīd ʿĪd. *Shubuhat Ḥawl Qaḍāyā Al-Mar'ah al-Muslimah* (*al-Alūkah al-Sharīʿah,* 2013), https://www.noor-book.com/en/ebook-شبهات-حول-قضايا-المراه-المسلمه-والرد-عليها--pdf.

Al-ʿAzāwī, Fāris. "Al-Mahr wa Āthāruhu" (*al-Alūkah al-Sharīʿah*, 2014), https://www.alukah.net/social/0/74965.

Azizah Y, Al-Hibri, Muslim Women's Rights in the Global Village: Challenges and Opportunities, 15 J. L. & Religion 37 (2000).

Al-Aẓam, ʿĀbidah al-Mu'ayyad. *Sunnah al-Tafāḍul*. Beirut, Lebanon: Dār Ibn Ḥazm for Printing & Publication & Distribution, 2000.

Al-Aẓam, ʿĀbidah al-Mu'ayyad. *Mā Ḥudūd Ṭāʿah al-Zawj?* https://abidaazem.com/حدود-طاعة-الزوج/.

Badawi, Jamal. "Series • Jamal Badawi - Social System of Islam." Muslim Central, 2017. https://muslimcentral.com/series/jamal-badawi-social-system-of-islam/.

Al-Banna, Jamal. *Al-Mar'ah al-Muslimah bayn Taḥrīr al-Qur'ān wa Taqyīd al-Fuqahā'* (Cairo, Egypt: Dār al-Shurūq, 2007).

Barroso, Amanda, and Juliana Menasce Horowitz. "The Pande mic Has Highlighted Many Challenges for Mothers, but They Aren't Necessarily New." Pew Research Center, March 22, 2021. https://www.pewresearch.org/fact-tank/2021/03/17/the-pandemic-has-highlighted-many-challenges-for-mothers-but-they-arent-necessarily-new/.

Al-Basal, ʿAlī Abū. "Al-Rujūʿ fī al-Hibah fī al-Fiqh al-Islāmī [Backing Off from a Given Gift Based on Islamic Law]" (*al-Alūkah al-Sharīʿah*, 2016), https://www.alukah.net/sharia/0/98047/.

Blenkhorn, Lindsey E. "Note Islamic Marriage Contracts in American Courts: Interpreting Mahr Agreements as Prenuptials and Their Effect on Muslim Women." *Southern California Law Review* 76, no. 189 (n.d.): 46.

Britannica, T. Editors of Encyclopedia. "Coverture." Encyclopedia Britannica, October 8, 2007. https://www.britannica.com/topic/coverture.

Britannica, T. Editors of Encyclopedia. "Custom." Encyclopedia Britannica, February 4, 2018. https://www.britannica.com/topic/custom-English-law.

Britannica, T. Editors of Encyclopedia. "Married Women's Property Acts." Encyclopedia Britannica, September 8, 2010. https://www.britannica.com/event/Married-Womens-Property-Acts-United-States-1839.

Brown, Emily & Phojanakong, Pam & Patel, Falguni & Chilton, Mariana. (2020). Financial health as a measurable social determinant of health. PLOS ONE. 15. e0233359.10.1371/journal.pone.0233359.

Al-Bukhārī, Muhammad ibn Ismā'īl. *Ṣaḥīḥ al-Bukhārī.* Cairo, Egypt: Dar al-Ta'ṣīl, 2012.

Al-Būrīnī, ʿĀtikah. "Mā Hiya Sūrah al-Farā'iḍ" (Mawḍūʿ, 2019), https://mawdoo3.com/ما_هي_سورة_الفرائض.

Chapman, Aliya R., and Lauren Bennett Cattaneo. "American Muslim Marital Quality: A Preliminary Investigation." *Journal of Muslim Mental Health* 7, no. 2 (2013). https://doi.org/10.3998/jmmh.10381607.0007.201.

Charrad, Mounira M., "Tunisia at the Forefront of the Arab World: Two Waves of Gender Legislation," 64 WASH. & LEE L. REV. 1513 (2007), 1516, https://scholarlycommons.law.wlu.edu/wlulr/vol64/iss4/11.

Chou, Eileen Y., Bidhan L. Parmar, and Adam D. Galinsky. "Economic Insecurity Increases Physical Pain." Psychological Science 27, no. 4 (April 2016): 443–54. https://doi.org/10.1177/0956797615625640.

Coniglio, Amber, "American Muslim Women: Feminism, Equality, and Difference" (2018). Honors Theses. 2997. https://scholarworks.wmich.edu/honors_theses/2997.

Conner, Dana Harrington, *Financial Freedom: Women, Money, and Domestic Abuse*, 20 Wm. & Mary J. Women & L. 339 (2014), https://scholarship.law.wm.edu/wmjowl/vol20/iss2/4, 394.

Al-Dabbagh, Maryam, Suleiman Omar, Tahir Roohi and Elshinawy Mohammed, "Mā Kunnā Nu'idd li al-Nisā' Amran: Musāwah al-Jinsayn wa Buzūgh Fajr al-Islam [We Never Used to Give Women Any Value: Gender Equality and the Rise of Islam] (Yaqeen Institute, 2020), https://yaqeeninstitute.org/read/paper/نُع-كُنَا-ما%D9%90د-للنساء%D9%90-أمرا-مساواة-ال.

Dado, Natasha, "Muslim Women Left to 'Shop' for an Imam When They Need a Religious Divorce," *New America Media* (2013), https://www.pri.org/stories/2013-09-26/muslim-women-left-shop-imam-when-they-need-religious-divorce.

D'Almeida, Massan "Marriage and Divorce in Tunisia" (AWID, 2010), https://www.awid.org/news-and-analysis/marriage-and-divorce-tunisia-womens-rights.

Dana Harrington Conner, Financial Freedom: Women, Money, and Domestic Abuse, 20 Wm. & Mary J. Women & L. 339 (2014), 394, https://scholarship.law.wm.edu/wmjowl/vol20/iss2/4.

Dār Al-Iftā' al-Miṣriyyah, "The Obligation for a Woman to Obtain Her Husband's Permission to Travel for Hajj" (22 October 2020)https://www.dar-alifta.org/Foreign/ViewFatwa.aspx?ID=8119.

Davis, Christopher & Mantler, Janet & Doyle, Brian & Sc, B & Ca, Mba & Cirp, Cfe & Or, Paul & Salewski, (2004). The Consequences of Financial Stress for Individuals, Families, and Society.

"Demographic Portrait of Muslim Americans." Pew Research Center's Religion & Public Life Project, May 30, 2020.

https://www.pewforum.org/2017/07/26/demographic-portrait-of-muslim-americans/.

Dāwūd, Muhammad ʿAbd al-Maqṣūd. "Al-Qiwāmah ʿalā al-Mar'ah bayn al-Ḥaqā'iq al-Fiqhiyyah wa al-Mafāhīm al-Maghlūṭah", *al-Sharīʿah wa al-Qānūn*, No. 34, Part 2 (2019), https://jlr.journals.ekb.eg/article_80480_64728356f601db4917d41f278405b1d2.pdf.

Dew, J. P., & Stewart, R. (2012). A Financial Issue, a Relationship Issue, or Both? Examining the Predictors of Marital Financial Conflict. Journal of Financial Therapy, 3 (1) 4. https://doi.org/10.4148/jft.v3i1.1605.

Ewerling, Fernanda & Lynch, John & Victora, Cesar & Van Eerdewijk, Anouka & Tyszler, Marcelo & J D Barros, Aluisio. (2017). The SWPER index for women's empowerment in Africa: Development and validation of an index based on survey data. The Lancet Global Health. 5. 10.1016/S2214-109X(17)30292-9.

Fadʿaq, ʿAbdullāh. "Al-Mar'ah wa Ḥaqquhā al-Mahḍūm fī Al-Kadd wa al-Siʿāyah [The Woman and Her Absorbed Right to Al-Kadd and Siʿāyah]." (Al-Watan, 2020). https://www.alwatan.com.sa/article/1062472.

Fajar, Abbas Sofwan Matlail. "Criticism of Gender Mainstreaming According to Abdul Karim Zaidan in 'Al-Mufassol Fi Ahkam Al-Mar'ah wa Bayt Al-Muslim'," AHKAM Jurnal Ilmu Syariah 19(2) DOI: 10.15408/aiis v19i2.10852, 2019, 271, https://www.researchgate.net/publication/338259095_Criticism_of_Gender_Mainstreaming_according_to_Abdul_Karim_Zaidan_in_Al-Mufassol_Fi_Ahkam_Al-Mar'ah_wa_Bayt_Al-Muslim/link/5e0eb1b74585159aa4adb897/download.

Farooqi, Sadaf. "The Power of Economics in Marriage." About Islam, March 31, 2021. https://aboutislam.net/family-life/laying-foundations/in-marriage-money-does-matter/.

Fīdah, Saḥar. "Shakṣiyyah Mulhimah" (Sayyidaty, 2016), https://www.sayidaty.net/node/442021/أسرة-ومجتمع/شخصية-اليوم/عابدة-العظم-سليلة-العثمانيين-وحفيدة-الطنطاوي#photo/1.

Fry, Richard, Carolina Aragão, Kiley Hurst and Kim Parker. "In a Growing Share of U.S. Marriages, Husbands and Wives Earn About the Same." Pew Research Center, April 13, 2023. https://www.pewresearch.org/social-trends/2023/04/13/in-a-growing-share-of-u-s-marriages-husbands-and-wives-earn-about-the-same/.

Galloway, Sonia D. "The Impact of Islam as a Religion and Muslim Women on Gender

Equality: A Phenomenological Research Study". Doctoral dissertation. Nova Southeastern University. Retrieved from NSUWorks. Graduate School of Humanities and Social Sciences, 141, https://nsuworks.nova.edu/shss_dcar_etd/14/.

Al-Ghazālī, Muhammad. *Qaḍāyā al-Mar'ah bayn al-Taqālīd al-Rākidah wa al-Wāfidah* [*Women's Issues Between Stagnant and Expatriate Traditions*] Cairo, Egypt: Dār Al-Shurūq, 2012.

Gennari, Marialuisa, Cristina Giuliani, and Monica Accordini. "Muslim Immigrant Men's and Women's Attitudes towards Intimate Partner Violence." *Europe's Journal of Psychology* 13, no. 4 (2017): 688–707. https://ejop.psychopen.eu/index.php/ejop/article/view/1411.

"Global Connections. Roles of Women." PBS. Public Broadcasting Service. Accessed September 12, 2020. http://www.pbs.org/wgbh/globalconnections/mideast/questions/women/.

Goleen Samari (2019) Women's empowerment in Egypt: the reliability of a complex construct, Sexual and Reproductive Health Matters, 27:1, 146-159, DOI: 10.1080/26410397.2019.1586816.

Al-Gousi, Hiam Salah Al-din Ali. "Women's Rights in Islam and Contemporary Ulama," 2010, 57, https://etheses.whiterose.ac.uk/15221/1/535101.pdf.

Groenewald, Thomas. "A Phenomenological Research Design Illustrated." *International Journal of Qualitative Methods* 3, no. 1 (2004): 42–55. https://doi.org/10.1177/160940690400300104.

Abd el-Qadir, Hamd al-Neel Abd el-Sayed, "Hadith Umm Zar: Dirasah fi al-Tarakeeb wadallalah," *Mugalit Kulayit al-Ulum wal-Adab bil-Ula*, Tibah University, February 2018, https://mkda.journals.ekb.eg/article_123451_dae35f260cc11128d490c0e32c6887dd.pdf, 227-29.

Haddad, Gibril Fouad. *The Biographies of the Elite Lives of the Scholars, Imams & hadith Masters: Biographies of The Imams & Scholars*. No city: Zulfiqar Ayub, 2015.

Hammad, Ahmad Zaki, *Islamic Law, Understanding Juristic Differences*, Washington,

Indianapolis: American Trust Publications & the Author, 1992, 10-37.

Haqqani, Shehnaz, "Gendered Expectations, Personal Choice, and Social Compatibility in Western Muslim Marriages." University of Texas at Austin, 2013, 53-5, https://repositories.lib.utexas.edu/bitstream/handle/2152/22208/HAQQANI-THESIS-2013.pdf?sequence=1&isAllowed=y.

Al-Ḥarrānī, Ibn Taymiyyah. *Al-La'āli al-Lāmi'āt fī Aḥkām al-Mu'āmalāt.* Beirut, Lebanon, Sharikah Binā' Sharīf al-Anṣārī for Printing and Publication and Distribution, 2011.

Hāshimī Muḥammad 'Alī. *The Ideal Muslimah: The True Islamic Personality of the Muslim Woman as Defined in the Qur'an and Sunnah. Internet Archive.* Riyadh: International Islamic Pub. House, 2005, 191-92, https://archive.org/details/TheIdealMuslimah-alhamdulillah-library.blogspot.in.pdf.

Ḥatḥūt, Ḥassān. *Bihādhā Alqā Allāh.* Kuwait: Al-Marzūk Printing & Publishing Establishment.

Ḥijāzī, Muṣṭafā. *Al-Takhalluf al-Ijtimāʿī: Madkhal ilā Sīkūlūjiyyah al-Insān al-Maqhūr* [*Social Backwardness: An Entrance to the Psychology of an Abused Human Being*]. Casablanca, Morocco: al-Markaz al-Thaqāfī al-ʿArabī, 2005.

Ḥijāzī, Saʿīd and ʿĪsā, ʿAbd al-Wahhāb. "Al-Azhar: Ṭalab al-Khulʿ la Yatawaqqaf ʿalā Riḍā al-Zawj [The Request of Khulʿ Is not Based on the Husband's Consent] (El Watan News, 2018), https://www.elwatannews.com/news/details/2990337.

Al-Hilālī, Saʿd al-Dīn. *Al-Islām wa Insāniyyah al-Dawlah.* Cairo, Egypt: al-Hay'ah al-Miṣriyyah al-ʿĀmmah, 2012.

Hussain, Justice Aftab, *Status of Women in Islam.* Lahore, Pakistan: Law Publishing Al-aama lil-Kitab, 2012, 161-261.Company, 1987, 204-05.

Hussain, Rahmin, Ahmad, Arifuddin, Siti, Kara and Alwi, Zulfahmi "Polygamy in the Perspective of hadith", *Madania Jurnal Kajian Keislaman*, 10.29300/madania.v23.1954:95, https://www.researchgate.net/publication/335221025_Polygamy_in_the_Perspective_of_hadith_Justice_and_Equality_among_Wives_in_A_Polygamy_Practice.

Ibn Ḥayyān, Muhammad ibn Yūsuf ibn ʿAlī ibn Yūsuf. *Tafsīr al-Baḥr al-Muḥīt.* Beirut, Lebanon: Dār Iḥyā' al-Turāth al-ʿArabī, 2002.

Ibn Ḥazm, Abū Muhammad ʿAlī ibn Aḥmad ibn Saʿīd. *Al-Muḥallā bi al-Āthār.* Beirut, Lebanon: Dār al-Kutub al-ʿIlmiyyah, 2003.

Ibn Ḥazm, Abū Muhammad ʿAlī ibn Aḥmad ibn Saʿīd. *Al-Muḥallā fī Sharḥ al-Mujallā bi al-Ḥujaj wa al-Āthār*. Amman, Jordan: International Idea Home, n.d.

Ibn al-Jawzī, *Aḥkām Al-Nisā'* [*Laws Regarding Women*] (Cairo, Egypt: Maktabah Ibn Taymiyyah, 1997). Net Library E-Book Retrieved from https://archive.org/details/FP38344/page/n3/mode/1up?view=theater.

Ibrahim, Adnan. 2019. "Women's Rights in Islam." Dr. Adnan Ibrahim's Official Website. March 8, 2019. http://www.adnanibrahim.net/حقوق-المرأة-في-الإسلام.

Ibn Kathīr, Abū al-Fiḍā'. *Mukhtaṣar Tafsīr Ibn Kathīr*, ed. Muhammad ʿAlī al-Ṣābūnī. Beirut, Lebanon: Dār al-Qur'ān al-Karīm, 1981.

Ibn Kathīr, Abū al-Fiḍā'. *Tafsīr al-Qur'ān al-ʿAẓīm*. Riyadh, Saudi Arabia: Dār Ṭaybah Publications, 1997.

Abeer Idlaby, "*Al-Zawja Tas'al Wal Shar' Yujeeb.*" Dimishq, Beirut, Al-Yamamah for Printing, Publications & Distribution, 2010, 15, 16

Al-Khateeb, Maha, Islamic Marriage Contracts, A Resource Guide for Legal Professionals, Advocates, Imams & Communities, 2012, https://bwjp.org/assets/documents/pdfs/islamic_marriage_contracts_resource_guide_apiidv.pdf, 27, 29.

Killawi, Amal; Daneshpour, Manijeh; Elmi, Arij; Dadrus, Iman and Shamoon, Zain, Community Brief: Promoting Healthy Marriages & Preventing Divorce in the American Muslim Community, Institute for Social Policy and Understanding (Dearborn, Michigan, 2014), https://www.ispu.org/wp-content/uploads/2016/08/ISPU_Marriage_Divorce-Brief_Final.pdf.

Ibn al-Hamam, Fath al-Qadeer. Beirut, Lebanon: Dār al-Kutub al-ʿIlmiyyah, 2003, 275, https://ia802801.us.archive.org/22/items/waq72501/02_72502.pdf.

Ibn Manẓūr, Abū al-Faḍl Jamāl al-Dīn Muhammad ibn Mukarram. *Lisān al-ʿArab*. Beirut, Lebanon: Dar Ṣādir.

Ibn al-Nujaym, Zayn al-Dīn. *Al-Baḥr al-Rāʾiq fī Sharḥ Kanz al-Daqāʾiq*, ed. Zakariyyā al-ʿUmayrāt, 9 (Beirut: Dār al-Kutub al-ʿIlmiyyah, 1997).

Ibn Qudāmah, *Al-Mughnī*. Riyadh, Saudi Arabia: Dār ʿAalam al-Kutubʿ Publications, 1986, https://ia801609.us.archive.org/23/items/WAQmogni/mogni04.pdf.

Ibn Rushd. *The Distinguished Jurist's Primer*. Translated by Imran Ahsan Khan Nyazee. Reading, United Kingdom: Garnet Publishing Limited, 1996.

Adnan Ibrahim, "Huquq al-Mar'ah fī al-Islām [The Rights of Women in Islam]" (*Adnan Ibrahim*, 2019), http://www.adnanibrahim.net/حقوق-المرأة-في-الإسلام/.

Idlibī, Abīr, *Al-Zawjah Tas'al wa al-Sharʿ Yujīb*. Beirut, Lebanon: Al-Yamamah Printing & Publication & Distribution, 2010.

Al-ʿIlmī, ʿAlī ibn al-Ḥusnī. *Kitāb al-Nawāzil.* Rabat, Morocco: Wizārah al-Awqāf fi Al-Shu'ūn al-Islāmiyyah, 1983.

Islam Web. "Ma Hiya al-Nafaqah ʿalā al-Zawj" [What is the Nafaqah Expected of the Husband], (*Islamweb*, 2008), https://www.islamweb.net/ar/fatwa/113285/ماهية-النفقة-الواجبة-على-الزوج.

Ismāʿīl, Abū ʿAbd al-Raḥmān Ayman. "Al-ʿAqd al-Bāṭil wa al-ʿAqd al-Fāsid" (*al-Alūkah al-Sharīʿah*, 2020), https://www.alukah.net/sharia/0/138890/.

Ismāʿīl, Muhammad Bakr, *Al-Fiqh al-Wāḍiḥ* (Cairo, Egypt, Dār al-Manār Publications, 1997).

Al-ʿĪsah, Inās ʿAbbād. "Qirā'ah fī Waḍʿiyyah al-Mar'ah fī al-Mujtamaʿ al-ʿArabī [A Reading on the Situation of the Woman in the Arab Society]" (*Ākhir al-Akhbār*, 2020), https://translate.google.com/translate?hl=en&sl=ar&tl=en&u=https%3A%2F%2Fwww.wattan.net%2Far%2Fnews%2F317604.html&anno=2&prev=search&sandbox=.

Jarrār, Alā'. "Waṣiyyah al-Rasūl ilā al-Nisā' [The Bequest of the Messenger Regarding Women]" (*Mawḍūʿ*, 2021), https://mawdoo3.com/وصية_الرسول_بالنساء.

Al-Jazā'irī, Abū Bakr Jābir. *Minhāj al-Muslim*. Riyadh, Saudi Arabia: Darussalam Global Leader in Islamic Books, 2001.

Al-Jazīrī, ʿAbd al-Raḥmān. *Kitāb al-Fiqh ʿalā al-Madhāhib al-Arbaʿah* (Beirut, Lebanon: Dār al-Fikr, 1986).

Jewett, Jennifer. *The Recommendations of International Conference on Population and Development: The Possibility of the Empowerment of Women in Egypt*, 29 Cornell INT'LL.J., 1996, 191, 203.

Al-Jibaly, Muhammad. *The Quest for Love & Mercy*. Beirut, Lebanon: Al-Kitaab & as-Sunnah Publishing, 2000.

Karamah: Muslim Women Lawyers for Human Rights. "Answer to Alimony Question". Ask Zahra Advice Column. 07/2015.

Al-Kurdī, Aḥmad al-Ḥijī. "Al-Mahr" (Shabakat al-Fatāwā al-Shar īʿah, 2020), http://www.islamic-fatwa.com/library/book/8/136.

Al-Kāsānī, ʿAlā' al-Dīn Abū Bakr ibn Masʿūd, *Al-Badā'iʿ al-Ṣanā'iʿ fī Tartīb al-Sharā'iʿ*. Beirut, Lebanon: Dār al-Kutub al-ʿIlmīyyah, 2003. https://ia801201.us.archive.org/11/items/waq75041/03_75043.pdf.

Khan, Muhammad Farooq, *Islam and Women*, Model Town, Lahore, Pakistan: Dar-Ul-Ishraq, 2002, 12-14.

Kia, Amir. "The Concept of Responsibility of Men and Women in Islam." *Arts & Humanities Open Access Journal* 3, no. 5 (2019). https://doi.org/10.15406/ahoaj.2019.03.00137.

Killawi, Amal, Manijeh Daneshpour, Arij Elmi, Iman Dadrus, and Zain Shamoon. n.d. "Community Brief: Promoting Healthy Marriages & Preventing Divorce in the American Muslim Community, Institute for Social Policy and Understanding." *Institute for Social Policy and Understanding: RESEARCH MAKING AN IMPACT*. https://www.ispu.org/wp-content/uploads/2016/08/ISPU_Marriage_DivorceBrief_Final.pdf.

Kozak, Janet. "6 Hidden Abuses of Muslim Woman's Rights." About Islam, October 13, 2019. https://aboutislam.net/family-life/gender-society/6-hidden-abuses-of-muslim-womens-rights/.

Lerner, Gerda, *The Creation of Patriarchy.* Volume One. New York, Oxford, Oxford University Press, 1986, 216, https://garrafeminista.files.wordpress.com/2018/04/gerda-lerner-the-creation-of-patriarchy.pdf.

Lewis, A. D.E., Glendon, Mary Ann and Kiralfy, Albert Roland. "Common law."

Encyclopedia Britannica, October 30, 2020. https://www.britannica.com/topic/common-law.

Lugo, Karen. "American Family Law and Sharia-Compliant Marriages." *The Federalist Society Engage*, July 14, 2012. https://fedsoc.org/commentary/publications/american-family-law-and-sharia-compliant-marriages.

Al-Madinah News, "Taqrīr: Thulthay Fuqarā' al-'Ālam min al-Nisā' [Report: One Third of the Poor in the World are Women]" (Al-Madīnah al-Ikhbāriyyah, October 17, 2018), https://www.almadenahnews.com/article/701459--تقرير-ثلثي-فقراء-العالم-من-النساء.

Maine, Sir Henry Sumner. Lectures on the Early History of Institutions. 7th edition. London, John Murray, 1914. Lecture XI. The Early History of the Settled Property of Married Women, 310, https://oll.libertyfund.org/title/maine-lectures-on-the-early-history-of-institutions.

Mālik, Ibn Anas, *Muwaṭṭa' li Imām Mālik*. Shubra, Egypt: Al-Andalus al-Jadīdah for Publications and Distributions, 2009.

Manīsī, Samiyyah. "Ahammiyyah Taʿlīm al-Mar'ah [The Importance of Educating Women]" (*al-Alūkah al-Sharīʿah*) https://www.alukah.net/social/0/116019/.

Mason, Miles. "Financial Abuse, Narcissists & Money: A Divorce Lawyer's Perspective." Miles Mason Family Law Group, PLC. Miles Mason Family Law Group, PLC, September 7, 2021. https://memphisdivorce.com/tennessee-divorce-law/financial-abuse-narcissists-money-a-divorce-lawyers-perspective/.

Al-Māwardī, Abū al-Ḥasan ʿAlī ibn Muhammad ibn Ḥabīb. *Kitāb al-Nafaqāt*. Beirut, Lebanon: Dar Ibn Ḥazm Publications, 1998.

Al-Mazīnī, Khālid ibn ʿAbdullāh. "Nafaqah Al-Zawja fī al-ʿAsr al-Ḥāḍir (2/2)" (almoslim.net, 2017). https://almoslim.net/node/275160.

Meisenbach, Rebecca. (2010). The Female Breadwinner: Phenomenological Experience and Gendered Identity in Work/Family Spaces. Sex Roles. 62. 2-19. 10.1007/s11199-009-9714-5.

Al-Mubārak, Fayṣal. "Ḥukm al-Nafaqah ʿalā al-Zawjah [The Legal Ruling of Maintenance for the Wife]" (*al-Alūkah al-Sharīʿah*, 2017), https://www.alukah.net/sharia/0/112941/.

Al-Mubārak, Fayṣal. "Iʿsār Al-Zawj [The Withholding of the Husband]" (*al-Alūkah al-Sharīʿah*, 2017), https://www.alukah.net/sharia/0/113501/.

Al-Mubārak, Sayyid. "Ṣadāq al-Zawjayn bayn al-ʿUrf wal-Sharʿ" (*al-Alūkah al-Sharīʿah*, 2018), https://www.alukah.net/social/0/132617/.

Al-Mubārakfūrī, Ṣafī al-Raḥmān. *Al-Raḥīq al-Makhtūm*. Al-Mansura, Egypt: Dār al-Wafā' for Printing, Publications and Distribution, 1999.

Muhammad, ʿAbdullāh Najīb. "Al-ʿAmal bi Sahm al-Mu'allafah Qulūbuhum" (*al-Alūkah al-Sharīʿah*, 2015), https://www.alukah.net/sharia/0/88911/.

Muhammad, Maḥmūd Bandar ʿAlī, "Nafaqah al-Zawjah fī al-Sharīʿah wa al-Qānūn," Kuliyyat al-ʿUlūm Al-Islāmiyyah Magazine, 16th edition, https://www.iasj.net/iasj/download/329e2c58ffa1c074, 377.

Al-Munajjid, Muhammad Ṣāliḥ. "Did the Prophet (Blessings and Peace of Allah Be upon Him) Ever Hit His Wife 'Aa'ishah (May Allah Be Pleased with Her)?" Islam Question & Answer. Question 164216. Publication: 06-12-2013. https://islamqa.info/en/answers/164216/did-the-prophet-blessings-and-peace-of-allah-be-upon-him-ever-hit-his-wife-aaishah-may-allah-be-pleased-with-her.

Al-Munajjid, Muhammad Ṣāliḥ. "Dafʿ al-Zakāh li al-Mar'ah al-Faqīrah Idhā Kāna Zawjuhā la Yunfiq ʿAlayhā [The Obligatory Charity for the Poor Woman When Her Husband Abstains From Spending on Her]." Al-Islām Su'āl wa al-Jawāb. Publication: 06-05-2007. https://islamqa.info/ar/answers/102755/دفع-الزكاة-للمراة-الفقيرة-اذا-كان-زوجها-لا-ينفق-عليها.

Al-Munajjid, Muhammad Ṣāliḥ. "The Difference Between Khul', Tallaq and Faskh (Ways of Ending a Marriage)." Islam Question & Answer, Question 133859. Publication: 31-03-2016. https://islamqa.info/en/answers/133859/

the-difference-between-khul-talaaq-and-faskh-ways-of-ending-a-marriage.

Musawah: For Equality in the Family, "Positive Developments in Muslim Family Laws," (2019), https://www.musawah.org/wp-content/uploads/2019/02/Positive-Developments-Table-2019_EN.pdf, 13, 14.

Nāṣif, Naʿīmah. "Umm Zarʿ: Al-Zawjah Al-Wafiyyah fī Turāthina al-Islāmī [Umm Zarʿ: the Sincere Wife in our Islamic Heritage]" (*al-Alūkah al-Sharīʿah*, 2007), https://www.alukah.net/social/0/1062/.

Al-Najīrī, Maḥmūd Maḥmūd. "Tanāzuʿ al-Zawjayn fī Matāʿ al-Bayt" (Al-Multaqā al-Fiqhī, 2008), https://feqhweb.com/vb/threads/796/.تنازع-الزوجين-في-متاع-البيت/.

Al-Nawawī, Yaḥyā ibn Sharaf. *Riyāḍ al-Ṣāliḥīn* (Sunnah.com, 2020), https://sunnah.com/riyadussalihin.

Offenhauer, P. (2015). Women in Islamic Societies: A selected review of social scientific literature.

Philips, Abu Ameenah Bilal, *The Evolution of Fiqh*. Edition Riyadh: Saudi Arabia: International Islamic Publishing House, 1995.

Qāsim, Yūsuf. "Ḥuqūq al-Usrah fī al-Fiqh al-Islāmī (The Family Rights Within Islamic Derived Laws)" (*al-Alūkah al-Sharīʿah*, 2010), https://www.alukah.net/sharia/0/23148/.

Al-Qaṭṭān, Mannāʿ. *Mabāḥith fī ʿUlūm al-Qur'ān*. Cairo, Egypt: Maktabah Wahbah, 2000.

Al-Qurṭubī, Abū ʿAbdullāh Muhammad ibn Aḥmad al-Anṣārī. *Al-Jāmiʿ li Aḥkām al-Qur'ān* (Dār ʿUlūm Al-Qur'ān).

Qutb, Sayyid. *Fī Ẓilāl Al-Qur'ān*. Cairo, Egypt: Dār al-Shurūq, 1972.

Qutb, Sayyid. In The Shade of The Qur'an *Fī Ẓilāl Al-Qur'ān*, Translated and Edited by Adil Salahi & Ashur Shamis.

Markfield, Leicester LE67 9SY, United Kingdom, The Islamic Foundation, Markfield Conference Centre, 2001.

Rahman, Md. Habibur Rahman, "A Juristic Analysis on Hibah al-Umra and al-Ruqba and Their Applications." International Islamic University Malaysia, 2012, https://www.academia.edu/10710931/Hibah_al-Umra_and_al-Ruqba_and_Their_Applications.

Ratner, Carl. Subjectivity and Objectivity in Qualitative Methodology [29 paragraphs]. *Forum Qualitative Sozialforschung / Forum: Qualitative Social Research*, *3*(3), Art. 16, 2002. http://nbn-resolving.de/urn:nbn:de:0114-fqs0203160.

Al-Rāzī, Muhammad Fakhr al-Dīn. *Tafsīr al-Fakhr al-Rāzī*. Beirut, Lebanon: Dār al-Fikr Printing and Publication.

Renan Barzilay, Arianne, Power in the Age of In/Equality: Economic Abuse, Masculinities, and the Long Road to Marriage Equality (January 29, 2018). Akron Law Review, Vol. 52, 2018, Available at SSRN: https://papers.ssrn.com/sol3/papers.cfm?abstract_id=3117817.

Al-Rifāʿī, Khālid ʿAbd al-Munʿim. "Ḥukm Akhdh al-Zawj Ratib al-Zāwjah (Ruling of a Husband Taking the Wife's Paycheque)" (*Ṭarīq Al-Islam*, 2012), https://ar.islamway.net/fatwa/36835/حكم-أخذ-الزوج-راتب-الزوجة.

Riḍwān, Amīnah. "Ḥaqq al-Kadd wa al-Siʿāyah Fi al-Qānūn al-Maghribī." المعلومة القانونية [The Right to Kadd and Si'ayah Based on Morocco Law] October 2, 2019. https://alkanounia.info/?p=7676.

Al-Ṣabāḥ, Rīnād. "Ma Huwa Faskh Al-Nikāḥ [What is the Invalidation of the Marriage Contract]" (Mawḍūʿ, 2020), https://mawdoo3.com/ما_هو_فسخ_النكاح.

Ṣādiq, Muhammad ʿAbd al-Raḥmān. "Manẓūmah al-Shūrā fī al-Islām [The Shūrā System in Islam]" (al-Alūkah al-Sharīʿah, 2016), https://www.alukah.net/sharia/0/108384/منظومة-الشورى-في-الإسلام/.

Al-Ṣaffār, Ḥasan. "Al-Ṣadāq" (Maktab Samāḥah al-Shaykh Ḥasan al-Ṣaffār, 2001), https://www.saffar.org/?act=artc&id=957.

Sahih International, *The Qur'an, The Quranic Arabic Corpus,* (Kais Dukes, 2009-2017), https:// corpus.quran.com.

Ṣalāḥ, Razān. "Maʿlūmāt ʿan ʿAbd al-Malik ibn Marwān" (Mawḍūʿ, 2019), https://mawdoo3.com/معلومات_عن_عبد_الملك_بن_مروان.

Salahi, Adil. "Imam Ali ibn Hazm." Muslim Heritage. Foundation for Science, Technology and Heritage, 2005. https://muslim heritage.com/imam-ali-ibn-hazm/.

Salahi, Adil, Imam Ali ibn Hazm. Muslim Heritage, Accessed 2020.

Al-Sammān, ʿAbd al-Fattāḥ. *Nafaqāt al-Nabī Ṣallā Allāh ʿAlayhi wa Sallam ʿalā Zawjātihi fī Hayātihi wa Baʿd Mamatihi* [The Expenses of the Prophet Muhammad on His Wives During His Life and After His Death]" (Cairo, Egypt: Dār al-Fikr, 2018); https://dergipark.org.tr/tr/download/article-file/572586.

Al-Sammān, ʿAbd al-Fattāḥ. "Zawjī Hal Uqriḍuhu Mālī? [My Husband Should I Lend Him my Money?]" (2019), Kayf Maluk TV Programme, https://www.youtube.com/watch?v=d2F-73nUPulc.

Sandstrom, Heather, and Sandra Huerta. "The Negative Effects of Instability on Child Development: A Research Synthesis. Low Income Working Families: Discussion Paper 3." Urban Institute, September 2013. https://www.urban.org/sites/default/files/publication/32706/412899-The-

Negative-Effects-of-Instability-on-Child-Development-A-Research-Synthesis.PDF.

Al-Ṣanʿānī, Muhammad ibn Ismāʿīl. *Subul al-Salām: Sharḥ Bulūgh al-Marām min Adillah al-Aḥkām*. Riyadh, Saudi Arabia: Darussalam Publishers & Distributors, 2002.

Al-Sawy, Salah. "The Assembly's Family Code for Muslim Communities in North America." The Assembly of Muslim Jurists of America the Assembly's Family Code for Muslim Communities in non-Muslim Societies, 2012. https://www.amjaonline.org/declaration-articles/the-assemblys-family-code-for-muslim-communities-in-north-america/.

Sayf, ʿAbdullāh ibn Mubārak ʿAlī. "Min Aḥkām al-Liʿān fī al-Fiqh al-Islāmī [Amongst the Legal Rulings Regarding Imprecation Within Islamic Fiqh]" (*al-Alūkah al-Sharīʿah*, 2014), https://www.alukah.net/web/abdullah-ibn-mubarak/0/76957/#_ftnref2.

Al-Sirjānī, Rāghib. "Shurayḥ al-Qāḍī (Qiṣṣah al-Islām, 2019), https://islamstory.com/ar/artical/3408542/شريح-القاضي.

Al-Shāfiʿī, Muhammad ibn Idrīs al-Shāfiʿī. *Al-Umm*. Cairo, Egypt: Dār al-Ḥadīth, 2008.

Al-Shawkānī, Muhammad ibn ʿAlī ibn Muhammad. *Nayl al-Awṭār*. Beirut, Lebanon: Dār al-Maʿrifah, 2002.

Al-Shaykh, ʿĀrif. "Hal al-Mahr Sharṭ fī Ṣiḥḥah al-Nikāḥ [Is the Mahr a Condition for the Validity of the Marriage Contract?]" (*al-Khalīj*, 2020), https://www.alkhaleej.ae/عالم-متجدد/هل-المهر-شرط-في-صحة-النكاح؟.

Al-Shirbīnī, Shams al-Dīn Muhammad ibn Muhammad al-Khaṭīb. *Mughnī al-Muḥtāj* (Cairo, Egypt: Dar al-Ḥadīth Publications, Printing and Distribution, 2006).

Al-Sibāʿī, Muṣṭafā. *Al-Mar'ah bayn al-Fiqh wa al-Qānūn*. Cairo, Egypt: Dār Al-Salām for Printing and Publications and Distribution and Translation.

Silva, Brady (2019) "The Importance of Muslim Fathers in America," Spectrum: Vol. 8: Iss. 1, Article 7. Available at: https://scholars.unh.edu/spectrum/vol8/iss1/7/. 3.

Smith, Jane I. *Islam in America*. New York, United States: Columbia University Press, 2010.

Al-Ṭabarī, Abū Jaʿfar Muhammad ibn Jarīr, *Jāmiʿ al-Bayān ʿan Ta'wīl āy al-Qur'ān*. Beirut, Lebanon: Mu'assasah al-Risālah Printing and Publications, 1994.

Al-Tarīqī, ʿAbdullāh ibn ʿAbd al-Muḥsin. "Al-Nafaqah al-Wājibah ʿalā al-Mar'ah li Ḥaqq al-Ghayr" (*al-Alūkah al-Sharīʿah*, 2007), http://cp.alukah.net/web/turaiqi/0/363/.

Thanwi, Ashraf 'Ali. *Ashraf's Blessings of Marriage*. Dewsbury, United Kingdom: Amanah Studio, 2008.

Thanwi. Ashraf 'Ali. *Tafsīr Bayān al-Qur'ān*. Lahore, Pakistan: Maktaba Rehmania, n.d.

Timmons, Jacquette M., *Financial Intimacy*. Chicago, Illinois: Chicago Review Press, 2010, 73-8.

Al-Tirmidhī, Abu Muhammad. "12 The Book on Suckling." *Jāmiʿ al-Tirmidhī* 1163, The Book on Suckling (sunnah.com, 2020), https://sunnah.com/tirmidhi:1163.

Usmani, Mufti Muhammad Taqi, "Shaykh Mufti Muhammad Shafi, The Grand Mufti of Pakistan." December 4, 2011, https://www.scribd.com/document/94954972/Shaykh-Muhammad-Shafi-The-Mufti-of-Pakistan.

Walton, L. M., Akram, RDMS, BS, F., & Hossain, BBA, F. (2014). Health Beliefs of Muslim Women and Implications for Health Care Providers: Exploratory Study on the Health

Beliefs of Muslim Women. Online Journal of Health Ethics, 10(2). http://dx.doi.org/10.18785/ojhe.1002.05.

Wehr, Hans. A Dictionary of Modern Written Arabic. Spoken Language Services, Inc., Ithaca, New York, 1976, https://www.ghazali.org/books/wehr-cowAl-76.pdf, 318; https://context.reverso.net/translation/arabic-english/رئيس.

Williams, Glanville L. The Legal Unity of Husband and Wife, *Modern Law Review*. Vol. 1. Issue 1, 1947, 18, https://onlinelibrary.wiley.com/doi/pdf/10.1111/j.1468-2230.1947.tb00034.x.

"Women." *The Chancellor, Masters, and Scholars of the University of Cambridge* 28, 11th ed., 28:816–20. Cambridge etc., New York: The Univ. Press, 1910.

Yūsuf, Umm ʿAbd al-Raḥmān. "Sakan wa Mawaddah wa Rahmah" [Tranquillity, Love, and Mercy]" (*Qiṣṣah al-Islām*, 2012), https://islamstory.com/ar/artical/24806.

Zain, Syed Abu Zafar, *The Prophet of Islam the Ideal Husband*. Bombay, India: Bilal Books, 1997. 51.

Zarabozo, Jamaal. "Fiqh of Marriage." Shakeel Mahate, 2013. http://www.smahate.com/islamic-classes/2013-winter/fiqh-of-marriage.

Zarabozo, Jamaal, "Life Insurance and the Extent to which it is Permitted in Case of Need.

Houston, Texas: The Assembly of Muslim Jurists of America 16th Annual Imams Conference, 2019, 48. https://www.amjaonline.org/wp-content/uploads/2019/04/Life-Insurance-and-the-Extent-to-which-it-is-Permitted-in-a-Case-of-Need-Zarabozo.pdf.

Zaydān, ʿAbd al-Karīm. *Al-Jāmiʿ fī al-Fiqh al-Islāmī al-Mufaṣṣal fī Aḥkām al-Mar'ah wa al-Bayt al-Muslim*. Beirut, Lebanon: al-Risālah Publications, 1993.

Al-Zuḥaylī, Wahbah. *Al-Fiqh al-Islāmī wa Adillatuhu*. Beirut, Lebanon: Dār al-Fikr, 2014.

Al-Zuḥaylī, Wahbah. *Al-Wajiz Fi al-Fiqh al-Islami*. Beirut, Lebanon: Dār Al-Khair Publications and Distribution, 2006. Volume 1, 492. Net E-Book Library Retrieved from https://ia601302.us.archive.org/14/items/FP87019/01_87018.pdf.

Appendix A. Glossary of Arabic Terms

Abū	Father.
al-ḥawāshī	Successors and those of collateral kinship.
Al-Mulāʿanah (or Liʿān)	An oath pronounced by two spouses due to the husband's accusation of his wife committing adultery while being the only witness.
Aḍāḥī	Sacrifices.
Allah	God in Islam, who is unique, omnipotent and the only deity and creator of the universe.
Al-ʿUmrā wa al-Ruqbā	Gifts for survival.
Al-Walā'	Loyalty.
Al-Waqf	Islamic endowment.
ʿAqīdah	Creed.
Ahliyyat al-Wujūb	The rights that come along with one's mere existence.
Ahliyyat al-Adā'	The rights upon reaching adulthood.
Awāq	One *awāq* (the weight of pure silver) is equal to forty dirhams.
Bint	Daughter.
Bayt al-Māl	The state's public treasury.
Dinar	An ancient gold coin.
Dirham	A silver coin weighing 50 grains of barley with cut ends. It is equal to 1/12 of one *Uqiyyah* of gold in value.
Diyah	Monetary compensation.
Eid al-Aḍḥā	A four-day feast or festival for Muslims that begins on the tenth day of the Islamic month Dhul-Hijjah.

Eid Al-Fiṭr	A feast or festival for Muslims on the first day of the Islamic month of Shawwal. Shawwal is the month that follows the month of Ramadan in which Muslims are obligated to fast. The literal meaning of *fiṭr* is to breakfast.
Farā'iḍ	Fixed shares for the relatives of a deceased. In the Qur'an (4:11, 12, 176) they are stated as 1/2, 1/4, 1/3, 1/6, 1/8 or 2/3.
Fāsid	Invalid or corrupt.
Faskh	Annulment of marriage.
Fatwa	Religious verdict.
Fiqh	Islamic Jurisprudence.
Furūʿ	Branches.
Hajj	Pilgrimage to Mecca. One of the obligatory five pillars of Islam.
Halal	Lawful.
Hadith	(plural: *aḥādīth*) The sayings, deeds and approval accurately narrated from the Prophet ﷺ.
Haram	Unlawful and punishable in Islam
Henna	A type of plant used for dyeing or colouring the hair. Also used on body parts for beautification.
Hibah	A gift given to someone for the sake of Allah.
Ḥudūd	The boundaries or limits of Allah ﷻ of the permissible *(halal)* and impermissible (*haram*).
Ibn	Son.
Ibṭāl or Faskh	Annulment.
ʿIddah	The waiting time period prescribed by Allah for women after they were divorced or upon the death of their husbands. Once it is complete, a woman can remarry.
Iḥtibās	Confinement; trapping.
Iḥsān	All forms of giving.
Iḥtiwā'	Being secured or protected.
Ijārah	Earnings through renting property.
Ijtihād	Jurisprudence.
Īlā'	An oath taken by the husband that he would not have sexual relation with his wife for a certain time period.

Islam	The name of the Religion of Submission to One God.
Iṣṭilāḥ	Providing enough.
Kadd and Si'āyah	One's right to the fruit of their striving, hard work, and contribution to accumulating the family wealth.
Kaffārāt	Expiations.
Kāfir	Disbeliever.
Khul'	A type of divorce in which a wife seeks from her husband by returning back her *mahr* or compensation.
Kifāyah	That which is satisfactory.
Li'ān (or al-Mulā'anah)	An oath taken by both the husband and wife if the husband accuses his wife of committing adultery while being the only witness. It results in their eternal separation.
Mahr	Bridal gift given by the husband to his wife upon contracting the marriage.
Mahr Mithl	A stipulated mahr set according to what other female family members got married upon.
Ma'rūf	Appropriate kindness.
Madhāhib	Schools of Thought.
Mu'akhkhar Mahr	A specified *mahr* or marital gift that is to be paid upfront upon the contractual marriage signatures without any mention of it being expedited or deferred. Based on some schools of thought (Abū Ḥanīfah), the husband is required to immediately pay it off to his wife and in the event of non-payment, he loses rights over her while expected to provide for her.
Mulā'anah	The act of performing *li'an*.
Mut'at al-Bayt	Household belongings.
Mudd	A measure of two thirds of a kilogram. It can be a bit less or more.
Muqaddam	Prompt.
Nafaqah	Maintenance.
Nafaqat al-Walad	Post-divorce for providing child support.
Niḥlah	Graciously or in good will.
Nisā'	Women.

Niṣāb	The minimum amount of property liable to payment of the *zakāh*, e.g., *niṣāb* of gold is twenty *mithqāls* i.e., approx. 94 grams. *Niṣāb* of silver is two hundred dirhams, i.e., approx. 640 grams.
Niṣāb	Of food grains and fruit is 5 awsaq i.e., 673.5 kg. *Niṣāb* of camels is 5 camels. *Niṣāb* of cows is 5 cows, and *niṣāb* of sheep is 40 sheep.
Nushūz	Recalcitrant.
Nudhūr	Vows.
Qiṣāṣ	Laws of equality in punishment for wounds etc. in retaliation.
Qur'an	The Islamic sacred book believed to be the word of God.
Qiwāmah	Charge.
Riḍā'ah	Breastfeeding.
Ramadan	The month of observing fasts. It is the ninth month of the Islamic calendar. This is the month in which the Holy Qur'an was revealed upon Prophet Muhammad ﷺ. It was sent on a particular night in the last ten nights of the month, called the night of Qadr.
Rizquhunna	Their blessings.
Ruqbā	It is the house which is gifted to someone for lifetime only to live in and does not belong to them.
Ṣadaqah	Voluntary alms or anything given as charity.
Ṣadāq (Mahr)	A unique charity.
Ṣadaqat al-Fitr	Breaking fast for charity.
Ṣadaqah Jāriyah	Voluntary charity
Ṣalāh	Prayer.
Shariah	Islamic law derived directly from the Qur'an and authentic Prophetic traditions.
Ṣulb	The location of a man's reproduction system responsible for producing semen.
Sunnah	The legal way or ways, orders, acts of worship and statements of the Prophet ﷺ, that have become models to be followed by the Muslims.
Sunni	The larger of the two main branches of Islam based on Islamic traditions.

Tafsīr	Exegesis of the Qur'an.
Ṭalāq	Divorce.
Ṭaqwā	Being conscious and cognizant of God.
Ujrat al-Ḥadānah	Post-Divorce Compensation for Providing Childcare.
'Urf	Everything that is considered customary in a society whether is related to peoples' sayings or actions. The acceptable *'urf* in Islam must be in accordance to the Islamic Shariah and does not allow what is forbidden nor disallow what is permitted.
Uṣūl	Origin.
Umm	Mother.
'Umrah	Pilgrimage to Mecca of a lesser nature. It is called 'lesser Hajj.'
Walā'	A right to inherit the property of a freed slave to the person who has freed him.
Walī	Representative, protector, guardian, supporter, helper or friend.
Waqf	Religious endowment.
Waṣiyah	Rights to Making and Receival of a Bequest.
Yamīn	A sworn statement.
Zakāt	Obligatory charity: A certain fixed proportion of the wealth and of every kind of property liable to *zakāh* of a Muslim to be paid yearly for the benefit of the poor in the Muslim community. The payment of *zakāh* is one of the obligatory five pillars of Islam. It is a major economic means for establishing social justice and leading the Muslim society to prosperity and security.
Zakāt al-Fiṭr	Obligatory alms to be given by Muslims before the prayer of al-Fitr feast (Eid al-Fiṭr).
Zakāt al-Mal	Obligatory charitable financial giving of two and a half percent of one's saved possessions.
Ẓihār	An oath that requires expiation.
Dhimmah	Legally qualified.

Appendix B. Index of Terms Bestowing Honor

: *Jalla wa ʿAlā*	"The All-High and Exalted"
: *Ṣallā Allāh ʿAlayhi wa Sallam*	"Blessings and peace be upon him"
: *ʿAlayhi (or ʿalayha) al-Salām*	"May peace be upon him (or her)"
: *Raḍiyā Allāhu ʿAnha*	"May Allah be pleased with her"
: *Raḍiyā Allāhu ʿAnhu*	"May Allah be pleased with him"

Appendix C. Qur'an Index

1	*Al-Fātiḥah* (The Opening)	1	In the name of Allah, Most Gracious, Most Merciful.	بِسۡمِ ٱللَّهِ ٱلرَّحۡمَٰنِ ٱلرَّحِيمِ
4	*Al-Nisā'* (The Women)	135	O you who have believed, be persistently standing firm in justice, witnesses for Allah, even if it be against yourselves or parents and relatives. Whether one is rich or poor, Allah is more worthy of both. So follow not [personal] inclinations, lest you not be just. And if you distort [your testimony] or refuse [to give it], then indeed Allah is ever, with what you do, Acquainted.	۞ يَٰٓأَيُّهَا ٱلَّذِينَ ءَامَنُواْ كُونُواْ قَوَّٰمِينَ بِٱلۡقِسۡطِ شُهَدَآءَ لِلَّهِ وَلَوۡ عَلَىٰٓ أَنفُسِكُمۡ أَوِ ٱلۡوَٰلِدَيۡنِ وَٱلۡأَقۡرَبِينَۚ إِن يَكُنۡ غَنِيًّا أَوۡ فَقِيرٗا فَٱللَّهُ أَوۡلَىٰ بِهِمَاۖ فَلَا تَتَّبِعُواْ ٱلۡهَوَىٰٓ أَن تَعۡدِلُواْۚ وَإِن تَلۡوُۥٓاْ أَوۡ تُعۡرِضُواْ فَإِنَّ ٱللَّهَ كَانَ بِمَا تَعۡمَلُونَ خَبِيرٗا ١٣٥
4	*Al-Nisā'* (The Women)	4	And give the women [upon marriage] their [bridal] gifts graciously. But if they give up willingly to you anything of it, then take it in satisfaction and ease.	وَءَاتُواْ ٱلنِّسَآءَ صَدُقَٰتِهِنَّ نِحۡلَةٗۚ فَإِن طِبۡنَ لَكُمۡ عَن شَيۡءٖ مِّنۡهُ نَفۡسٗا فَكُلُوهُ هَنِيٓـٔٗا مَّرِيٓـٔٗا ٤
34	*Saba'* (Sheba)	39	Say, "Indeed, my Lord extends provision for whom He wills of His servants and restricts [it] for him. But whatever thing you spend [in His cause] - He will compensate it; and He is the best of providers."	قُلۡ إِنَّ رَبِّي يَبۡسُطُ ٱلرِّزۡقَ لِمَن يَشَآءُ مِنۡ عِبَادِهِۦ وَيَقۡدِرُ لَهُۥۚ وَمَآ أَنفَقۡتُم مِّن شَيۡءٖ فَهُوَ يُخۡلِفُهُۥۖ وَهُوَ خَيۡرُ ٱلرَّٰزِقِينَ ٣٩

4	*Al-Nisā'* (The Women)	3	And if you fear that you will not deal justly with the orphan girls, then marry those that please you of [other] women, two or three or four. But if you fear that you will not be just, then [marry only] one or those your right hand possesses. That is more suitable that you may not incline [to injustice].	وَإِنْ خِفْتُمْ أَلَّا تُقْسِطُوا۟ فِى ٱلْيَتَٰمَىٰ فَٱنكِحُوا۟ مَا طَابَ لَكُم مِّنَ ٱلنِّسَآءِ مَثْنَىٰ وَثُلَٰثَ وَرُبَٰعَ ۖ فَإِنْ خِفْتُمْ أَلَّا تَعْدِلُوا۟ فَوَٰحِدَةً أَوْ مَا مَلَكَتْ أَيْمَٰنُكُمْ ۚ ذَٰلِكَ أَدْنَىٰٓ أَلَّا تَعُولُوا۟ ﴿٣﴾
65	*Al-Ṭalāq* (The Divorce)	6	Lodge them [in a section] of where you dwell out of your means and do not harm them in order to oppress them. And if they should be pregnant, then spend on them until they give birth. And if they breastfeed for you, then give them their payment and confer among yourselves in the acceptable way; but if you are in discord, then there may breastfeed for the father another woman.	أَسْكِنُوهُنَّ مِنْ حَيْثُ سَكَنتُم مِّن وُجْدِكُمْ وَلَا تُضَآرُّوهُنَّ لِتُضَيِّقُوا۟ عَلَيْهِنَّ ۚ وَإِن كُنَّ أُو۟لَٰتِ حَمْلٍ فَأَنفِقُوا۟ عَلَيْهِنَّ حَتَّىٰ يَضَعْنَ حَمْلَهُنَّ ۚ فَإِنْ أَرْضَعْنَ لَكُمْ فَـَٔاتُوهُنَّ أُجُورَهُنَّ ۖ وَأْتَمِرُوا۟ بَيْنَكُم بِمَعْرُوفٍ ۖ وَإِن تَعَاسَرْتُمْ فَسَتُرْضِعُ لَهُۥٓ أُخْرَىٰ ﴿٦﴾
2	*Al-Baqarah* (The Cow)	233	Mothers may breastfeed their children two complete years for whoever wishes to complete the nursing [period]. Upon the father is the mothers' provision and their clothing according to what is acceptable. No person is charged with more than his capacity. No mother should be harmed through her child, and no father through his child. And upon the [father's] heir is [a duty] like that [of the father]. And if they both desire weaning through mutual consent from both and consultation, there is no blame upon either of them. And if you wish to have your children nursed by a substitute, there is no blame upon you if you give payment according to what is acceptable. And fear Allah and know that Allah is Seeing of what you do.	۞ وَٱلْوَٰلِدَٰتُ يُرْضِعْنَ أَوْلَٰدَهُنَّ حَوْلَيْنِ كَامِلَيْنِ ۖ لِمَنْ أَرَادَ أَن يُتِمَّ ٱلرَّضَاعَةَ ۚ وَعَلَى ٱلْمَوْلُودِ لَهُۥ رِزْقُهُنَّ وَكِسْوَتُهُنَّ بِٱلْمَعْرُوفِ ۚ لَا تُكَلَّفُ نَفْسٌ إِلَّا وُسْعَهَا ۚ لَا تُضَآرَّ وَٰلِدَةٌۢ بِوَلَدِهَا وَلَا مَوْلُودٌ لَّهُۥ بِوَلَدِهِۦ ۚ وَعَلَى ٱلْوَارِثِ مِثْلُ ذَٰلِكَ ۗ فَإِنْ أَرَادَا فِصَالًا عَن تَرَاضٍ مِّنْهُمَا وَتَشَاوُرٍ فَلَا جُنَاحَ عَلَيْهِمَا ۗ وَإِنْ أَرَدتُّمْ أَن تَسْتَرْضِعُوٓا۟ أَوْلَٰدَكُمْ فَلَا جُنَاحَ عَلَيْكُمْ إِذَا سَلَّمْتُم مَّآ ءَاتَيْتُم بِٱلْمَعْرُوفِ ۗ وَٱتَّقُوا۟ ٱللَّهَ وَٱعْلَمُوٓا۟ أَنَّ ٱللَّهَ بِمَا تَعْمَلُونَ بَصِيرٌ ﴿٢٣٣﴾

4	*Al-Nisā'* (The Women)	23	Prohibited to you [for marriage] are your mothers, your daughters, your sisters, your father's sisters, your mother's sisters, your brother's daughters, your sister's daughters, your [milk] mothers who nursed you, your sisters through nursing, your wives' mothers, and your stepdaughters under your guardianship [born] of your wives unto whom you have gone in. But if you have not gone in unto them, there is no sin upon you. And [also prohibited are] the wives of your sons who are from your [own] loins, and that you take [in marriage] two sisters simultaneously, except for what has already occurred. Indeed, Allah is ever Forgiving and Merciful.	حرمت عليكم أمهاتكم وبناتكم وأخواتكم وعماتكم وخالاتكم وبنات الأخ وبنات الأخت وأمهاتكم التي أرضعنكم وأخواتكم من الرضاعة وأمهات نسائكم وربائبكم التي في حجوركم من نسائكم التي دخلتم بهن فإن لم تكونوا دخلتم بهن فلا جناح عليكم وحلائل أبنائكم الذين من أصلابكم وأن تجمعوا بين الأختين إلا ما قد سلف إن الله كان غفورا رحيما ﴿٢٣﴾
86	*Al-Ṭāriq* (The Piercing Star)	7	Emerging from between the backbone and the ribs.	يخرج من بين الصلب والترائب ﴿٧﴾
2	*Al-Baqarah* (The Cow)	83	And [recall] when We took the covenant from the Children of Israel, [enjoining upon them], "Do not worship except Allah; and to parents do good and to relatives, orphans, and the needy. And speak to people good [words] and establish prayer and give zakāh." Then you turned away, except a few of you, and you were refusing.	وإذ أخذنا ميثاق بني إسرائيل لا تعبدون إلا الله وبالوالدين إحسانا وذي القربى واليتامى والمساكين وقولوا للناس حسنا وأقيموا الصلاة وآتوا الزكاة ثم توليتم إلا قليلا منكم وأنتم معرضون ﴿٨٣﴾

31	*Luqmān*	15	But if they endeavour to make you associate with Me that of which you have no knowledge, do not obey them but accompany them in [this] world with appropriate kindness and follow the way of those who turn back to Me [in repentance]. Then to Me will be your return, and I will inform you about what you used to do.	وَإِن جَٰهَدَاكَ عَلَىٰٓ أَن تُشْرِكَ بِى مَا لَيْسَ لَكَ بِهِۦ عِلْمٌ فَلَا تُطِعْهُمَا ۖ وَصَاحِبْهُمَا فِى ٱلدُّنْيَا مَعْرُوفًا ۖ وَٱتَّبِعْ سَبِيلَ مَنْ أَنَابَ إِلَىَّ ۚ ثُمَّ إِلَىَّ مَرْجِعُكُمْ فَأُنَبِّئُكُم بِمَا كُنتُمْ تَعْمَلُونَ ﴿١٥﴾
65	*Al-Ṭalāq* (The Divorce)	1	O Prophet, when you [Muslims] divorce women, divorce them for [the commencement of] their waiting period and keep count of the waiting period, and fear Allah, your Lord. Do not turn them out of their [husbands'] houses, nor should they [themselves] leave [during that period] unless they are committing a clear immorality. And those are the limits [set by] Allah. And whoever transgresses the limits of Allah has certainly wronged himself. You know not; perhaps Allah will bring about after that a [different] matter.	يَٰٓأَيُّهَا ٱلنَّبِىُّ إِذَا طَلَّقْتُمُ ٱلنِّسَآءَ فَطَلِّقُوهُنَّ لِعِدَّتِهِنَّ وَأَحْصُوا۟ ٱلْعِدَّةَ ۖ وَٱتَّقُوا۟ ٱللَّهَ رَبَّكُمْ ۖ لَا تُخْرِجُوهُنَّ مِنۢ بُيُوتِهِنَّ وَلَا يَخْرُجْنَ إِلَّآ أَن يَأْتِينَ بِفَٰحِشَةٍ مُّبَيِّنَةٍ ۚ وَتِلْكَ حُدُودُ ٱللَّهِ ۚ وَمَن يَتَعَدَّ حُدُودَ ٱللَّهِ فَقَدْ ظَلَمَ نَفْسَهُۥ ۚ لَا تَدْرِى لَعَلَّ ٱللَّهَ يُحْدِثُ بَعْدَ ذَٰلِكَ أَمْرًا ﴿١﴾
65	*Al-Ṭalāq* (The Divorce)	6	Lodge them [in a section] of where you dwell out of your means and do not harm them in order to oppress them. And if they should be pregnant, then spend on them until they give birth. And if they breastfeed for you, then give them their payment and confer among yourselves in the acceptable way; but if you are in discord, then there may breastfeed for the father another woman	أَسْكِنُوهُنَّ مِنْ حَيْثُ سَكَنتُم مِّن وُجْدِكُمْ وَلَا تُضَآرُّوهُنَّ لِتُضَيِّقُوا۟ عَلَيْهِنَّ ۚ وَإِن كُنَّ أُو۟لَٰتِ حَمْلٍ فَأَنفِقُوا۟ عَلَيْهِنَّ حَتَّىٰ يَضَعْنَ حَمْلَهُنَّ ۚ فَإِنْ أَرْضَعْنَ لَكُمْ فَـَٔاتُوهُنَّ أُجُورَهُنَّ ۖ وَأْتَمِرُوا۟ بَيْنَكُم بِمَعْرُوفٍ ۖ وَإِن تَعَاسَرْتُمْ فَسَتُرْضِعُ لَهُۥٓ أُخْرَىٰ ﴿٦﴾

2	*Al-Baqarah* (The Cow)	241	And for divorced women is a provision according to what is acceptable - a duty upon the righteous.	وَلِلْمُطَلَّقَٰتِ مَتَٰعُۢ بِٱلْمَعْرُوفِ ۖ حَقًّا عَلَى ٱلْمُتَّقِينَ ﴿٢٤١﴾
2	*Al-Baqarah* (The Cow)	237	And if you divorce them before you have touched them and you have already specified for them an obligation, then [give] half of what you specified - unless they forego the right or the one in whose hand is the marriage contract foregoes it. And to forego it is nearer to righteousness. And do not forget graciousness between you. Indeed Allah, of whatever you do, is Seeing.	وَإِن طَلَّقْتُمُوهُنَّ مِن قَبْلِ أَن تَمَسُّوهُنَّ وَقَدْ فَرَضْتُمْ لَهُنَّ فَرِيضَةً فَنِصْفُ مَا فَرَضْتُمْ إِلَّآ أَن يَعْفُونَ أَوْ يَعْفُوَا۟ ٱلَّذِى بِيَدِهِۦ عُقْدَةُ ٱلنِّكَاحِ ۚ وَأَن تَعْفُوٓا۟ أَقْرَبُ لِلتَّقْوَىٰ ۚ وَلَا تَنسَوُا۟ ٱلْفَضْلَ بَيْنَكُمْ ۚ إِنَّ ٱللَّهَ بِمَا تَعْمَلُونَ بَصِيرٌ ﴿٢٣٧﴾
24	*Al-Nūr* (The Light)	4	And those who accuse chaste women and then do not produce four witnesses - lash them with eighty lashes and do not accept from them testimony ever after. And those are the defiantly disobedient	وَٱلَّذِينَ يَرْمُونَ ٱلْمُحْصَنَٰتِ ثُمَّ لَمْ يَأْتُوا۟ بِأَرْبَعَةِ شُهَدَآءَ فَٱجْلِدُوهُمْ ثَمَٰنِينَ جَلْدَةً وَلَا تَقْبَلُوا۟ لَهُمْ شَهَٰدَةً أَبَدًا ۚ وَأُو۟لَٰٓئِكَ هُمُ ٱلْفَٰسِقُونَ ﴿٤﴾
24	*Al-Nūr* (The Light)	6	And those who accuse their wives [of adultery] and have no witnesses except themselves - then the witness of one of them [shall be] four testimonies [swearing] by Allah that indeed, he is of the truthful.	وَٱلَّذِينَ يَرْمُونَ أَزْوَٰجَهُمْ وَلَمْ يَكُن لَّهُمْ شُهَدَآءُ إِلَّآ أَنفُسُهُمْ فَشَهَٰدَةُ أَحَدِهِمْ أَرْبَعُ شَهَٰدَٰتٍۭ بِٱللَّهِ ۙ إِنَّهُۥ لَمِنَ ٱلصَّٰدِقِينَ ﴿٦﴾
24	*Al-Nūr* (The Light)	7	And the fifth [oath will be] that the curse of Allah be upon him if he should be among the liars.	وَٱلْخَٰمِسَةُ أَنَّ لَعْنَتَ ٱللَّهِ عَلَيْهِ إِن كَانَ مِنَ ٱلْكَٰذِبِينَ ﴿٧﴾

4	*Al-Nisā'* (The Women)	12	And for you is half of what your wives leave if they have no child. But if they have a child, for you is one fourth of what they leave, after any bequest they [may have] made or debt. And for the wives is one fourth if you leave no child. But if you leave a child, then for them is an eighth of what you leave, after any bequest you [may have] made or debt. And if a man or woman leaves neither ascendants nor descendants but has a brother or a sister, then for each one of them is a sixth. But if they are more than two, they share a third, after any bequest which was made or debt, as long as there is no detriment [caused]. [This is] an ordinance from Allah, and Allah is Knowing and Forbearing.	۞ وَلَكُمْ نِصْفُ مَا تَرَكَ أَزْوَاجُكُمْ إِن لَّمْ يَكُن لَّهُنَّ وَلَدٌ فَإِن كَانَ لَهُنَّ وَلَدٌ فَلَكُمُ الرُّبُعُ مِمَّا تَرَكْنَ مِن بَعْدِ وَصِيَّةٍ يُوصِينَ بِهَا أَوْ دَيْنٍ وَلَهُنَّ الرُّبُعُ مِمَّا تَرَكْتُمْ إِن لَّمْ يَكُن لَّكُمْ وَلَدٌ فَإِن كَانَ لَكُمْ وَلَدٌ فَلَهُنَّ الثُّمُنُ مِمَّا تَرَكْتُم مِّن بَعْدِ وَصِيَّةٍ تُوصُونَ بِهَا أَوْ دَيْنٍ وَإِن كَانَ رَجُلٌ يُورَثُ كَلَالَةً أَوِ امْرَأَةٌ وَلَهُ أَخٌ أَوْ أُخْتٌ فَلِكُلِّ وَاحِدٍ مِّنْهُمَا السُّدُسُ فَإِن كَانُوا أَكْثَرَ مِن ذَٰلِكَ فَهُمْ شُرَكَاءُ فِي الثُّلُثِ مِن بَعْدِ وَصِيَّةٍ يُوصَىٰ بِهَا أَوْ دَيْنٍ غَيْرَ مُضَارٍّ وَصِيَّةً مِّنَ اللَّهِ وَاللَّهُ عَلِيمٌ حَلِيمٌ ﴿١٢﴾
4	*Al-Nisā'* (The Women)	11	Allah instructs you concerning your children: for the male, what is equal to the share of two females. But if there are [only] daughters, two or more, for them is two thirds of one's estate. And if there is only one, for her is half. And for one's parents, to each one of them is a sixth of his estate if he left children. But if he had no children and the parents [alone] inherit from him, then for his mother is one third. And if he had brothers [or sisters], for his mother is a sixth, after any bequest he [may have] made or debt. Your parents or your children - you know not which of them are nearest to you in benefit. [These shares are] an obligation [imposed] by Allah. Indeed, Allah is ever Knowing and Wise.	يُوصِيكُمُ اللَّهُ فِي أَوْلَادِكُمْ لِلذَّكَرِ مِثْلُ حَظِّ الْأُنثَيَيْنِ فَإِن كُنَّ نِسَاءً فَوْقَ اثْنَتَيْنِ فَلَهُنَّ ثُلُثَا مَا تَرَكَ وَإِن كَانَتْ وَاحِدَةً فَلَهَا النِّصْفُ وَلِأَبَوَيْهِ لِكُلِّ وَاحِدٍ مِّنْهُمَا السُّدُسُ مِمَّا تَرَكَ إِن كَانَ لَهُ وَلَدٌ فَإِن لَّمْ يَكُن لَّهُ وَلَدٌ وَوَرِثَهُ أَبَوَاهُ فَلِأُمِّهِ الثُّلُثُ فَإِن كَانَ لَهُ إِخْوَةٌ فَلِأُمِّهِ السُّدُسُ مِن بَعْدِ وَصِيَّةٍ يُوصِي بِهَا أَوْ دَيْنٍ آبَاؤُكُمْ وَأَبْنَاؤُكُمْ لَا تَدْرُونَ أَيُّهُمْ أَقْرَبُ لَكُمْ نَفْعًا فَرِيضَةً مِّنَ اللَّهِ إِنَّ اللَّهَ كَانَ عَلِيمًا حَكِيمًا ﴿١١﴾

2	*Al-Baqarah* (The Cow)	180	Prescribed for you when death approaches [any] one of you if he leaves wealth [is that he should make] a bequest for the parents and near relatives according to what is acceptable - a duty upon the righteous.	كُتِبَ عَلَيْكُمْ إِذَا حَضَرَ أَحَدَكُمُ الْمَوْتُ إِن تَرَكَ خَيْرًا الْوَصِيَّةُ لِلْوَالِدَيْنِ وَالْأَقْرَبِينَ بِالْمَعْرُوفِ ۖ حَقًّا عَلَى الْمُتَّقِينَ ﴿١٨٠﴾
9	*Al-Tawbah* (The Repentance)	60	Zakah expenditures are only for the poor and for the needy and for those employed to collect [zakah] and for bringing hearts together [for Islam] and for freeing captives [or slaves] and for those in debt and for the cause of Allah and for the [stranded] traveler - an obligation [imposed] by Allah. And Allah is Knowing and Wise.	۞ إِنَّمَا الصَّدَقَاتُ لِلْفُقَرَاءِ وَالْمَسَاكِينِ وَالْعَامِلِينَ عَلَيْهَا وَالْمُؤَلَّفَةِ قُلُوبُهُمْ وَفِي الرِّقَابِ وَالْغَارِمِينَ وَفِي سَبِيلِ اللَّهِ وَابْنِ السَّبِيلِ ۖ فَرِيضَةً مِّنَ اللَّهِ ۗ وَاللَّهُ عَلِيمٌ حَكِيمٌ ﴿٦٠﴾
33	*Al-Aḥzāb* (The Confederates)	35	Indeed, the Muslim men and Muslim women, the believing men and believing women, the obedient men and obedient women, the truthful men and truthful women, the patient men and patient women, the humble men and humble women, the charitable men and charitable women, the fasting men and fasting women, the men who guard their private parts and the women who do so, and the men who remember Allah often and the women who do so - for them Allah has prepared forgiveness and a great reward.	إِنَّ الْمُسْلِمِينَ وَالْمُسْلِمَاتِ وَالْمُؤْمِنِينَ وَالْمُؤْمِنَاتِ وَالْقَانِتِينَ وَالْقَانِتَاتِ وَالصَّادِقِينَ وَالصَّادِقَاتِ وَالصَّابِرِينَ وَالصَّابِرَاتِ وَالْخَاشِعِينَ وَالْخَاشِعَاتِ وَالْمُتَصَدِّقِينَ وَالْمُتَصَدِّقَاتِ وَالصَّائِمِينَ وَالصَّائِمَاتِ وَالْحَافِظِينَ فُرُوجَهُمْ وَالْحَافِظَاتِ وَالذَّاكِرِينَ اللَّهَ كَثِيرًا وَالذَّاكِرَاتِ أَعَدَّ اللَّهُ لَهُم مَّغْفِرَةً وَأَجْرًا عَظِيمًا ﴿٣٥﴾
2	*Al-Baqarah* (The Cow)	215	They ask you, [O Muhammad], what they should spend. Say, "Whatever you spend of good is [to be] for parents and relatives and orphans and the needy and the traveler. And whatever you do of good - indeed, Allah is Knowing of it.	يَسْأَلُونَكَ مَاذَا يُنفِقُونَ ۖ قُلْ مَا أَنفَقْتُم مِّنْ خَيْرٍ فَلِلْوَالِدَيْنِ وَالْأَقْرَبِينَ وَالْيَتَامَىٰ وَالْمَسَاكِينِ وَابْنِ السَّبِيلِ ۗ وَمَا تَفْعَلُوا مِنْ خَيْرٍ فَإِنَّ اللَّهَ بِهِ عَلِيمٌ ﴿٢١٥﴾

5	Al-Māʾidah (The Table Spread)	89	Allah will not impose blame upon you for what is meaningless in your oaths, but He will impose blame upon you for [breaking] what you intended of oaths. So, its expiation is the feeding of ten needy people from the average of that which you feed your [own] families or clothing them or the freeing of a slave. But whoever cannot find [or afford it] – then a fast of three days [is required]. That is the expiation for oaths when you have sworn. But guard your oaths. Thus does Allah make clear to you His verses that you may be grateful.	مَا يُؤَاخِذُكُمُ اللّٰهُ بِاللَّغْوِ فِىۤ أَيْمَانِكُمْ وَلٰكِن يُؤَاخِذُكُم بِمَا عَقَّدتُّمُ الأَيْمَانَ فَكَفّٰرَتُهُ إِطْعَامُ عَشَرَةِ مَسَاكِينَ مِنْ أَوْسَطِ مَا تُطْعِمُونَ أَهْلِيكُمْ أَوْ كِسْوَتُهُمْ أَوْ تَحْرِيرُ رَقَبَةٍ فَمَن لَّمْ يَجِدْ فَصِيَامُ ثَلٰثَةِ أَيّٰمٍ ذٰلِكَ كَفّٰرَةُ أَيْمَانِكُمْ إِذَا حَلَفْتُمْ وَاحْفَظُوۤا أَيْمَانَكُمْ كَذٰلِكَ يُبَيِّنُ اللّٰهُ لَكُمْ ءَايٰتِهِ لَعَلَّكُمْ تَشْكُرُونَ ۝
58	Al-Mujādilah (The Argument)	2	Those who pronounce ẓihar among you [to separate] from their wives - they are not [consequently] their mothers. Their mothers are none but those who gave birth to them. And indeed, they are saying an objectionable statement and a falsehood. But indeed, Allah is Pardoning and Forgiving	الَّذِينَ يُظٰهِرُونَ مِنكُم مِّن نِّسَآئِهِم مَّا هُنَّ أُمَّهٰتِهِمْ إِنْ أُمَّهٰتُهُمْ إِلَّا الّٰۤئِى وَلَدْنَهُمْ وَإِنَّهُمْ لَيَقُولُونَ مُنكَرًا مِّنَ الْقَوْلِ وَزُورًا وَإِنَّ اللّٰهَ لَعَفُوٌّ غَفُورٌ ۝
108	Al-Kawthar (The Abundance)	2	So, pray to your Lord and sacrifice [to Him alone].	فَصَلِّ لِرَبِّكَ وَانْحَرْ ۝
4	Al-Nisāʾ (The Women)	32	And do not wish for that by which Allah has made some of you exceed others. For men is a share of what they have earned, and for women is a share of what they have earned. And ask Allah of his bounty. Indeed, Allah is ever, of all things, Knowing.	وَلَا تَتَمَنَّوْا مَا فَضَّلَ اللّٰهُ بِهِ بَعْضَكُمْ عَلٰى بَعْضٍ لِّلرِّجَالِ نَصِيبٌ مِّمَّا اكْتَسَبُوا وَلِلنِّسَآءِ نَصِيبٌ مِّمَّا اكْتَسَبْنَ وَاسْأَلُوا اللّٰهَ مِن فَضْلِهِ إِنَّ اللّٰهَ كَانَ بِكُلِّ شَىْءٍ عَلِيمًا ۝

5	*Al-Māʾidah* (The Table Spread)	45	And We ordained for them therein a life for a life, an eye for an eye, a nose for a nose, an ear for an ear, a tooth for a tooth, and for wounds is legal retribution. But whoever gives [up his right as] charity, it is an expiation for him. And whoever does not judge by what Allah has revealed – then it is those who are the wrongdoers.	كَتَبْنَا عَلَيْهِمْ فِيهَآ أَنَّ ٱلنَّفْسَ بِٱلنَّفْسِ وَٱلْعَيْنَ بِٱلْعَيْنِ وَٱلْأَنفَ بِٱلْأَنفِ وَٱلْأُذُنَ بِٱلْأُذُنِ وَٱلسِّنَّ بِٱلسِّنِّ وَٱلْجُرُوحَ قِصَاصٌ فَمَن تَصَدَّقَ بِهِۦ فَهُوَ كَفَّارَةٌ لَّهُۥ وَمَن لَّمْ يَحْكُم بِمَآ أَنزَلَ ٱللَّهُ فَأُوْلَٰٓئِكَ هُمُ ٱلظَّٰلِمُونَ ۝
4	*Al-Nisāʾ* (The Women)	92	And never is it for a believer to kill a believer except by mistake. And whoever kills a believer by mistake - then the freeing of a believing slave and a compensation payment presented to the deceased's family [is required] unless they give [up their right as] charity. But if the deceased was from a people at war with you and he was a believer - then [only] the freeing of a believing slave; and if he was from a people with whom you have a treaty - then a compensation payment presented to his family and the freeing of a believing slave. And whoever does not find [one or cannot afford to buy one] - then [instead], a fast for two months consecutively, [seeking] acceptance of repentance from Allah. And Allah is ever Knowing and Wise.	وَمَا كَانَ لِمُؤْمِنٍ أَن يَقْتُلَ مُؤْمِنًا إِلَّا خَطَـًٔا وَمَن قَتَلَ مُؤْمِنًا خَطَـًٔا فَتَحْرِيرُ رَقَبَةٍ مُّؤْمِنَةٍ وَدِيَةٌ مُّسَلَّمَةٌ إِلَىٰٓ أَهْلِهِۦٓ إِلَّآ أَن يَصَّدَّقُواْ فَإِن كَانَ مِن قَوْمٍ عَدُوٍّ لَّكُمْ وَهُوَ مُؤْمِنٌ فَتَحْرِيرُ رَقَبَةٍ مُّؤْمِنَةٍ وَإِن كَانَ مِن قَوْمٍ بَيْنَكُمْ وَبَيْنَهُم مِّيثَٰقٌ فَدِيَةٌ مُّسَلَّمَةٌ إِلَىٰٓ أَهْلِهِۦ وَتَحْرِيرُ رَقَبَةٍ مُّؤْمِنَةٍ فَمَن لَّمْ يَجِدْ فَصِيَامُ شَهْرَيْنِ مُتَتَابِعَيْنِ تَوْبَةً مِّنَ ٱللَّهِ وَكَانَ ٱللَّهُ عَلِيمًا حَكِيمًا ۝
4	*Al-Nisāʾ* (The Women)	1	O mankind, fear your Lord, who created you from one soul and created from it its mate and dispersed from both many men and women. And fear Allah, through whom you ask one another, and the wombs. Indeed, Allah is ever, over you, an Observer.	يَٰٓأَيُّهَا ٱلنَّاسُ ٱتَّقُواْ رَبَّكُمُ ٱلَّذِي خَلَقَكُم مِّن نَّفْسٍ وَٰحِدَةٍ وَخَلَقَ مِنْهَا زَوْجَهَا وَبَثَّ مِنْهُمَا رِجَالًا كَثِيرًا وَنِسَآءً وَٱتَّقُواْ ٱللَّهَ ٱلَّذِي تَسَآءَلُونَ بِهِۦ وَٱلْأَرْحَامَ إِنَّ ٱللَّهَ كَانَ عَلَيْكُمْ رَقِيبًا ۝

4	*Al-Nisā'* (The Women)	2	And give to the orphans their properties and do not substitute the defective [of your own] for the good [of theirs]. And do not consume their properties into your own. Indeed, that is ever a great sin.	وَءَاتُوا۟ ٱلْيَتَٰمَىٰٓ أَمْوَٰلَهُمْ ۖ وَلَا تَتَبَدَّلُوا۟ ٱلْخَبِيثَ بِٱلطَّيِّبِ ۖ وَلَا تَأْكُلُوٓا۟ أَمْوَٰلَهُمْ إِلَىٰٓ أَمْوَٰلِكُمْ ۚ إِنَّهُۥ كَانَ حُوبًا كَبِيرًا ﴿٢﴾
4	*Al-Nisā'* (The Women)	32	For men is a share of what the parents and close relatives leave, and for women is a share of what the parents and close relatives leave, be it little or much - an obligatory share.	لِّلرِّجَالِ نَصِيبٌ مِّمَّا تَرَكَ ٱلْوَٰلِدَانِ وَٱلْأَقْرَبُونَ وَلِلنِّسَآءِ نَصِيبٌ مِّمَّا تَرَكَ ٱلْوَٰلِدَانِ وَٱلْأَقْرَبُونَ مِمَّا قَلَّ مِنْهُ أَوْ كَثُرَ ۚ نَصِيبًا مَّفْرُوضًا ﴿٧﴾
4	*Al-Nisā'* (The Women)	19	O you who have believed, it is not lawful for you to inherit women by compulsion. And do not make difficulties for them in order to take [back] part of what you gave them unless they commit a clear immorality. And live with them in kindness. For if you dislike them - perhaps you dislike a thing and Allah makes therein much good.	يَٰٓأَيُّهَا ٱلَّذِينَ ءَامَنُوا۟ لَا يَحِلُّ لَكُمْ أَن تَرِثُوا۟ ٱلنِّسَآءَ كَرْهًا ۖ وَلَا تَعْضُلُوهُنَّ لِتَذْهَبُوا۟ بِبَعْضِ مَآ ءَاتَيْتُمُوهُنَّ إِلَّآ أَن يَأْتِينَ بِفَٰحِشَةٍ مُّبَيِّنَةٍ ۚ وَعَاشِرُوهُنَّ بِٱلْمَعْرُوفِ ۚ فَإِن كَرِهْتُمُوهُنَّ فَعَسَىٰٓ أَن تَكْرَهُوا۟ شَيْـًٔا وَيَجْعَلَ ٱللَّهُ فِيهِ خَيْرًا كَثِيرًا ﴿١٩﴾
4	*Al-Nisā'* (The Women)	21	And how could you take it while you have gone in unto each other and they have taken from you a solemn covenant?	وَكَيْفَ تَأْخُذُونَهُۥ وَقَدْ أَفْضَىٰ بَعْضُكُمْ إِلَىٰ بَعْضٍ وَأَخَذْنَ مِنكُم مِّيثَٰقًا غَلِيظًا ﴿٢١﴾
4	*Al-Nisā'* (The Women)	24	And [also prohibited to you are all] married women except those your right hands possess. [This is] the decree of Allah upon you. And lawful to you are [all others] beyond these, [provided] that you seek them [in marriage] with [gifts from] your property, desiring chastity, not unlawful sexual intercourse. So, for whatever you enjoy [of marriage] from them, give them their due compensation as an obligation. And there is no blame upon you for what you mutually agree to beyond the obligation. Indeed, Allah is ever Knowing and Wise.	۞ وَٱلْمُحْصَنَٰتُ مِنَ ٱلنِّسَآءِ إِلَّا مَا مَلَكَتْ أَيْمَٰنُكُمْ ۖ كِتَٰبَ ٱللَّهِ عَلَيْكُمْ ۚ وَأُحِلَّ لَكُم مَّا وَرَآءَ ذَٰلِكُمْ أَن تَبْتَغُوا۟ بِأَمْوَٰلِكُم مُّحْصِنِينَ غَيْرَ مُسَٰفِحِينَ ۚ فَمَا ٱسْتَمْتَعْتُم بِهِۦ مِنْهُنَّ فَـَٔاتُوهُنَّ أُجُورَهُنَّ فَرِيضَةً ۚ وَلَا جُنَاحَ عَلَيْكُمْ فِيمَا تَرَٰضَيْتُم بِهِۦ مِنۢ بَعْدِ ٱلْفَرِيضَةِ ۚ إِنَّ ٱللَّهَ كَانَ عَلِيمًا حَكِيمًا ﴿٢٤﴾

2	*Al-Baqarah* (The Cow)	236	There is no blame upon you if you divorce women, you have not touched nor specified for them an obligation. But give them [a gift of] compensation - the wealthy according to his capability and the poor according to his capability - a provision according to what is acceptable, a duty upon the doers of good.	لَّا جُنَاحَ عَلَيْكُمْ إِن طَلَّقْتُمُ ٱلنِّسَآءَ مَا لَمْ تَمَسُّوهُنَّ أَوْ تَفْرِضُوا۟ لَهُنَّ فَرِيضَةً ۚ وَمَتِّعُوهُنَّ عَلَى ٱلْمُوسِعِ قَدَرُهُۥ وَعَلَى ٱلْمُقْتِرِ قَدَرُهُۥ مَتَٰعًۢا بِٱلْمَعْرُوفِ ۖ حَقًّا عَلَى ٱلْمُحْسِنِينَ ﴿٢٣٦﴾
4	*Al-Nisā'* (The Women)	20	But if you want to replace one wife with another and you have given one of them a great amount [in gifts], do not take [back] from it anything. Would you take it in injustice and manifest sin?	وَإِنْ أَرَدتُّمُ ٱسْتِبْدَالَ زَوْجٍ مَّكَانَ زَوْجٍ وَءَاتَيْتُمْ إِحْدَىٰهُنَّ قِنطَارًا فَلَا تَأْخُذُوا۟ مِنْهُ شَيْـًٔا ۚ أَتَأْخُذُونَهُۥ بُهْتَٰنًا وَإِثْمًا مُّبِينًا ﴿٢٠﴾
30	*Al-Rūm* (The Romans)	21	And of His signs is that He created for you from yourselves mates that you may find tranquillity in them; and He placed between you affection and mercy. Indeed, in that are signs for a people who give thought.	وَمِنْ ءَايَٰتِهِۦٓ أَنْ خَلَقَ لَكُم مِّنْ أَنفُسِكُمْ أَزْوَٰجًا لِّتَسْكُنُوٓا۟ إِلَيْهَا وَجَعَلَ بَيْنَكُم مَّوَدَّةً وَرَحْمَةً ۚ إِنَّ فِى ذَٰلِكَ لَءَايَٰتٍ لِّقَوْمٍ يَتَفَكَّرُونَ ﴿٢١﴾
4	*Al-Nisā'* (The Women)	34	Men are in charge of women by [right of] what Allah has given one over the other and what they spend [for maintenance] from their wealth. So righteous women are devoutly obedient, guarding in [the husband's] absence what Allah would have them guard. But those [wives] from whom you fear arrogance - [first] advise them; [then if they persist], forsake them in bed; and [finally], strike them. But if they obey you [once more], seek no means against them. Indeed, Allah is ever Exalted and Grand.	ٱلرِّجَالُ قَوَّٰمُونَ عَلَى ٱلنِّسَآءِ بِمَا فَضَّلَ ٱللَّهُ بَعْضَهُمْ عَلَىٰ بَعْضٍ وَبِمَآ أَنفَقُوا۟ مِنْ أَمْوَٰلِهِمْ ۚ فَٱلصَّٰلِحَٰتُ قَٰنِتَٰتٌ حَٰفِظَٰتٌ لِّلْغَيْبِ بِمَا حَفِظَ ٱللَّهُ ۚ وَٱلَّٰتِى تَخَافُونَ نُشُوزَهُنَّ فَعِظُوهُنَّ وَٱهْجُرُوهُنَّ فِى ٱلْمَضَاجِعِ وَٱضْرِبُوهُنَّ ۖ فَإِنْ أَطَعْنَكُمْ فَلَا تَبْغُوا۟ عَلَيْهِنَّ سَبِيلًا ۗ إِنَّ ٱللَّهَ كَانَ عَلِيًّا كَبِيرًا ﴿٣٤﴾

4	*Al-Nisā'* (The Women)	128	And if a woman fears from her husband contempt or evasion, there is no sin upon them if they make terms of settlement between them - and settlement is best. And present in [human] souls is stinginess. But if you do good and fear Allah - then indeed Allah is ever, with what you do, Acquainted.	وَإِنِ امْرَأَةٌ خَافَتْ مِن بَعْلِهَا نُشُوزًا أَوْ إِعْرَاضًا فَلَا جُنَاحَ عَلَيْهِمَا أَن يُصْلِحَا بَيْنَهُمَا صُلْحًا وَالصُّلْحُ خَيْرٌ وَأُحْضِرَتِ الْأَنفُسُ الشُّحَّ وَإِن تُحْسِنُوا وَتَتَّقُوا فَإِنَّ اللَّهَ كَانَ بِمَا تَعْمَلُونَ خَبِيرًا ﴿١٢٨﴾
58	*Al-Mujādilah* (The Pleading Woman)	11	O you who have believed, when you are told, "Space yourselves" in assemblies, then make space; Allah will make space for you. And when you are told, "Arise," then arise; Allah will raise those who have believed among you and those who were given knowledge, by degrees. And Allah is Acquainted with what you do.	يَا أَيُّهَا الَّذِينَ آمَنُوا إِذَا قِيلَ لَكُمْ تَفَسَّحُوا فِي الْمَجَالِسِ فَافْسَحُوا يَفْسَحِ اللَّهُ لَكُمْ وَإِذَا قِيلَ انشُزُوا فَانشُزُوا يَرْفَعِ اللَّهُ الَّذِينَ آمَنُوا مِنكُمْ وَالَّذِينَ أُوتُوا الْعِلْمَ دَرَجَاتٍ وَاللَّهُ بِمَا تَعْمَلُونَ خَبِيرٌ ﴿١١﴾
30	*Al-Rūm* (The Romans)	21	And of His signs is that He created for you from yourselves mates that you may find tranquillity in them; and He placed between you affection and mercy. Indeed, in that are signs for a people who give thought	وَمِنْ آيَاتِهِ أَنْ خَلَقَ لَكُم مِّنْ أَنفُسِكُمْ أَزْوَاجًا لِّتَسْكُنُوا إِلَيْهَا وَجَعَلَ بَيْنَكُم مَّوَدَّةً وَرَحْمَةً إِنَّ فِي ذَٰلِكَ لَآيَاتٍ لِّقَوْمٍ يَتَفَكَّرُونَ ﴿٢١﴾
2	*Al-Baqarah* (The Cow)	280	And if someone is in hardship, then [let there be] postponement until [a time of] ease. But if you give [from your right as] charity, then it is better for you, if you only knew.	وَإِن كَانَ ذُو عُسْرَةٍ فَنَظِرَةٌ إِلَىٰ مَيْسَرَةٍ وَأَن تَصَدَّقُوا خَيْرٌ لَّكُمْ إِن كُنتُمْ تَعْلَمُونَ ﴿٢٨٠﴾

2	*Al-Baqarah* (The Cow)	229	Divorce is twice. Then, either keep [her] in an acceptable manner or release [her] with good treatment. And it is not lawful for you to take anything of what you have given them unless both fear that they will not be able to keep [within] the limits of Allah. But if you fear that they will not keep [within] the limits of Allah, then there is no blame upon either of them concerning that by which she ransoms herself. These are the limits of Allah, so do not transgress them. And whoever transgresses the limits of Allah - it is those who are the wrongdoers.	ٱلطَّلَٰقُ مَرَّتَانِ ۖ فَإِمْسَاكٌۢ بِمَعْرُوفٍ أَوْ تَسْرِيحٌۢ بِإِحْسَٰنٍ ۗ وَلَا يَحِلُّ لَكُمْ أَن تَأْخُذُوا۟ مِمَّآ ءَاتَيْتُمُوهُنَّ شَيْـًٔا إِلَّآ أَن يَخَافَآ أَلَّا يُقِيمَا حُدُودَ ٱللَّهِ ۖ فَإِنْ خِفْتُمْ أَلَّا يُقِيمَا حُدُودَ ٱللَّهِ فَلَا جُنَاحَ عَلَيْهِمَا فِيمَا ٱفْتَدَتْ بِهِۦ ۗ تِلْكَ حُدُودُ ٱللَّهِ فَلَا تَعْتَدُوهَا ۚ وَمَن يَتَعَدَّ حُدُودَ ٱللَّهِ فَأُو۟لَٰٓئِكَ هُمُ ٱلظَّٰلِمُونَ ﴿٢٢٩﴾
53	*Al-Najm* (The Star)	39	And that there is not for man except that [good] for which he strives	وَأَن لَّيْسَ لِلْإِنسَٰنِ إِلَّا مَا سَعَىٰ ﴿٣٩﴾
53	*Al-Najm* (The Star)	41	Then he will be recompensed for it with the fullest recompense	ثُمَّ يُجْزَىٰهُ ٱلْجَزَآءَ ٱلْأَوْفَىٰ ﴿٤١﴾
3	*Āl ʿImrān* (The Family of Imran)	180	And let not those who [greedily] withhold what Allah has given them of His bounty ever think that it is better for them. Rather, it is worse for them. Their necks will be encircled by what they withheld on the Day of Resurrection. And to Allah belongs the heritage of the heavens and the earth. And Allah, with what you do, is [fully] Acquainted.	وَلَا يَحْسَبَنَّ ٱلَّذِينَ يَبْخَلُونَ بِمَآ ءَاتَىٰهُمُ ٱللَّهُ مِن فَضْلِهِۦ هُوَ خَيْرًا لَّهُم ۖ بَلْ هُوَ شَرٌّ لَّهُمْ ۖ سَيُطَوَّقُونَ مَا بَخِلُوا۟ بِهِۦ يَوْمَ ٱلْقِيَٰمَةِ ۗ وَلِلَّهِ مِيرَٰثُ ٱلسَّمَٰوَٰتِ وَٱلْأَرْضِ ۗ وَٱللَّهُ بِمَا تَعْمَلُونَ خَبِيرٌ ﴿١٨٠﴾
2	*Al-Baqarah* (The Cow)	43	And establish prayer and give *zakah* and bow with those who bow [in worship and obedience]	وَأَقِيمُوا۟ ٱلصَّلَوٰةَ وَءَاتُوا۟ ٱلزَّكَوٰةَ وَٱرْكَعُوا۟ مَعَ ٱلرَّٰكِعِينَ ﴿٤٣﴾

92	*Al-Layl* (The Night)	4	Indeed, your efforts are diverse.	إِنَّ سَعْيَكُمْ لَشَتَّىٰ ﴿٤﴾
92	*Al-Layl* (The Night)	3	And [by] He who created the male and female,	وَمَا خَلَقَ الذَّكَرَ وَالْأُنثَىٰ ﴿٣﴾
28	*Al-Qaṣaṣ* (The Story)	23	And when he came to the well of Madyan, he found there a crowd of people watering [their flocks], and he found aside from them two women driving back [their flocks]. He said, "What is your circumstance?" They said, "We do not water until the shepherds dispatch [their flocks]; and our father is an old man."	وَلَمَّا وَرَدَ مَاءَ مَدْيَنَ وَجَدَ عَلَيْهِ أُمَّةً مِّنَ النَّاسِ يَسْقُونَ وَوَجَدَ مِن دُونِهِمُ امْرَأَتَيْنِ تَذُودَانِ قَالَ مَا خَطْبُكُمَا قَالَتَا لَا نَسْقِي حَتَّىٰ يُصْدِرَ الرِّعَاءُ وَأَبُونَا شَيْخٌ كَبِيرٌ ﴿٢٣﴾
5	*Al-Mā'idah* (The Table Spread)	38	[As for] the thief, the male and the female, amputate their hands in recompense for what they committed as a deterrent [punishment] from Allah. And Allah is Exalted in Might and Wise.	وَالسَّارِقُ وَالسَّارِقَةُ فَاقْطَعُوا أَيْدِيَهُمَا جَزَاءً بِمَا كَسَبَا نَكَالًا مِّنَ اللَّهِ وَاللَّهُ عَزِيزٌ حَكِيمٌ ﴿٣٨﴾
95	*Al-Tīn* (The Fig)	4	We have certainly created man in the best of stature.	لَقَدْ خَلَقْنَا الْإِنسَانَ فِي أَحْسَنِ تَقْوِيمٍ ﴿٤﴾
13	*Al-Ra'd* (The Thunder)	41	Have they not seen that We set upon the land, reducing it from its borders? And Allah decides; there is no adjuster of His decision. And He is swift in account.	أَوَلَمْ يَرَوْا أَنَّا نَأْتِي الْأَرْضَ نَنقُصُهَا مِنْ أَطْرَافِهَا وَاللَّهُ يَحْكُمُ لَا مُعَقِّبَ لِحُكْمِهِ وَهُوَ سَرِيعُ الْحِسَابِ ﴿٤١﴾
22	*Al-Ḥajj* (The Pilgrimage)	46	So have they not travelled through the earth and have hearts by which to reason...?	أَفَلَمْ يَسِيرُوا فِي الْأَرْضِ فَتَكُونَ لَهُمْ قُلُوبٌ يَعْقِلُونَ بِهَا أَوْ آذَانٌ يَسْمَعُونَ بِهَا فَإِنَّهَا لَا تَعْمَى الْأَبْصَارُ وَلَٰكِن تَعْمَى الْقُلُوبُ الَّتِي فِي الصُّدُورِ ﴿٤٦﴾

Appendix D. Prophetic Traditions Index

Prophetic Traditions

ʿUqbah ibn ʿĀmir ﷺ narrated: "The Messenger ﷺ married me to so-and-so, but I never specified for her the obligatory *mahr* and I never gave her anything, so now I bear you to witness that I gift her with my share from (the booties of the battle of) Khaybar, so she took it and sold it for one hundred thousand."

The Prophet ﷺ said: "No money is due for you: if you spoke the truth, then indeed you consummated the marriage (already), and if you lied then it is further from you then you can imagine."

The Prophet ﷺ said: "Allah ﷻ said: 'Spend (on others) O son of Adam, and I will spend on you.'"

The Prophet ﷺ said: "Begin with yourself then with those under your responsibility."

The Prophet ﷺ said, "Indeed good wealth is in the hands of a good person."

The wife of Ibn Masʿūd ﷺ, asked the Messenger ﷺ: "Is it possible for me to spend on my poor husband and some orphans under my care? And he ﷺ replied: "Yes, and for you is double the reward, one for helping a family member and one for giving charity."

The Prophet ﷺ said: "Your husband and your children are more deserving of your *ṣadaqah*."

A man asked the Messenger ﷺ: "O Messenger of Allah, I have one dinar." the Messenger ﷺ replied, "Spend it on yourself." The man then said, "I have another dinar." The Messenger ﷺ said: "Spend it on your wife." The man then said: "I have another." The Messenger ﷺ said: "Spend it on your children." The man said: "I have one more." The Messenger ﷺ said, "Spend it on your servant." The man said, "I have one more." Then the Messenger ﷺ said: "Spend it on whatever you please."

The Prophet ﷺ said, "O young men, whoever amongst you can afford to get married, let him do so, and whoever cannot afford, let him fast, for that will be a shield for him.

Hind bint 'Utbah ﵉ once complained to the Prophet ﷺ that her husband, Abū Sufyān, did not supply her with enough money to care for herself and child. The Prophet ﷺ replied, "Take [from your husband] what is sufficient for yourself and your child."

A man asked the Prophet ﷺ, "Who is most deserving of my care?" And he ﷺ replied: "Your mother, then your mother, then your mother, then your father, then close family members."

The Prophet ﷺ said, "It is the duty of a Muslim who has something that is to be given as a bequest not to keep it for two nights without having his will written down regarding it."

The Companion Ibn 'Umar said, "The Prophet ﷺ commanded for *zakāh al-fiṭr* to be amounted to a *sa'* of dates or a *ṣā'* of barely upon the slave and the free, the male and the female, the young and the old from amongst the Muslims. And he commanded that it is paid before the people's outing to the prayer (of Eid al-Fiṭr)."

The Prophet ﷺ said, "When a man dies, his deeds come to an end except for three things: ceaseless charity (*ṣadaqah jāriyah*);

a knowledge which is beneficial, or a virtuous descendant who prays for him (for the deceased)."

Ibn 'Umar ⊛ said his father went to the Messenger ﷺ and asked, "O Messenger of Allah, I have acquired property more valuable than any I ever had before so what do you advise me to do with it (to please Allah)." And the Messenger replied, "If you wish you may keep the corpus intact and give its produce as *sadaqah*." So, Ibn 'Umar narrated, "Thus, 'Umar gave it (land acquired in Khaybar) as *sadaqah* declaring that this property must not be sold, gifted or inherited. He devoted it for the poor and close family members and the emancipation of slaves and for the sake of Allah and for those visiting. It is also permissible for the one managing it to eat from its goodness and feed his friends from it in a reasonable manner."

The Prophet ﷺ said, "Whoever makes a vow to obey Allah must obey Him, and whoever makes a vow to disobey Him must not disobey Him."

The Prophet ﷺ said, "Muslims are equal regarding the sanctity of their blood."

The Prophet ﷺ said, "Whoever has two wives and is more inclined towards one of them (in material or immaterial matters), he will come on the Day of Judgment with half of his body leaning."

The Prophet ﷺ said, "Indeed Allah had granted each person their due share of rights, so there is no bequest for an heir."

The Prophet ﷺ said, "Your mother got jealous."

Abū Bakr al-Ṣiddīq ⊛, while standing on the doorstep of the home of the Prophet ﷺ and getting ready to enter, overheard his daughter 'Ā'ishah ⊛, who was also the wife of the Prophet ﷺ,

raising her voice over her husband. Once he had received permission to enter, Abū Bakr ﷺ strode in, grabbed his daughter out of anger and exclaimed, "How dare you raise your voice like that to the Messenger ﷺ!" The Prophet ﷺ quickly intervened, pulling Abū Bakr ﷺ away from ʿĀ'ishah ﷺ and calming him down. Once Abū Bakr ﷺ had left, the Prophet reinforced the way in which he had defended ʿĀ'ishah ﷺ by saying to her, "Did you see how I stood up for you in front of him?"

ʿĀ'ishah ﷺ said: Once Sawdah bint Zamʿah went out at night for some need, and ʿUmar saw her, and recognising her, he said (to her), "By Allah, O Sawdah! You cannot hide yourself from us." So, she returned to the Prophet ﷺ and mentioned that to him while he was sitting in my dwelling taking his supper and holding a bone covered with meat in his hand. Then the Divine Inspiration was revealed to him and when that state was over, he ﷺ said, "O women! You have been allowed by Allah to go out for your needs."

The Prophet ﷺ said, "[There is] no obedience to any creation upon a sinful act, and to not perform one's mandated Hajj would be a sin."

The Prophet ﷺ said, "No Muslim inherits a disbeliever (*kāfir*), nor a disbeliever a Muslim."

The Prophet ﷺ said, "Islam increases and does not decrease."

The Prophet ﷺ made a visit to Saʿd ibn Abī Waqqās, who was very ill and approaching his death. He asked, "O Messenger of Allah, my ailment has overcome me as you can see, and I have wealth, but no one inherits me except my only daughter. Should I bequest two thirds of my wealth in charity?" The Messenger ﷺ

replied, "no." The man asked, 'How about half?" He ﷺ replied, "No." Then the Messenger ﷺ said, "You may give one-third, but this is (still) too much (*kathīr*), for indeed for you to leave your heirs rich is better than to leave them in poverty dependent on (other) people. And you will not give anything for the sake of Allah except that you will be rewarded for it, even a tiny crumb that you feed your wife."

Ibn ʿAbbās ؓ said, "If the people came down in their bequest from a third to a fourth it would be dearer to me, as the Messenger ﷺ said, 'A third, and a third is too much.'"

The Prophet ﷺ said, "Whoever has the luxury of having someone at their back should use it towards those who do not have a back, and whoever has sustenance should give it to those who do not have sustenance.

The Messenger ﷺ said, "I am more deserving (to take responsibility) of the believers than their own selves. Thus, whoever dies while in debt and does not leave anyone who can pay it for him, then it becomes our duty to pay it off and whoever leaves behind wealth then it is handed to his (or her) heirs."

The Prophet ﷺ said, "Whoever is made wealthy by Allah and does not pay the *zakāh* of his wealth then on the Day of Resurrection his wealth will be made like a bald-headed poisonous male snake with two black spots over his eyes. The snake will encircle his neck and bite his cheeks and say, 'I am your wealth; I am your treasure.'" Then the Prophet ﷺ recited verse 180 of Sūrah Āl ʿImrān.

The Prophet ﷺ said in his final Hajj sermon at the Mount of ʿArafah, "Fear Allah in your dealings with women, for you have taken them as your wives under Allah's trust and consummated the marriage by His permission…and it is your responsibility to feed them and clothe them in a goodly manner…O people, there shall be no prophet after me nor a nation after you, so worship your Lord and perform your five prayers and fast your month of Ramadan and pay off your due *zakāh* from your wealth to cleanse with it your souls and perform Hajj and obey your leaders. You do this, and you shall enter your Lord's Paradise (Jannah)."

The Prophet ﷺ said to Bashīr (al-Nuʿmān's father), "So fear Allah and practice equality between your children."

The Prophet ﷺ advised women to give charity during Eid al-Fiṭr, and they pulled off their jewelled valuables and placed it into Bilāl's dress sack.

Asmā' – the daughter of Abū Bakr ﷺ – asked the Prophet ﷺ, "O Messenger of Allah, I have no wealth except what al-Zubayr brings home; am I able to give charity from it?" He ﷺ replied, "Give charity (for the sake of Allah) as much as you could and do not hoard, lest Allah would withhold (His blessings) from you."

Ibn ʿAbbās ﷺ narrated that the Prophet ﷺ said, "Treat your children equally regarding gifts, and if I was to favour anyone, I would certainly favour the females."

The Prophet ﷺ said, "It is not permissible to give a gift and take it back except for a father taking back a gift he gave his offspring."

The Prophet ﷺ who said, "Al-ʿUmrah is for whomever it was gifted to."

Abū Hurayrah ﷺ said, "A man broke his fast in Ramadan, so the Messenger ﷺ commanded him to expiate by freeing a slave or fasting two consecutive month or feeding sixty poor people."

Asmā' bint Abī Bakr said, "Al-Zubayr married me, and he had no wealth, no slaves, nothing except his horse. I used to feed his horse, looking after it and exercising it. I crushed date-stones to feed his camel. I used to bring water and repair the bucket, and I used to make bread, but I could not bake it, so some of my Anṣārī neighbors, who were kind women, used to bake it for me. I used to carry the dates from the garden that the Prophet had given to al-Zubayr on my head, and this garden was two-thirds of a *farsakh* away. One day I was coming back with the dates on my head. I met the Messenger of Allah, who had a group of his Companions with him. He called me, then told his camel to sit down so that I could ride behind him, but I felt embarrassed to ride with the men and I remembered al-Zubayr and how jealous he was for he was more jealous than all the people. So, the Messenger understood that I was shy, so he just left. When I got home to al-Zubayr I told him what happened…he said, 'It is worse for me to see you carrying the dates on your head than to see you riding behind him.' Later, Abū Bakr sent me a servant, who relieved me of having to take care of the horse; it was as if I had been released from slavery."

Jābir ibn 'Abdullāh said, "My maternal aunt was divorced, and she wanted to collect the harvest from her date-palm trees. A man rebuked her for going out to the trees. She went to the Prophet who said: 'No, go and collect the harvest from your trees, for perhaps you will give some in charity or do a good deed with it.'" The Prophet said, "Seeking knowledge is an obligation upon every Muslim."

The Messenger wrote a statement to the Companion 'Amr ibn Ḥazm saying, "The man is killed for the woman (whom he kills)."

The Prophet said, "For whomever one of his or her family member is killed, his family may choose between two; if they chose, they may retaliate (*qiṣāṣ*), and if they chose, they may receive compensation (*diyah*)."

The Companion 'Aṭā' 🏵 said, "The Messenger of Allah 🏵 imposed *diyah* on people according to their wealth, whatever it was: On the possessors of camels, a hundred camels, on the possessors of sheep, one thousand sheep, on the possessors of cows, two hundred cows and on the possessor or textiles, a hundred dresses."

The Prophet 🏵 said, "For the believing soul is one hundred camels."

'Ā'ishah 🏵 said, "(One day) there sat together eleven women making an explicit promise amongst themselves that they would not conceal anything about their spouses. The first woman said, 'My husband is…' The eleventh woman said, My husband is Abū Zar', and what is Abū Zar' (i.e., what should I say about him)? He has given me many ornaments and my ears are heavily loaded with them and my arms have become fat (i.e., I have become fat). And he has pleased me, and I have become so happy that I feel good about myself. He found me with my family who were mere owners of sheep and living in poverty and brought me to a respected family having horses and camels and threshing and purifying grain. Whatever I say, he does not rebuke or insult me. When I sleep, I sleep till late in the morning, and when I drink water (or milk), I drink my fill. The mother of Abū Zar', and what may one say in praise of the mother of Abū Zar'? Her saddle bags were always full of provision and her house was spacious…" The Messenger ﷺ then said to me, "I am to you as Abū Zarʿ was to his wife Umm Zarʿ…The Messenger ﷺ said, 'I am to you as Abū Zarʿ was to his wife Umm Zarʿ.'" ʿĀ'ishah ﷺ replied, "O Messenger of Allah, you are much better to me than Abū Zarʿ."

The Prophet ﷺ said, "Every one of you is a shepherd and is responsible for his flock."

ʿĀ'ishah ﷺ said, "He ﷺ used to keep himself busy serving his family," and "He ﷺ was like any human being, patching his garments, milking his sheep, and serving his own self."

The Prophet ﷺ said, "The most complete of the believers in faith is the one with the best character among them, and the best of you are those who are best to your women."

The Prophet ﷺ said to men, "I advise you to take care of the women, for they are created from a rib and the most bent portion of the rib is its upper part; if you try to straighten it, it will break, and if you leave it, it will remain bent, so I urge you to take care of women."

The Prophet ﷺ said, "She will not change to fit your wishes."

The Prophet ﷺ said, "[Cause] no harm to oneself nor to others."

The Prophet ﷺ said, "I have not seen anyone with reductions in mind and religion more capable of removing reason from a resolute man than you."

The Prophet's wife Umm Ḥabībah ﷺ said, "The Prophet ﷺ married her while she resided in Abyssinia (Ethiopia today) and the King Negas married them (by a power of attorney that he ﷺ sent him), and (given the situation of the Messenger living under siege in Mecca at the time) Negas gave her a *mahr* of four thousand dirham and spent on all her bridal expenses, a matter that was not disapproved of by the Messenger ﷺ."

Appendix E: Assembly of Muslim Jurists of America (AMJA) Family Codes

Selected Articles

The Right to Set Conditions or Prenuptial Agreement.

Article 14: The wife has the right to stipulate in the marriage contract, or her husband can stipulate for her, whatever involves a lawful benefit for the woman that does not contradict the essence of marriage – such as completing her studies, remaining in her job, him not marrying another alongside her, him not relocating her outside her hometown or country, and the likes. If the husband does not uphold this condition, then the wife is entitled to demand an annulment or legally enforced divorce. She can also determine, by mutual consent with the husband, other forms of penalties that don't violate the Shariah, such as monetary compensation, in exchange for foregoing her right to litigation upon acquiring the agreed upon settlement.

If a Husband is Not Properly Spending on His Wife:

Article 87: If the husband becomes insolvent in terms of spending, and his wife demands it, the judge can determine a monetary allowance to her, which would be a debt that the husband is responsible for, after confirming that a valid marriage is ongoing between them. He will also permit the wife to take a loan in her husband's name.

If a Husband Did Not Fulfill His Financial Obligation, it Becomes a Debt Upon His Death:

Article 90: The obligation to spend on the wife ends with its payment, or being absolved of it, or either spouse dying. However, this obligatory spending being absolved by death does not controvert the previously established debt he had become liable for [towards her].

Marrying Women from the People of the Book:

Article 15: When a Muslim is marrying a woman from the People of the Book outside the lands of Islam, he must stipulate in the marriage contract that Islam is the religion of the children, and that the spouses will seek judgment from the Islamic Sharia in the matters related to family law such as marriage, divorce, inheritance, bequests, and custody – and that decisions will be sought with an Islamic entity in times of dispute. This is what is Islamically binding on the Muslim, and it will be finally up to the other party to accept such clause or reject it.

Article 19: The Muslim judge in the lands of Islam, or those in his position abroad (namely the arbitrators and those appointed by the Muslim community to perform marriages and are licensed by the state to carry out marriage contracts), should undertake the marrying of new Muslim sisters who have no paternal relatives upon Islam. If no entity exists that is responsible for performing such marriage contracts, then she would delegate in that case any man from the Muslim community whom she accepts to represent her.

Article 20: A woman from the People of the Book is married off by her guardian from the People of the Book, or the Muslim judge, or those in his position. Her marriage should not be annulled if she marries herself off, or if she appoints a Muslim to marry her off, or a Muslim agrees to marry her through a judge from the People of the Book.

Marrying More than One Wife in America is Unlawful:

Article 39: When warranted, a man is entitled to combine between more than one wife, but it is forbidden for him to increase beyond four. However, to avoid harm to themselves and their communities, Muslims should adhere to the local laws and rulings on marriage restrictions.

Article 43: A Muslim man marrying a chaste woman from the People of the Book is lawful, on the condition that it be stipulated in the contract that the Shariah rulings are the reference point during disagreements, and that Islamic arbitration is sought to judge in the disputes that take place between the spouses. This is what is Islamically binding on the Muslim, and it will be finally up to the other party to accept such clause or reject it.

The Assembly Derived to the Following Rulings Regarding the *Mahr* or Bridal Marital gift:

Article 48: The *ṣadāq* becomes binding upon a valid contract, and the parties cannot agree on dismissing it. This *ṣadāq* becomes all due upon consummation or an actual seclusion – unless both spouses affirm that no consummation took place. It also becomes all due upon the death [of either party], regardless of whether the death was before or after consummation.

Immediate and Deferred *Ṣadāq* or *Mahr*

Article 49: The *ṣadāq* is completely the woman's entitlement. Therefore, she can deal with it as she pleases, and can agree to either demand it (or part of it) immediately or defer it to an appointed term. She has the right to refuse consummation until the immediate portion of her *ṣadāq* is paid to her, and if she accepts consummation before receiving it, then it becomes a debt upon the husband that he is liable for.

Article 50: The deferred portion of the *ṣadāq* becomes due upon the first of the two terms; death or divorce, unless the contract states otherwise.

Article 51: Before consummation, the divorcee is entitled to half the *ṣadāq* if it was specified, unless the separation was due to the marriage being dissolved or annulled for a defect, in which case she would not be entitled to any of the *ṣadāq*. If no *ṣadāq* had been specified, the judge or those in his position allot her an alimony, which is an amount of wealth or benefit paid to a divorcee that is determined by the customs and norms, while taking into consideration the solvency and insolvency of both spouses.

Article 52: If the *mahr* or *ṣadāq* was not specified before or during the contract, and the spouses did not agree on it thereafter, or it was an invalid form of *ṣadāq*, or consummation had taken place in an invalid or mistaken marriage, then it will be referred to the *ṣadāq* of her peers.

Article 53: If someone gets married during his terminal illness, for a *ṣadāq* equivalent to that of the bride's peers, and he was in need of that, then this *ṣadāq* is to be taken from his inheritance after death. If it exceeds the *ṣadāq* of the bride's peers, then the excess is governed by the rules of the bequest. If he was not in need of that, then it is taken entirely from the 1/3rd of his inheritance after his death and is given precedence over the other bequests.

The Assembly Ruled the Furnishing of the Household as Part of the Wife's Due Right of *Nafaqah:*

Article 54: The default is that the husband is completely responsible for furnishing the marital home, within the bounds of reasonability. In turn, that becomes his property, unless he makes this furniture a portion of the *ṣadāq*. The wife is not responsible for any of that, unless she willingly contributes, and she reserves the right [of ownership] for whatever she contributes.

General Marital Rights and Obligations Shared by the Spouses:

Article 59: The rights and obligations that are shared by both spouses are:

a) Living together in harmony, caring for the welfare of the family, consulting one another about the decisions related to it, avoiding everything that scathes the other's dignity, respecting the other's relatives, upholding kinship ties on both sides, visiting family, and inviting them to visit according to what is appropriate.

b) Living together Islamically, which includes marital intimacy, and each being loyal to the other in terms of protecting their religion, honor, progeny, and wealth.

c) Caring for the children and rearing them in a righteous fashion.

d) Concealing marital secrets.

e) Observing the rights of inheritance between them.

f) Husband and Wife Financial Rights.

Article 60: The wife's rights upon her husband are:

a) The *mahr/ṣadāq*, which is what the husband pays to the wife for the sake of marrying her, whether it be wealth or another benefit qualified by the Shariah.

b) Spending on her food, clothing, treatment, housing, and everything necessary to sustain a livelihood, to the degree of his solvency or insolvency, without extravagance or stinginess.

c) Not touching any of her wealth except with her permission.

Husband's Rights upon His Wife

Article 61: The husband's rights upon his wife are:

a) Recognizing his position as a maintainer, director, and advisor, in order to protect her religiosity and secure her hereafter. Part of that is keeping her chaste and modest, having her abide by the Islamic attire, and preventing her from everything that is considered evil in the Shariah.

b) Obeying him in that which is good, namely everything permissible in the Shariah that will not inflict harm upon her.

c) Looking after the marital home, managing its affairs, and safeguarding is possessions.

d) Prudently dealing with the husband's wealth, namely by spending from it in proportion to her need, and the need of her children, according to that which is appropriate, without being extravagant and wasteful. She should not spend any of his wealth unless he permits, or it's within the bounds of what is customarily acceptable.

e) Caring for his children which she mothered and nursing them unless she cannot.

Nushūz:

Article 86: If the husband is absent, or travels, or disappears, and leaves his wife without money, and the wife chooses to refer her affair to the judge, then a monetary allowance is determined for her which becomes a debt that the husband is responsible for. This is contingent upon the judge confirming that a valid marriage is ongoing between them, and after he confirms via testimony that her husband did not leave money for her expenses, and that she is not rebellious (nāshiz), nor is she a divorced woman whose *ʿiddah* has ended.

Article 89: The obligatory spending on a wife is absolved when she refuses to move into the marital home for a reason that deems the woman rebellious (*nāshiz*).

The Extent of Each Spouse's Right to House Their Dependents When There Is a Need:

Article 92: It is impermissible for either spouse to house with the other, in the marital home, anyone of his/her relatives, even if s/he is liable for spending on that person – unless that takes place based on mutual consent and consultation, in order to safeguard for each spouse their right to privacy in the marital home.

Spending on the Relatives:

a) Spending on the Children

Article 93: a) Spending on the child that has no wealth for himself is obligatory upon his father. The obligation to spend on the girl is not absolved until she no longer needs to be spent on; either because her husband is now obligated to spend on his wife, or because she has become financially independent to an extent that suffices her needs. The obligation to spend on the son is not absolved until he becomes capable to earn, or possesses wealth that suffices his expenses, unless he is a student that is currently continuing his studies, in which case his right to sustenance will continue until he is customarily capable of earning a living.

b) Spending on the older son/ daughter that is incapable of earning due to a handicap or otherwise is obligatory upon his/ her father, unless s/he possesses wealth from which s/he can spend.

c) If a woman is divorced, or her husband dies, and she has no wealth nor a job to earn from, her sustenance becomes incumbent upon her father, unless her expenses are shouldered by someone else.

Article 99: If the relatives qualified for being spent on are multiple, and there is not enough wealth for everybody, precedence is given to spending on the wife, and then spending on the children, while including his parents that qualify for spending to his family – if his finances allow for spending on them alongside his wife and children. Then, there comes spending on the remaining relatives.

Types of Divorce

Article 136: An irrevocable divorce terminates the marriage contract from the moment it takes place, and it has two types:

a) A minor irrevocable divorce, which terminates the current marriage, and that divorced woman does not become lawful for her divorcer except with a new contract and new *mahr* (wedding gift). This type of divorce results from a divorce before consummation, or a legally enforced divorce carried out by a judge, or the *ʿiddah* following a revocable divorce ending without revocation, or a divorce [initiated by the wife] in return for compensation.

b) A major irrevocable divorce, which results from the third divorce, and immediately terminates the current marriage. In this case, that divorced woman does not become lawful for her divorcer except after completing her *ʿiddah* from another husband that actually consummated with her in a valid marriage that was not merely to make her lawful [for the original divorcer].

Divorce:

Article 141: If the husband forces his wife out of the house, or if she leaves due to an emergency that necessitates that, or if it was an irrevocable divorce, the judge or those in his position outside the lands of Islam should – based on her request – issue instructions about how much she must be given for her expenses throughout her *ʿiddah*, and the expenses of the children, and who is entitled to custody and the visitation of those in custody. This judicial order is considered binding from moment of its issuance.

Article 142: A woman who is divorced before consummation or actual seclusion is entitled to alimony if no *mahr* has been decided for her. If a *mahr* has been decided for her, then she is entitled to half of it, as well as a recommended alimony. Once there is consummation, this alimony is mandatory for every divorce, even if her *mahr* had been decided at the time of the marriage contract. The alimony is determined based on the solvency of the divorcer, as well as the status of the woman and what is customary for her likes. It is impermissible to use this as a means to justify what the man-made laws permit of dividing all the possessions acquired after the marriage in half between the two parties.

Wife Initiated Divorce (*Khul*ʿ)

Article 143: *Khul*ʿ is a termination of the marriage contract in exchange for a compensation that is paid by the wife, or without compensation if the severing takes place using the term *khul*ʿ. This happens when a woman hates her husband, and is incapable of bearing to live with him, without a just cause, because that would warrant a legally enforced divorce due to harm.

Article 144: For a valid *khul*ʿ, it is stipulated that the wife be competent in her dealings, and that the husband qualifies to effect a divorce.

Article 145: Any permissible compensation in the Sharia qualifies to be the compensation for the *khul*ʿ, without being deliberately incapacitating or excessively exorbitant, although there is no minimum or maximum for this compensation.

Article 146: A *khul*ʿ is considered a minor irrevocable divorce which grants the wife independence of her affairs following it. Thereafter, her husband has no access to her except with a new contract and new *mahr*.

Article 147: It is impermissible for the *khul*ʿ compensation to be forsaking custody of the children or their expenses. If that happens, the *khul*ʿ is valid and its terms are dismissed.

Article 148: The wife is entitled to retrieve the amount she paid for *khul*ʿ if she proves that this *khul*ʿ was resultant of her being forced or harmed by the husband. As for divorce, it is effective in all cases.

Article 149: The default is that *khulʿ* happens by agreement from both spouses. If the husband does not accommodate her request in order to deliberately incapacitate her, the wife refers her matter to the Islamic judge or those in his position outside the lands of Islam, and he decides between them after the arbiters he sends to reconcile between them are incapable of doing so. If the discord was due to misbehavior from the wife's end, the two arbiters are to determine a compensation for the *khulʿ* that can be less or more than the *mahr* amount. If the discord was due to misbehavior from the husband's end, the two arbiters are to suggest to the judge that he separate between them without a compensation.

Article 150: Those in the position of an Islamic judge outside the lands of Islam should not rush to issue the documents for a *khulʿ* or legally enforced divorce due to harm before the civil divorce papers are issued, in order to avoid the harm that could be provoked by spiting this angered husband.

Article 151: If the two spouses agree on the concept of proceeding with a *khulʿ*, but disagree on the compensation amount, then the matter should be referred to a judiciary to determine it after the attempts to reconcile between the spouses fail. When calculating this amount, of what should be considered is the *mahr* amount, the duration of the marriage, the reasons for seeking a *khulʿ*, and the financial status of the two spouses.

Article 152: If the wife seeks a *khulʿ* before consummation and seclusion, and she surrenders the *mahr* she received, and what the husband spent for the marriage, but the husband still refuses and the judge and those in his position fail to reconcile, then a verdict of dissolving the marriage is granted.

Demanding Divorce for Not Paying the Currently Owed *Ṣadāq or Mahr*

Article 157: Before consummation, the wife can be granted a legally enforced divorce for not being paid the currently owed *ṣadāq* if her husband has no apparent wealth from which the *ṣadāq* can be taken, or he is apparently insolvent, or has unknown circumstances, and has not paid the *ṣadāq* by the deadline set by the judge for its payment and has no guarantor from either an entity or a solvent individual. Ideally, the likes of these cases should be sponsored by the public treasury.

Article 158: After consummation, a legally enforced divorce is not to be granted to the wife for not being paid her currently owed *ṣadāq*, and it remains as a debt that the husband is liable for.

Annulment or *Faskh* of Contract

Article 179: The default in a marriage contract is it being a binding agreement, one that does not become null by mutual exoneration. However, it can be annulled in exceptional circumstances, when it involves that which contradicts its very essence, or when factors surface that prevent its continuity.

Article 180: The marriage does not take effect when one of its pillars are absent, or when it involves that which hinders its validity, such as marrying one of the *mahram* relatives. In such cases, it becomes obligatory to separate between the spouses, and the *mahr* (wedding gift) is not entitled if separation takes place before consummation or seclusion, and is entitled if the separation happens thereafter.

Article 181: The marriage contract is annulled when there surfaces that which prevents its continuity in the Sharia, such as either spouse apostatizing from Islam, or when the woman embraces Islam and her husband refuses Islam until her *ʿiddah* expires.

Article 182: Separation due to *liʿān* (public imprecation) is an annulment, and it is unlawful for the two spouses who practiced *liʿān* against one another to ever get married together again.

Article 183: Annulling the marriage due to a defect in the wife disqualifies the *ṣadāq* if the annulment takes places before consummation. When it takes place after it, she remains entitled to the *ṣadāq* and the husband is to pursue it from the one who deceived him, while seeking the aid of a medical entity that is specialized in the defects that warrant separation.

Article 184: Annulling the marriage due to a defect in the husband does not disqualify the woman's right to *ṣadāq*. If the annulment takes place before consummation, then she is entitled to half the *ṣadāq*, and if it takes place after it, then she is entitled to the *ṣadāq* in full.

Article 185: Annulment is not considered a divorce, and hence it does not decrease the number of divorces allotted by the Sharia[h] to the husband.

Author's Note

As I complete this book, I find myself asking what this book did for me. My answer, without a doubt, is that it provided me with a sense of self-fulfillment. The idea that this book will be read by men and women and guide them to become better partners within matrimony fulfills me in ways I could not have ever imagined. A woman who is a wife, mother, daughter, and grandmother spends her entire adulthood giving in order to fulfill her families' needs; it too is important that she find ways of self-fulfillment, and this is my way of doing so. I do hope that the men who read this book can understand this and take care not to hinder the women in their lives from achieving whatever it is that may provide them with a true sense of self-fulfillment.